PIER PAOLO PASOLINI

SELF-PORTRAIT (1947)

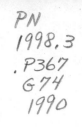

PIER PAOLO PASOLINI

CINEMA AS HERESY

Naomi Greene

PRINCETON UNIVERSITY PRESS   PRINCETON, NEW JERSEY

Library of Congress Cataloging-in-Publication Data

Greene, Naomi, 1942–
Pier Paolo Pasolini : cinema as heresy / Naomi Greene.
p.   cm.
ISBN 0-691-03148-7 (alk. paper)
1. Pasolini, Pier Paolo, 1922–1975—Criticism and interpretation.
I. Title.
PN1998.3.P367G74 1990
858'.91409—dc20   89-37066

The real Marxist must not be a good Marxist. His function is to put orthodoxy and codified certainties into crisis. His duty is to break the rules.

—*Pier Paolo Pasolini (1975)*

Contents

Illustrations _____

Photographic credits: Fondo Pier Paolo Pasolini, The Museum of Modern Art/Film Stills Archive, Angelo Novi, Angelo Frontoni, Mario Tursi, Angelo Pennoni, Divo Cavicchioli, Cineteca Nazionale/Centro Sperimentale di Cinematografia (Rome).

Frontispiece. Self-portrait (1947).

Illustrations follow page 114.

1. Echoes of neorealism: Accattone and his family in the *borgata*.

2. *Accattone*: A "frontal, massive, romantic, chiaroscuro world."

3. Pasolini with Anna Magnani at his side on the set of *Mamma Roma*.

4. The two "directors" of *La ricotta*: Pasolini and Orson Welles.

5. Jacopo da Pontormo's *Deposition*.

6. Pasolini's re-creation of Pontormo's *Deposition* in *La ricotta*.

7. "Documentary movements" of *Il Vangelo*: (a) the Flight from Egypt (The Museum of Modern Art/Film Stills Archive), (b) Salome prepares for her dance.

8. Painterly influences upon *Il Vangelo*: (a) the Pharisees as seen by Piero della Francesca and (b) by Pasolini.

9. The Christ of *Il Vangelo*: distant, "hieratic," and violent.

10. Pasolini's mother, Susanna (center), as the aged Mary in *Il Vangelo*.

11. The three travelers of *Uccellacci e Uccellini*: Totò, Ninetto, and the Marxist crow. (The Museum of Modern Art/Film Stills Archive)

12. Totò and Ninetto "talk" with the sparrows in the medieval episode of *Uccellacci e Uccellini*. (The Museum of Modern Art/Film Stills Archive)

13. *Uccellacci e Uccellini*: the need for Marxism to embrace new realities such as the Third World.

14. Totò embraces a "life force" in the shape of a prostitute. (The Museum of Modern Art/Film Stills Archive)

15. *La terra vista dalla luna*: "Lacking a language or style to express in writing, verbally, this type of comedy, I was forced to write the screenplay

Acknowledgments

LOOKING BACK, I realize how many people had a part in this book. I would like to thank just a few of them here: Maria and Cesare Vesco in Rome—Cesare for the many times he patiently discussed Pasolini and Italian politics with me, Maria for her boundless generosity and hospitality; Ivano Rovere in Casarsa for showing me, in word and deed, what Pasolini loved about Friuli and its people; Dina Grazoni in Creil for the many times we discussed Pasolini together; Lucienne Frappier-Mazur, Anna Brusatti, Natasha Durovícová, and Ruth Longworth for reading parts of this manuscript and offering valuable advice and criticism; Allen Cohen, Lou Smitheram, and Kitty Ute of the library at the University of California at Santa Barbara for their constant help; Paul Slater for the many tasks that only an ardent bibliophile could have performed; and my parents, as always, for their continuing support.

I would also like to thank Laura Betti and the staff of the Fondo Pier Paolo Pasolini in Rome for permitting me to consult their invaluable collection, as well as the Rockefeller Foundation for a grant that allowed me to spend a month—during which I completed the first draft of this book—at the Villa Serbelloni at Bellagio, Italy.

A special thanks to my editor, Joanna Hitchcock, without whose faith and enthusiasm this book would never have been written.

PIER PAOLO PASOLINI

I

Under the Sign of Rimbaud

> but I,
>   from poetry's skies,
>   plunge into communism
> because
>   without it
>   I feel no love.
>   —Vladimir Mayakovsky (1925)

IN THE SUMMER of 1987 I found myself on a train headed for Casarsa delle Delizie, a small Italian town in the region of Friuli, northeast of Venice. Since the town of Casarsa is intimately associated with the late writer and director Pier Paolo Pasolini, the trip represented a cultural pilgrimage for me. My interest in Pasolini had been sparked years earlier on a rainy afternoon in Paris—a city where he was always much admired—when a friend persuaded me to see one of his films. This led to a stay in Rome in the early 1970s—a time when Pasolini was probably the most polemical figure in Italian cultural and political life.

The route from Rome to Casarsa was one that, in reverse, marked important stages of Pasolini's career. After a literary debut as a poet in Casarsa, he settled in Rome. There he achieved fame: first as a poet, novelist, and essayist, then as a filmmaker, and, finally, as a highly controversial political commentator. In November 1975 a brutal assassination—apparently at the hands of a young male prostitute—ended the life of a man who, by the time of his death, was generally recognized not only as a great *poète maudit* but one of the most important intellectuals of postwar Europe, occupying a position in Italy comparable, perhaps, to that of Sartre in France.

In the small cemetery of Casarsa, Pasolini lies buried near his adored mother and many of her relatives since it was she, a gentle schoolteacher of modest rural stock, who came from the region of Friuli. His father, on the other hand, was of minor nobility from Ravenna. After exhausting his patrimony (with some dispatch), Pasolini *père* went into the military. Living on his father's meager salary meant that Pasolini, who was born in 1922 (the year Mussolini came to power), experienced a "petit-bourgeois" childhood, marked by what he called "dignified poverty."

His parents' differing social origins presaged other differences—temperamental and ideological—that would divide them and, much later, would be reflected in Pasolini's persistently binary view of the world. Theirs was not a happy marriage: one of Pasolini's cousins, Nico Naldini, suggests that Pasolini's mother, Susanna, bestowed upon her young son, Pier Paolo, all the love she refused his father.[1] Pasolini himself confessed to feeling an "antagonistic, dramatic tension" between his father and himself from childhood on. His mother's gentleness contrasted with what Pasolini deemed his father's "violent" and "possessive" nature. And while she did not question the social order, she was anti-Fascist, unlike her authoritarian husband, who embraced Mussolini's regime from the beginning. Speaking of the parental arguments that deeply marked his youth, Pasolini noted that his whole life was "influenced by the scenes my father made with my mother. These scenes awakened in me the desire to die. . . . He reproached her with having her head in the clouds. The simple truth is that he was a Fascist, she was not. Being in the clouds meant, for him, being anti-conformist, in disagreement with the laws of the State, with the ideas of those in power."[2]

Memories of childhood would always haunt Pasolini. When he was nearly fifty, he remarked to a friend, the writer Dacia Maraini: "Until the time I was thirty I longed for my childhood and I narcissistically relived it. . . . Because it was the most heroic period of my life. I longed for it desperately."[3] Although this "heroic period" was seen in a different light as he grew older, Pasolini always found it easier to express his great love for his mother (with whom he lived all his life) than his deeply ambivalent and disturbing emotions concerning his father. An avid reader of Freud, he never ceased to probe the implications of his relationship to his parents. As he noted in the course of a long series of interviews with Jean Duflot, a French journalist:

> I almost regret that you're not a psychoanalyst because . . . I'm very curious about this method of investigation, and I have read enough to question the possibility of speaking about my relations with my parents in terms that are simply poetic or even in a way which is purely anecdotal. . . . I will say simply that I experienced a great love for my mother. Her physical "presence," her way of being, of speaking, her tact and gentleness governed my childhood. For a long time I thought that my entire emotional and erotic life was exclusively determined by this excessive passion which I even perceived as a monstrous form of love. Now, quite recently, I have discovered that my sentimental rela-

[1] Pasolini, *Lettere: 1940–1954*, ed. Nico Naldini (Turin: Einaudi, 1986), p. xviii.
[2] Cited by Dacia Maraini in *E tu, chi eri?* (Milan: Bompiani, 1973), pp. 267–268.
[3] Ibid., p. 269.

tions with my father have also had their importance and one which is far from negligible. It is not only a question of rivalry and hatred.[4]

Pasolini's "monstrous" love for his mother meant that her idealism—her belief in "heroism, in charity, in piety, in generosity"—shaped his most fundamental attitudes.[5] Absorbing her beliefs in an almost "pathological way," he was especially influenced by her respect for "authority"—a respect that would impel both his conformism and, perhaps, his need to rebel. Speaking of himself in the third person, years later, he declared:

> He sought the Authority *feared* by his mother
> not the Authority exerted by his father—a fascist. . . .
>
> Therefore: his conformism—let us repeat, of *maternal and*
> *not paternal origin*—stopped him, for longer than is
> normal, from understanding what liberty and rebellion were,
> Because liberty and rebellion were his bread.[6]

At the heart of this deeply ambivalent nexus of conformism and rebellion lay his homosexuality. In his eyes the cast his sexuality would assume was apparent even in earliest childhood. An entry in a diary Pasolini kept in his mid-twenties describes the violence of his reactions when, as a three-year old, he was attracted by the knees of some young boys at play. Even as these lines suggest the nature of his first sexual stirrings, they also reveal the fascination that words would always hold for him—in this case, *teta veleta*, which, as he later learned, suggested the Greek word for sex, *tetis*.

> Now I know that it was an intensely sensual feeling. If I re-experience it I feel precisely in my insides the melting, sadness, and violence of desire. It was the sense of the unobtainable, of the carnal—a sense for which no name had yet been invented. I invented it then and it was "teta veleta." Just seeing the legs bent in the throes of the game I said to myself that I felt "teta veleta," something which was like a tickling, a seduction, a humiliation.[7]

The hint of "humiliation" that comes at the end of this passage becomes the focus of a diary entry describing a second experience which occurred two years later (when he was five) at the sight of a gruesome film poster of a man being mauled by a tiger. Recalling this scene in later years, he

[4] Cited by Jean Duflot in *Entretiens avec Pier Paolo Pasolini* (Paris: Belfond, 1970), pp. 11–12.

[5] Cited by Maraini, *E tu, chi eri?* p. 262.

[6] Pasolini, "Coccodrillo," in *Il sogno del centauro* (Rome: Riuniti, 1983), p. 176. In addition to "Coccodrillo," this volume contains the Italian translation of Duflot's *Entretiens avec Pier Paolo Pasolini*, followed by additional interviews conducted in 1975.

[7] Pasolini, *Lettere*, p. xvi.

observed that this, his first experience with the cinema, had an "erotic-sexual" cast.

> The young adventurer seemed to be still alive and conscious of having been half-eaten by the splendid tiger. He lay with his head down, almost in the position of a woman, defenseless, nude. Meanwhile the animal was ferociously swallowing him. . . . I was seized by a feeling similar to that which I had experienced seeing the young boys playing at Belluno two years earlier, but it was more murky and insistent. I felt a shiver within me like a kind of surrender. Meanwhile I began to wish that I myself were the explorer being devoured alive by the beast.[8]

The sensitivity and introspection revealed in these passages led Pasolini—almost inevitably—to poetry, and at a tender age. When he was seven, a few days after his mother gave him a poem expressing her love for him, he composed *his* first verses containing—significantly—highly literary words such as "nightingale" and "verdure." At fourteen, as he told Dacia Maraini, he "read *Macbeth*, discovered secondhand bookstores and stopped believing in God"[9]; the following year, his view of the world changed after reading the French poet Arthur Rimbaud. Entranced, certainly, by Rimbaud's adolescent genius, Pasolini was also drawn to Rimbaud's youthful passion and rebellion, his scandalous and doomed love affair with the married poet Paul Verlaine, and, finally, his romantic flight from Europe into the dark heart of Africa. Pasolini's discovery of the great *poète maudit*, says his cousin Nico, was both a "literary and a political baptism that in one blow fractured [Pasolini's] academic and provincial culture, his Fascist conformism, and placed into crisis even the social identity of the adolescent poet."[10] In 1941, at university in Bologna—where he wrote a literary thesis on the poet Pascoli—he and a number of friends tried to start a literary magazine called *Eredi*. They saw themselves as the heirs, or the "eredi," of the Italian modernist tradition represented by writers such as Ungaretti and Montale. Wartime restrictions on paper doomed the project; the following year (1942), however, he contributed to a new review, *Il Setaccio*. Although officially sponsored by University Fascist Youth, *Il Setaccio* attempted to attract young intellectuals by offering them relative freedom to express personal views. Foreshadowing his later rejection of all orthodoxy, Pasolini soon took advantage of this freedom. After attending two great assemblies of Fascist youth—one in Florence, the other in Weimar—he wrote an article for *Il Setaccio* in which he contrasted Nazi propaganda with the great traditions of European culture.

[8] Ibid., p. xx.
[9] Cited by Maraini, *E tu, chi eri?* p. 266.
[10] Pasolini, *Lettere*, p. xxvii.

By 1943 the war had reached Bologna. Along with his mother and younger brother, Guido, Pasolini left the city and took refuge in Friuli—a region he knew and loved from boyhood summers spent in and around Casarsa. The rural landscape became the scene of his erotic initiation. Diary entries reveal the intensity of his first passion for a peasant lad, Bruno, whom he saw as "violent" and "coarse." The discovery that boys were not merely "angels without sex," the fierceness of his desire, forced him to see himself and the world in a new—and disquieting—way. Noting that his loss of "innocence" seemed a "betrayal" of his more "sensitive" and "generous" nature, he confided to his diary that even the natural world had taken on a different cast for him—one that was highly physical, insistent, and "impure." Diary entries in which he describes erotic longings hint at a deeply religious sensibility perturbed and distraught by passion: "In a mystical nakedness," he confesses, "the terror-creating nakedness of the soul, perhaps I can find some way of justifying myself: I *had to* sin, that is to follow the road of the Christian in reverse. It is known that a convert normally has one obstacle to overcome: the state of sin. I had . . . to go from an innocence that was imposed to one that was willed."[11]

Pasolini's personal drama played itself out against the background of the war. Casarsa itself, as an important railroad depot, was subject to Allied bombings and scenes of intense fighting. "The war stinks of shit," wrote Pasolini to a friend in March 1944, "everything stinks of shit, it makes you sick to your stomach to think that these men [the Nazis] shit here. I would like to spit on this stupid earth that keeps sending forth green grasses, and yellow and blue flowers, and buds on the alder trees. . . . Everything stinks of shooting and boots."[12] Young men were subject to being seized by the Fascists and forcibly conscripted into the army. To escape these roundups, in 1944 Pasolini left Casarsa for the nearby hamlet of Versuta, where a plaque in the church square now bears one of his early poems. In this tiny village, Pasolini—revealing the pedagogical bent that informs his essays and articles—managed to establish a little school for children who, because of the war, could no longer travel in safety to their normal schools. The previous year, along with some friends, he had launched a similar school in Casarsa. His hours in the classroom were a source of deep joy. "I believe," he remarked in his diary, "that I never gave of myself with such dedication as I did to these students . . . during the lessons of Italian and history."[13]

Only a few months before peace was announced, the war took its terrible toll of the Pasolini family. In the summer of 1944, Pier Paolo's be-

[11] Ibid., p. lxx.
[12] Ibid., pp. 190–191.
[13] Ibid., p. lxxiii.

loved younger brother, Guido, had left home—with a "revolver hidden in a book of poems"—to join the Resistance. Little more than six months later, in February 1945, Guido died in an atrocious, absurd combat between conflicting partisan groups, apparently killed in cold blood by Yugoslav (and even Italian) partisans who were struggling to annex Friuli to Tito's Communist Yugoslavia. A grief-stricken Pasolini may have felt partly responsible for his brother's death: he had suggested to Guido which partisan group to join. Twenty years later he was to write:

> I still cry, every time that I think
> about my brother Guido,
> a partisan killed by other partisans, Communists
> (he was in the Partito d'Azione, but upon my advice
> he joined the Resistance as a Communist),
> at the accursed mountains of a frontier.[14]

Soon afterward his father, who had left for the African theater in 1941, only to spend much of the war in an English prisoner-of-war camp in Kenya, returned home. He was broken by defeat, drink, and now the death of his son. Bored and embittered, he would pass long hours in a local café, drinking constantly. His alcoholism and drink-induced crises created an unbearably tense atmosphere at home. "I work a great deal," Pasolini wrote to a friend in 1948, "to maintain a state (between erotic and mystical) of joy and to avoid thinking of the future. My father's 'paranoid syndrome' [thus diagnosed by one psychiatrist] makes our family life an inferno; it is a problem without solution. Believe me, there are no words to express certain situations that are created at home during my father's moments of crisis."[15]

At the end of the war, Pasolini chose to remain in Friuli. He was understandably disturbed about his father, but relatively content with his friends and with the life he was carving out for himself. The little schools he had started gave way to a salaried teaching post when he received his degree. To him, Friuli seemed a "bit like an ideal country, almost outside space and time, a kind of sentimental and poetic Provence for me who was writing poetry like Rimbaud, Verlaine, or Lorca."[16] He had, in fact, continued to write throughout the war; his first collection of poems, *Poesie a Casarsa* (originally intended for the ill-fated review *Eredi*), was published in 1942 and, to Pasolini's surprise and delight, elicited praise from a famous man of letters, Gianfranco Contini.

Significantly, Pasolini's first collection was not written in standard Ital-

---

[14] Pasolini, "Io, poeta delle Ceneri," *Nuovi Argomenti* No. 67–68 (July–December 1980), p. 3.

[15] Pasolini, *Lettere*, p. 338.

[16] Pasolini, *Le belle bandiere* (Rome: Riuniti, 1977), p. 136.

ian, but in the Friulian dialect spoken mainly by peasants. (The bourgeois Pasolini household spoke a Venetian dialect which his cousin has described as "dry and impoverished" in comparison with Friulian.) Pasolini's choice of Friulian was important for a variety of reasons. On a personal level, it revealed his attachment to the region with its age-old way of life, its rural and mystical Christianity. In his cousin's eyes, Pasolini's "intimacy with the peasant world" was also imbued with nostalgia "for a language that, before the influx of Venetian, had sprung forth from antic lyrical sources, and for religious liturgies full of feelings of charity."[17] Years later Pasolini would analyze his attraction to the language and world of the Friulian peasants as the first manifestation of a lifelong nostalgia for past civilizations which, as he aged and the nostalgia grew more acute, became increasingly more remote in time and place. As with Friulian, this nostalgia always contained linguistic and ideological components: the longing he felt for dialects and past civilizations was the reverse side of the linguistic and cultural crisis he experienced in his own civilization. Observing that perhaps only an outsider, one who was "marginal and not too Friulian," could be fully aware of what the conscious or literary use of dialect implied, he wrote:

> The "return," that essential vocation of dialect . . . should come about for complex reasons . . . both internal and external, and take place from one language (Italian) to another (Friulian) that has become the object of a mournful nostalgia which is sensual in origin (in all the breadth and depth of the term); but [this return] also coincides with the nostalgia of one who lives—and knows it—in a civilization that has reached a linguistic crisis, the desolation and violence of a Rimbaudian "je ne sais plus parler."[18]

Pasolini's attraction to Friulian also reflected what proved to be a lifelong interest in philology and linguistics. In 1945, in fact, he helped found an organization devoted to the study of the Friulian language, the Academiuta di Lenga Furlana. But as the above quote suggests, literary sensibilities—in particular, his love of symbolist poets and especially Rimbaud—were probably even more important. The choice of a dialect quite distinct from Italian, where the language itself compelled attention, automatically meant embracing the "absolute" language of poetry. Viewing his decision to write in dialect as "the height of hermeticism, of obscurity, of the refusal to communicate," he observed that he had learned Friulian as

[17] Nico Naldini, *Nei campi dei Friuli: La giovanezza di Pasolini* (Milan: Pesce d'Oro, 1984), pp. 24–25.

[18] Pasolini, *Passione e ideologia* (Milan: Garzanti, 1977), pp. 132–133. Originally published in 1960.

a mystic act of love, a kind of *félibrisme*, like the Provençal poets. The first poems I wrote in Friulian were when I was about seventeen. . . . As you know, at that time hermeticism was in vogue in Italy, which was a kind of provincial current of symbolism; Mallarmé was the principal influence and symbolism was widely taken up in Italy. . . .

The central idea of hermetic poetry was the idea of the language of poetry as an absolute language.[19]

Foreshadowing the intimate link between politics and culture that would become one of the defining characteristics of all his work, the literary/linguistic choice of Friulian had political and social ramifications. Pasolini's embrace of dialect represented a defiance of Fascism, which scorned marginal regions and dialects, seeing in them "a form of real life it wanted to conceal." To the Fascist mentality, culture itself was suspect. Speaking of the way his literary sensibility both shaped and reflected his growing political awareness, Pasolini told one interviewer:

I followed the only two paths that could take me to anti-Fascism: that of hermeticism . . . and decadentism, that is, essentially [the path] of good taste . . . and, secondly, the path which led me into contact with the humble and Christian way of life of the peasants in my mother's region, a way of life expressing a mentality totally different from the style of Fascism.[20]

The political awareness implicit in Pasolini's choice of Friulian also had a pronounced Freudian cast. In what he deemed a "bold gesture," one undoubtedly infused with complex and ambivalent emotions, Pasolini dedicated *Poesie a Casarsa* to his father. As a Fascist with a "racist" contempt for "anything that came from the margins of the country," the latter might well have been hurt by his son's use of dialect. Referring to the poem and its dedication nearly a quarter century later, Pasolini wrote:

It's the sign of our hatred, the indisputable sign,
the sign that could not mislead a scientific inquiry,
—that could not mislead it—
this book dedicated to him
was written in Friulian dialect!
The dialect of my mother!
The dialect of a small
world, that he had to scorn,
—or else accept with a father's patience.[21]

[19] Cited by Oswald Stack in *Pasolini on Pasolini* (Bloomington and London: Indiana University Press, 1969), pp. 15–16.

[20] Cited by Ferdinando Camon in *Il mestiere di scrittore* (Milan: Garzanti, 1973), p. 95.

[21] Pasolini, "Io, poeta delle Ceneri," p. 4.

But his father, it appears, did not take *Poesie a Casarsa* as a "sign of hatred." Quite the contrary. Pasolini's diary reveals that the book was greeted not only by paternal "patience" but even paternal pride: "Despite the absurdity of the language used, it was dedicated to him, and this consoled him, made him rejoice."[22]

Other consequences, both personal and political, stemmed from the choice of Friulian: using the dialect spoken by the peasants, Pasolini gradually came closer to them and to the very real problems of their difficult existence. His realization that everything about their life distinguished it from his own ("their psychology, their education, their mentality, their soul, their sexuality were all different"[23]) heightened his class consciousness, his acute awareness of his own bourgeois core. Before long his depiction of peasant life assumed a populist cast, a "sentimental and vaguely Socialist halo of a Romantic Christian sort."[24] As this "Socialist halo" began to interact with his linguistic fascination, the decadent or hermetic aspect of his poems lessened even as their earlier Christianity gave way to more "concrete sociological forms." Gradually the use of dialect became less an aesthetic device and more a political and social one. Although he turned to Friulian as a "special language for poetry," his contact with dialect inevitably

> had an effect. . . . It was through Friulian that I came to understand some of the real world of the peasantry. Of course, at first I understood it imperfectly in an aesthetic way. . . . Yet once I'd taken this step I couldn't stop and so I started using dialect not as a hermetic-aestheticist device but more and more as an objective and realist element: this reached its culmination in my novels, where Roman dialect is used in a way which is the exact opposite of how I used Friulian at the beginning.[25]

Moved by his attachment to Friuli as well as a growing social awareness, Pasolini before long joined a group devoted to Friulian autonomy. Around the same time he also began attending meetings of a local Communist group; in 1948 he officially joined the Communist party and was named secretary of the Communist Section of San Giovanni, a town close to Casarsa. The fact that the Communists did not support the aims of the Friulian group did not seem to disturb him. As if foreshadowing the many conflicts he would have with the party, Pasolini remained committed to both the ideal of regional autonomy and to Communist aims. Nor was this the only issue in dispute. Hinting at what would become a firmly held and lifelong conviction, in 1948 he made a speech in which he questioned

[22] Pasolini, *Lettere*, p. xl.
[23] Cited by Stack, *Pasolini*, p. 26.
[24] Cited by Camon, *Il mestiere di scrittore*, p. 95.
[25] Cited by Stack, *Pasolini*, pp. 16–17.

the party's tendency to judge literature solely in political and ideological terms. "There is a tendency to the right and a tendency to the left even in literature," he declared, "and for reasons that are purely literary. But those who are on the left in literature are not always to the left in politics, etc.: there is therefore a double play of relations between political and literary avant-gardism."[26]

Around the time that Pasolini joined the party, the left-wing groups of a nearby town, San Vito al Tagliamento, organized a demonstration to protest the failure of tenant farmers and unemployed workers to receive aid and jobs promised them as compensation for damages suffered during the war. Dramatically taking to the streets, many of the younger protesters besieged a large estate owned by absentee landlords. These scenes of stark class confrontation, of day laborers, or *braccianti*, pitted against big landlords, so moved Pasolini that he later wove a novel around them: *Il sogno di una cosa* (1962). "Never so much as at that moment," comments his cousin Nico, "did the idea of a peasant revolution seem such a realizable dream."[27] Much later, in a column written for a Communist periodical, Pasolini would describe this peasant protest as a "crucial moment" in his life, a moment that confirmed him in his belief that ideology stems not from pure reason but from lived experience. "The direct experience of the problems of others," he was to observe, "radically transformed my own problems: for this reason I feel that at the root of the communism of a bourgeois there is always an ethical, in some sense, an evangelical, impulse."[28]

As the decisive elections of 1948 approached, Pasolini and his comrades were swept up in a wave of political activity: debates, meetings, and newspaper articles became the order of the day. Even the bitter defeat suffered by the Left at the polls did not lessen their political fervor. Dismayed by Pasolini's politics, some old friends fell away; new ones took their place. Pasolini began to read theoretical texts: parts of *Das Kapital* and, more importantly, works by Antonio Gramsci, a founder of the Italian Communist party. Noting that he found Marx "distant" for various reasons, Pasolini remarked that "Gramsci's ideas coincided with mine; they won me over immediately, and he had a fundamental role in my formation."[29]

It was, in fact, Pasolini's growing activism that triggered the first and, perhaps, the most traumatic of the many "scandals" he would endure. Like all those to come, this first drama sprang from a mix of sex and

[26] Pasolini, "Un intervento rimandato," in *Dialogo con Pasolini: Scritti 1957–1984* (Rome: Rinascita, 1985), p. 109.

[27] Pasolini, *Lettere*, p. civ.

[28] Pasolini, *Le belle bandiere*, p. 136.

[29] Cited by Stack, *Pasolini*, p. 23.

politics. A number of Catholics who, naturally, supported the Christian Democrats and may have hoped that Pasolini would prove a friend rather than a Communist adversary viewed his political activities with hostility. As a respected teacher and intellectual who wrote articles for the local papers, Pasolini was highly visible and hence threatening. Well aware of their hatred, in March 1949 Pasolini wrote to a very close woman friend, Silvana Mauri, that the "priests of the area . . . slander me from the altars." But, he continued, "for me believing in Communism is a great thing."[30] He held fast to his idealism even after an important prelate warned him that he would be ruined if he did not cease his political activities. This threat was made good in the fall of 1949. On September 30, during a local rural festival, Pasolini disappeared into the bushes with three young lads; on October 22 he stood accused of "corrupting minors and obscene acts in public."

In recounting the incident, Nico Naldini says simply that "a masturbation" took place that night. This fairly commonplace act apparently led first to an anonymous letter and then to a police report that Pasolini's political enemies were quick to escalate into legal charges. Although acquitted of the corruption charge, Pasolini *was* convicted of obscene acts. Two years later—in a pattern that would recur in all his trials—he was declared innocent; the appeals court reversed the conviction for insufficient evidence. But by then the damage had been done. Forbidden to teach in the state schools, he lost his livelihood; in a second, and perhaps even more devastating blow, he was also expelled from the Communist party.

In retrospect, the Communists emerge from this incident scarcely less tainted than the Christian Democrats. Given the climate of the cold war, the Communists' reluctance to defend a known homosexual is understandable. But the tone of the expulsion, which was published in the Communist paper *L'Unità*, hints at something more. Imbued with the moralism and intolerance that would always pursue Pasolini, the journal stated:

> The facts which have provoked a serious disciplinary measure against the poet Pasolini give us the opportunity to once again denounce the deleterious influence of certain ideological and philosophical currents [represented] by Gide, Sartre, and other decadent poets and men of letters who try to seem progressive but who, in reality, take on the most harmful aspects of bourgeois degeneration.[31]

Stricken by the political excommunication, Pasolini responded with a moving letter to Ferdinando Mautino, author of the expulsion decree.

[30] Pasolini, *Lettere*, pp. 353–354.
[31] Ibid., p. cix.

After reminding Mautino that the scandal had been engineered by their common political enemies, Pasolini continued in a more personal vein, declaring his outrage, his anguish, and his continuing political faith:

Yesterday morning my mother almost went crazy, my father is in an indescribable state—I heard him crying and moaning all night long. I'm without work, that is, reduced to begging. Simply because *I am a Communist*. While I'm not astonished by the diabolical perfidy of the Christian Democrats, I am astonished by your inhumanity. You must understand that any talk of ideological deviation is idiotic. In spite of you, I remain and shall remain a Communist, in the most authentic meaning of the word. . . . Until yesterday, I was sustained by the thought of having sacrificed my life and my career to an ideal; now there is nothing to sustain me. In my place, someone else would have committed suicide; unfortunately, I must live for my mother. . . . For this I have betrayed my class and what you people call my bourgeois education; now those betrayed have revenged themselves in the most ruthless and frightful way. And I remain alone with the mortal grief of my father and mother.[32]

What little sympathy Pasolini received came not from his former political allies but from the townspeople of Casarsa. But this could do little to alleviate the despair he experienced in the weeks following the scandal. Deeming himself a "Rimbaud without genius," the young poet wrote to a friend, "My future is not even black; it does not exist."[33] Despondency and isolation made him cling to his writing—to what he called the "prison of [his] vocation"—with ever greater singleness of purpose and fury. Without a means of support, tortured by the idea of taking money from his alcoholic father, Pasolini finally made a move that was to prove momentous for his life, his work, and the world of Italian culture. Writing to his good friend Silvana Mauri that he sought even the "humblest" job somewhere ("they tell me that I will not die of hunger"), he joined his mother in abandoning his father and, on January 28, 1950, left Casarsa for the home of one of his uncles in Rome. Years later he would describe that fateful period:

With the end of the war began the most tragic period of my life . . . my brother's death and my mother's superhuman grief; my father's return from prison—an ill veteran, poisoned by the defeat of Fascism . . . destroyed, ferocious, a powerless tyrant, crazed by bad wine, more and more in love with my mother who had never loved him very much and who was now wrapped up in her own grief. And to all this was added the problem of my life and flesh. As in a novel, in the winter of '49 . . . I fled with my mother to Rome.[34]

[32] Ibid., pp. 368–369.
[33] Ibid., p. 375.
[34] Pasolini, "Al lettore nuovo" in *Poesie* (Milan: Garzanti, 1970), p. 9.

The Rome they fled to was still the city depicted in neorealist films—a city of work shortages, hunger, poverty. Life was so difficult initially that Pasolini later remarked: "For two years I was a desperate person out of work, like those who wind up killing themselves."[35] To his great humiliation, his mother accepted work as a live-in governess. "We arrived in Rome," he wrote years later,

> helped by my gentle uncle,
> who gave me a little of his blood:
> I lived as one condemned to death
> always "with that thought" dragging me down
> — dishonor, lack of work, misery.
> My mother was reduced for a while to being a maid.
> And I'll never recover from this pain.
> Because I'm a petit-bourgeois.[36]

Finding work seemed at first almost impossible: a despairing Pasolini beseeched friends for any possible leads or contacts, put himself on the list of film extras at the studios of Cinecittà, did some proofreading. Money was so scarce that he was compelled to sell cherished books. His father's arrival in Rome did nothing to alleviate the situation: "My father is always there, alone in the poor little kitchen, elbows on the table, face in his hands, immobile, mean, grieving; he fills up the space of the tiny room with the huge size of dead bodies."[37] But through it all he continued writing furiously; paradoxically, the first journalistic pieces the young Communist managed to place were in right-wing and Catholic papers.

Very slowly life started to improve. Nearly two years after his flight from Casarsa, he finally obtained a teaching post in a private school. Although he received a miserable wage and was forced to spend nearly four hours a day commuting by bus, his mother was able to stop working. He also obtained his first literary contract—one commissioning an anthology of poetry in dialect. The result, his massive *Poesia dialettale del Novecento*, received an enthusiastic welcome in 1953, and a second anthology, devoted to popular Italian poetry, was published two years later. In 1953 he also published a volume of verse in Friulian as well as a short story, "Ragazzi di vita," that would later become a chapter in his first novel. Gradually, too, he made literary acquaintances, such as Ungaretti and Gadda, and friends; he became especially close to the novelists Elsa Morante and Alberto Moravia. He was friendly, too, with the writer Attilio Bertolucci, father of Bernardo the filmmaker. For a time he lived in the

---

[35] Cited by Luciano de Giusti in his *I film di Pier Paolo Pasolini* (Rome: Gremese, 1983), p. 28.

[36] Pasolini, "Io, poeta delle Ceneri," p. 7.

[37] Pasolini, *Lettere*, p. cxxi.

same apartment building as the Bertolucci family. Reminiscing about his deep friendship with Pasolini during those years, Bernardo Bertolucci has written:

> I wrote poems and I was used to a kind of ritual: as soon as I finished writing them, I ran from the fifth floor where we lived to the second floor where Pier Paolo lived. I rang his door and if Pier Paolo was home, I immediately had him read them. . . . In a certain way I even saw Pier Paolo as a paternal figure. . . . I tended . . . to absorb his way of seeing reality and even a little of his style. There are certain poems of mine that I believe I never published because they were very Pasolinian, really written in Pasolini's manner.[38]

Friendships were not all that attached Pasolini to the Eternal City. After the "mystical Christianity" of Friuli, Rome seemed to exude a pagan sensuality: erotic adventures were easy, inconsequential, and daily occurrences (thus began the pattern of random and numerous encounters that would continue throughout his life). This aspect of the city helped lighten, perhaps, Pasolini's dark feelings about his own sexuality (this "dragon with a thousand heads"), feelings elegantly expressed in an oft-quoted letter to Silvana Mauri written soon after his arrival in Rome. Still under the shock of the scandal, in this letter Pasolini analyzes both the obsessive cast of his sexuality and what critics would later see as his exhibitionism. "Like me," he writes, "those who are destined not to live according to the norm wind up by overestimating its value. A normal person might resign himself (terrible word) to chastity, to lost opportunities; but, in me, the difficulty of loving has made the need for loving an obsession." His feeling of shame about his sexuality, he continues, makes him want to tell others —like Silvana—about it; only through confession can he make his former "honest and good" self pardon him for what he has become. Placing his future life under the "sign of Rimbaud or Campana or Wilde," he tells her: "I have never accepted my sin, I have never made a truce with my nature and I am not even used to it. I was born to be calm, balanced, and natural: my homosexuality was something extra, it was outside, it had nothing to do with me. I always saw it beside me like an enemy, I never felt it within me."[39] Happily, this letter's pessimism and self-deprecation were not constant; feelings changed from day to day, from letter to letter. In the summer of 1952, as the terrible hardships of the first years were drawing to a close, Pasolini wrote Silvana in a totally different mood, exuberant about Rome and the way it had changed him:

> Rome has made me pagan enough to lose faith in the validity of certain scruples which are typically northern and do not make much sense in this climate. . . .

---

[38] Bernardo Bertolucci, "Un ladro alla porta," *Cinema e cinema* No. 43 (May–August 1985), pp. 11–12.
[39] Pasolini, *Lettere*, pp. 389–392.

Here I am in a life that is all muscles, turned inside out like a glove, which always unfurls like one of those songs that I used to hate . . . in human organisms so sensual as to be almost mechanical; here none of the Christian attitudes—forgiveness, humility, etc.—are known, and egotism takes legitimate, virile forms. . . . Rome, ringed by its inferno of *borgate*, is stupendous right now: the fixity, so stripped, of the heat is what is needed to dampen its excesses.[40]

By *borgate*, Pasolini was referring to Rome's barren outlying districts. These desolate wastelands were populated by the poorest of the poor, by an underclass or sub-proletariat composed mainly of southerners who had migrated to the capital city. Pasolini, who lived in these impoverished neighborhoods during his early days in the great city, knew these districts well and had many of his adventures with youths encountered there. Some of these young men would become friends; two in particular were to be closely associated with his cinema: Sergio Citti (who later became a director in his own right) frequently worked with him behind the camera, while Ninetto Davoli (to whom Pasolini remained deeply attached throughout his life) became a familiar face to audiences of Pasolini's films. (Like Davoli, Sergio's brother Franco Citti also became one of Pasolini's favorite actors.) As if reenacting his sentimental and linguistic attraction to the peasants of Friuli, once in Rome Pasolini began to write about the *borgate* youths and to use their Romanesque dialect. ("My biography," he told Silvana Mauri, "always winds up by identifying itself with literature."[41]) His first novels, *Ragazzi di vita* (*Boys of Life*, 1955) and *Una vita violenta* (*A Violent Life*, 1959), were subsequently set in the world of the *borgate*—a world that, before then, had remained hidden even to most Romans.

These novels, along with a major collection of poetry, *Le ceneri di Gramsci* (*The Ashes of Gramsci*, 1957), finally brought Pasolini the literary acclaim that he had been dreaming of for more than a decade. But with success came scandal and notoriety. When *Ragazzi di vita* first appeared, it was charged with being an "obscene publication." The accusation was later withdrawn, but it was a forerunner of the persistent, and increasingly numerous, charges Pasolini would face as his fame grew. "I could write", he once observed, "a 'white paper' on my relations with Italian justice." After his death, a "white paper"—in fact, a "white book"—detailing the *thirty-three* legal accusations made against him was written: *Pasolini: cronaca giudiziaria, persecuzione, morte* (Milan: Garzanti, 1977). In addition to constant attacks in the right-wing press and charges of obscenity leveled against his books and films (nine of his films encountered censorship problems), on more than one occasion Pasolini

---

[40] Ibid., pp. 489–491.
[41] Ibid., p. 513.

was brought to court by unstable individuals who made extravagant, fanciful—and always unproven—charges against him. This extraordinarily mild man—so regarded by many people who were familiar with Pasolini's gentleness—was accused of starting a public brawl, corrupting minors, and possessing a dangerous weapon.

The success of Pasolini's first novel also drew him into the film world as it resulted in a number of offers to write or collaborate on screenplays. Pasolini had, in fact, worked on his first screenplay, Mario Soldati's *La donna del fiume*, the year before *Ragazzi di vita* was published. Although, in this way, literary activities led him to cinema, his interest in film was not new by any means. As a student in Bologna, he had seen many film classics through a cinema club and had even thought briefly of going to Rome to study film at the national film school, the Centro sperimentale di cinematografia. "As a youth," he remarked, "I thought of becoming a director. Then I forgot it . . . the war came, and so many other things. But it was my first vocation."[42] While circumstances and literary activities meant that he abandoned this "first vocation" for many years, he always saw writing and directing as "analogous experiences." In his view, for example, his novels reflected the early love he felt for cinema, especially for directors such as Chaplin, Eisenstein and Dreyer: "If you take certain pages of *Ragazzi di vita*, you realize that they're already visual. That is, my literary works contain a strong dose of cinematographic elements."[43] Conversely, he was also convinced that he made all his films "as a poet": "Comparing some of my poems with some of my shots, you cannot deny that a *certain way of feeling something* was identical."[44]

As a screenwriter, Pasolini worked with a number of respected directors such as Mario Soldati, Mauro Bolognini, Franco Rossi, and Florestano Vancini. But the best-known film he had a hand in was probably Fellini's *Le notti di Cabiria* (*The Nights of Cabiria*, 1956). With Sergio Citti as "linguistic consultant," Pasolini was responsible for the "low life" parts:

> As there were these kind [*sic*] of characters in *Ragazzi di vita* Fellini thought I knew that world, as indeed I did because I had lived out at Ponte Mammolo, where lots of pimps and petty thieves and whores live; all the setting [*sic*], and Cabiria's relations with the other whores and especially the episode about Divine Love are all done by me. . . . My main contribution was in the dialogue, which has been a bit lost because Fellini's use of dialect is fairly different from mine.[45]

[42] *Con Pier Paolo Pasolini*, ed. Enrico Magrelli (Rome: Bulzoni, 1977), p. 24.
[43] Cited by Massimo d'Avack in his *Cinema e letteratura* (Rome: Canesi, 1964), p. 111.
[44] Pasolini, "Al lettore nuovo," p. 10.
[45] Cited by Stack, *Pasolini*, pp. 31–32.

In all likelihood, Fellini did more than change Pasolini's dialogue. The characters of *Le notti di Cabiria*, particularly the heroine herself, exude a pathos and melancholy absent from Pasolini's films or novels. Similarly, the director Mauro Bolognini probably softened Pasolini's portrayal of proletarian youths in the script the latter wrote for Bolognini's 1959 film, *La notte brava*. While the young men in Pasolini's own films or novels move in a world apart—a world marked by a special language and code of behavior—Bolognini's youths are little more than impoverished versions of their bourgeois counterparts. Noting that *La notte brava* was the first film that he conceived and wrote by himself, Pasolini went on to observe that the completed film differed from what he had imagined while writing: "I tend to an almost obsessive realism; Bolognini tends to an elegant stylization."

Pasolini's understandable wish not to have others change his screenplays—his desire to have "facts, people and scenes realized" as he saw them—was certainly one of the factors that promoted him to try his hand at directing. It is also clear that he chafed at the limited role accorded the screenwriter; while acknowledging that the writer's task could be a beautiful one, he went on to complain: "Unfortunately, you work with ignorant, stupid people who never know what they want. A scriptwriter is not presumed to know anything about producing or distributing: he is simply supposed to work with the director."[46] In addition to these factors, even more fundamental reasons drew him to cinema. It was his conviction that the desire to make films reflected a need to "escape obsession" by experimenting and adopting "new, innovating technique[s]." In the case of cinema, this "innovating" technique had two important aspects. One was historical, for by the late 1950s he sensed that he had reached a cultural and ideological impasse in literature. The "new novel" and other avantgarde experiments just then coming into vogue held no interest for him. His other motive was, instead, more profoundly existential. He would always feel that cinema allowed him to come closer to reality. Like dialect, which offered what he called a "carnal approach" to the world of peasants, he believed that cinematic expression, that is, the "object-like concreteness of cinema," permitted him to "reach life more completely. To appropriate it, to live it through recreating it. Cinema permits me to maintain contact with reality—a physical, carnal contact, and even one, I'd say, of a sensual kind."[47]

Although, in retrospect, Pasolini's embrace of film clearly expressed deeply felt impulses, his transition from novelist to director nonetheless evoked a great deal of comment. To understand why this was so, one

[46] Pasolini, *Lettere*, pp. cxxvii–cxxviii.
[47] Cited by Duflot, *Entretiens*, p. 17.

must remember that by 1961, the year of Pasolini's first film, he had become a public figure—a recognized poet and novelist. This meant, as one critic put it, that when he began making films, it was "the first time that an intellectual of Pasolini's importance took on a completely different medium from that of literature, a medium whose origins and evolution were linked to the culture industry."[48] Even Jean Cocteau, the sole major poet-turned-filmmaker before him, had, unlike Pasolini, entered the world of cinema through the back door, that is, with a noncommercial, experimental short. Once immersed in the culture industry, Pasolini's fame grew as he came into contact with an international audience. It is to his films that I would like to turn now, viewing them against a superimposed, double backdrop: in relationship to Pasolini's other activities, both literary and political, and to historical and cultural moments and events. As I hope to show, Pasolini's films cannot be separated either from the body of his work or from the stage of European intellectual and artistic thought on which he himself was such a prominent player.

[48] Roberto Turigliatto, "Letteratura e cinema in Pasolini," in *Per Conoscere Pasolini* (Rome: Bulzoni e Teatro tenda, 1978), p. 99.

II

The Heritage of Neorealism

In fondo fare il cinema è una questione di sole.
  —Pier Paolo Pasolini (1962)

(In essence cinema is a question of the sun.)

WATCHING Pier Paolo shoot *Accattone* I felt as if I were present at the invention of cinema. It was the first time that Pier Paolo took the camera and handled it; it was also the first time that he raised questions and problems concerning cinematic language and style. He had very clear ideas on this point: he wanted a cinema composed of fixed framings and some traveling shots. . . . he was like someone who had not gone to school and was constrained to invent writing.[1]

So wrote Bernardo Bertolucci describing his initiation into cinema—an initiation that took place on the set of Pasolini's first film, *Accattone*. As soon as the film was released, it was clear that Pasolini's iconoclasm was not limited to what Bertolucci called the director's "deliberately naive" style. Indeed, the sharply divided critical opinion and right-wing disturbances that greeted *Accattone* in 1961 indicated that Pasolini would probably prove even more controversial as a filmmaker than as a novelist.

Discussing the debates that swirled around his first film, which is set in the Roman *borgate*, Pasolini suggested that he had chosen an inopportune time to depict the wretched existence of the city's sub-proletariat. Whereas, he implied, the portrayal of social misery in postwar neorealist films had reflected widespread poverty, the hunger and despair depicted in *Accattone* were, by the relatively affluent early 1960s, uncomfortable reminders of a past that most Italians preferred to forget. The protagonists of *Accattone* were no longer to be found in the mainstream of Italian life but on its ragged and miserable edges. And, he continued, if Italians were "shocked" by *Accattone*, it was precisely because they wanted to believe that the acute poverty of the postwar years had all but disappeared. By 1961, he observed,

[1] Bernardo Bertolucci, "Un ladro alla porta," *Cinema e cinema* 43 (May–August 1985), pp. 13–14. Incidentally, Bertolucci's first film, *La comare secca*, was based on a subject proposed by Pasolini.

Everyone—bourgeois critics and even Communists—had wound up convincing themselves that the world of the sub-proletariat no longer existed. And what about them? What was I to do with these twenty million people of the sub-proletariat? Put them in a concentration camp? Gas them? There was still a racist attitude toward the sub-proletariat—as if they came from a world that no longer existed. A headstone had been placed above their graves but they, poor souls, they continued to exist.[2]

Pasolini's observations were both true and false—socially acute yet deliberately simplistic. He was correct, of course, that Italy had changed considerably, even dramatically, in the sixteen years since the end of the war. At least partially as a result of these changes, the historical and ideological concerns that had dominated film in the late 1940s and early 1950s had been eclipsed by other issues. The characters of Fellini's *La dolce vita* (1960) and his *8 1/2* (1963), or of Antonioni's *L'avventura* (1959) and *L'eclisse* (1962) suffer not from poverty but from spiritual alienation and ennui. By the early 1960s, even films made by directors associated with the heyday of postwar neorealism—directors like Rossellini, De Sica, and Visconti—revealed new concerns and different directions.

Still, despite these changes, there was no sense of an abrupt rupture in the world of film. In this respect, Italy was very different from France, where, toward the end of the 1950s, the Young Turks of the New Wave turned on their elders, showing little mercy for the generation of filmmakers that had preceded them. Nothing remotely similar to this oedipal break occurred in Italy. On the contrary, neorealism, and its tradition of social commitment, remained visibly influential. Neorealist echoes are present, after all, in Fellini's *La strada* (1954) and in his *Le notti di Cabiria* (1956). And the work of some younger directors offered ample proof that social concerns had not vanished by any means: for example, the year 1961 witnessed not only *Accattone* but also Ermanno Olmi's *Il posto* and Francesco Rosi's *Salvatore Giuliano*.

True, Pasolini's characters are much lower on the social scale than Olmi's struggling clerks or Rosi's Sicilian bandits. Nonetheless, in light of the strong political tradition and the heterogeneous cast of Italian cinema, Pasolini's contention that Italy was "shocked" by the indictment of social misery in *Accattone* had a hollow, indeed polemical, ring. Certainly critics on the left—who were, in any case, far more influential and numerous than those on the right—were not "shocked" by Pasolini's depiction of social injustice. And, in fact, they objected not to Pasolini's depiction of the sub-proletariat per se but rather to the way he chose to portray it. Many of them even echoed complaints from the right that Pasolini's char-

[2] Pasolini, "Una visione del mondo epico-religiosa," *Bianco e Nero* (June 1964), p. 21.

acters were "amoral" and "depraved," consumed by "instincts" and "sensuality."

Unlike critics on the right, moreoever, those on the left, and in particular those associated with the Communist party, were distressed not only for moral reasons but for political ones as well. They feared, for example, that Pasolini's "depraved" sub-proletarians conveyed an erroneous, even dangerous, impression of an oppressed social class. Most of all, however—and this was at the root of the controversy surrounding the film—*they felt that Pasolini's poetic and fatalist vision actually subverted the Marxist impetus for social change and improvement.* Although couched in a variety of ways, this fundamental complaint was voiced by the majority of critics on the left. For example, one wrote that Pasolini never exhibits any "thust toward the conquest of an authentic and free humanity." Returning to this theme, still harsher critics accused him of a "bitter fatalism [that] signaled the end of human values," of not "combating or confronting the outer world," of depicting a "violence and desolation [outside] of any human rule." Observing that *Accattone* displayed a kind of existentialist ennui, one critic spoke for many when he remarked that "Pasolini is not only a phenomenon of literary fashion and Marxist journalism. He is something more. He is a poet, and he is a symptom of this era, a forerunner of leaden times—times without faith."[3]

One of the reasons, though by no means the only one, why reaction from the left was so strong may have been that *Accattone*—and, later, Pasolini's second film, *Mamma Roma* (1962)—first raised the hopes of those who wanted a socially conscious cinema but then quickly disappointed them. Such hopes were aroused initially, perhaps, not only because Pasolini himself was regarded as a Marxist but because his cinema had deep affinities with the intensely political cinema of the early neorealists. It was these affinitios certainly that at first viewing masked dissimilarities—as leftist critics soon realized to their dismay—that were perhaps even more profound. Like, for example, Rossellini's *Roma, città aperta* (*Rome, Open City*), both *Accattone* and *Mamma Roma* were shot on location and populated by nonprofessional actors. And both films concerned characters who lead even more desperate lives than the unemployed workers in De Sica's *Ladri di biciclette* (*Bicyle Thief*, 1948) or the impoverished fishermen in Visconti's *La terra trema* (1948).

Accattone—the central character in the film of that title—is a pimp, the lowest of the low. (He is played by Franco Citti.) When the film opens, Accattone is living off Maddalena, a prostitute who betrayed her former

[3] For these remarks (as well as further critical reactions to Pasolini's films) see *Da Accattone a Salò*, eds. Vittorio Boarini, Pietro Bonfiglioli, and Giorgio Cremonini, *Quaderni della Cineteca* (Bologna) No. 4 (May 1982), pp. 16–20.

boyfriend (also a pimp) to the police in order to be with Accattone. She is soon severely beaten by pals of the abandoned boyfriend and, refusing to identify her attackers for fear of her life, lands in jail. Accattone, left without any means of support, wanders about his desolate neighborhood. He meets a girl, Stella, and for the first time in his life, to his surprise—and ours—falls in love. She is as innocent as Accattone is corrupt. But despite his love for her, Accattone, urged on by inner demons he hates yet cannot control, sends her out to walk the streets. At the last moment she refuses the role she has been assigned. Meanwhile, Maddalena, learning of Accattone's love for another woman, denounces him to the police and he is placed under official surveillance. As a result, when he and his pals attempt the theft of a truck, the police are on hand. Accattone alone escapes on a stolen motorcycle only to collide with a truck and be killed.

Mamma Roma also deals with people on the lowest level of Roman life. After years of prostitution, Mamma Roma, the title character (played by Anna Magnani), has accumulated sufficient savings to establish herself and her teenage son, Ettore, in an apartment house in the barren outskirts of Rome. To compensate for years of being a social pariah, she is consumed by petit-bourgeois desires. Thus when Ettore falls in love with a young girl, Bruna—a figure of redemption similar to Accattone's Stella—Mamma Roma does her best to end the affair because Bruna is a poor unmarried mother. But Mamma Roma's past catches up with her in the sinister person of Carmine, an old boyfriend (played by Franco Citti), who forces her back to the streets. As for Ettore, he is traumatized when he learns of his mother's profession and he begins to steal. Caught in an act of petty thievery, he is brought to prison where he dies, delirious, strapped to a bed in his cell. When she hears the news, a devastated Mamma Roma must be prevented by her neighbors from committing suicide.

It is not merely the milieu of these films—one populated by whores, petty thieves, and unwed mothers—that recalls neorealist dramas. Like the filmmakers of a preceding generation, Pasolini emphasizes the economic and social chains that bind the characters. Mamma Roma's poverty-stricken parents virtually sold her, at the age of fourteen, to an elderly husband. After her husband was led away by police on their wedding day, she was forced onto the streets. Asked why her husband, Ettore's father, was no good, she replies that he was a thief and his mother a moneylender, and that he was descended from "beggars, hangmen, thieves and spies." How, then, we ask ourselves, could Ettore be other than what he is? And when Accattone attempts to break the cycle of poverty by working, and even by stealing—which, in his eyes and those of his friends, is a step above pimping—it is clear that the fates are against him. His inevitable descent suggests to Adelio Ferrero, author of an excellent study of Pasolini's cinema, the trajectory or "parabola" taken by characters in neorealist films. Like them, observes Ferrero, Accattone is portrayed in a "marginal and dependent condition as he follows his parabola of desperation and defeat; he is virtually never [seen] in a moment of awareness and protest. The lost protagonist of *Bicyle Thief* and the frustrated petit-bourgeois of *Umberto D* . . . come from the same matrix."[4]

But if Pasolini never lets us forget Accattone's desperate social condition, he also—and here we begin to see why traditional leftists were so disturbed by the film—underscores, even luxuriates in, the tragic, fatalistic, and even religious elements that constantly threatened to subvert the political thrust of neorealism itself. Accattone's "parabola of desperation and defeat"—a parabola that might have been confined to the social sphere—is imbued with a sense of tragic inexorability that virtually proclaims the futility of social or political struggle. The sense of tragic destiny that hovers around the edges of De Sica's *Bicycle Thief*, and that confronts—more starkly still—the doomed fishermen of Visconti's *La terra trema*, infuses every moment of Pasolini's film. Hope and struggle have no place in the world of *Accattone* because everything has been determined from the beginning. And the fate so implacably reserved for his characters is not—as in neorealist melodrama—merely economic or social ruin. Rather, as in high tragedy, it is nothing less than death itself.[5]

Premonitions of death, in fact, haunt *Accattone* from the outset. In the very first scene Accattone and his friends are discussing the death of a companion who died from a jump into the river. Soon, when Accattone decides that he will attempt a similar dive, they begin to joke about his possible death, asking who will inherit his woman, what kind of funeral he would like, and so on. Their remarks have an apocalyptic ring: "We are doomed men," they say, or "This is the end of the world." As befits this world of doom, funerals constitute an important motif: the sight, midway through the film, of a funeral procession dominated by a cross outlined against the sky is later echoed by a silent, hallucinatory sequence in which Accattone dreams of his own death and funeral, to which, iron-

---

[4] Adelio Ferrero, *Il cinema di Pier Paolo Pasolini* (Venice: Marsilio, 1977), p. 9.

[5] Concerning the central role played by death in Pasolini's films, one of the director's most acute critics, Lino Miccichè, writes: "Death in Pasolini is not only, or not so much, the biochemical conclusion of biological existence but, rather, the defining law of existence, the sovereign drive, the necessary and definitive conclusion (the only definitive one and therefore the only really necessary one) of every discourse and every existence: it alone is therefore the dominant tension in reality. Such a conception of Thanatos (which governs every human action) is metahistorical by definition because it only coincides in one moment (that of physical death) with historical existence (with existence in history). At the same time the only way of exorcising such a haunting phantom is by inserting it into a mythical web, making it the ultimate, conclusive stitch." See Lino Miccichè, *Il cinema italiano degli anni '60* (Venice: Marsilio, 1975), p. 158.

ically, he is denied admittance. At the end, like all of Pasolini's protagonists, Accattone meets a death that is both definitive and absolute
("There's only death," remarked Pasolini, "there's nothing beyond") and,
at the same time, or for that very reason, ennobling: "The only thing that
gives a true greatness to man is the fact that he will die."[6]

Far more haunted by death than most neorealist films, both *Accattone*
and *Mamma Roma* are also—and this, too, must have disturbed leftists—
far more overtly Christian. The religious dimension of *Accattone* is announced from the outset: the chords of Bach's *Passion according to St.
Matthew* accompany the credits, setting the stage as for a religious tragedy or sacred drama. Christian iconography infuses both gestures (Accattone crosses himself before diving into the Tiber) and mise en scène (before he dives, we glimpse a marble angel behind him on the bridge). Again
and again, Accattone's martyrdom is implicitly compared to that of
Christ. When he is faint from lack of food, the published script tells us
that his "head rolls on his back like that of Christ," and when he attempts
to work he appears bent over with a burden like "Christ under the cross."
Echoes of the Passion are particularly strong at the close of the film: the
two friends with Accattone at his death are—handcuffed, heads bowed—
reminiscent of the two thieves. Similar iconography infuses *Mamma
Roma*. There the arrangement of the banquet table and guests in the
opening scene suggests the Last Supper, while Mamma Roma, pushing
her fruit and vegetable cart before her, seems to be mounting the hill of
Calvary. Like Accattone's death, Ettore's agony is likened to that of
Christ: as he lies dying with hands and legs outstretched on his prison
bed, the camera pans up and down his body three times with a wide-angle
lens, foreshortening him like the dead Christ in Mantegna's painting
Cristo morto.

In *Accattone*, in particular, metaphysical and Christian overtones are
reinforced by allusions to the *Divine Comedy*. Presaging the downward
Dantesque spiral that would inform Pasolini's cinematic trajectory—and
that would culminate in the peculiarly modern inferno of *Salò*—*Accattone* is prefaced by a quote from the *Purgatory*. Drawn from canto V—
which concerns the late conversion and, consequently, the possible salvation of those who die a violent death (the "penitents of the last
hour")—the quote underscores the struggle that takes place in the soul of
a sinner torn between Satan and God, between sin and salvation. It reads:
"God's angel took me, and he from Hell cried: 'O thou from Heaven,
why dost thou rob me? Thou carriest off with thee this man's eternal part
for a little tear that takes him from me.' "

As *Accattone* progresses, the significance of this quote becomes ines-

---

[6] *Con Pier Paolo Pasolini*, ed. Enrico Magrelli (Rome: Bulzoni, 1977), pp. 59–60.

capable: Accattone may belong to an oppressed social class but he is also—and perhaps above all—a soul in purgatory.[7] He journeys through Dantesque circles populated by whores and thieves until he meets Stella, who, like Dante's Beatrice, beckons him toward salvation. By making him aware of his degradation, she compels him to question the manner of his life. From that moment on, he is torn beween his desire to change, on the one hand, and the forces that bring him back to his sordid existence. As in the work of modern Catholic writers or directors such as Robert Bresson or Georges Bernanos, in Pasolini's films the characters must reach bottom before they can be redeemed. And Accattone's abasement *is* total: not only does he rob his young son of a religious medal but he attempts to turn his beloved into a prostitute even as he prays to the Virgin to save him from himself. His tormented struggle can be ended only by a welcome death, a death that offers him, in Pasolini's words, "a pallid act of redemption. There is no other solution for him, as for a huge number of people like him."[8]

Save for a few observations to the effect that Accattone's Catholicism was "pagan" or "pre-bourgeois," Pasolini did not really discuss the pronounced religious and even specifically Christian aspects of *Accattone*. But this very silence bespoke deep ambivalence, perhaps even defensiveness, where his own faith was concerned. Deeply religious as an adolescent, he had experienced mystical longings so intense that—as he confessed in his diary—at times he seemed to see "images of the Madonna move and smile."[9] The ideological awakening he experienced in young manhood, his discovery of Marx and Gramsci, challenged this faith even as it altered his view of the world. Still, although he later declared himself (and probably was) an atheist, although he never ceased to struggle against harsh clerical laws, he never denied that Christianity was deeply rooted within him. In 1961, the year of *Accattone*, he observed movingly in the Communist paper *Vie nuove*: "As for me, I'm not afraid to say that I'm anticlerical, but I know that within me there are two thousand years of Christianity. With my prayers, I have constructed Romanesque churches, and then Gothic churches and then Baroque churches: these are my patrimony in content and style. I would be crazy if I denied what a

---

[7] *Accattone* is so permeated by the presence of Dante that one critic, Pio Baldelli, sees the film as the "itinerary of a sinner," marked by the following four stages: (1) the inferno of the borgata (Accattone and his friends); (2) the blessed woman (Accattone's meeting with Stella); (3) purgatory (Accattone torn between his desire for wealth and his love for Stella); and (4) Calvary of redemption and desperate apotheosis (Accattone's humiliation and death). See Pio Baldelli, *Film e opera letteraria* (Padua: Marsilio, 1964), pp. 350–353.

[8] Pasolini, *Accattone* (Rome: Edizioni FM, 1961), p. 22.

[9] Pasolini, *Lettere* (Turin: Einaudi, 1986), p. xxvi.

strong force they are within me—if I left the monopoly of Good to the priests."[10]

It is this deeply ambivalent, deeply felt "Christian patrimony" that marks his early films, a patrimony that, waxing and waning, took various forms as time passed. In 1964, what he called a furious "wave of irrationalism" impelled him to make a film about Christ, *Il Vangelo secondo Matteo (The Gospel according to St. Matthew)*. While he never returned to explicitly Christian themes or iconography after that work, his films were always peopled with saints and martyrs, infused with a sense of guilt and sin. As the years went by, his Manichaean vision offered less and less hope of salvation: at its best, life would always be felt, as he once admitted, as "imperfection." "If," he wrote in 1964,

> a work of art is in some deep and mysterious way a self-therapy, what is it curing us of if not life itself [since] life is imperfection, a sense of postponement, a sense of incompleteness. In the end, the artistic process has not succeeded in liberating me from these famous, harmful, burning, and incomprehensible "religious elements" [that] are still there, still intact.[11]

If, as this remark suggests, Pasolini always experienced his religious ambivalence in a deeply problematical way, for his critics—particularly his orthodox Communist critics—the issue was, of course, far simpler. For them, Pasolini's religious or mystical longings, his quest for the absolute, were still another sign of his "decadence" and his "irrationalism"—qualities in their eyes, that stood sharply opposed to "rational" Marxism and ideological commitment. His first films only confirmed the worst fears that his poems and novels had earlier evoked in such critics. As suggested earlier, the funereal tone and metaphysical context of both *Accattone* and *Mamma Roma* imply certainly the vanity of social struggle. After all, in a Jansenist world where human dramas are played out in terms of sin and salvation, where the *borgata* becomes not a "sociological" sphere but an absolute one,[12] nothing—certainly no change in the social or economic order—can halt the downward spiral that destiny assumes. Furthermore, Pasolini's subversion went beyond merely putting into question the worth and value of political action. *Accattone*, in particular, seems implicitly to denounce the middle-class or bourgeois aspirations, that is, the desire to better oneself and one's children, that traditional leftists—including, of course, the Communist party—hold for workers. For Accattone himself—and in this he is profoundly different

---

[10] Pasolini, *Le belle bandiere* (Rome: Riuniti, 1977), p. 170.

[11] Cited in "Spirito e lettera nel film di Pier Paolo Pasolini," *Cineforum* No. 4 (December 1964), p. 971.

[12] Franco Brevini uses these terms to describe the *borgata* in "Il cinema," in *Pasolini*, ed. Brevini (Milan: Mondadori, 1981), p. 378.

not only from the poor people of neorealist films but even from Mamma Roma—has no wish to improve his standing in the world, to better his condition. Indeed, as one critic observed, it is precisely his "pride, his refusal of salaried work, his hatred of order, and his retrograde conception of honor [that] seem the last bastion in the face of an egalitarian, but also reductivist, civilization."[13] At the deepest level this means—and I shall return to this issue when I discuss Pasolini's style—that *Accattone* exalts the sub-proletariat for the very "misery" that political activists wish to eradicate.

In the face of a film that denounced social misery and yet somehow ennobled it, that questioned the value of political action, it is hardly surprising that many orthodox leftists were apprehensive and wary. Still, politics alone can scarcely account for the often vituperative and violent epithets that were applied to Pasolini's first film. *Accattone* was denounced not only for irrationalism and aestheticism but also for "violence," "pathology," "morbidness," "fatalism," "egoism," "ideological capriciousness," "complicity in degradation," "anti-historicism," and—that all-encompassing word—"decadence." Judging by the critic Angelo Guglielmi, the far left was no less forgiving than mainstream Communists: calling Pasolini "our crudest and most vulgar" writer, Guglielmi condemns the poet for his "licentiousness" as well as his "hopelessly decadent" and "narcissistic" characters.[14]

The hysterical edge one senses in such remarks reveals not only political differences but a deep homophobia. "Decadence," of course, has often been a code word for homosexuality,[15] but even terms like "pathology" and "narcissism"—when used by Pasolin's critics—had sexual overtones. Without even being consciously aware of it, many critics were probably disturbed by Pasolini's depiction of the *borgata* less for political reasons than because, as they (and everyone else) knew full well, it was frequently the scene of his sexual encounters. And if such leftists denounced Pasolini's insistence on emotions and instincts, it was at least partially because such "instincts" included sexual impulses perceived as ungovernable and unforgivable.

Pasolini did not directly confront his critics on the issue of homosexu-

[13] Annie Goldmann, "L'exilé," in *Pasolini*, special issue of *La revue d'esthéthique* N.S. No. 3 (1982), p. 56.

[14] Cited in *Il dialogo, il potere, la morte: la critica e Pasolini*, ed. Luigi Martellini (Bologna: Cappelli, 1979), p. 55.

[15] Harold Beaver makes this point about the use of the word "decadence" in his "Homosexual Signs," *Critical Inquiry* (Autumn 1981), p. 104. Ironically, the moralistic tone of the Italian critics who charged Pasolini with "decadence" reappeared, attenuated, in a latter-day reversal when a number of British critics debated whether or not Pasolini's images of men were "self-oppressive." On this issue, see Richard Dyer's "Pasolini and Homosexuality," in *Pier Paolo Pasolini*, ed. Paul Willemen (London: British Film Institute, 1977).

ality until the late 1960s. But while for years they continued to deplore his "decadence" and "narcissism," he repeatedly and emphatically decried what he called their "moralism"—a moralism, in his eyes, that was one of the quintessential traits of the bourgeoisie. ("Being moralistic," he once declared unequivocally, "means being bourgeois in the most horrendous way."[16]) And in an important passage written as early as 1960 he sought to analyze—from a Freudian perspective—the motives, and nature, of such moralism. Insisting, as always, on the profound and often irrational impulses that govern thought and action, on the "personal and psychological factors" that underlie even philosophy and ideology, in this passage Pasolini suggests that it was precisely the petit-bourgeois origins of many Communist critics—*origins they seek to repress*—that made them leery of Freudianism, the subconscious, and, implicitly, everything (like homosexuality) that is not "normal." Although, he remarks, Communists "disassociate" themselves from their own origins by accepting the class struggle,

> they do not delve deeply enough into personal and psychological factors. . . . Marxism has never confronted the problem of irrationality in a satisfactory way. While logic can explain Gramsci's thought and actions, it cannot explain the "sentiment," the "faith" that enabled him to endure prison and death. . . . Communists have a conventional diffidence toward psychology and, in this case, toward psychoanalysis. . . . In renouncing introspection, the militant Marxist critic is often the victim of his own unconscious.[17]

This passage underscores one of the profound differences between Pasolini and traditional leftists even as it hints at the roots of the controversy stirred up by *Accattone*. While the attacks directed against Pasolini became, perhaps, more intense when he turned to cinema (and its potentially vast audience), his profound iconoclasm had begun to emerge years earlier. The chasm separating him from those he called "orthodox Marxists"—that is, from Communists—had first become apparent in the course of a series of important cultural and political debates that took place throughout the 1950s. Thus before returning to *Accattone* and *Mamma Roma* for a closer look at Pasolini's style, I shall briefly examine these debates. Not only did they set the stage for later controversies but they also gave Pasolini the opportunity to voice some of the ideological and stylistic impulses that would inform his work for decades to come.

At the heart of these debates lay changing attitudes toward social and cultural ideals which had been inspired largely by the experience of the war and the Resistance. With the passage of time, postwar hopes for a

---

[16] Cited by Ferdinando Camon in *Il mestiere di scrittore* (Milan: Garzanti, 1973), p. 118.

[17] Cited by Michel Davíd in his *La psicoanalisi nella cultura italiana* (Turin: Boringhieri, 1966), p. 560.

new society, a new culture—hopes embodied in neorealism, in the notion of "committed" intellectuals—began to fade. As they did so, the left itself became less cohesive: if most Communists followed the increasingly hard line taken by the party during the cold war, others were prey to a growing unease and disillusionment. And decisive political events—particularly, in 1956, the brutal repression of the Hungarian Revolution and Khrushchev's speech revealing Stalinist atrocities—fueled this unease even as they gave rise to renewed debates concerning the political role that committed left-wing intellectuals should, or could, continue to play in Italy. Years later, looking back at these debates, Franco Fortini, a leading Italian intellectual who had participated in them, began an article entitled "The Writer's Mandate and the End of Anti-Fascism" with a concise summary of the issues discussed:

> Between 1945 and 1953, and again in 1956, there was a lot of discussion in Italy on the relationship between cultural and political activity. Particular attention was paid to the theme of defining the status of writers and artists within a country, within a party and within a socialist political perspective. All Italian intellectuals were involved in the discussion, which went through stages determined by national and international events—the polemic over the demise of *Il Politecnico* (1947), Zhadanov's theses on art and literature (1947), the publication of the works of Gramsci (1947–1949) and of Lukács (1953–1956), the debates on commitment (1945–1947), the 'cultural front' (1948), 'neorealism' (1945–1950) and 'socialist realism' (1955).
>
> These debates implied, in general, finding an answer to the question of what sort of leading role was or could be assumed by the Communist party in the cultural life of our country.[18]

The fact that, as Fortini suggests, the Italian Communist party was a pivotal player in these debates, and certainly the single most important cultural force on the left, meant that the positions taken by others tended to define themselves in relationship to that of the party. Despite his iconoclasm, Pasolini was no exception to this general rule. There is no doubt that the implicit presence of the party is felt throughout his essays: when, for example, he spoke of "orthodox Marxists" in his essays of the 1950s, or of the "office boys" of the party in the 1960s, or of the "New Power" in the 1970s (when the Communists had become very strong), it was always clear to his readers that he had the party in mind. As Geoffrey Nowell-Smith observes:

> Although [Pasolini] has often taken what seems at first sight to be rather arbitrary and individualistic political positions—irresponsible even—they are al-

---

[18] Franco Fortini, "The Writer's Mandate and the End of Anti-Fascism," trans. in *Screen* 15, No. 1 (Spring 1974), p. 33.

ways . . . *political* positions, adopted in light of the politico-cultural situation
and in particular of the role being played in that situation by the PCI. Sometimes
the position was hostile to the PCI, sometimes favorable, but either way the
Party is always a co-ordinate. He fights it, he supports it, he opens a "dialogue"
with it . . . he may ostentatiously turn his back on it. But the very ostentation
only serves to prove the point that his interlocutor, real or imagined, was always the same.[19]

If the party's position is felt implicitly in Pasolini's essays, it also informed—in a far more direct and unequivocal fashion—the attacks that
"orthodox Marxists," that is, Communist critics, launched against him
throughout the 1950s. Marked by the party's own cold-war intransigeance, these attacks also revealed the extent to which the party's position
on cultural matters in the 1950s had been shaped by the Hungarian philosopher Gyorgy Lukács. Italian critics did not merely echo Lukács's terminology; they also tended—alas—to reproduce the harsh, dogmatic
tone that casts such a long shadow over much of his later work. For example, in one such work, *Realism in Our Time*, the Hungarian critic
sweepingly condemns the "ideology of Modernism" even as he charges
"subjective" and "decadent" writers like Beckett and Kafka with creating
an "angst-ridden" view of reality from which man and the world have
disappeared. This vision of an absurd world, contends Lukács, does more
than obscure the facts of historical and social oppression: it also paralyzes
the will to act and to improve man's situation. To replace this literature
of exacerbated subjectivity, Lukács calls for a "realistic" literature, one
in which "typical" and positive characters confront the outside world as
they struggle for economic and social progress.

In this rigidly ideological and strangely puritanical climate—a climate
in which Kafka and Beckett were placed in the dock, in which "subjectivity" and "decadence" (to say nothing of sexuality) constituted cultural
crimes—it is hardly surprising that Pasolini came under fire. Lukácsian
motifs run throughout one of the best-known attacks against him, written
by Alberto Asor Rosa, a left-wing intellectual. Amplifying criticisms he
had directed against Pasolini's novels and poems throughout the 1950s,
Asor Rosa discussed the poet at length in an influential work published
in 1965, *Scrittori e popolo*. Here Asor Rosa contends that Pasolini's writings—along with certain works by Moravia and Visconti (who, like Pasolini, tend to emphasize sexuality)—cannot be considered part of the
"ideal patrimony of the workers' movement"; far from being "progressive and positive," these writings are merely the "petrified remains of
bourgeois culture." In fact, says Asor Rosa, the only aspect of Marxism

[19] Geoffrey Nowell-Smith, "Pasolini's Originality," in *Pier Paolo Pasolini*, ed. Paul Willemen, p. 6.

"which counts for something in [Pasolini's] narrative work" is his populism,[20] that is, his portrait of the sub-proletariat. But even this populism, Asor Rosa is quick to note with veiled allusions to the poet's homosexuality, is suspect for at least two important reasons: (1) the motives that drew Pasolini to the people were misplaced since they sprang not from ideology but from "sentimental necessity"; (2) by giving instincts and sensuality a "quasi-sacred" role, Pasolini renders the people not only incapable of political action but even "sub-human." Referring to one of Pasolini's most famous poems, "Le ceneri di Gramsci," Asor Rosa adamantly declares:

> Here the proletariat becomes . . . the only thing it can be in the depths of Pasolini's inspiration: a religious symbol, an object of psychological and spiritual analysis, a projection of hate and love which is moved by the "heat of instincts and esthetic passion." It becomes a totally arbitrary living creature which reflects only Pasolini's own mania to identify with the world.[21]

It is significant that *Scrittori e popolo* indicts not only Pasolini but also—and perhaps above all—Antonio Gramsci. As the quote by Fortini cited earlier suggests, the postwar discovery of Gramsci's works (like those of Lukács) had repercussions on Italian cultural life well into the 1950s and, to judge by Asor Rosa's book, into the 1960s. Gramsci was not only a great political thinker and activist but also an important theorist of Marxist aesthetics—and one who differed from Lukács in almost every respect.[22] (Not surprisingly, in the cold-war climate of the 1950s the Communist party's admiration for Lukács was matched by its wariness toward Gramsci.) Gramsci exhibits virtually none of the prescriptive moralism—the moralism that Pasolini deemed "horrendous"—that permeates the work of Lukács and "orthodox Marxists" like Asor Rosa. Gramsci never judges; he never suggests, for example, that political considerations render one artistic style or movement—be it "realism" or "modernism"—better or more "positive" than another. In Gramsci's eyes, the writer is not a privileged being, untouched by history or culture, who is free to decide upon a given course; rather, like everyone else, he is emmeshed in a web of social, economic, and cultural conditions that are inevitably reflected in his work. Consequently, for Gramsci, the critic's task is not to judge a work of art but to explore its "hidden ideologies"— to see what political and historical tendencies they call into question on

---

[20] Alberto Asor Rosa, *Scrittori e popolo* (Rome: Samonà e Savelli, 1965), p. 426.

[21] Ibid., p. 402.

[22] Interestingly, too, in light of the tremendous affinity Pasolini felt for Gramsci, the latter was one of the rare early Marxist theoreticians open to psychoanalysis. See Jennifer Stone's "Italian Freud: Gramsci, Giulia Schucht, and Wild Analysis," *October* No. 28 (Spring 1984).

the part of both writer and audience. These ideologies, argues Gramsci, must be deciphered before they can be changed in order to further a new cultural hegemony.

Unlike Lukács, too, whose focus is almost entirely upon content, Gramsci—and here he foreshadows the socio-linguistic approach that would characterize Pasolini—analyzes the *language* of literary works. In this, of course, he reflects issues that were of particular importance in Italy, where the centuries-old lack of a national language meant that the ensuing division between "written" and "spoken" language, and the presence of dialects, had noteworthy historical dimensions. In a passage that almost seems to foreshadow Barthes's notion of "écriture," Gramsci observes: "In addition to its given cultural and sentimental world, the work of art contains other 'historical' elements [such as] its language, perceived not only as a purely verbal expression which could be fixed in a certain grammatical time and place, but as an ensemble of images and modes of expression not encompassed by grammar."[23]

It is Gramsci's deeply historical, deliberately nonjudgmental view of literature, together with his emphasis on style and language, that subtends Pasolini's critical essays of the 1950s. Offering an implicit challenge to the prescriptive literary moralism of "orthodox Marxists" like Asor Rosa, these essays were first published in *Officina*, a review that Pasolini helped found, which, in general, had a distinctly Gramscian cast. Looking back at his involvement with *Officina*, in 1969 Pasolini remarked to one interviewer:

> The post-war period produced a flood of sentimentalism, with the discovery of everyday humdrum life and all that. Yet along with this there was also the first serious rethinking of a rationalist-ideological kind, and I think I can fairly say that this coincided with the review *Officina*, which was founded by me and several friends of mine, Leonetti, Roversi, Fortini and others in the mid fifties. *Officina* provided the first critical revision of a rationalist kind of neorealism and of the whole of Italian literature, naturally in a fairly sporadic and fragmentary way. This rationalism had marxist origins, but with heterodox tendencies, and although it had marxist origins it was very much in polemic with the Communist Party.[24]

For Pasolini and the others at *Officina*, a "critical revision" of literature, and especially of neorealism, implied a kind of Gramscian or socio-historic analysis of writers and/or literary movements. Moreoever, their investigation of the inextricable links between culture and politics did not

---

[23] Gramsci, *Letteratura e vita nazionale* (Rome: Riuniti, 1977), pp. 25–26.
[24] Cited by Oswald Stack in *Pasolini on Pasolini* (Bloomington and London: Indiana University Press, 1969), pp. 80–81.

limit itself to the past: acutely aware of their own place in the historical process, the *Officina* critics also constantly examined which, if any, ideological and artistic choices remained open to left-wing writers and artists who, like themselves, came from the bourgeoisie.

This is not to suggest that the political/cultural nexus of the past and that of the present were approached separately: if Pasolini, in particular, was so intent on examining past culture, it was largely so that he could situate himself within a continuum that was at once literary, social, and historical. And, as one might have expected of this most personal and poetic of critics, he viewed this literary continuum largely in stylistic terms. For him, then, the "critical revision" of past literature meant, above all, reexamining the *language* used by earlier writers and literary movements. In this sense, his *Officina* essays, like Roland Barthes's 1953 work, *Le degré zéro de la littérature*, were animated by a desire to probe the ideological implications of style. (Like Barthes, too, Pasolini's analyses of language and style would lead him, less than a decade later, to the study of semiology.[25]) Gian Carlo Ferretti, who has devoted a book to the phenomenon of *Officina*, suggests that Pasolini's essays of the 1950s combine Gramsci's (Marxist) cultural historicism with Leo Spitzer's (formal) stylistic analyses. In Ferretti's view, the combination of these two approaches allowed Pasolini to pursue a

> socio-politico-linguistic analysis concerning the link between the problems of style and language and the history of intellectuals and social classes. This approach is clearly distinct from both . . . stylistic or hermetic-modernist criticism and the [content-oriented] critics who were inspired by Marxism.[26]

For the most part, Pasolini applies this "socio-politico-linguistic" approach to the two major Italian literary movements of the twentieth century: on the one hand, he is concerned with the hermetic, formalist, "irrational" tradition (so marked in his own early poetry) that stems from Mallarmé and other French symbolists and, on the other, with the neorealist reaction to it. A formal, stylistic analysis of the language that characterizes these two, apparently so opposed, literary movements leads him into the realm of ideology and history. Examining, for example, the irrational, mystical, and precious language of hermetic/modernist literature, Pasolini notes that it was totally suited to express emotions and the inner self. But, he continues, its corresponding *inability* to deal with the outer

---

[25] Unlike Pasolini, however, Barthes did try to envision a style that would be free of determinants. But in thus trying to place himself outside history, Barthes fell into the trap history reserves for such audacious attempts: in retrospect, what he saw as the "neutral" style of Robbe-Grillet or Camus is undeniably linked to a given historical moment.

[26] Gian Carlo Ferretti, *Officina: Cultura, letteratura e politica negli anni cinquanta* (Turin: Einaudi, 1975), p. 22.

world, history, or the class struggle also made it the perfect literature for the Fascist state. Even its so-called stylistic liberty was historically determined—a result, he asserts, of the collapse of "bourgeois ideology"—and hence merely illusory.

> Anti-Fascist involution was the result of the same decadence of liberal and romantic bourgeois ideology that led to the literary involution of stylistic research done for its own sake, to a formalism filled only with its own aesthetic consciousness. . . . In a period of reactionary, centralist State politics, language achieved a maximum of "fixation" perhaps never before seen in Italy.[27]

But what of neorealism, which reacted against the precious rhetoric, the "fixed" language, of hermetic literature? Here, perhaps, it should be noted that while Pasolini's discussion of neorealism bears more upon writers—Pavese, Vittorini, Pratolini—than upon filmmakers, his attempts to situate the phenomenon in cultural and political terms are clearly applicable to cinema. And one must also keep in mind that neorealist cinema did not by any means follow parameters laid out first by literature. In fact, as Pasolini pointed out, quite the contrary was true: "Since about 1936, the year of *Modern Times*, cinema has been ahead of literature. . . . Cinematic neorealism (*Rome, Open City*) prefigured all the literary Italian neorealism which came after the war and lasted into the 1950s."[28]

Whether discussing neorealist literature or cinema, Pasolini's analysis leads him to a disquieting conclusion: he is convinced that, despite its opposition to the hermetic literature of the Fascist era, neorealism was but the other face of bourgeois culture. He does not deny, of course, that neorealism made important innovations designed to capture everyday reality and express historical events: hence it mixed styles, reproduced the "direct discourse" of ordinary people, and emphasized the social and historical backdrop of events. (This last element, he notes, lent itself especially well to cinematic expression.) But he proceeds to argue that, despite its innovations and good intentions, neorealism could not avoid certain pitfalls since it was undermined by two important factors. One was the lack of a mass base; the other—which is clearly of great interest to him — was its unwillingness or inability to create a "new" language.

If, Pasolini now continues, neorealism did not create a "new" language, it was largely because it ignored issues related to style. As a result of this fatal indifference, neorealism was haunted by an involuntary tendency to incorporate some of the metaphorical, romantic, and even religious and decadent elements of past literary language. Proceeding as if its

---

[27] Pasolini, *Passione e ideologia* (Milan: Garzanti, 1960), pp. 335, 482.
[28] Pasolini, *Empirismo eretico* (Milan: Garzanti, 1972), p. 190.

literary, ethical, and phenomenological vision did not need to be questioned, neorealism wound up "readopting a linguistic material which was dated and often about to perish."[29] This meant that, in the end, neorealism fell back on the very language developed during the pre-Fascist period. And how, Pasolini asks, could the ideal of "national popular" culture, which neorealism sought to realize, be achieved in precisely the language created by the "conservative bourgeoisie . . . which gave us Fascism"?[30] Taking this one step further, he concludes one essay with the observation that neorealism fell prey to some of the irrational remnants of past culture that permeate Marxism itself: "The adoption of Marxist philosophy originally comes from a sentimental and moralistic impetus and is therefore continually permeable to the rising of the religious, and naturally of the catholic, spirit."[31]

After thus mapping out the principal literary strategies embraced by preceding generations, Pasolini comes, finally, to his own era. And once there he poses a fundamental existential and ideological question: what choices, what language(s), are possible for contemporary committed writers like himself who must reject both these earlier literary currents—that is, both hermetic/modernist literature and neorealism—because of the ideologies they carry within them? It is clear to him that whatever the personal cost—and given his love for the hermetic tradition, in his case the cost must have been high indeed—contemporary writers must avoid the "precious irrationalism" that inspired not only the involution of a Rimbaud, a Proust, but also the "private" literature of the Fascist state. The historical and ideological awareness that came with the experience of the Resistance and the Liberation, and the discovery of Marx and Gramsci, has, he declares, rendered this path impossible: "the world which was, at first, a pure source of sensations expressed by means of a ratiocinative and precious irrationalism, has now become an object of ideological, if not philosophical, awareness and, as such, demands stylistic experiments of a radically new type."[32] As for neorealism, despite the lure it still holds for many, it, too, uses a "superseded" language, a language permeated by "bourgeois ideology." Moreoever—and here the gap between Pasolini and "orthodox Marxists" becomes palpable—he maintains that neo-realism is built upon a "myth" that, given the climate of the mid-1950s, is no longer valid. Both the diminution of hopes for political change and historical events have, he argues, eroded the "official ideologies" of the postwar period. Implicitly taking issue with the Communist party, he contends that new political and social realities render any

[29] *Passione e ideologia*, p. 329.
[30] Ibid., p. 329.
[31] Ibid., p. 484.
[32] Ibid., p. 484.

fidelity to the "myth of the Resistance"—the myth, of course, underlying neorealism—"anti-historical."

Still, even as Pasolini rejects the past, he is only too well aware of the virtual impossibility of creating a new literature or culture when the society to which they would correspond has yet to be realized. Forced to reject a past that is ideologically compromised, unable to embrace an unknown future, the contemporary left-wing writer, he sadly admits, is caught in a kind of ideological and existential limbo. Hinting at the dilemma that would haunt him throughout his life, he describes this writer as someone who, trapped at a difficult historical moment and impossibly self-aware, can do little more than bear witness—through his own pain and struggle—to a period of unhappy transition. In an essay written in 1954, the only glimmer of hope he raises—and even this glimmer fades in later essays—is that from this very "pain" a new poetry will be born.

> Whether we cannot be, or do not want to be, Communists (it comes to the same thing), the very fact of having to face this new, implicit, social and moral measure, this new configuration of the past and this new perspective of the future . . . works within us. That is, it works within those of us who have remained bourgeois with the violence and the inertia of a psychology which has been historically determined. . . . But, in our view, the situation which confronts us daily—a situation of choices that are left unmade, of dramas left unresolved because of hypocrisy or weakness, of false "relaxation," of discontent for everything that may have given a fullness (however restless) to preceding generations—seems sufficiently dramatic to produce a new poetry.[33]

Voicing this crisis repeatedly in the poems and essays of the 1950s, Pasolini seems a Janus-like creature, torn between, on the one hand, the religious and cultural sensibilities of his "bourgeois heritage" and, on the other, a "new perspective of the future" for which he could find no artistic embodiment. A sense of limbo, of lacerating tension, informs the very title, *Passione e ideologia*, of an anthology of critical essays he published in 1957. On the side of "passion" lay his deep thirst for absolutes, his "sentimental" populism, and his love for the self-conscious and precious language of the symbolists—an outdated language, as he knew only too well, that reflected the "collapse of bourgeois ideology." On the side of ideology and reason lay, of course, the historical awareness that would have him jettison a beloved aesthetic tradition. Schematically summing up this dichotomy in 1961, the year of *Accattone*, he told the readers of a column he wrote for the Communist paper *Vie nuove*: "[My] political ideology is Marxist, but my aesthetic ideology, however modified, comes from the experience of the decadence and thus brings with it the debris of

[33] Ibid., p. 326.

a culture which has been superseded—that is, evangelism, humanitarianism, etc."[34]

As the above remark suggests, it is Pasolini's style, his "esthetic ideology," that reveals the full measure of his ties to the past and his "passion," the depth of the gap separating his cinema from one animated largely by social and ideological concerns. This gap is so profound, in fact, that one of Pasolini's most perceptive critics, Lino Miccichè, virtually dismisses the ideological component in Pasolini's films. Defending *Accattone* against those left-wing critics who attacked the film for its mistaken political ideology, Micchichè argues that the film cannot be judged solely on such terms:

> *Accattone* is not a film which contains or implies a mistaken or regressive political ideology for the very good reason that . . . it makes no claim to be an ideological representation of the condition of the proletariat. [Rather] it applies . . . the "ideology of death"—which torments and exalts Pier Paolo Pasolini, the bourgeois intellectual —to the proletariat world. Thus—and this points to the futility of a purely ideological discourse about the film—Accattone's death is not the death of a "historical" sub-proletarian of the borgata. It is, instead, the—formal—conclusion of a basic premise concerning death that springs from Pasolini's inner world.[35]

I would not go quite so far as Miccichè. Although I think that the balance between passion and ideology was, indeed, precarious—and the scales were always tipped toward passion—I also believe that much of the special tone of Pasolini's work comes, precisely, from this tension. Until the mid-1960s, he consciously sought to portray the world of social and historical realities, to prevent himself from taking refuge in the ivory tower of hermeticism or from giving in to what he would later call the "divine temptation" of mannerism—a temptation embodied in a precious and artificial language. Clearly, too, this tension inhabits his very first films, in which neorealist milieus and social concerns are filtered through a deeply religious, fatalistic sensibility. But at an even deeper level, as Pasolini himself suggested, this struggle or tension also gave rise to what was, perhaps, a "new stylistics." And if this stylistics did not point to the future, neither did it accept the past: for even as it evoked what could be called the "aesthetic" of neorealism, as critics sensed uneasily, it also subverted it.

Analyzing some of the essential features of the neorealist aesthetic, the French philosopher Gilles Deleuze makes several observations that offer

---

[34] Pasolini, *Le belle bandiere*, p. 160.
[35] Micciché, *Il cinema italiano degli anni '60*, p. 157.

a context in which to examine the precise nature of Pasolini's subversion. Reversing a fairly longstanding tradition that relegates neorealism to a very definite cinematic past, Deleuze argues instead that important aspects of neorealism characterize some of the most significant directors and moments of postwar cinema, that is, the French New Wave, German films of the 1970s, and American directors like Robert Altman and Martin Scorsese. For Deleuze, these examplars of modernist cinema share the neorealist outlook, which lies in depicting "reality as discursive and full of lacunae," composed of "fragmentary, broken meetings," and devoid of a "vector or a line . . . which lengthens or shortens events."[36] In his view, even a relatively late neorealist film like Fellini's *I Vitelloni* points not only to the "insignificance of events but also to the uncertainty of their linkage, and to their distance from those involved in them."[37]

If one agrees with Deleuze that these formal elements can be said to characterize neorealism, then the parameters of Pasolini's subversion begin to come into focus. Although, for example, Pasolini's tendency to go from one essential moment to the next means that his films are indeed marked by "lacanae," it is also true that the world he presents is one where everything is predestined, highly patterned, and controlled. Events and characters are inextricably and necessarily linked, ordinary transitions eschewed, and only important moments recorded. Here the illusion of real time and space that neorealism seeks to create through its "fragmentary meetings," and long takes of people in given environments, is conspicuously absent. In fact, if one were to isolate the governing element of Pasolini's films—the one that determines his choice of shots, editing, composition, music, and eventually narrative—it would have to be his aversion to the illusion of naturalism which lies at the core of neorealism.

As Pasolini repeatedly observed, his avoidance of naturalism, and the neorealist outlook this implied, was absolutely conscious and deliberate. "My fetishistic love for the 'things' of the world," he declared, "prevents me from considering them natural. It consecrates them or desecrates them, violently, one by one: it does not link them in a correct flow, it does not accept this flow. Rather, it isolates them and idolizes them one by one more or less intensely."[38] It is this "fetishistic" love that impels his camera to break the sense of spatial and/or temporal continuity by lingering, mysteriously, on isolated fragments of reality. Scenes that the neorealists would have filmed in long takes in order to preserve the spatial relationships and "correct flow" of things are seen instead in a disconnected, even disjointed, fashion. For example, instead of using long takes for sequences where Accattone and his friends converse while seated around a table,

---

[36] Gilles Deleuze, *Cinéma I: L'image mouvement* (Paris: Minuit, 1983), pp. 285–286.
[37] Ibid., p. 286.
[38] Pasolini, *Empirismo eretico*, p. 235.

Pasolini pans from one face to another as each character speaks. Filmed in a medium shot or a close-up, each person speaks not to the others but, rather, into the camera in a very nonnaturalistic and even abrupt fashion. Whereas, to borrow a metaphor from André Bazin, the neorealists waited patiently for reality to unveil itself, a brutal Pasolini meets it head-on. As he remarked:

> The main feature of neorealism is the long take; the camera sits in one place and films a scene as it would be in real life. . . . Whereas I never use a long take (or virtually never). I hate naturalness. I reconstruct everything. I never have somebody talking in a long shot away from the camera, I have to have him talking straight into the camera, so there is never a scene in any of my films where the camera is to one side and the characters are talking away among themselves. They are always in *champ reverse champ.*[39]

Discussing still other ways in which he sought to avoid any semblance of naturalism, Pasolini often focused on precisely those aspects of neorealism discussed by Deleuze. His terms and what he chose to emphasize are, of course, slightly different: for example, what Deleuze describes as "discursive reality" was perceived by Pasolini as "anecdotal suggestions of reality." And of these he had this to say:

> Certain elements which are present in *Accattone* and *Mamma Roma*—elements such as the lack of immediate anecdotal suggestions of reality, the way in which the film is shot, or the conception of framing, sequences and the whole of the work (which is closed rather than open, an epic whole rather than an ensemble of anecdotes and lyrical suggestions of reality)—all mean that *Accattone* and *Mamma Roma* no longer belong, although they are rooted in it, to the neorealist sphere, to the neorealist outlook.[40]

On the other hand, Deleuze's "vector . . . which lengthens or shortens events," inconspicuous or absent in neorealism, is extraordinarily strong in Pasolini's films, where one senses that everything is accorded a prescribed weight and duration from the beginning. "It does not seem to me," Pasolini observed, "that my films contain the documentary or lyrical moments which are essentially the most important part of neorealist films."[41] His is a world where banal or trivial events have been banished, and where characters are not gradually established but, instead, captured at moments of crisis when lives and souls are always in the balance.

Although, at least at the beginning, Pasolini worked with nonprofessionals, as did the neorealists, it was for totally different reasons: while they believed this would add to the realism of their films, Pasolini turned

[39] Cited by Stack, *Pasolini on Pasolini*, p. 132.
[40] Pasolini, "Una visione del mondo epico-religiosa," p. 18.
[41] *Con Pier Paolo Pasolini*, p. 26.

to nonprofessionals because their acting did *not* seem "real." Conversely, he usually eschewed professional actors because they sought to appear natural. Working with the great actress Anna Magnani in *Mamma Roma* posed problems precisely because she had been trained to *seem* natural and spontaneous, to artfully capture sentimental nuances and slight changes in mood. Hence she resisted Pasolini's approach which strove to capture "feelings, expressions, and psychological changes at culminating, absolute, and immobile moments."[42]

The irony, of course, is that, from a conventional viewpoint, Anna Magnani was far more convincing in her role than the nonprofessional actors who—like the young man who played her son, or Franco Citti in *Accattone*—did, in fact, come from the borgata. Often, too, the lack of naturalism they brought to their roles was further heightened by Pasolini, who had them dubbed by still other nonprofessionals in order to attain a kind of unreal, "polyvalent" speech. Lastly, the fact that these nonprofessionals were often Pasolini's friends or well-known acquaintances also worked against naturalism. Each appearance of, say, Ninetto Davoli reminded Italian audiences—that is, audiences who knew the personalities involved—of Davoli's close relationship to Pasolini. The presence of these "mascot-faces," to use a term proposed by Jean Sémoulé,[43] thus became a kind of artistic signature signaling the presence of the author within his film.

A lack of naturalism was not the only reason why nonprofessionals appealed to Pasolini. Their presence also meant that cinematic effects would be created more through *his* means—that is, through the use of camera, framing, and editing—than through artful performances. In this way performers became "fragments of reality" to be manipulated. "I like to be in charge of my own work," Pasolini remarked, "as if I were writing a book or a poem. The actor, instead, by his training, adds something of himself."[44] Short takes and frequent close-ups were another way of fragmenting the actor's performance, of preventing him from "adding something of himself." By filming in this manner, observed Pasolini, "the actor's playing is mutilated or, rather, chopped up so that he can no longer try for his usual effects. Besides, I attach such importance to editing that nothing much remains of a personal acting style."[45]

[42] Pasolini, *Mamma Roma* (Milan: Rizzoli, 1962), p. 140.

[43] Jean Sémoulé, "Après *Le Décaméron* et *Les Contes de Canterbury*: réflexions sur le récit chez Pasolini," special issue of *Etudes cinématographiques* No. 112–114 (1977), p. 137.

[44] Pasolini, "En tant que marxiste, je vois le monde sous un angle sacré," *Les lettres françaises*, September 23, 1965, p. 20.

[45] Cited by Jean Duflot in *Entretiens avec Pier Paolo Pasolini* (Paris: Belfond, 1970), p. 123.

In addition to editing, another means over which Pasolini had total control—and used in a similarly nonnaturalistic fashion—was music. Instead of functioning in what he called a conventional "horizontal" manner—in which images are reinforced through the addition of "rhythmic values"—music is applied contrapuntally or "vertically" to *transform* the sense of images.[46] In his first films, Bach (especially *The Passion according to St. Matthew*) and Vivaldi become the agents of this transformation. The decision to use Bach as a "commentary" in *Accattone* was, said Pasolini, both a fundamental and "irrational" choice. He felt that he could not "comment upon the film in any other way than with Bach's music— a little because he is the composer I love best, a little because Bach's music is music incarnate, music in an absolute sense. . . . When I thought about a musical commentary, I always thought irrationally about Bach."[47] What Pasolini called a kind of "contamination" emerges from the contrast between the cultural and historical resonances evoked by Bach's music and the terrible brutality of sub-proletarian life from which culture and history—or at least an awareness of history—are banished. In the case of a sequence depicting a sordid street fight, for example, Bach's grandiose music makes viewers aware that they are not witnessing a "kind of picturesque quarrel à la neorealism, but an epic fight which opens onto the sacred and the 'religious.' "[48]

The words "sacred" and "religious" are important: behind Pasolini's antinaturalism lay, undoubtedly, a desire to exchange the social and historical world of the neorealists for a universe that opens upon the sacred, the mythic, the epic. His taste for such absolutes was, he once confessed, only "completely satisfied by the act of death, which seems to me the most mythic and epic aspect there is—all this, however, at a level of pure irrationalism."[49] Similarly "irrational" perhaps—and certainly controversial—was his belief that only "prehistoric" cultures like the sub-proletariat could achieve the mythic or epic sense which, he felt, had vanished from the contemporary world. To film students who questioned him about *Accattone*, he once declared:

My vision of the world is essentially of an epic-religious sort. Thus, epic-religious elements play a very important role—especially in characters who are wretched, devoid of historical awareness and, in this case, of bourgeois consciousness. Misery is always—because of its deepest nature—epic. In a certain

---

[46] Cited in Antonio Bertini's *Teoria e tecnica del film in Pasolini* (Rome: Bulzoni, 1979), p. 115.

[47] *Con Pier Paolo Pasolini*, p. 36.

[48] Cited by Duflot, *Entretiens*, p. 117.

[49] Cited by Stack, *Pasolini on Pasolini*, p. 56.

sense, the elements at work in the psychology of someone who is wretched, poor, and sub-proletarian are always pure.[50]

In Pasolini's view, the epic-religious dimension of *Accattone* and *Mamma Roma*, the sense of life "seen under the sign of eternity," went beyond the presence of death, and that of the sub-proletariat, beyond, even, religious music and Christian allusions. Insisting—as he would do for all his films—that the real "message" of *Accattone* lay in its style, he declared that the sacred quality of the film was found

> less in the character's overwhelming need for personal salvation (from pimp to thief!), or in the external fatality that determines and concludes everything . . . than in the way of "seeing the world": in the technical sacredness of seeing it. . . . nothing is more sacred, technically, than a slow panorama. . . . Sacredness, front view [frontalità]. And thus religion.[51]

If the film's "technical sacredness" is created by prolonged frontal shots and slow panoramas, it is further underscored by a deliberate avoidance of motion. A pervasive sense of immobility gives a hieratic and ritualistic cast to Pasolini's films even as it, too, works against the illusion of naturalism. (Film theorists have long observed that filmed movement—which reproduces both the nonmateriality and temporality of real movement—heightens the "illusion of reality" created by cinema. "The combination of the *reality* of motion and the *appearance* of forms," writes Christian Metz, quoting Edgar Morin, "gives us the feeling of concrete life and the perception of objective reality."[52]) In Pasolini's films, immobility extends to performers and camera movements alike: "There is never a character," he observed of *Accattone*, "who enters the shot and then leaves it; the dolly, with its 'impressionistic,' sinuous movements is never used."[53] On the rare occasions when movements are filmed, it is in a slow, symmetrical, and rhythmic fashion: two such scenes in *Accattone*—when Accattone walks down a long desolate road, first with Maddalena and later with Stella—stand out, establishing echoes with each other. The figures in his film, as he noted, "always move . . . in as symmetrical a manner as possible: close-up against close-up, pan to the right against pan to the left, regular rhythms (possible ternary) of shots."[54]

Measured rhythms, slow camera movements, frontal shots, and long and frequent close-ups all create a hieratic and stylized poetic universe that is, as Pasolini remarked, "a frontal, massive, romantic, chiaroscuro

---

[50] Pasolini, "Una visione del mondo epico-religiosa," p. 13.

[51] Pasolini, *Uccellacci e Uccellini* (Milan: Garzanti, 1966), pp. 44–45.

[52] Christian Metz, *A Semiotics of the Cinema: Film Language* (New York: Oxford University Press, 1974), p. 7.

[53] Pasolini, *Mamma Roma*, p. 145.

[54] Ibid., p. 145.

world." As these adjectives suggest, this world is also deeply imbued with plastic and painterly values. A great lover of art, a man who sketched and drew throughout his life, Pasolini possessed an immense visual culture. Before completing his thesis on literature, in fact, he studied art history under a famous critic, Roberto Longhi. And echoes of schools of paintings, even allusions to specific works, play an important role throughout his films. Drawn, above all, to the nonnaturalistic art of the Middle Ages and early Renaissance, he once observed that "the pictorial paradigm is represented for me by Byzantine frescoes or Romanesque art, that is, by the most frontal and hieratic pictorial or plastic representation which exists."[55] It is, of course, precisely this paradigm that sets its seal on his early films. "What I have in mind visually," he observed in the course of a discussion of *Mamma Roma*,

> are the frescoes of Masaccio, of Giotto—the painters that I love the most, together with certain mannerists (for example, Pontormo). I cannot conceive of images, landscapes, or compositions of figures outside of my initial passion for 14th-century paintings where man was the center of all perspective.... I always conceive of the background as the background of a painting ... and therefore I always attack it frontally. The figures in long shots are the background, and the figures in close-ups move against this background, followed by pans which are, I repeat, almost always symmetrical. ... My camera moves over backgrounds and figures which are essentially seen as immobile and profoundly chiaroscuro.[56]

As in paintings by Giotto and Masaccio, in Pasolini's early films man is both at the center of the frame and, as befits the director's "fetishistic" vision, isolated or cut off from surrounding reality. This is accomplished in a variety of ways. In addition to long and frequent close-ups, Pasolini shoots into the light so that backgrounds are obscured, outlines characters by placing them against white or black backgrounds (*Accattone* is often viewed against the sky or against dark tenement walls), or uses spotlights upon them in night scenes. In *Mamma Roma*, for example, during an interminable nighttime walk, the protagonist is seen against a black sky, "punctuated by lights," that becomes an "abstract background."[57] By fixing and isolating segments of what is visible, Pasolini creates the sense that what we see is merely one part of reality, and that the truly essential—and sacred—remains unseen. Analyzing this phenomenon, Antonio Bertini, author of a book on Pasolini's style, observes that the director's "fixed frame" deliberately reveals merely a segment of "physical

---

[55] Cited by Michel Mangois, "Interview with Pier Paolo Pasolini," *Zoom* (October 1974), p. 23.
[56] Pasolini, *Mamma Roma*, p. 145.
[57] *Con Pier Paolo Pasolini*, p. 49.

continuity." As a result, continues Bertini, "between the person framed and what the framing 'excludes' is created a link that, precisely because it is based on the 'not seen,' the 'not revealed' . . . has an implicit sacredness."[58]

The relationship between the seen and the unseen in film—an issue often discussed by critics in the past—has been addressed once again in recent years by Gilles Deleuze. Although Deleuze pays particular attention to Dreyer in this context, much of what he says seems equally applicable to Pasolini, who readily acknowledged the important influence that Dreyer exerted upon him. (Tonino Delli Colli, cameraman for most of Pasolini's films, recounts that before making *Accattone*, Pasolini insisted on taking him to see Dreyer's *Joan of Arc* "to have a model, since he couldn't manage to explain to me what he wanted."[59]) Discussing the relationship between what is inside and outside the frame, Deleuze remarks that the stronger the link between these two spaces, the more does off-screen reality fulfill its primary function which is to "add space to space." But the weaker the link, that is, the more close-ups and other devices cut off the seen from the unseen, the more the filmed fragment suggests not known realities but a "trans-spatial and spiritual whole," a "radical Elsewhere, outside homogenous space and time."[60] In other words, the more the image is spatially closed or reduced to two dimensions, "the more it is apt to open upon a fourth dimension which is that of time, and upon a fifth which is Spirit, the spiritual decision of Joan of Arc or Gertrud."[61]

In *La passion de Jeanne d'Arc*, Dreyer films Joan's trial and martyrdom largely through a series of extreme close-ups of the suffering face of Falconetti, the actress who plays Joan. It is these close-ups, suggests Deleuze, that create a sense of closure, of two-dimensionality, and, ultimately, of spirituality. By emphasizing individual features rather than the face as a whole, these close-ups suppress any sense of individuality even as they make us acutely aware of separate features and the emotions they convey. Forgetting Joan as an individual subject, we are struck, above all, by her overwhelming and absolute torment: "The event itself [Joan's passion] overflows its own causes and suggests only other emotions while the causes fall by the wayside."[62] Through her suffering, Joan transcends the historical: she enters into a "virtual connection" with the role of Christ even as her social/civil trial and the metaphysical Passion become inseparable.

[58] Bertini, *Teorica e tecnica del film in Pasolini*, p. 20.
[59] Cited in Bertini's *Teoria e tecnica del film in Pasolini*, p. 203.
[60] Deleuze, *Cinéma I*, p. 30.
[61] Ibid., p. 31.
[62] Ibid., p. 151.

Just as Dreyer likens Joan's martyrdom to that of Christ, so, too, does Pasolini endow Accattone's agony with a mythic dimension. Echoing Dreyer's austere visual style, through frontal shots and obsessive close-ups Pasolini separates his characters from the known world even as he suggests the (invisible) presence of spiritual realities, of what Deleuze calls a "radical Elsewhere." As he does so, the miserable Roman borgata becomes the scene of a primal drama in which a miserable pimp reenacts the sacred Passion of Christ.

While the influence exerted both by Dreyer and by neorealism upon *Accattone* and *Mamma Roma* was clear from the outset, the relationship between Pasolini's films and those of his most important contemporaries was, instead, far more problematical. In fact, it would hardly be an exaggeration to say that Pasolini's first films appeared strangely out of place in the climate of the early 1960s. After all, as Pasolini himself remarked, his mythic sub-proletarians had little in common with the alienated and affluent characters who peopled the films of Antonioni and Fellini. Centuries, and not kilometers, seemed to separate the Roman world of Fellini's *dolce vita* from Pasolini's *borgata*. From the standpoint of film history, too, Pasolini's austere and imposing "technical sacredness" seemed, at first glance, to admit few points of comparison with the cinema of, say, the emerging French New Wave—a cinema marked by playful allusions, a mobile and intrusive camera, and deliberate attempts to solicit audience complicity.

Still, in retrospect, it is clear that there *were* indeed resemblances, which brought Pasolini no less than, say, Antonioni or Godard squarely into the modernist camp. As I shall demonstrate in a later chapter, Pasolini was deeply influenced by the "obsessive" relationship to reality that he perceived in Antonioni. As for Godard, Pasolini certainly shared one of the French director's most characteristic traits: a tremendous preoccupation with past culture. Unlike Godard, of course, he did not strew his films with bits and pieces—quotes, titles, and snips of music—torn from the vast body of Western culture. Rather, in Pasolini, such references were evoked as in filigree, in the mode of "contamination." Mention has already been made, for example, of the way Bach's music or Renaissance painting "contaminates" some of the most brutal moments in his early films, as fragments of a (sacred) past are superimposed upon a (profane) present. While this meant that the references and allusions were somehow muted, especially when compared with Godard's flamboyant citations, their role was still central. In fact, in Pasolini's view, his films were characterized *not* by stylistic unity but, rather, by the "degree of intensity" he brought to the contamination and mixture of "borrowed" material. Deeming his cinema "eclectic," he remarked that it is composed of elements, of material borrowed from different cultural sectors: borrowings from dialects, popular verses, popular or classical music, references to pictorial art and architecture. . . . I do not claim to create and impose a style. What creates the stylistic magma with me is a kind of fervour, a passion which impels me to seize any material, any form which seems to me necessary to the economy of a film.[63]

This "stylistic magma" took many forms, but, as in Godard, it always involved a self-reflective meditation not only on culture and style but even on cinema itself. True, references to cinema are not as central or prominent in Pasolini's films as in many of those of the New Wave. With a few important exceptions he did not, for example, pay homage to specific directors or films. Still, the deliberately naive frontal shots and unconnected tableaux of his early films hark back to a cinema even more primitive than that marked by the iris shots lovingly recalled by Godard and Truffaut. And if they flashily "reread" Hollywood gangster films, then a more subtle Pasolini "reread" neorealism, evoking it not in Godard's parodic mode but in what Adelio Ferrero has called "an oneiric and funereal fashion."[64] This rereading meant that specific codes associated with neorealism were altered, imbued with a different significance. Dubbing Pasolini's aesthetic one of "transgression" for this very reason, Joël Magny analyzes the way Pasolini transforms, or "transgresses," the "plan-séquence" (a long take or entire sequence shot without editing) so dear to the neorealists. "For Rossellini," writes Magny,

> it was a question of capturing the continuous appearance of reality, of avoiding ruptures and manipulation. With Pasolini it is often a question of a frontal, slow, reverse travelling shot which accompanies one or several characters who are walking. This is the case of Mamma Roma's nighttime walk where different men approach her, accompany her, and leave her while she is recounting her life. Far from giving the impression of continuity or spatial-temporal homogeneity, this movement is in fact broken by shadows who appear in the shot only to disappear into the night, while Anna Magnani is silhouetted against a black background, almost without decor.[65]

Frequently, too, Pasolini's transgression—like that of the New Wave directors—goes beyond specific codes, such as those associated with neorealism, in its drive to subvert even more general cinematic rules and conventions. In *Accattone*, for example, despite the advice of experts, Pasolini insisted on shooting into the light to create a sense of the violent sun

[63] Cited by Duflot, *Entretiens*, p. 119.
[64] Ferrero, *Il cinema di Pier Paolo Pasolini*, p. 39.
[65] Joël Magny, "Une écriture mythique," in *Pasolini: le mythe et le sacré*, special issue of *Etudes cinématographiques* No. 109–111 (1976), pp. 18–19.

and burning heat of a Roman summer. Or, to give another example, *Accattone* begins with a disorienting series of close-ups. This unconventional opening, as Marc Gervais observes, tells us that we are dealing with a "cinema dominated by an abrupt tonality, where faces look at us and speak to us directly. . . . *Accattone* marks the beginning of a style of confrontation, even of assault."[66]

Most of all, perhaps, it is the narrative, marked by mysterious ruptures and ellipses, that reflects this style of "assault." And here Pasolini's rule-breaking becomes even more radical, if less obvious, than that of his French contemporaries. For Godard's cuts, however abrupt and unconventional, usually lend themselves to some explanation: in general it might be said that they reflect a Brechtian impulse to distance the audience, that is, to make it reflect upon the philosophical and intellectual (rather than narrative and psychological) connections between shots. In a similar manner, explanations also come to mind for Alain Resnais's startling and dramatic cuts: it has often been suggested, for example, that they correspond to the logic of the unconscious, of memory and dream. When we come to Pasolini, however, it is precisely such explanations that are lacking. Not only does he fragment the narrative flow by isolating shots from each other, but such shots may depict nothing more than isolated fragments of reality that have caught Pasolini's painterly, "fetishistic," imagination. These fragments may simply be unrelated to each other in any way that can be "explained." As Geoffrey Nowell-Smith succinctly observes:

> The image track of *Accattone* really does consist literally of images, loosely linked to each other via the content of what is being narrated, but visually dislocated from each other and, singly, often bizarre. The faces in close-up, for example, do not, as in a classic action film, serve to express the thoughts of the character relevant to the action at that point in the plot. Nor are they there as portraits of social types, as so often in neorealism. They seem, rather, to be just faces, expressions of the enigma that is the human face. . . . [The] smile means nothing in the context of the action, except that whoever is looking into that face (maybe another character, maybe the director, maybe just the audience) cannot read that face.[67]

Similarly struck by the enigmatic smiles of Pasolini's characters, Alberto Moravia remarks that they seem to lack the "diegetic motives [normally] furnished by preceding shots."[68] As an "autonomous" diegetic or narrative moment, an expression without discernible motivation, each

[66] Marc Gervais, *Pier Paolo Pasolini* (Paris: Seghers, 1973), p. 15.

[67] Nowell-Smith, "Pasolini's Originality," pp. 10–11.

[68] Alberto Moravia, "Pasolini poète civil," in *Pasolini*, ed. M. A. Macciocchi (Paris: Grasset, 1980), p. 93.

smile is profoundly ambiguous, connoting, perhaps, joy, seduction, or even menace. Nor do we know—and this, of course, heightens the unease—*who* is the object of the smile; it may be the spectator, another character, or someone/something that is visible to the character but not to the spectator. And these psychological ambiguities are intensified still further by a disconcerting gap—which is especially marked where objects of love or desire are concerned—between what the narrative tells us and what the images convey. For example, although the hero of *Accattone* is supposedly in love with Stella, the camera caresses not Stella, the object of *his* desire, but Accattone himself.

A camera that lingers on male bodies is, perhaps, only the most obvious and specific sign of Pasolini's attraction to men. His very taste for ambiguity—an ambiguity expressed through smiles we cannot interpret, gaps between narrative and image—may well be still another indication of a homosexual sensibility. In fact, Pasolini seems to share the attraction to hidden meanings that, in the eyes of Harold Beaver, has frequently marked homosexual writers in the past. In a very interesting article entitled "Homosexual Signs," Beaver argues that the taste for hidden codes—a taste epitomized, perhaps, by Proust—reflects the way homosexuals experience reality itself: living in a "duplicate culture of constantly interrupted and overlapping roles," they see the world as an ambiguous one "wholly devoted to a switching of signs based on switching of context. . . . For to be homosexual in Western society," he writes,

entails a state of mind in which all credentials, however petty, are under unceasing scrutiny. The homosexual is beset by signs, by the urge to interpret whatever transpires, or fails to transpire, between himself and every chance acquaintance. He is a prodigious consumer of signs—of hidden meanings, hidden symbols, hidden potentiality. Exclusion from the common code impels the frenzied quest: in the momentary glimpse, the scrabbled figure, the sporadic gesture, the chance encounter, the reverse image, the sudden slippage, the lowered guard. In a flash meanings may be disclosed; mysteries wrenched out and betrayed.[69]

No less than the world of Proust or Cocteau, Pasolini's cinema is one of hidden codes, of "sudden slippages" and reversals of meaning. His films demand to be read and deciphered even as they render interpretation not only difficult but, at times, impossible. This is a world where known reference points are destroyed by frequent and obsessive close-ups and where pools of gloom contain mysterious secrets. Here juxtaposed codes and different stylistic strands generate moments of pastiche and overlays of meaning that demand (re)interpretation. Permeated by a baroque in-

[69] Beaver, "Homosexual Signs," p. 105.

stability, this cinema constantly keeps us off balance: the life of a pimp may turn into an epic drama of sin and salvation, and the death of a petty thief may take on the dimensions of Christ's final agony.

Impelled by the hermeneutical urge that led Proust's narrator to probe the recesses of memory, or that lured Cocteau's poet into "another" world (the world behind the mirror in *Le sang d'un poète*), Pasolini, too, was driven to discover what lay behind appearances. His evocation of the sacred implied a will to transcend the world of social and historical truths just as the insistences of his lingering and "fetishistic" camera betrayed a desire to go beyond the seeming "naturalness" of reality. His sensibility, shaped by an early love of symbolist poetry, was essentially hostile to an aesthetic of naturalism, an aesthetic that embraces the world as it seems. Drawn instead to decipher the hidden meanings behind phenomena, and to art and style seen as a transformation of the "real," this sensibility was prone to see the world in terms of the "signs" offered by previous culture—signs that provided the impetus and the material for still further pastiche and stylization, for still greater transgression.

Despite, then, an almost desperate longing to embrace reality (a longing, he maintained, that led him from literature to cinema), Pasolini could no more breach the gap between art and life than could a Wilde, a Cocteau, a Proust. In the emphasis he placed upon the fundamental dichotomy between art and life, as in so many other respects, he embodied that current of modernism that flows from the symbolist-decadent experience. But this current itself—as the profound affinities between Proust, Cocteau, and Pasolini suggest (and as the puritanical Lukács may well have sensed when he attacked the "ideology of modernism")—cannot be separated from the homosexuality that characterized so many of its central figures. Addressing this important issue, that is, the ways in which the experience of homosexuality informs the very shapes and impulses assumed by modernism, George Steiner begins with the following observation:

> Since about 1890 homosexuality has played a vital part in western culture and perhaps even more significantly, in the myths and emblematic gestures which that culture has used in order to arrive at self-consciousness. . . . The tonality of the 'modern movement', the theories of the creative act implicit in important branches of twentieth-century arts and letters, cannot be dissociated from the lives and work of Oscar Wilde, Proust, André Gide, Stefan George, and Cocteau.[70]

After these remarkably succinct and incisive passages, Steiner goes on to note that much of what we consider vital to modernism—its rejection of

[70] George Steiner, *A Reader* (New York: Oxford University Press, 1984), pp. 329–330.

the outer world in favor of a self-referential art, its wish to shock and transgress (to *épater les bourgeois*), its will to explore and unearth the sometimes violent turnings of a desire that is frequently "death haunted"—is the result of what he calls "homosexual strategies." As Beaver also suggests, such strategies stem from the way homosexual writers experienced, or were forced to experience, the world. Their exclusion from a middle-class society ruled by utilitarian values, their flight to inwardness, "made possible," writes Steiner, "that exercise in solipsism, that remorseless mockery of philistine common sense and bourgeois realism which is modern art."[71]

The lineage that Steiner establishes, which goes from Proust and Wilde to Gide and Cocteau, unmistakably reaches as far as, encompasses, Pasolini. Unlike these earlier writers, however—*and this makes Pasolini's drama such a distinctive one*—he was pulled not only toward "passion" (toward what they might have called "art for art's sake") but also toward "ideology." He was always suspicious of, defensive toward, the self-conscious aestheticism that they, in the main, embraced. Still, the strategies that Steiner describes so eloquently *were* determining presences in Pasolini's work—presences that came into ever sharper focus as his political hopes began to fade. His "indefatigable pursuit of meaning," to borrow a phrase from Roland Barthes, gave rise, by the late 1960s, to difficult and self-referential cinematic parables that foregrounded a hermeneutical core. As everything came under renewed scrutiny, essential texts of Western culture were reread in controversial, even scandalous, ways. Contamination often verged upon, turned into, pastiche and parody, while desire assumed ever more transgressive forms. In the end, Pasolini's constant urge to reject appearances in favor of another, "truer" world—a world often coextensive with art and stylization—became the target of ferocious satire in his last film, *Salò*. But, as the following chapters will show, many twistings and turnings preceded that desperate admission of ultimate defeat.

[71] Steiner, *A Reader*, p. 331.

III

The End of Ideology

Nessuno dei problemi degli anni cinquanta
Mi importa più! Tradisco i lividi
moralisti che hanno fatto del socialismo un cattolicesimo
Ugualmente noioso! Ah, ah, la provincia impegnata!
Ah, ah, la gara a essere uno più poetà razionale dell'altro
La droga, per professori poveri, dell'ideologia!
    —Pier Paolo Pasolini, "Poema per un verso di Shakespeare" (1964)

(None of the problems of the 1950s
Matter to me any longer! I betray the livid
moralists who have turned socialism into an equally
boring Catholicism! Ah, ah! provincial commitment!
Ah, ah, the race to be the most rational poet
For poor professors, the drug of ideology!)

WITH *Accattone* and *Mamma Roma*, Pasolini had created for himself a recognizable niche in Italian cinema. If Antonioni was the anatomist of middle-class alienation, and Fellini the master of spectacle, then Pasolini was the poet of the Roman *borgata*. But just when audiences knew, or thought they knew, what to expect, Pasolini took a surprising turn. His films of the mid-1960s are not only markedly different from *Accattone* and *Mamma Roma*, but also quite distinct from one another. In this respect, they stand apart from all his other films, which fall into definite groups: the sub-proletarian duo of *Accattone* and *Mamma Roma*, the mythic quartet of the late 1960s, and the still later "trilogy of life." Although some critics have attempted to link one or two of these heterogeneous works to *Accattone* and *Mamma Roma*, they probably have more in commmon with one another than with his first films.[1] But what they share is less a similar style—unless stylistic experimentation is itself a

---

[1] Sandro Petraglia closes the first phase of Pasolini's cinema with the short film *La ricotta* (1963), while Adelio Ferrero extends this phase to include Pasolini's 1964 feature film about Christ, *Il Vangelo secondo Matteo* (*The Gospel according to St. Matthew*). Ferrero argues that, like his earlier films, *Il Vangelo* concerns the "myth of the sub-proletariat" even as it uses elements associated with neorealism. See Sandro Petraglia, *Pier Paolo Pasolini* (Florence: Nuova Italia, 1974), p. 51; Adelio Ferrero, *Il cinema di Pier Paolo Pasolini* (Venice: Marsilio, 1977), p. 64.

common denominator—than an analogous set of social and political concerns.

In general, these concerns have a distinctly Gramscian cast. As suggested earlier, the discovery of Gramsci's writings after the war did much to inspire the revolutionary hopes, and to shape the political vision, of Pasolini and his contemporaries. To Pasolini, in particular, Gramsci seemed a kindred spirit: the young poet's love of the peasant world, the lifelong nostalgia for the "cultivated soil" left in him by the years in Friuli, found political support in Gramsci's work. One of the rare early theoreticians of Marxism to attribute a revolutionary role to the peasantry, Gramsci—like Pasolini—came from the margins of the country: as a Sardinian, he, too, had firsthand experience of rural life. "By means of Gramsci," Pasolini observed years later,

> I situated the position of the intellectual—a petit-bourgeois by origin or choice—between the party and the masses, a true mediating linchpin between classes, and especially, I verified, theoretically, the importance of the peasant world in a revolutionary perspective. The resonances of Gramsci's work within me were decisive.[2]

When Pasolini speaks of the intellectual as a "mediating linchpin between classes," he is referring to Gramsci's concept of "organic" intellectuals—a concept that, after the war, became transformed into that of the intellectual's "mandate," or social mission. Although the term "organic" came to designate any intellectual who was politically and socially committed, for Gramsci it was rather more precise. In his view, the ideal intellectual was one who stood ready to renounce his traditional ivory tower in favor of "organic" links with the working class. By voicing the people's deepest needs and desires, such intellectuals would be instrumental in creating a homogeneous, proletarian mass—a mass marked by an ideology of its own. At the level of the superstructure, this new ideology, or "hegemonic apparatus" would correspond to new relations of production. Changing both the economic structure and the ideological superstructure would give rise to what Gramsci called a new "historical bloc" (*blocco storico*); and this, in turn, would pave the way for political revolution. For this reason, Gramsci urged that a cultural battle, led by organic intellectuals and aimed at the subversion of bourgeois ideology, be fought in certain vital domains: the schools, the media, and the arts. Designed to alter the way men think, this battle was, he believed, especially critical in the West, where governments depend as much upon "spontaneous consensus" as upon force.

For committed intellectuals of Pasolini's generation, this ideological

---

[2] Cited by Jean Duflot in *Entretiens avec Pasolini* (Paris: Belfond, 1970), p. 20.

battle seemed to imply the creation of a new "national-popular" culture. This referred to still another fundamental Gramscian concept which, once again, was fairly precise. By "national," Gramsci did not mean the nation-state, but all those—especially the common or "humble" people, the *umili*—sharing the same history and traditions. As for "popular," unlike many Marxist critics, Gramsci did not use the term to denote the representation of the working class—like that, say, found in Dickens— but in the more modern sense both of "popularity" and "popular culture." It was his belief that nineteenth-century novelists such as Alexandre Dumas and Eugène Sue generated widespread and popular appeal precisely because they were in touch with "profound currents of national-popular life." (In Gramsci's view, a novel such as *The Count of Monte Cristo* revealed the people's deep need to avenge its "complex of social inferiority.") Rooted in the "humus of popular culture," in touch with a great collective nerve, these popular novels were in a position to disclose hidden beliefs ("the conceptions of the world predominating in the 'silent' multitudes") and even, at times, to diffuse or create new ideologies. As an example of the latter phenomenon, Gramsci observed that the concept of the "superman" was spread less by the "high" culture of Nietzsche than through the widely read works of Balzac and Dumas. Finally, he argued that not only popular novels but even the greatest art—that of the Greek dramatists, Shakespeare, or Tolstoy—must reach down into the sub-soil of national-popular culture. For a work to be truly popular and artistically valid,

> "beauty" is not enough: it needs a given intellectual and moral content which would express, in the fullest and completest possible way, the deepest aspirations of a given public, that is, of the nation-people at a certain phase of its historical development. Literature must be at once a contemporary element of civilization as well as a work of art: otherwise, mass-produced literature, which is, in its way, a contemporary element of culture—of a culture which may be degraded but which is keenly felt—will be preferred to literary art.[3]

Such a passage sheds still further light on the reasons Pasolini was so deeply drawn to Gramsci. Not only did the great political thinker underscore the importance of the peasantry but he also ascribed a revolutionary role to culture and intellectuals. Moreoever, he did so without denying— and this must have been crucial for Pasolini—the value of "beauty" and art. In light of these affinities, it is not difficult to understand why Pasolini was always haunted by the figure of Gramsci. But with the passage of time, this figure underwent a sea change: as Gramsci's political and social ideals appeared increasingly less relevant, he became less a determining

[3] Antonio Gramsci, *Letteratura e vita nazionale* (Rome: Riuniti, 1977), pp. 97–98.

political presence than a mythic and symbolic icon in the depths of Pasolini's poetic imagination. By the 1950s, Gramsci had come to embody not
only the rational Marxism that Pasolini could never fully embrace but
also a historical moment—that of the Resistance and Liberation—that
was sadly, irretrievably, over. In a famous poem that would forever link
his name with Gramsci's in the minds of many Italians, Pasolini mourn-
fully described the blend of nostalgia and ambivalence, the conflict between "passion" and "ideology," evoked in him by the memory of the
great Marxist thinker.

The poem, entitled "Le ceneri di Gramsci" ("The Ashes of Gramsci"),
begins with Pasolini in the so-called Protestant or English cemetery of
Rome, contemplating Gramsci's grave, that is, his "ashes." The poet's
thoughts drift from the political hopes and illusions of earlier times—
hopes represented first by Gramsci, then by Resistance partisans—to the
bitter disillusionment and hopelessness of the postwar decade. Against
the backdrop of history, Pasolini describes an intense inner drama: he is
torn between ideological awareness and commitment (also represented by
Gramsci) and the "exquisite" bourgeois heritage that attracts him to the
"innocence" and "primitive joy" of an ahistorical working-class world.
Reason and history (understood as Marxism, ideology, and the class
struggle) make him side with Gramsci and the hopes for social progress;
instincts and passion attach him to a mythic and popular world. Para-
lyzed by this lacerating conflict, he confesses to the dead Gramsci that he
suffers from

> The scandal of contradicting myself, of being
> with you and against you; with you in my heart,
> in the light, against you in my dark entrails.
>
> A traitor—in thought, in the shadows
> of action—to my paternal state,
> knowing myself attached to it by the
>
> heat of instincts and aesthetic passion;
> attracted by a proletarian life
> which preceded you. Its joy,
>
> not its age-old struggle, is
> religion for me; its nature,
> not its consciousness.[4]
>
> (Lo scandalo del contraddirmi, dell'essere
> con te e contro te; con te nel cuore,
> in luce, contro te nelle buie viscere;

[4] Pasolini, *Poesie* (Milan: Garzanti, 1975), p. 73.

del mio paterno stato traditore
—nel pensiero, in un'ombra di azione—
mi so ad esso attaccato nel calore

degli istinti, dell'estetica passione;
attratto da una vita proletaria
a te anteriore, è per me religione

la sua allegria, non la millenaria
sua lotta: la sua natura, non la sua
coscienza.)

As the poem draws to a close, the personal and the political commingle as Pasolini lucidly confronts his feelings of estrangement and his impossible dilemma: unlike the humble people of Rome who embrace life fervently without thinking, he—a bourgeois intellectual—is unable to live with "pure passion," knowing that revolutionary hopes ("our history") are "finished."

> As for me, with the conscious heart
>
> of one who lives only in history,
> can I ever again act with pure passion,
> when I know that our history is finished?[5]
>
> (Ma io, con il cuore cosciente
>
> di chi soltanto nella storia ha vita,
> potrò mai più con pura passione operare,
> se so che la nostra storia è finita?)

"Le ceneri di Gramsci" was written in 1954. (It gave its title to the collection of poems published by Pasolini in 1957.) By the early 1960s, social changes and historical events had brought the existential ambivalence and profound historical pessimism expressed in the poem to a critical point. These years saw Pasolini prey to a growing political disillusionment—a disillusionment that, before erupting in his 1966 film, *Uccellacci e Uccellini (The Hawks and the Sparrows)*, could be traced almost from one week to the next in the pages of a column he wrote, from 1960 to 1965, for the Communist periodical *Vie nuove*. Introducing an anthology of these journalistic essays, the Italian critic and cultural historian Gian Carlo Ferretti observes:

> The years from 1960 to 1965 signal a crucial phase in the career of Pier Paolo Pasolini: a phase whereby he went from the era [which was] set under the sign of the *Ceneri di Gramsci* (1957), [an era] marked by an active and contradic-

[5] Ibid., p. 80.

tory clash between "passion" and "ideology" . . . to the explosion of a profound crisis . . . and to the first formulation of the desperate and lucid discourse
on future capitalism that he would pursue until his death.[6]

What Ferretti calls Pasolini's "profound crisis" stemmed, in great measure, from the director's bitter conviction that the revolutionary hopes of
the postwar years were finished, part of an era that had come to a definitive close. His fear that traditional Marxism—the Marxism of the Resistance and Liberation—had outlived itself seemed to find confirmation
wherever he looked. Events abroad—the revelation of Stalinist atrocities,
the brutal suppression of the Hungarian Revolution—were a clear indication that Marxism was "blocked" in the countries of Eastern Europe.
As for Italy, it was undergoing profound social and economic changes
that radically altered traditional Marxist hopes and expectations. In the
industrial North, the economic boom of the 1960s was erasing the sharp
class divisions of the postwar years even as it rendered the workers vulnerable to the lure of consumer capitalism. The Communist party itself,
which was becoming increasingly moderate and centrist, generally favored the new consumerism, the new social (and hardly revolutionary)
lines being drawn. For Pasolini, the party—imbued with traces of "opportunism and bourgeois morality"—was not keeping up with the battle
and the enemy: continuing to speak in traditional class terms, it was ignoring the mental changes wrought by consumerism and technology
("Neocapitalism tends to put the most specialized workers to sleep . . . or
to make them become fixed in rigid positions"), as well as the revolutionary potential of the southern sub-proletariat (a "virgin and mature mass
that should be called to its historical function"[7]). For Marxism to remain
a vital force, he asserted, it had to take into account three major areas of
social and political change: "1) the atomic bomb and the conquest of
space; 2) the presence of the Third World and the end of the old colonial-
ism; 3) the evolution of capitalism toward new technocratic forms."[8]

But how *should* committed intellectuals react to these vital changes?
How could they combat a capitalism that was becoming ever more international, technocratic, and monolithic? What stance could they take in
light of the immense problem posed by the Third World? For someone
like Pasolini, who had been so deeply influenced by the notion of "organic" intellectuals, these questions were critical. And increasingly, as the
pages of his *Vie nuove* column made clear, they were questions to which
he had no answer. He was by no means alone in his growing conviction

[6] See Gian Carlo Ferretti's introduction to Pasolini's *Le belle bandiere* (Rome: Riuniti,
1977), p. 7.
[7] Pasolini, *Le belle bandiere*, p. 159.
[8] Ibid., p. 291.

that the postwar "mandate" of writers and intellectuals had no place in a world dominated by the media and mass consumption, a world where, as a pessimistic Franco Fortini wrote, the "road" to socialism had become "invisible."[9] Still, Pasolini's passionate commitment to the cause of social justice, the aversion he felt for the new society he saw emerging about him, meant that he suffered from the disappearance of a social mission in a particularly acute manner. As early as 1961, discussing a collection of his verse, *La religione del mio tempo*, he told the readers of his *Vie nuove* column that as political hope receded it left behind a terrible "existential void":

> *La religione del mio tempo* expresses the crisis of the 1960s. . . . On the one hand the neocapitalist siren, on the other, the fading of the revolution: and the void, the terrible existential void that comes as a result. When political action weakens, or becomes uncertain, then one experiences either the desire for evasion and dream . . . or a moralistic resurgence.[10]

A few years later, in 1964, he returned, significantly, to the notion of emptiness as he told his readers that "we are in a 'zero' historical moment marked by the end of one historical moment and the beginning of another."[11] The final acknowledgment of failure came the following year when he decided to abandon both the column and the "organic" role it had automatically conferred upon him—a role in which, not surprisingly, he had never felt very comfortable. In his last column for *Vie nuove* he bid adieu not only to his faithful readers but to the very notion of commitment. Proclaiming the end of an era, he offered himself as the living embodiment of a painful moment of transition:

> In the 1950s [the writer] was a kind of guardian of the sacred flame who discussed the common hopes of humanity with his working-class readers. Although now such discussions appear spent, many, many comrades do not want to acknowledge this and therefore continue . . . to expect from a writer the types of discussion and solidarity that were expected some years ago. Moreover the new "figure" of the writer has not yet defined itself: needs are still

[9] Franco Fortini, "The Writer's Mandate and the End of Anti-Fascism," *Screen* Vol. 15, No. 1 (Spring 1974), p. 57. Fortini goes on to say that, if socialism has become impossible, "it is absurd (and criminal) to engage in any nostalgic or rebellious move aiming to restore to the writer the social status inherited from romanticism, which made him the voice of national conscience or the historian of private life. Equally impossible and illusory is the return to the mandate and the status which the working class movement offered to the writer, whether (over the period of transition from nineteenth to twentieth century) as an inheritance of the mission of the bourgeois enlightenment, or (during the years from 1935 to just recently) through the formation of the anti-fascist fronts."

[10] Pasolini, *Le belle bandiere*, p. 164.

[11] Ibid., pp. 269–271.

fluctuating. It can be said that I, through my column in *Vie nuove*, found myself living this transformation *in corpore vili*.[12]

Like a current of despair, the bitter existential "transformation" expressed in the pages of his *Vie nuove* column runs throughout the films made by Pasolini between 1963 and 1966. Both the varying themes and the heterogeneous form of these films—which include one fictional short, three quasi-documentaries, and two features—attest to a moment of transition, of uncertainty. In general, his shorts, whether fictional or documentary, align themselves with one moment of the inner dialectic expressed in "Le ceneri di Gramsci." While *La ricotta* (1963) bears witness to the private Pasolini, prey to the "passion" of a mannered aestheticism, *La rabbia* (*Rage*, 1963) and *Comizi d'amore* (*Let's Talk about Love*, 1964) reveal him as an "organic" intellectual grappling with ideology. In the two features, however—*Il Vangelo secondo Matteo* (1964) and *Uccellacci e Uccellini* (1966)—public and private concerns merge even as Pasolini returns to the styles and tones that were the subject of experimentation in his shorts. Thus the self-irony of *La ricotta* prevails in *Uccellacci e Uccellini*, while the documentary, even *cinéma vérité*, technique of *Comizi d'amore* is used to great effect in *Il Vangelo*. But if these two important features differ sharply in tone and subject, both reveal a Pasolini torn between, on the one hand, a desire for social justice and, on the other, the bitter awareness—implicit in *Il Vangelo*, explicit in *Uccellacci e Uccellini*—that the age of revolutionary hope, of the intellectual's mandate, is no more.

                              il gusto
          del dolce e grande manierismo
          che tocca col suo capriccio dolcemente robusto
          le radici della vita vivente.
              —Pasolini, "La Guinea" (1964)

                         (the taste
          for sweet and great mannerism
          that touches with its sweetly robust whim
          the roots of living life.)

Considered one of the high points of Pasolini's cinema, *La ricotta* is one of four episodes in a collective film known as *Laviomoci il cervello* or *Rogopag*—thus named after its four contributing directors: Rossellini, Godard, Pasolini, and Gregoretti. Initially banned as an "attack upon

12 Ibid., p. 367.

religion," *La ricotta* resulted first in a trial and then in a four month suspended prison sentence for Pasolini. "I still can't say exactly why they tried me at all," he observed years later, "but it was a terrible period for me. I was slandered week after week, and for two or three years I lived under a kind of unimaginable persecution."[13] Even under the harsh clerical laws then in force, Pasolini's sentence seemed harsh. In retrospect, of course, it is even more shocking—especially since *La ricotta* deals less with religion per se than with the degraded position it occupies in contemporary society and, especially, with the way(s) it is represented.[14]

The problem of representation is clearly at the heart of *La ricotta*, for this highly metacinematic film concerns a film crew engaged in shooting a life of Christ. The announcement that we are watching a film about a film comes at the very outset—and in a startling manner. After a solemn preface with quotes from the Gospels, Pasolini cuts suddenly to shots of a Felliniesque acting troupe, grotesquely dressed in Biblical costumes and dancing to pop music. The dichotomy between the sacred and the profane, the "real" and the "unreal," is followed by a series of shots that underscore still another major opposition of the film: the contrast between the frivolous concerns of the bourgeoisie (represented by the Roman film world) and the very real needs of the proletariat (needs incarnated in a poor extra named Stracci). A close-up of beautiful food carefully arranged for the film-within-a-film (the luscious grapes, in particular, might have been drawn by Caravaggio) is followed by one depicting the face of poor Stracci talking about his hunger.

As the film unfolds, it becomes clear that the real "passion" of *La ricotta* is not the one being filmed but that lived by Stracci. Cast symbolically in the role of the Good Thief, Stracci is consumed by hunger: he particularly loves ricotta cheese—hence *La ricotta*. Like an animal, he hides whatever food he receives as an extra in a cave only to find, at one point, that the star's pampered dog—who, of course, eats far better than he or his hungry family—has stolen it from him. Although his deepest fear is that he will perish of hunger, Stracci expires, instead, of overeating. Close-ups of his death agony—which occurs on the set where he is nailed to a raised cross—are accompanied by special effects of thunder and light-

---

[13] Cited by Oswald Stack in *Pasolini* (Bloomington and London: Indiana University Press, 1969), p. 63.

[14] Luigi Faccini feels that the problem of representation is so fundamental to *La ricotta* that he takes this film as the point of departure for Pasolini's increasingly metacinematic filmic universe. In this film, asserts Faccini, Pasolini confronts "the objective material of representation" for the first time even as he "begins to liberate himself from the (traditional) narrative structure and the painterly allusions of his earlier films." See Faccini, "Le strutture stilistiche omologhe della realtà," *Cinema e film* Vol. I, No. 1 (Winter 1966–1967), pp. 60–61.

ning created for the filmed Passion so that the "real" and the "unreal," life and art, are grotesquely juxtaposed. Close-ups of his last prayers are intercut with scenes showing the arrival of the film's all-powerful producer as we hear, in ironic counterpoint, an aria from *La Traviata*. Forced to take notice of poor Stracci when the latter fails to respond to a cue, the producer sadly observes that the poor extra "had to die to remind us that he was alive."

The implicit allusion to the Passion of Christ in both *Accattone* and *Mamma Roma* becomes, then, totally explicit in *La ricotta*. But at the same time Pasolini introduces a new and unsettling note of irony. Stracci himself is as much a comic figure as a tragic one: he is weirdly dressed in a modern shirt and a Biblical loin cloth, his comic aspect emphasized by a camera that films him in the fast motion of early silent comedies. Like Christ who was mocked at the temple gates by the Philistines, Stracci becomes a figure of fun for the rest of the cast. After discovering him in his cave, his fellow actors treat him like a caged animal by throwing food at him—food that he wolfs down in a bizarre version of the Last Supper. The film's strange blend of tragedy and irony, of grotesque need and real hunger, of the sacred and the profane, is disquieting, making us unsure of how to react: how do we, or should we, feel about this absurd but desperate clown? The unease *La ricotta* provokes in us gives a foretaste of later films where the excesses inspired by frustrated and monstrous hungers will assume ever more outrageous forms (such as cannibalism and coprophagy), even as the link between hunger, transgression, and sexuality will be made explicit. One very rapid, explicitly autobiographical sequence of *La ricotta* does, in fact, hint at this link: while nailed to the cross, Stracci is first fed mockingly by other members of the cast and then forced to witness a striptease. Pasolini crosscuts between this erotic display—a degraded, modern version of Salome's dance—and shots of a sensual youth clad in the scanty costume of an angel: shots that obviously reveal *his*, and not Stracci's desire.

If Stracci's plight has a disturbing tragicomic cast, Pasolini's real irony, as in later films, is reserved for the bourgeoisie, that is, for the vulgar troupe members, and for himself. In his view, the fictional director was a "caricature" of himself, a "cynical" portrait of what he might become if he "went beyond certain limits." The first of many authorial characters in Pasolini's cinema, the director is a looming, solitary, Felliniesque figure. As if to underscore the self-reflective nature of *La ricotta*, he is played by Orson Welles, who, suggests one critic, was chosen by Pasolini as an "hommage" to someone whose artistic vocation was always thwarted by commercial restraints.[15] But if Welles *was* chosen for this reason, he is

---

[15] See Adelio Ferrero, *Il cinema di Pier Paolo Pasolini*, p. 46.

also the target of tremendous (self) irony: the film he is making is clearly both futile—designed, as it is, for a profane society—and completely removed from reality, particularly, from the reality lived by Stracci. And the enormous, indeed ontological, gap between Stracci's "real" passion and that filmed by Welles is further emphasized by the contrast between the poor extra, who coincides with his role until the very moment of death, and the other actors, who could not be further removed from the Biblical characters they are asked to represent. The vulgarity of Christ, for example, is matched only by the bitchy egotism of Mary Magdalene, who is played, in still another layer of self-conscious irony, by a close friend of Pasolini's, the actress-singer Laura Betti.

The essential contrast between the "real" and the "unreal" is, in turn, buttressed by a series of stylistic differences that set the filmed Passion apart from the rest of *La ricotta*. In the film-within-a-film, Pasolini mocks what he called the "worst" side of his own art: he greatly exaggerates, and thereby parodies, his "mannerist" taste for startling contrasts and hieratic poses, for cultural echoes and layers of pastiche, for a deeply aestheticized and stylized reconstruction of reality. While Stracci, for example, is usually seen in natural settings that evoke the rounded volumes and harmony of Renaissance paintings, the film-within-a-film re-creates paintings—close-ups even suggest the enlarged details found in art books—by Pontormo and Rosso Fiorentino, two Italian mannerists. Virtually a *tableau vivant* of Pontormo's *Deposition from the Cross*, the filmed Passion is composed of shots of languid, motionless figures carefully poised against a depthless space. Strikingly unlike the rest of *La ricotta*, the mannerist film-within-a-film is shot in color: backdrop and costumes were carefully chosen to echo Pontormo's garish and anemic shades of turquoise, pink, and sickly green.

The maker of an "artificial" film, Welles resembles Pasolini in still other respects. He, too, is a lonely intellectual cut off from the very people who need him most. Welles may be the only one to understand the real nature of Stracci's plight, but he is powerless to close the gap between them. As Lino Miccichè observes, the contrast could hardly be greater between the "verbal gifts of the Artist who recites his own ideology and the . . . anguished mumblings of this poor man who is dying of hunger; between the director's monumental static quality and the parody of sub-proletarian vitality; between the possibility of a representation without suffering and the reality of a suffering which no representation can render."[16]

The "verbal gifts" of Welles/Pasolini, as well as the indissoluble link between Pasolini and his fictional counterpart, are made very clear in a scene where Welles grants an interview to an eager and foolish reporter.

---

[16] Lino Miccichè, *Il cinema italiano degli anni '60* (Venice: Marsilio, 1975), p. 162.

The journalist—whom Welles scornfully dubs an "average guy" (the worst of insults for him and, of course, for Pasolini)—is allowed four questions:

> Journalist: What do you want to express with this new work of yours?
> Director: My profound, inmost, archaic Catholicism.
> Journalist: And what do you think of Italian society?
> Director: [We have] the most illiterate masses, the most ignorant bourgeoisie in Europe.
> Journalist: And what do you think about death?
> Director: As a Marxist, it is a fact which I do not take into consideration.
> Journalist: Fourth and last question: what is your opinion . . . of our great Federico Fellini?
> Director: He dances![17]

In these most personal of responses, as always in *La ricotta*, confession is veiled in irony, mixed with humor. Half-mockingly, Welles/Pasolini confesses to his "archaic Catholicism," his scorn for the Italian bourgeoisie, and his despairing view of the people. He then proceeds to satirize his intransigeant critics who, as Marxists, "refuse to take death into consideration." After raising these important issues, Pasolini injects the light-hearted, enticingly ambiguous remark that "Fellini dances"—a remark that may refer to the artistry of Fellini's films, to the Felliniesque nature of *La ricotta*, and/or even to an unfortunate episode in which Fellini apparently retracted a half-promise to help finance *Accattone* after seeing the initial rushes for the film. And this, in turn, is followed by the most serious and explicitly autobiographical moment of the film: holding up a volume of *Mamma Roma*, Welles reads from it one of Pasolini's poems, a poem that expresses his—and Pasolini's—nostalgic melancholy for eras long past:

> I am a force of the Past. Tradition is my only love.
> I come from ruins, from Churches,
> from altarpieces, from forgotten
> villages of the Apennines and the Prealps
> where my brothers lived.
> I wander around the Tuscolana like a madman
> and around the Appian Way like a homeless dog.
> . . . . An adult fetus, more modern than
> all the moderns, I roam in search
> of brothers that are no more.[18]

[17] Pasolini, *Alì dagli occhi azzurri* (Milan: Garzanti, 1965), p. 473.
[18] Ibid., pp. 474–475.

(Io sono una forza del Passato.
Solo nella tradizione è il mio amore.
Vengo dai ruderi, dalle Chiese,
dalle pale d'altare, dai borghi
dimenticati sugli Appennini e sulle Prealpi,
dove sono vissuti i fratelli.
Giro per la Tuscolana come un pazzo,
per l'Appia come un cane senza padrone.
. . . . E io, feto adulto, mi aggiro
più moderno di ogni moderno
a cercare fratelli che non sono più.)

Foreshadowing the political and existential crisis that Pasolini would experience a few years after making *La ricotta*, these verses also echo the
feelings of impotence and frustration he had voiced so lyrically nearly a
decade earlier in "Le ceneri di Gramsci." And Welles, of course, embodies
all the ambivalences Pasolini had expressed not only in that poem but
throughout his essays of the 1950s. It is clear that this most cerebral of
directors could never play an "organic" role; and it is just as clear that
his subjective, aestheticized art has little or nothing in common with true
national-popular culture. But how, the film seems to ask, can an artist
create authentic culture in a consumer society that renders everything
profane and grotesque—a society where, as Luigi Faccini suggests, "religious values can be recuperated only through cultural images?"[19]

The essential role played by "cultural images" in the film-within-a-film
brings us back, finally, to the issue of representation. At the heart of Pasolini's film essays of the late 1960s, the problem of representation was
one that apparently began to torment him when he was barely an adolescent. At the age of twelve or thirteen, his youthful diary tells us, he attempted to draw some scenes inspired by the "other world" of adventure
books. Suddenly faced with the gap between the real and the represented—that is, the gap between the "real" scenes described by Homer
and Jules Verne and his own illustrations or representations of them—he
was filled with anguish:

The kitchen was the scene of my unbridled adventures; I saw myself bent over
the pages, tortured simply by the *pure* problem of the relationship between the
real and the artificial. The fact of representation appeared to me then as something terrible and primordial, precisely because in a pure state the equivalent
would have to be definitive. Faced with the problem of reproducing a meadow
I went crazy. The question for me was: should I draw all the blades of grass? I
did not know then that, by filling up the whole space with a green crayon, I

[19] Faccini, "Le strutture stilistiche omologhe della realtà," p. 60.

could have conveyed the *mass* of the meadow and . . . neglected the blades of grass. I was still far removed from such hypocrisies.[20]

The child's desire to capture every "blade of grass" persisted in the adult—the adult who, in fact, turned to cinema believing somehow that it was more concrete, closer to reality, than literature. Pasolini's attraction to mannerist art with its implied distance from reality was, perhaps, but the infernal mirror image of this intense desire to apprehend the real in a total and tangible way.[21] If art cannot grasp the real, Pasolini's mannerism seems to imply, let it show itself for what it is: an artifice, a simulacrum, a world of pure form. Haunted, always, by this dilemma, even as he made *La ricotta*, Pasolini was writing a poem in which he expressed his almost mystical longing to go beyond the screen or veil posed by the various "representations of Christ"—that is, beyond "cultural images"—in order to seize the "reality" of Christ directly. What he really wanted was to evoke

> an idea of Christ
> which precedes every style, every twist of history,
> every fixation, every development; virgin;
> reality reproduced with reality; without
> a single echo of poetry or painting;
> I want not only to be unaware of Dante, or Masaccio
> or Pontormo who have long dominated
> my eyes, my heart,
> my senses: I do not even want
> to know language and painting.
> I want this Christ to appear as did Christ in reality.[22]

> (un' idea di Cristo
> anteriore a ogni stile, a ogni corso della storia,
> a ogni fissazione, a ogni sviluppo; vergine;
> realtà riprodotta con la realtà; senza
> un solo ricordo di poemi o pitture;
> Voglio non solo non conoscere il Dante, o il Masaccio

[20] Pasolini, *Lettere* (Milan: Einaudi, 1986), pp. xxiv–xxv.

[21] Adriano Aprà offers still another interpretation of the tension at work in Pasolini between, on the one hand, an intense desire to grasp the real and, on the other, a taste for stylization. In a review of *Comizi d'amore*, Aprà remarks that "Pasolini's cinema shows a constant conflict between a realistic substance (faces, things, noises) and compositional stylization (editing, framings) which represents the concrete form of a masked relationship with reality, a kind of diffidence and fear, of tenderness and rage." See Aprà, "Il film testimonianza," *Filmcritica* No. 161 (1965), p. 503.

[22] Pasolini, "Bestemmia," *Cinema e film* Vol. I, No. 2 (Spring 1967), p. 225. Pasolini had thought to make a film about a heretical medieval saint named Bestemmia (i.e., "Blasphemy"), but this project was never realized.

o il Pontormo che a lungo hanno dominato
i miei occhi, il mio cuore,
i miei sensi: ma non voglio
neanche conoscere la lingua e la pittura
Voglio che quel Cristo si presenti come Cristo in realtà.)

In light of the desire expressed in this poem, the film-within-a-film of *La ricotta*—a film that seems defiantly to embody the simulacrum at the heart of all art—takes on the unmistakable color of defeat. Vulgar and unreal, this mannerist Passion suggests that, as in his adolescent days, Pasolini would always view the world of representation as a "hypocrisy," a fall from grace.

The desire to foreswear culture in favor of "reality" may well have been one of the impulses that led Pasolini to a dramatic change of direction in his next few films. Among his most committed works, *La rabbia* (1963) and *Comizi d'amore* (1964) embody one of the dialectical swings that would punctuate his career. Whereas *La ricotta* pirouetted around the dilemmas of the artist and his aesthetic "passion," these two films look outward to the world of "ideology"—to the world of social mores, politics, and history. Renouncing the cultural echoes and mannered pastiche of *La ricotta*, *La rabbia* and *Comizi d'amore* use, instead, techniques associated with documentary. But as the unconventional blend of poetry and documentary in *La rabbia* indicates, even at his most political Pasolini was not ready to renounce his penchant for stylistic experimentation.

A deeply personal and poetic short, *La rabbia* had an even more unfortunate history than *La ricotta*. Upon its completion, the producer—either for commerical reasons or fear of censorship—decided it should be released together with a second short film to be made by a director on the other side of the political spectrum, that is, on the right. The man chosen for this segment was Giovanni Guareschi. When the two shorts were eventually released, they were prefaced by the following remark:

> *La rabbia* is a film in two parts: the first by Pier Paolo Pasolini, the second by Giovanni Guareschi. Two ideologies, two opposing doctrines, respond to dramatic questions: why is our life dominated by discontent, anguish, fear of war, and war itself?

Pasolini, however—apparently for reasons that were more aesthetic than political—found Guareschi's episode "unacceptable." He withdrew his name from the film—partly as a result of this, partly because, as he said, "people were not interested in such highly political material"—and it had an extremely brief commercial run.

La rabbia is less an attempt to answer the "dramatic questions" posed by the preface than what Pasolini called "a Marxist denunciation of so-

ciety and recent events," or even a "cry of rage" against human suffering
and man's inhumanity to man. Composed entirely of photographs and
clips from newsreels and shorts, *La rabbia* was edited, he said, "according
to a chronological-conceptual line which took the shape of an act of in-
dignation against the *unreality* of the bourgeois world and the historical
irresponsibility to which it gives rise."[23]

As the clips and photographs of *La rabbia* pass briefly before us, a poetic commentary, often in counterpoint with the images, is read by two
friends of the director—a writer, Giorgio Bassani (the voice of peace and
sorrow), and a painter, Renato Guttuso (the voice of rage). No less than
in *Accattone* and *Mamma Roma*, classical music constitutes an important
presence: the lamenting violins of Albinoni's *Adagio in G minor* accompany scenes of war and devastation, global suffering and torture—in
Hungary, Korea, Algeria, and the Suez. These scenes are interspersed
with images of the two superpowers: Eisenhower at the Republican convention, Kennedy and Khrushchev, the atomic bomb. Repeatedly, the
commentary exhorts us not to close our eyes to the problem of the Third
World—the "emergence of men of color"—and its suffering millions. "A
new problem is exploding in the world," says the commentary, "it is
called: color. . . . We must accept infinite stretches of real lives which ask,
with a ferocious innocence, to enter our world."

The political images of *La rabbia* are punctuated by those drawn from
the many worlds of culture, suggesting, of course, the inseparability of
the two realms. Ava Gardner gives an interview in Italy; the rich are seen
at the opera; left-wing paintings by Ben Shawn are eclipsed by shots of
jazz musicians, as the commentary tells us that "Armstrong triumphed
over Marx." One of the film's longest sequences—and the one Pasolini
liked best—is devoted to the death of Marilyn Monroe. Like so many
others, Pasolini was drawn to the star's beauty and vulnerability; amidst
images of the "old" world (tribal ceremonies, folklore) and the "new"
(skyscrapers, the Oscar awards) the same photographs of her return obsessively, as the text, now a funeral dirge, addresses both Marilyn and us:
"Of the fearful ancient world and the fearful future world/ only beauty
was left, and you/ wore it like an obedient smile. . . . She vanished like a
golden dove."[24]

The political and social perspective of *La rabbia* is global; that of *Comizi d'amore*, Italian. Revealing an ethnological, even sociological bent,
in this film Pasolini uses *cinéma vérité* techniques to explore an issue close
to his heart and to that of his countrymen: Italian attitudes towards sex.
Revealing the fascination with faces that would characterize *Il Vangelo*,

[23] Cited by Carlo di Carlo in Antonio Bertini's *Teoria e tecnica del film in Pasolini* (Rome:
Bulzoni, 1979), p. 147.
[24] Pasolini, *Il cinema in forma di poesia*, ed. Luciano de Giusti (Pordenone: Cinemazero,
1979), pp. 121–122.

Pasolini interviews all kinds of Italians—of different regions, ages, classes —as he travels the length and breadth of Italy. Wherever he goes he patiently solicits his countrymen's views on sex and marriage, on divorce and homosexuality. Children are asked if they know where babies come from; soldiers are made to decide if they would rather be "Don Juans" or "good family men"; a young woman must ask herself what she would do if her child were homosexual. Surprisingly, perhaps, in this era of transition—on the eve of what Michel Foucault called the "grey mornings of tolerance"[25]—people are defensive and embarrassed about sex. Most of the Italians who consent to speak before the camera do so defensively, defiantly telling us they have no sexual problems, no interest in the questions posed. In the face of their supposed indifference and complacency, even their homophobia, an amazingly mild Pasolini remains imperturbable, encouraging.

Within the film, Pasolini periodically discusses his "findings," that is, the results of his interviews, with several friends and acquaintances—the novelist Alberto Moravia; a psychiatrist, Cesare Musatti; two journalists, Oriana Fallacci and Camilla Cederna. All express dismay at the portrait of sexual ignorance, hypocrisy, and prejudice that emerges from the interviews. (When I saw *Comizi d'amore*, it was presented by a critic who reminded Italian high-schoolers in the audience how fortunate they were not to have known the bigoted Italy of those years.) In Pasolini's eyes, the film revealed the "myths and taboos of a society full of the archaic strata and primitive cultural levels typical of under governed countries."

A portrait of prejudice and conformism, *Comizi d'amore* also illustrates how widely Italians differ: southerners and northerners, peasants and bourgeoisie might belong to different civilizations. One cannot help but share Pasolini's preference for the common people and peasants whose frank and direct answers contrast sharply with the snickers and evasiveness of the middle-class interviewees. "The South," comments Pasolini, "appears archaic but intact; the North new but confused." The chasm between North and South is matched by that separating social and legal realities. In a segment shot in Sicily, the men's conversation makes it clear that a "liberal" law closing the brothels has made their life very difficult: they can no longer, as Pasolini notes, hide from themselves sexual imperatives. The discrepancy between material and social progress leads a saddened Pasolini to conclude: "If this inquiry has a value, it is the negative one of demystification. The essence of this Italy of material well-being is dramatically contradicted by these real Italians."

[25] Michel Foucault, "Grey Mornings of Tolerance," in *Pier Paolo Pasolini: The Poetics of Heresy*, ed. Beverly Allen (Saratoga, Calif.: Anma Libri, 1982), p. 73. Originally in *Le Monde*, March 23, 1977.

Unlike *La rabbia* or *Comizi d'amore*, Pasolini's last nonfeature film of this period, *Sopraluoghi in Palestina* (*On the Scene in Palestine*, 1964) is clearly a minor work—virtually a cinematic afterthought. According to Pasolini, Alfredo Bini, the producer of *Il Vangelo secondo Matteo*, wanted to promote that film before its release and thought it might be useful to show some work-in-progress. Since a cameraman had followed Pasolini to the Holy Land, where he had initially gone in search of locations for *Il Vangelo*, it was decided to edit this footage and add a commentary to it. "I did not even have the time to write the commentary," observed Pasolini, "we went into the dubbing room and while the material was unfolding before my eyes, I became an improvised *speaker*."[26] In the course of this hastily improvised commentary, Pasolini explains that once he saw the Holy Land he realized that it would be impossible to film *Il Vangelo* there: everything—buildings, kibbutzes, faces—was far too modern. As we see him visit one legendary site after another, he begins to compare the landscape of the Holy Land with that of southern Italy, where he would actually film *Il Vangelo secondo Matteo*. But if Palestine did not yield desired locations, the journey did have one very important consequence: it was here that Pasolini filmed the first of the savage desert landscapes (in this instance, the untouched and "tremendous lunar landscape" near the Dead Sea) whose visual presence would dominate several films of the late 1960s—stark and forbidding symbols, in his view, of both eternal power and human alienation.

The intensity of Pasolini's emotions upon viewing the historic and tragic landscapes associated with Christ does much to explain his decision to make a film based on St. Matthew's version of the Gospel. It was, after all, a decision that many found surprising coming from someone who was seen, on the one hand, as "decadent" and "amoral" and, on the other, as a Marxist. Pasolini himself acknowledged that the film was impelled by a "furious wave of irrationalism"—a wave due, in no small measure, to his growing fear that traditional Marxism had reached an impasse. "In me," he told one interviewer "[ideological uncertainty] took the form of this regression to certain religious themes which, nonetheless, have been constant in all my work."[27] But despite his political "uncertainty," he also hoped—and this hope, too, subtends *Il Vangelo*—that Marxism might yet be revitalized. And one of the ways that this might be

---

[26] *Pier Paolo Pasolini: Una vie future*, eds. Laura Betti and Sergio Vecchio (Rome: River Press, 1987), p. 103.

[27] *Con Pier Paolo Pasolini*, p. 67. In the same conversation, Pasolini described the ideological climate surrounding *Il Vangelo* thus: "All the ideological rationalism elaborated in the 1950s, not only in me but in all of literature, is in crisis; an air of crisis is everywhere—in the avant-gardes, in the silence of many writers, in the ideological uncertainties of writers like Cassola or Bassani—and it is also in me."

accomplished, he felt, was through a radically unconventional alliance or "dialogue" with Christianity.

There is little doubt that Pasolini's deeply religious sensibility—the inability, as he wrote to a friend in 1954, to abandon the "bourgeois and Catholic" world of his youth in order to make the "virile and definitive" choice of communism[28]—fueled his desire for such an alliance. But he was also encouraged in this hope by historical factors, in the early 1960s, that seemed to lessen the traditional chasm between Marxists and Catholics: the emergence of a less rigid Communist party at this time coincided with the presence of a compassionate and socially aware pope. *Il Vangelo* is, in fact, dedicated to the memory of Pope John XXIII, "the first to understand that a Marxist is not a *bête noire* and that it is possible to create a dialogue between Marxists and Catholics."[29]

Above and beyond these historical factors, however, lay something even more fundamental: Pasolini's belief that, at the deepest level, Marxism and Christianity had profound affinities. He was convinced that, in the modern world, perhaps only these two forces stood opposed to the materialist values of neocapitalism. "The great enemy of Christianity," he wrote,

> is not communist materialism, but bourgeois materialism. The former—because it is theoretical, philosophical, and speculative—*contains* the most absolute moments of religion. The latter—totally practical, empirical, and functional—excludes . . . every sincerely religious or cognitive moment of reality. . . . In the former one can always find moments of idealism, of desperation, of psychological violence, of cognitive desire, and of faith—moments that, however disparate, are elements of religion. In the latter one finds nothing but mammon.[30]

This great affinity led him to hope that these two movements—historically opposed yet spiritually akin—might each emerge stronger, more essential, purer, from a "dialogue" that would force each to confront its deepest impulses. In an interview published in the Communist newspaper *L'Unità* on December 22, 1964, Pasolini reiterated the need for this alliance even as he expressed the fundamental themes of *Il Vangelo*:

> Catholicism must be capable . . . of taking into account the problems of the society in which we live; and so too must Marxism face the religious moment of humanity. There will always be an irrational, religious moment. Improving the social sphere will place the moment of the religious problem in a different

[28] Pasolini, *Lettere*, p. 695.
[29] Cited by Marisa Rusconi, "4 Registri al magnetofono," *Sipario* (October 1964), p. 16.
[30] Pasolini, *Le belle bandiere*, p. 259.

perspective; once class oppression is over, man will confront only his own human nature—death.[31]

The initial surprise many experienced at the thought of a Marxist filming the life of Christ receded when *Il Vangelo* was released. Not only did
the film win international acclaim but, for once, Pasolini seemed to please
Italians on both sides of the spectrum: both Catholics and, to a lesser
extent, Marxists had high praise for *Il Vangelo*. Although—as I would
like to show in a moment—some leftists were disturbed by the film, most
acknowledged that *Il Vangelo* maintained a very fine balance between
religion and politics. Discussing the deliberate ways in which he sought
to create this balance, Pasolini remarked that he did not try to please
"official Marxists" by portraying Christ as a totally secular social agita-
tor. "It is against my nature," he said, "to desacralize things and people."[32] But while he refused to ignore the mystical side of Christ, he also
gave him the deep moral and social sensibility, with all its secular resonances, that underscores *La rabbia* and *Comizi d'amore*. Pasolini's Christ
shares his own "rage" against the philistines and the powerful, his love
for the poor and oppressed. One can hardly tell, as Sandro Petraglia observes, whether Pasolini "began with Christ in order to arrive at Marx or,
vice versa, if in fact his love for the story of the Passion took him . . . to a
version of the myth profoundly renewed by a populist, sub-proletarian,
or Third World current."[33] Still another critic, Edoardo Bruno, explicitly
deems *Il Vangelo* a national-popular work: "After [*La ricotta*] and especially, after the brief, intense, enlightening montage film *La rabbia* . . .
Pasolini's mournful poetry had to approach themes of a religious, epic
nature, themes that reflected the nature—popular and national, ideological and civil—of his mandate."[34]

Bruno obviously touched a chord dear to Pasolini's heart. For the director himself felt that, despite some "decadent elements," *Il Vangelo* was
indeed infused with great "bursts of a national-popular sort." In his view,
the film successfully transformed the private and "stylistically precious"
aspects of his earlier religious works into "faith, myth, and collective mythology."[35] In fact, he was particularly drawn to St. Matthew's version of
the Gospel largely because it was the only one, he believed, that possessed
a "national-popular epic" quality. "Mark's seemed too crude, John's too
mystical, and Luke's sentimental and bourgeois."[36] Once he had chosen

[31] "Cristo e il Marxismo: Dialogo Pasolini-Sartre," *L'Unità*, December 22, 1964, p. 26.

[32] Cited by Duflot, *Entretiens*, p. 27.

[33] Petraglia, *Pasolini*, p. 58.

[34] Edoardo Bruno, "*Il Vangelo secondo Matteo*," *Filmcritica* No. 147–148 (July–August
1964), p. 356.

[35] Pasolini, *Il Vangelo* (Milan: Garzanti, 1964), p. 297.

[36] Cited by Rusconi, "4 Registri al magnetofono," p. 16.

this version of the Gospel, he remained scrupulously faithful to it, avoiding additional explanations and transitions in the belief that "inserted words or images could never reach the poetic heights of the text."[37] The resulting film thus reflected not only St. Matthew's elliptical and frequently mysterious text but also Pasolini's constant desire to capture characters and events only at "absolute" moments. At the same time, Pasolini felt that the elliptical, even staccato, nature of both the text and the film corresponded to what he saw as the fundamental "violence" of Christ:

> By literally following Matthew's "stylistic accelerations"—the barbaric-practical workings of his narration, the abolition of chronological time, the elliptical jumps within the story which inscribe the "disproportions" of the didactic, static moments such as the stupendous, interminable, discourse on the mountain—the figure of Christ should finally assume the violence inhering in any rebellion which radically contradicts the appearance and shape that life assumes for modern man: a gray orgy of cynicism, irony, brutality, compromise and conformism . . . of hatred for anything that is different and teleological rancor without religion.[38]

Pasolini's fidelity to Matthew's text was, in fact, one of the factors that disturbed his more intransigeant critics on the left. This was the case, for example, of French student Marxists who—convinced that the left-wing Pasolini had betrayed them by making a religious work—vehemently attacked the film when it opened in Paris. In particular, they objected to Pasolini's literal depiction of the supernatural—a depiction, it must be admitted, that was given added credibility by the very fact of being seen. No literary description found in the Gospels can compete with a filmic sequence where Christ walks calmly upon the water or cures lepers of their sores. (And Pasolini's matter-of-fact style only heightened this believability: for example, the angel who appears "in a dream" in Matthew's text becomes, in the film, a totally real, albeit androgynous, being.) Stung by the reactions of the young Parisian Marxists, Pasolini—who had accompanied the film to the French capital—accused his critics of being impelled by a "strange hysterical fury," a fury stemming from their supposed "duty to 'reject' a religious work or, to use more boldly psychoanalytic terms, to erase a religious work."[39] In a less polemical vein, he defended his portrayal of the supernatural on the grounds that what he called the "subjective reality" of miracles exists. "It exists," he said, "for the peasants of Southern Italy, as it existed for those in Palestine. Miracles

[37] Pasolini, *Il Vangelo*, p. 16.
[38] Ibid., pp. 14–15.
[39] Pasolini, *Le belle bandiere*, p. 336.

are the innocent and naive explanation of the real mystery which lives in man, of the power hidden within him."[40] And it was precisely this "subjective reality" that he sought to convey in *Il Vangelo* where, he maintained, the life of Christ is seen through the eyes of a "believer." While discussing the film with Sartre in Paris, he declared:

> I have been faithful to myself and I have created a national-popular work in the Gramscian sense. Because the believer through whom I see Christ as the son of God is a humble Italian [*un personnagio popolare italiano*] . . . seeing the world through his eyes I came close to Gramsci's national-popular conception of art.[41]

Without denying either the "subjective reality" of miracles or (at least for the moment) the national-popular character of *Il Vangelo*, Pasolini's argument that the film is seen through the eyes of a believer does appear strained: it says more, perhaps, about his deep ambivalence toward Catholicism than about the way *Il Vangelo* is shot. One would be hard pressed, indeed, to distinguish, at least in any conventional sense, two points of view in *Il Vangelo*. For this reason I find myself agreeing with an observation made by a priest, Father Fantuzzi, who also happened to be a friend of Pasolini's. It was the opinion of Father Fantuzzi that, although Pasolini called himself an atheist, he "didn't know exactly what he was. He preferred to say that he wasn't a believer and that to make this film he had taken the point of view of a hypothetical believer. In fact, there is no difference between the two points of view."[42]

If the profound religious impulse at work in *Il Vangelo* testifies to the strength of Pasolini's "bourgeois heritage," its unconventional style reveals, instead, his need to innovate, perhaps to rebel. As if the mannerist film of *La ricotta* constituted a kind of exorcism, *Il Vangelo* scrupulously avoids the traditional iconography and cultural echoes that Welles/Pasolini found irresistible. The only noticeable exception to this are the costumes of the Pharisees and the Roman soldiers, which evoke a specific painter, Piero della Francesca. Otherwise, as Pasolini noted:

> whenever I realized from behind the camera that something might recall the composition of a painting, I destroyed it immediately. I sought to do everything the most cinematographically possible. Naturally there are some painterly echoes—there's Duccio, there's Mantegna—but certainly not a precise painting or school, simply generic references.[43]

[40] Cited by Duflot, *Entretiens*, p. 28.
[41] "Cristo e il marxismo," p. 26. Sartre, incidentally, asked that *La ricotta* be shown alongside *Il Vangelo* to make Pasolini's position clearer.
[42] Jean-Luc Muracciole, "Interview with Father Fantuzzi," *Art Press*, September 1984, p. 37.
[43] *Con Pier Paolo Pasolini*, pp. 70–71.

The absence of precise visual allusions means that while both *La ricotta* and *Il Vangelo secondo Matteo* work against traditional representations of Biblical scenes, they do so in almost opposing ways. In its film-within-a-film, *La ricotta* reproduces familiar iconography only implicitly to denounce its falsity and distance from reality; *Il Vangelo* deliberately, and consistently, rejects such iconography. Its Virgin is not the pious and luminous Madonna of Renaissance paintings but a very pregnant, bewildered young peasant woman who might well have stepped out of a neorealist film. Equally naturalistic, Joseph is unshaven, squat, and balding; Salome is not the erotic goddess of Hollywood films but a graceful, almost timid adolescent; Christ's followers, including St. John the Baptist, resemble Accattone's sub-proletarian comrades.

The counterpoint or play of oppositions characterizing Pasolini's early films is, in fact, reversed in *Il Vangelo*, where the subject is mythic and epic; the style realistic. Although this was not Pasolini's initial intention, once on location he soon found that the epic style of *Accattone* was excessive when applied to an equally epic story.

> Using a reverential style for *The Gospel* was gilding the lily: it came out rhetoric. Reverential technique and style in *Accattone* went fine, but applied to a sacred text they were ridiculous; so I got discouraged and was just about to give the whole thing up, and then when I was shooting the baptism scene near Viterbo I threw over all my technical preconceptions. I started using the zoom, I used new camera movements, new frames which were not reverential, but almost documentary. A completely new style emerged. In *Accattone* the style is consistent and extremely simple, as in Masaccio or in Romanesque sculpture. Whereas the style in *The Gospel* is very varied: it combines the reverential style with almost documentary movements, an almost classic severity with moments that are almost Godardian—e.g., the two trials of Christ shot like *cinéma vérité*.[44]

Once Pasolini realized that a documentary style suited *Il Vangelo*, the short focal-length lenses used for the sharply defined facial close-ups of *Accattone* and *Mamma Roma* were often replaced by long focal-length lenses that created a documentary, neorealist look. And, as he suggests, he also returned to some of the *cinéma vérité* techniques used in *Comizi d'amore*: a hand-held camera that shoots Christ acclaimed by the people gives the viewer the sense of being among the crowd; Christ's two trials are shot from a certain distance, as if by a television reporter held at bay. The film's look of raw documentary is enhanced by the use of nonprofessional actors, including a number of Pasolini's friends and relatives: his mother, Susanna, plays the aged mother of Christ; the writer Natalia

---

[44] Cited by Stack, *Pasolini*, pp. 83–84.

Ginzburg, Mary of Bethany; Pasolini's friend and biographer, Enzo Siciliano, Simon of Canaan; one of his *Officina* colleagues, Francesco Leonetti, Herod. Whereas his intellectual friends play those in power, all the
minor characters are drawn, as he phrased it, from the "agricultural and
pastoral proletariat of Southern Italy."[45]

The quasi-documentary approach of *Il Vangelo* may well have reflected
Pasolini's desire to capture reality (to seize, as he said, the "idea of Christ
which precedes every style, every twist of history"), but it also had a political dimension. By giving Biblical events and people a modern, earthy
cast, Pasolini underscores, and often creates, important analogies between the contemporary world and that of Christ—analogies, as he once
remarked, that are at the very heart of the film. For example, the landscapes and peasant faces found in *Il Vangelo* were inspired by Pasolini's
trips to the Third World (India and North Africa, in particular, suggested
to him the "brutally alive world of Biblical times"[46]), while the film's portrayal of the Scribes and the Pharisees—who are often seen in hieratic
groups and shot from a low angle to heighten their massive, static, and
imposing appearance—suggests the rigidity and power that adhere to any
reigning Establishment. And several analogies were even more specific:

> As far as the Roman soldiers during Christ's sermon at Gethsemane were con-
> cerned, I had to think of the Celere [tough anti-riot police]; for Herod's soldiers
> before the slaughter of the innocents, I had to think of Fascist hoods; Joseph
> and the Virgin Mary in flight were suggested by so many similar dramas of
> flight in the modern world (for example, in Algeria).[47]

Political analogies are frequently reinforced by music. Bach and Mozart
emphasize solemn moments; Negro spirituals intensify scenes of exaltation. In one particularly complex moment the music evokes overlying
strands of both film and history: we see Herod's massacre of Jewish in-
fants while hearing the Prokofiev music Eisenstein used in *Alexander
Nevsky* to accompany scenes of a battle on the ice in which Russian soldiers defend their homeland. In a similar manner, a Resistance song is
played during one of Christ's diatribes, with the result that, in the words
of René Prédal, "the martyrdom of the son of God . . . announces and
rejoins that of all victims to come in the revolutionary struggle."[48]

Above all, however, the political dimension of *Il Vangelo*—implicit in
the music and the analogies between past and present—is incarnated in
Christ himself. A decade earlier, Pasolini had written to a friend that

[45] Ibid., p. 77.
[46] Pasolini, *Il Vangelo*, p. 14.
[47] Pasolini, *Uccellacci e Uccellini* (Milan: Garzanti, 1966), p. 49.
[48] René Prédal, "L'évangile selon saint-Matthieu: de l'évènement au sacré," *Avant-scène
du cinéma* No. 175–176, p. 8.

Christ's injunction to "love thy neighbor as thyself" is really an injunction to "make structural [i.e., political] reforms."[49] It is these "structural
reforms" in essence, that are demanded by the Christ of *Il Vangelo*. "Anyone," said Pasolini, "who walks up to a couple of people and says, 'Drop
your nets and follow me' is a total revolutionary."[50] Convinced that
Christ must always be seen as a figure of rebellion and scandal, Pasolini
felt that St. Matthew in particular rendered him "inflexible . . . overwhelming, without a moment of rest or peace."[51] Underscoring this intransigeance, Pasolini does not give his Christ the soft features of Renaissance paintings; he is, instead, "distant" and "hieratic," with a "face that
corresponds to the arid and rocky places in which his sermons took
place."[52] (On occasion, in fact, this "arid" Christ—who rarely smiles,
who harshly commands his followers to abandon all, who exhibits little
human warmth—has dismayed Christians more comfortable with the
idea of a mild and loving God.)

As he resolutely fights for social justice, this Christ leaves no doubt
that, as Pasolini noted, he brings "not peace but a sword." Absorbed by
his political struggle, Christ pays little attention to the sins of the flesh
that so concerned many of the church fathers. In this, he reflects Pasolini's deep conviction, which he expressed in an interview with moving
and revealing personal overtones, that Christ would have judged carnal
sins—which are unconscious and hence "inevitable"—less harshly than
the conscious "social" sins (i.e., greed, injustice, and hypocrisy) of the
powerful Pharisees.[53] It was precisely his struggle against "social sins,"
noted Pasolini, that gave the Christ of *Il Vangelo* a Marxist cast. In the
course of the heated discussion that took place with hostile leftists in Paris
Pasolini observed:

> For a Frenchman [*Il Vangelo*] may be a religious film. For an Italian proletarian,
> there is no ambiguity. Christ is a member of the sub-proletariat and is involved
> with others of this class. An historical relationship exists between Christ and
> the proletariat; he would not have done anything if he had not been followed
> by proletarians. The Pharisees would not have killed him. And the proletariat
> would have remained immersed in an unhearing darkness without the revolu-
> tionary teachings of Christ.[54]

No one doubted the moral fervor of Pasolini's Christ. But, significantly,
some of the most important critical objections to the film did bear on

[49] Pasolini, *Lettere*, p. 709.
[50] Cited by Stack, *Pasolini*, p. 95.
[51] Cited by Ferdinando Camon, *Il mestiere di scrittore* (Milan: Garzanti, 1973), p. 102.
[52] Pasolini, *Il Vangelo*, p. 300.
[53] Pasolini, "Colloqui sul *Vangelo*," *Il Popolo*, June 19, 1971.
[54] "Cristo e il marxismo," *L'Unità*, p. 26.

what Pasolini saw as *Il Vangelo*'s Marxist perspective. A number of thoughtful critics argued, in fact, that Pasolini ignored the specific historical realities of Christ's era—realities such as the complicated relations between Jews and Romans or the issue of Jewish uprisings. In their view, this meant that the conflict between Christ and the Pharisees in *Il Vangelo* was less a precise Marxist, or class, analysis of a given historical moment than a kind of mythic and abstract confrontation between oppressed and oppressor. Even Lino Miccichè, long an admirer of the director, felt that Pasolini had elevated his own "aversion to the present bourgeois rule" into abstract terms even as he grafted his own "intellectual solitude . . . haughty prophesying and violent transgression" onto Christ.[55] For Gianni Toti, one of Pasolini's harshest critics on the far left, the Palestine of *Il Vangelo* was decidedly not the real Palestine, which "teemed with founders of religion," a Palestine in which Christ "translated into terms of faith and religious hope the age-old discontent of the masses in the face of economic and social oppression."[56]

And objections went further than Pasolini's interpretation, or even his neglect, of history. Even the Gramscian cast, the national-popular dimension of *Il Vangelo*—so dear to Pasolini's heart—was called into question. Taking issue once again with Pasolini's populism, critics objected not only to his "lifeless" portrayal of the people but also to the gulf that separated Christ from his proletarian followers. A French critic, Marie-Claire Ropars-Wuilleumier, likened the Biblical sub-proletariat of *Il Vangelo* to a bunch of expressionless "film extras"; the ever severe Gianni Toti felt that the apostles of *Il Vangelo*, characterized by the same "mentally torpid physiognomies" as the sub-proletarians in the slums of *Accattone* and *Mamma Roma*, provided still another example of Pasolini's "tendency toward decadent taste."[57] Even years later Sandro Petraglia, author of a book on Pasolini's cinema, echoed these views, declaring that *Il Vangelo* did not contain "a single scene in which a character from the crowd succeeds in resisting the absolute fierceness of the messiah, not a single frame in which one of them emerges from a perspective which flattens and crushes the multitudes into a sub-human homogeneity."[58]

A number of these remarks—for example, Toti's use of the word "decadent"—hint, certainly, at the homophobic moralism associated with

[55] Miccichè, *Il cinema italiano degli anni '60*, pp. 163–165.

[56] Gianni Toti, "Cinema e scienza religiosa," in *Da Accattone a Salò*, special issue of *Quaderni della cineteca* (Bologna) No. 4 (May 1982), p. 37. Originally in *Cinema sessanta* No. 46 (October 1964).

[57] Marie-Claire Ropars-Wuilleumier, "La lettre et l'esprit," in her *L'écran de la mémoire* (Paris: Seuil, 1970), p. 143. Originally in *Esprit*, May 1965. Toti, *Da Accattone a Salò*, p. 37.

[58] Petraglia, *Pasolini*, pp. 61–62.

Asor Rosa. Still, in several respects, the issues raised by these critics *are* valid: they pointed not only to the ambiguities that infuse the national-popular dimension of the film but to even deeper tensions. There is little doubt that Pasolini does indeed drain the people of life and vitality. While, for example, his decision to allow only Christ to speak may have been dictated by his fidelity to St. Matthew's text, the silence of Christ's followers in *Il Vangelo* helps reduce them to an indistinguishable mass. Totally dominated and overwhelmed by Christ, his followers, as critics also observed, are fatally removed from him. As if to underscore the emotional and intellectual distance separating this messiah from his followers, Pasolini consistently isolates Christ through visual means. For example, when Christ preaches on the mountain, only close-ups of his face are shown, so that we never see the effect of his words, that is, the reactions of others. Christ appears, in fact, as a kind of Biblical intellectual who, despite an intense desire to be "organically" linked to the people, cannot breach the immeasurable gap between them. One is left to wonder how his mute and passive followers will be able to further his teachings once he himself is gone.

In retrospect, it seems clear that the disquieting portrait of the people in *Il Vangelo*—a portrait that betrays a deep political pessimism—sprang from ambivalences and doubts of which Pasolini was not fully aware at the time. Five or six years after completing the film, he would admit that *Il Vangelo was* permeated by "violent" contradictions and "ambiguous and disconcerting" elements that were embodied, he felt, in the character of Christ.[59] Clearly, the intransigeance and loneliness of his messiah signaled not only his own sense of isolation but also a historical despair whose depths had still to be acknowledged. And his depiction of the people was also imbued with the "violent contradictions" that betray inner tensions—perhaps the very tensions he had expressed so eloquently in "Le ceneri di Gramsci." There he had confessed that he was always torn between, on the one hand, a rational desire to help the downtrodden and, on the other, an irrational attraction to the poor precisely because they embody certain moral and aesthetic virtues. It may well have been this "irrational" attraction that helped shape his portrait of Christ's meek and passive followers. In the eyes of at least one critic, Guido Frank, not only is this tension at the core of *Il Vangelo* but its *unacknowledged* presence works to undermine the film. Fink argues convincingly that in *Il Vangelo* Pasolini's love for the proletarian world

> wound up by being fatal: the harsh, unpleasant sub-proletariat and prehistorical reality is "redeemed". . . only on the sentimental . . . level and not at all on the critical one. . . . The results of this unfortunate *Vangelo* seem very different

[59] Cited by Stack, *Pasolini*, p. 77.

from those of *La ricotta* where the author and poet, far from identifying with the "exposed," humiliated, and martyred Christ, really crucified himself in his director's seat.[60]

But while the tensions underlying *Il Vangelo* were not acknowledged within the film, they were not to remain submerged for long. Indeed, in his next film, Pasolini would explicitly confront—and reluctantly dismiss—the Gramscian hopes and beliefs that he had nourished since his youth. The admission of political defeat would bring with it a return to the lucid self-irony of *La ricotta*: once again, Pasolini would "crucify" himself—not in the "director's seat" this time but in the strange, whimsical guise of a talking bird, a Marxist crow.

> My business
>   is
>   of a delicate nature:
>
> about the place
>   of the poet
>   in the workers' ranks.
>
>   —Vladimir Mayakovsky

The acute political and existential crisis Pasolini experienced in the mid-1960s is, precisely, the theme of *Uccellacci e Uccellini*. This most unusual of films—dubbed by one critic "a fable, an essay, a confession, a pamphlet, a sub-titled lesson, a picaresque saga"[61]—signaled a turning point in Pasolini's career even as it raised crucial questions concerning the direction of Italian Marxism. For Lino Miccichè, *Uccellacci e Uccellini* is not only one of the most beautiful films of 1966 but a "symptomatic document" of a critical moment in Marxist ideology—a moment in which the "ungrounded" hopes of the past seemed but the prelude to a very uncertain, if not "impossible," future.[62] Always playing against expectations, in *Uccellacci e Uccellini* Pasolini filters weighty historical and political issues through veils of whimsy and metaphor. This gives rise to what he called an "ironic and formal distance"—a "distance" sharply opposed to the passionate tone of *La rabbia* and *Il Vangelo*. Still, as *La ricotta* had made clear, Pasolini was never more engaged, certainly never more personal, than when deeply ironic.

The film's comic yet serious tone is apparent from the outset. The credits, sung as a kind of popular *chanson* against a shot of the moon,

---

[60] Guido Fink, "E il cinema e nato ieri," *Cinema Nuovo* Vol. 14, No. 176 (July–August 1965), p. 270.

[61] Mino Argentieri, "*Uccellacci e Uccellini*," in Luciano de Guisti's *I film de Pasolini* (Rome: Gremese, 1983), p. 77. Originally in *Rinascita*, May 21, 1966.

[62] Lino Miccichè, *Il cinema italiano degli anni '60*, p. 165.

tell us that the film was directed by a "certain Pier Paolo Pasolini who risked his reputation" by making the film. As the credits come to an end, a quote from Mao appears on the screen: "Where is humanity headed?" An indication of the film's serious theme, this citation also announces the important, almost Godardian, role that will be played by written words throughout *Uccellacci e Uccellini*. Here sub-titles often announce episodes and issues, while even street signs have ideological or symbolic weight. The streets of this Marxist fable, for example, do not bear the names of the famous and powerful but of the poor and humble: "Via Antonio Mangiapasta scopino" ("Via Antonio Pasta-eater, street cleaner").

The protagonists of the film—father and son, Totò and Ninetto—are played by people who do, in fact, come from a humble and popular milieu. Once a well-known and successful Neapolitan comedian, an aging Totò was rescued from inactivity by a Pasolini entranced with the comedian's "double" nature: "on the one hand, there's the Neapolitan subproletarian, and on the other, there's a pure and simple clown . . . [whose] unawareness of history is the unawareness of the innocent."[63] As for Ninetto, Totò's carefree and joyous son, he is played by Ninetto Davoli. A beloved friend from the Roman *borgata*, beginning with *Uccellacci e Uccellini*, Davoli would be the embodiment of joy and innocence in almost all of Pasolini's films.

As *Uccellacci e Uccellini* opens, these two "humble" Italians—modest representatives of mankind itself—are walking down an unidentified road. We are never told where they are from, nor where they are going, nor how long they have been traveling. They pass through a scarred urban landscape—marked by debris, shanties, yards full of automobile tires—reminiscent of the squalid Roman suburbs of *Accattone* and *Mamma Roma*. A cityscape that suggests, in the words of Adelio Ferrero, "the exhausted periphery of a world beyond history,"[64] these mournful surroundings convey the moral and physical leadenness, the sense of historical closure Pasolini had evoked more than a decade earlier in "Le ceneri di Gramsci":

autumnal May amid the old walls.
In it is the world's greyness,
the end of the decade which
saw our profound and naive effort to
remake life finish in ruins;
silence, sodden and barren.[65]

[63] Pasolini, "Ecco il mio Totò," *La Repubblica*, August 3, 1976, p. 11. From a 1974 interview.
[64] Ferrero, *Il cinema di Pasolini*, p. 68.
[65] Pasolini, *Poesie*, p. 67.

(tra le vecchie muraglie l'autunnale
maggio. In esso c'è il grigore del mondo,
la fine del decennio in cui ci appare

tra le macerie finito il profondo
e ingenuo sforzo di rifare la vita;
il silenzio, fradicio e infecondo.)

As in a novel by Samuel Beckett, Totò and Ninetto wander aimlessly through these gloomy surroundings, going from one metaphorical encounter to the next. Describing their adventures, Pasolini dubbed *Uccellacci e Uccellini* a special kind of picaresque fable where the characters obtain no "favors"—neither "kingdoms nor princesses"—after their many ordeals. Observing that while the characters and their adventures are imbued with the picaresque, he went on to say that the "ideology" of his fable, instead, "lies precisely in something which deeply contradicts any picaresque poetics. A fable which ends as it should not, a picaresque which does not say what it should."[66] What might be seen, in fact, as the film's "real" ideology—the one that contradicts any "picaresque poetics"—centers about a confirmed Marxist that Totò and Ninetto befriend in the course of their wanderings. And, as befits this "ideo-comic" fable, the Marxist turns out to be none other than a talking crow—one who speaks with the voice of Francesco Leonetti, an intellectual friend of Pasolini's.

Soon after his meeting with Totò and Ninetto, the crow tells them a story, which constitutes the middle part of the film. In this tale-within-a-tale, Totò and Ninetto appear as medieval friars who, inspired by the words of St. Francis, have set out to preach a message of love to the hawks and sparrows. Since the big hawks (i.e., *"uccellacci"*) and the little sparrows (*"uccellini"*) represent the division of society into oppressed and oppressor, the mission of the two friars—like that of Christ in *Il Vangelo secondo Matteo*—is both religious and social: they must teach the birds the nature of divine love and stop the powerful from preying on the poor. After long and arduous efforts, the saintly yet comic Totò—who reminds us now of Chaplin, now of Keaton—finally has a moment of triumph: he communicates with the birds by crying like a hawk and hopping like a sparrow. Lyrical music underscores his triumph as sub-titles tell us what he—and the birds—are saying. But victory is short-lived: no sooner does Totò deliver his Christian message to the birds than a hawk, ignoring all that he has said, swoops down to kill one of the little sparrows. Discouraged by their failure, the friars return home to relate their sad tale to St. Francis. Undaunted by their setback, the holy man urges them to try

[66] Pasolini, "Lettera aperta," *Occhio critico* Vol. I, No. 2 (November 1966), p. 57.

again. As Totò and Ninetto skip off down the road to begin anew, the film returns to the present day.

Once more in the modern world, the three travelers undergo a number of other adventures demonstrating, as the crow constantly reminds Totò and Ninetto, that—like the hawks and the sparrows—powerful and wealthy men prey on those who are weak and humble. Finally, the crow's obsession with ideology so irritates Totò and Ninetto that they turn on the bird and eat it. After this act of cannibalism, the two Italians, says Pasolini, "take to the road once more and, as in Chaplin's films, shoulder to shoulder, they go, go, go—along the white road toward their destiny."[67]

Given Pasolini's deep sense of self-irony, it is hardly surprising that he grafted his own features onto the unhappy crow: like Pasolini, the crow is at once a (Marxist) intellectual, a "teller of tales" (the narrator of the medieval episode), and even a kind of omniscient author in that he knows everything about Totò and Ninetto. If Pasolini mocked his aesthetic impulses in *La ricotta*, the crow allows him to satirize his devotion to theory, his inability to live life in an immediate and vital way. As the crow says, "I'm here because I'm nostalgic for the wonderful thing that I don't have—being part of life, simply being alive. . . . My parents are Signor Doubt and Signora Consciousness, my wife is Signora Culture and my family is Humanity."[68] The crow delivers a hymn to life and then goes on to express regret that living is not enough. But, for simple people like Totò and Ninetto, it is. Before the final act of cannibalism, for example, both go off with a woman who incarnates, as Pasolini noted, a life force—that is, the very force the crow lacks.

Throughout the film, in fact, the crow's intellectual musings—filled with theoretical preoccupations, with traces of doubt and guilt—contrast unfavorably with the vitality and spontaneity of Totò and Ninetto, whose "grace" and "innocence" the crow deems "religious." The tremendous gap between the crow and the two humble Italians is made clear, symbolically, when the three first meet. The crow introduces himself in somber tones, saying: "I come from far away. . . . I'm a stranger. . . . My country is called Ideology, I live in the capital, the City of the Future, on Karl Marx Street." And they, as if to emphasize the gulf between themselves and this portentous stranger, respond: "And we, we live in the Quarter of Garbage . . . on Dying-of-Hunger Street."[69] As a Marxist who is removed from life and caught up in intellectual dilemmas, the crow, said Pasolini, is an autobiographical figure, an "eccentric metaphor for the

---

[67] Pasolini, *Le belle bandiere*, p. 334.
[68] Pasolini, *Uccellacci e Uccellini*, p. 173.
[69] Ibid., pp. 170–171.

author. Marxism grafted like an innocent norm, a form of rebirth which is logical and not totally mad, onto a flaw in the norm, onto the trauma (i.e., nostalgia for life, compulsory detachment from it, solitude, poetry as compensation)."[70]

But the crow is not merely a self-ironic figure. In this film permeated by metaphor, where the serious and the comic commingle, the admirable yet laughable crow also embodies the dilemma of the committed intellectual whose postwar mandate has lost its force and direction in an era dominated by greed and the compulsion to consume. Seemingly unaware that his role is no longer valid, the poor crow gives one lesson in ideology after another to Totò and Ninetto to make them understand how their behavior has been shaped by the cruelties of capitalism. (Revealing Pasolini's taste for formal parallels, in the modern episode a bird "preaches" to mankind, while the medieval saints "preach" to the birds.) But Pasolini undercuts the crow's lessons with satire and irony. When, for example, an enraged man threatens the travelers after they relieve themselves on his property, the crow first explains how the system of private property leads to violence and war and then admonishes Totò and Ninetto to "carry away their shit and to reconcile in a single act of meekness the Communist revolution and the Church." Or, while Totò and Ninetto are moved and touched by the birth of a child, the crow—ever the ideologue—delivers a pedantic lecture on the need for birth control. The very insistence of the crow's ideological speeches, his seeming indifference to the realities of human emotion, reveals Pasolini's skepticism regarding the crow's brand of "rational," outdated Marxism. Like many ideologues, perhaps, the crow is both excessively linked to theory and removed from the very people, in this case Totò and Ninetto, he wants to help. His incessant teaching suffocates his companions, who kill and eat him as a lesson "not to meddle in the affairs of others." As for the audience, we may be shocked by the act of cannibalism, but, like Totò and Ninetto, we, too, are glad to be rid of the crow, to be free of his obsessive ideology that wants to explain everything and is woefully unable to do so.

If, on one level, Totò and Ninetto's brutal act puts an end to an annoying ideologue, on a more abstract plane, the crow's death symbolizes Pasolini's conviction—which had been growing steadily for over a decade—that the traditional Marxism of the postwar era had outlived itself. The crow's death echoes, in an ironic vein, the 1964 death of Palmiro Togliatti, co-founder and leader of the Italian Communist party. Within *Uccellacci e Uccellini*, the death of this important leader is evoked elegiacally through documentary clips of crowds weeping at Togliatti's bier as we hear the songs of Resistance partisans. In what might serve as a description of his own films, Pasolini referred to Togliatti's funeral as "politics

---

[70] Ibid., p. 58.

and death, united in a solemn, grave, infinite violence." Although Pasolini had never agreed with Togliatti's "authoritarian" policies,[71] he recognized that Togliatti had led the embattled party at a time when it was still inspired by the great social ideals of its members, many of whom had spent time in Fascist prisons and had fought as partisans. And he viewed Togliatti's death as the symbol of a tremendous change: "A historical epoch, the epoch of the Resistance, of great hopes for Communism, of the class struggle, has finished. What we have now is the economic boom, the welfare state, and industrialization."[72]

Despite his conviction that traditional Marxism had outlived itself, Pasolini continued to hope—as he repeatedly indicated in the pages of his *Vie nuove* column—that it might remain a vital force if it were willing to confront new realities, particularly the problem of the Third World. In *Uccellacci e Uccellini*, he hints at the fragile and tentative nature of this hope through the manner of the crow's death: by eating the bird, it is possible that Totò and Ninetto may absorb some of his teachings. Likening their act of cannibalism to a kind of Communion, Pasolini remarked that Totò and Ninetto "swallow the body of Togliatti (or of the Marxists) and assimilate it; after they have assimilated it they carry on along the road, so that even though you don't know where the road is going, it is obvious they have assimilated Marxism."[73] (A few comments made by Ninetto after he sees a road sign pointing to Cuba, that is, to the Third World, suggest that his view of the world has indeed been affected by the crow.) Discussing the ideological implications of *Uccellacci e Uccellini*, Pasolini observed:

> I never exposed myself as I did in this film. I never chose for the theme of a film one so explicitly difficult: the crisis of [the] Marxism of the Resistance and the 1950's . . . suffered and viewed from the inside by a Marxist who is not however ready to believe that Marxism is over. . . . Naturally it is not over insofar as it is able to accept many new realities hinted at in the film (the scandal of the Third World, the Chinese, and, above all, the immensity of human history and the end of the world, with the religiosity which this implies—and which constitutes the *other* theme of the film).[74]

What Pasolini calls the film's "other theme"—that is, its religiosity— emerges, of course, from the analogies between the Christian tale of the

[71] Observing that while he did not mean to accuse Togliatti of participating in Stalinist crimes, Pasolini did feel that in Italy Stalinism took the "form of Togliatti's policies, which were tacticist, diplomatic, authoritarian and paternalistic. The PCI [Italian Communist party] leadership always had a paternalistic attitude towards the rank and file, never going to the bottom of problems. . . . I have always been against Togliatti's policy." Cited by Stack, *Pasolini*, p. 23.

[72] Ibid., pp. 103–104.

[73] Ibid., p. 106.

[74] Pasolini, "Lettera aperta," p. 58.

two medieval saints and the modern, Marxist parable. By juxtaposing the two tales, Pasolini once again raises the issue of the fundamental relationship—at the heart of *Il Vangelo*—between Christianity and Marxism. (Once again, he also stresses the idea of a revolutionary or iconoclastic Christianity—incarnated here in the gentle St. Francis and his message of love—rather than the Church as an institution.[75]) But whereas these two great systems of belief were united in the towering Christ of *Il Vangelo*, in *Uccellacci e Uccellini* they are not only severed from one another but explicitly colored by doubt and irony. The unacknowledged ambivalences that fueled, perhaps, the terrible harshness of Pasolini's Christ come to the fore in *Uccellacci e Uccellini*, where, as he told one interviewer, he put "forward problems: the Church confronted with social problems, social problems confronted by mystery."[76] Pasolini leaves no doubt that neither the Marxist crow nor the saints can solve all of life's "problems": the crow's social dedication may be praiseworthy, but his obsession with reason and his refusal to confront life's "mysteries" are the object of satire. And while the saints' goodness is undeniable, their mission—to change the rapacious nature of the hawks—is obviously an impossible one.

If both the saints and the crow are at once comic and admirable figures, the film is nonetheless weighted in favor of the saints. Indeed, if one compares the two episodes, it becomes evident that a kind of historical degeneration has occurred. However naive, the Franciscans' goal revealed, as Pasolini noted, both the "goodness of a certain policy of the Church" and the "anti-bourgeois significance of every form of sacredness."[77] The aimless journey of the modern Totò and Ninetto is, instead, to use a phrase Pasolini borrowed from the French critic Lucien Goldmann, no more than a "degrading quest for authentic values in a degraded world." Sacredness, surely, has no place in this "degraded" world where even innocents like Totò and Ninetto have been tainted by opportunism and cynicism. Accepting the system as it stands, they are links in a chain of oppressed and oppressor: demanding payment from a starving woman who owes them money, in turn they cower before an affluent man to whom they are indebted. Wholly unaware of their greed and cruelty, they offer living proof of the ravages wrought by a corrupt and corrupting system.

[75] As Ugo Casiraghi writes: "[Pasolini's] target is both Stalinism as well as Catholic orthodoxy [*integralismo*]; he takes a stand for dialogue, for the free discussion of ideas, for the incessant play of thought. . . . Never did Pier Paolo Pasolini's Marxist Christianity or Christian Marxism find a clearer application in film than in *Uccellacci e Uccellini*." Casiraghi, "A proposito di *Uccellacci e Uccellini*," in *Da Accattone a Salò*, p. 55. Originally in *Civiltà dell'imagine*, July 1966.

[76] Cited by John Bragin in "Pasolini: A Conversation in Rome," *Film Culture* No. 42 (Fall 1966), p. 105.

[77] Pasolini, *Uccellacci e Uccellini*, p. 53.

The disabused portrait of Totò and Ninetto that emerges from the film points to still another dimension of the political crisis that assailed Pasolini at this time: his conviction that the humble people were destroyed, turned into "horrible petit-bourgeois," by the merciless growth of the media and consumer capitalism. It is true that Pasolini's attitude toward the people had always been deeply ambivalent: as suggested earlier, even in *Il Vangelo*, where he probably came closest to a national-popular cinema, he portrayed the masses as mute and lifeless. Still, the sub-proletariat (whether ancient or modern) *was* at the center of his earlier films. This changed after the mid-1960s—that is, after Pasolini became convinced that he could no longer continue to make films about a world, a people, that no longer existed. The disappearance of the people hinted at in *Uccellacci e Uccellini* signaled, then, nothing less than the end of the national-popular culture that had so profoundly influenced him and others of his generation after the war. Looking back at those years, in 1969 he told an interviewer that after *Uccellacci e Uccellini*

> I distanced myself from my Gramscian phase because objectively I no longer had the same world that Gramsci did in front of me. If there were no longer any people, for whom should national-popular stories be told? From now on the people and the bourgeoisie are fused into one and the same notion of the masses. Actually, I'm no longer working under the sign of Gramsci: my films are no longer epic-lyric, national-popular; they have become something else.[78]

Within *Uccellacci e Uccellini*, Pasolini expresses the end of his "Gramscian phase" through his explicit farewell to neorealism—the movement that, in the heady days of the postwar period, was often taken as the embodiment of national-popular culture. Playing a role that is at once stylistic, thematic, and even, to use Pasolini's word, "ideological,"[79] in *Uccellacci e Uccellini* neorealism—like paintings in *Accattone* and *Mamma Roma*—becomes a kind of cultural touchstone, a point of reference. Calling *Uccellacci e Uccellini* a "cinema born of another cinema" for this very reason, Pasolini went so far as to observe that his film

> is the product of a cinematographic rather than a figurative culture, unlike *Accattone*. It is about the end of neorealism as a kind of limbo, and it evokes the ghost of neorealism, particularly the beginning about two characters living out their life without thinking about it—i.e., two typical heroes of neorealism, humble, humdrum and unaware. All the first part is an evocation of neorealism, though naturally an idealized neorealism.[80]

---

[78] Pasolini, "Interview with Gian Piero Brunetta," *Cahiers du cinéma* No. 212 (May 1969), p. 15.
[79] "Entretien avec Pasolini," *Image et Son* No. 238 (April 1970), p. 76.
[80] Cited by Stack, *Pasolini*, p. 99.

What Pasolini calls the "ghost" of neorealism extends, in truth, way beyond the "humble, humdrum humble and unaware" characters of *Uccellacci e Uccellini*. Permeated by nostalgic allusions, indeed "hommages," to particular films and filmmakers, *Uccellacci e Uccellini* evokes neorealism in a variety of ways. Virtually the entire episode of the medieval saints, for example, harks back to Rossellini's film on St. Francis (*Francesco, Guillare di Deo*, 1950)—a film Pasolini loved and which he saw as the "extreme product" of neorealism. ("Rossellini," he wrote in 1959 after seeing *Il generale Della Rovere*, "is neorealism. . . . He was one of the first to see the poor face of the real Italy."[81]) As for the modern-day episode, scenes featuring a prostitute and some strolling players echo early Fellini films (that is, *Lo sceicco bianco, Le notti di Cabiria, La strada*) where the resonances of neorealism were still unmistakable. Even more explicitly, the crow himself announces at one point that "the age of Brecht and Rossellini is over."[82] Of course, given the film's elegiac mood and ironic tone, we hardly need the crow—whose *own* days are numbered—to tell us that the references to neorealism evoke shadows from a vanished past, shadows imbued with all the longing Pasolini felt for a bygone era. "If you will," Pasolini wistfully confessed to one interviewer,

> a kind of ambiguous homage to Rossellini [exists] in this film where contradictory feelings are at work: admiration for the Rossellini of *Francesco, Giullare di Dio* and irony toward this vision of an outdated world. The same might be said for the allusions to Fellini . . . whom I place with Rossellini insofar as both shared a similar vision during a whole neorealist epoch. That epoch is over and with it their vision of the world. Italy, like the rest of Europe, more quickly than the rest, has left the time of postwar deprivation and misery. The indictment of daily life is no longer valid, at least in the form that one finds in *Paisà* or *La strada*.[83]

Coda: Totò and Ninetto

Although *Uccellacci e Uccellini* was, in Pasolini's words, his final "national-popular work of Gramscian origins," it was not, happily, his last film with Totò and Ninetto. Fascinated by this "magical couple," even while engaged in far more ambitious projects, Pasolini found time to make two wonderful, totally unreal shorts with them: *La terra vista dalla luna* (*The Earth Seen from the Moon*, 1967) and *Che cosa sono le nuvole?*

[81] Pasolini, "Lo 'sguardo' di R.R.," *Filmcritica* No. 274–275 (April–May 1977), p. 131.

[82] Asked to comment on the crow's remark, Pasolini said: "I meant that the age of social denunciation and great ideological drama of the Brecht kind on the one hand and the day-to-day denunciation of the neorealist kind on the other are both finished." Cited by Stack, *Pasolini*, p. 109.

[83] Cited by Duflot, *Entretiens*, p. 40.

(*What Are Clouds Like?* 1968).[84] Discussing the genesis of the first of these works, Pasolini remarked:

> When I finished *Uccellacci e Uccellini* I realized that the ideology played a much greater part in it than I had expected: the ideology was not all absorbed by the story, it had not become transformed into poetry, lightness and grace. ... I really felt quite sorry about it because Totò and Ninetto were such a lovely couple, and so poetic *per se*; I felt they were full of possibilities. So I thought of making a film which would be all fables, and one of these was *La terra vista dalla luna*.[85]

Deliberately nonideological "fables," both *La terra vista dalla luna* and *Che cosa sono le nuvole?* present Totò and Ninetto, reduced to their most essential traits, living in what Pasolini called a "world of meta-historical surrealism." It is a lunar world of fantasy and popular tales—a world where, in the words of one critic, "every 'logical' infrastructure has been dissolved."[86] Once he had the idea for *La terra vista dalla luna*, in fact, Pasolini "wrote" the film through a series of sketches as if it were a kind of Italian comic book or *fumetto*: "Lacking a language or style to express in writing, verbally, this type of comedy [*comicità*], I was forced to write the screenplay ... by drawing Totò and Ninetto in various situations precisely as in *fumetti*."[87]

Like most of his nonfeature works, these shorts show Pasolini at his most innovative and experimental. Hence not only did the manner of its "writing" distinguish *La terra vista dalla luna* from preceding films but—with the exception of the brief film-within-a-film of *La ricotta*—it also marked his transition from black-and-white to color. (He felt, in fact, that it was largely the experience of making this short—where the comic-book format demanded a great precision about color—that helped him take this important step.) To underscore the cartoon-like nature of his tale, Pasolini used the bright and unreal hues of children's drawings: Ninetto's orangy-red hair, for example, is seen as a splash of contrast against walls painted improbable shades of pink, blue, and yellow. In its primary brightness, *La terra vista dalla luna* announces the stylized colors and varying palettes that, beginning with *Edipo Re* (1967), would become a defining characteristic of his feature films. In Pasolini's view, as he ob-

---

[84] Both shorts appeared in films composed of episodes by different directors: *La terra vista dalla luna* in *Le streghe* (other episodes were by Visconti, Mauro Bolognini, Franco Rossi, and Vittorio De Sica); *Che cosa sono le nuvole?* in *Capriccio all'italiana* (with other episodes by Steno, Mario Monicelli, Bolognini, and Pico Zac). Speaking of *Le streghe*, Pasolini remarked that his episode was "unassimilable" in a film where the other episodes were "anachronistic products of neorealism." He himself, he went on, considered it one of his best films, although it disconcerted audiences and critics alike. See Stack, *Pasolini*, p. 112.

[85] Ibid., pp. 112–113.

[86] Nuccio Lodata, "*Le streghe*," *Filmcritica*, April 1967, p. 184.

[87] Pasolini, *Il cinema in forma di poesia*, p. 54.

served in the course of a discussion concerning *La terra vista dalla luna*, color was less an integral part of film language (what he called a "semiological" or "grammatical" element) than an "aesthetic substance," like music, that is added to the film. Characteristically ironic toward the "formalist" preoccupations implicit in such a remark, he went on to say that, fortunately, the childlike, surreal nature of his fable somehow "legitimized" his taste for "chromatic aestheticism."[88]

In the brillantly colored world of *La terra vista dalla luna*, Totò and Ninetto once again appear as father and son. The opening scene finds them in a cemetery crying at the grave of their much beloved wife and mother. (In a cemetery filled with childlike statues, she is represented as a benevolent cook.) Eager to find another like her, they approach—in rapid succession and without success—a widow, a prostitute, and, finally, a mannequin. At last they meet a deaf mute named Assurda, who is played by the beautiful Italian star Silvana Mangano. With eloquent balletic gestures obviously inspired by Chaplin, Totò woos, and wins, the fair maiden. (Totò's implicit homage to the great comedian becomes explicit when Assurda comes upon a photograph of Chaplin while cleaning house.[89]) Totò and Assurda marry and are very happy in their colorful shanty dwelling until the day that Totò conceives of an evil plan. He has Assurda climb to the top of the Colosseum: from there she must threaten to jump to her death, pleading poverty, in the hope of eliciting money for a new house from sympathetic bystanders. Assurda plays her role to perfection until, suddenly, she slips on a banana peel and falls to the pavement. Bereaved and disconsolate once again, Totò and Ninetto sadly return home only to find—lo and behold!—Assurda. Although she is dead, she assures them, she can continue to care for them: after all, as the final titles tell us, "Being alive or dead is the same thing."

Che cosa sono le nuvole? presents an even stranger fable, one that Totò himself, within the film, calls a "dream within a dream." As the film opens, the credits are displayed on a poster for a puppet theater, where two life-size marionettes, played by none other than Totò and Ninetto, have just been created. Designed to star in a melodramatic version of *Othello*, Ninetto (colored brown) is to play the doomed moor while Totò (with a green face slashed by a bright-red tongue) will be the evil Iago. The play gets under way but, alas, before the puppets reach the end, they are set upon and destroyed by their audience, which has become incensed

---

[88] *Con Pier Paolo Pasolini*, p. 77.

[89] In the eyes of one critic, Chaplin's role in *La terra vista dalla luna* is as important as that of Pontormo and Rosso Fiorentino in *La Ricotta*. For him, Toto's gestural wooing of Assurda has "an illustrious precedent exactly in the idyll between Chaplin and the blind flower-seller of *City Lights*." See Paquito del Bosco, "*La terra vista dalla luna*," *Cinema e film* Vol. 1, No. 2 (Spring 1967), p. 242.

by Iago's perfidy. The poor marionettes are carried away and dumped ignominiously on a rubbish heap by a singing garbage man. As Ninetto rolls down heaps of refuse, he has his first glimpse of the sky, where feathery clouds race across a luminous blue expanse. Rendered grotesquely ecstatic by this beautiful sight, just before dying he exclaims: "Oh, the torturing and marvelous beauty of creation."

The sad end that greets the marionettes suggests that, even in his most lighthearted works, Pasolini could not escape the tragic view of the world so deeply rooted within him. Acknowledging that Italians did not, in truth, laugh much at his fables, he observed that the "underlying ideology" of his shorts was, indeed, "a picaresque one which, like everything of pure vitality, masks a deeper ideology which is that of death."[90] Just as the puppeteer of *Che cosa sono le nuvole?* turned *Othello* into a Punch and Judy melodrama, Pasolini's surreal fables replayed, in a grotesque and farcical key, the tragic dramas of Ettore and Accattone. Moreoever, the role accorded fateful performances in these shorts—a staged suicide attempt that becomes only too real, marionettes torn to death by an enraged public—foreshadowed the theatrical and ritualistic cast of Pasolini's mythic quartet of the late 1960s. Like the puppets of *Che cosa sono le nuvole?*—puppets who must act out their assigned roles before they can encounter what Lino Miccichè calls the "rapid and dazzling moment of death"[91]—the tragic heroes of the quartet will be compelled to follow a prescribed and fateful trajectory. And this trajectory will be propelled by the same dark forces of the unconscious that are at work even in the puppets: when, for example, a bewildered Ninetto turns to the puppeteer to ask why he must murder Desdemona, he is told: "Perhaps you want to kill her . . . perhaps she wants to be killed."

Before turning, however, to the violent and savage universe of the mythic quartet, I would like to examine several important essays on film Pasolini wrote in the mid- and late 1960s. Although existential and political concerns are never far below the surface in these essays, their principal concern is what Pasolini might have called a "formalist" one: that is, the very nature of cinematic language. But even as these essays raise issues of general theoretical concern, it is also clear that many of the ideas they contain both spring from, and lead back to, Pasolini's own filmic practice. He may have been, for a while, a director turned theoretician, but in his case neither the theoretician nor the director ever forgot the other's presence.

[90] Pasolini, *Il cinema di poesia*, p. 64.
[91] Miccichè, *Il cinema italiano degli anni '60*, p. 170.

IV

Theory: Toward a Poetics of Cinema

It has been said that I have three idols: Christ, Marx
and Freud. That's only a formula. In truth, my only
idol is reality. If I've chosen to be a filmmaker as well
as a writer, it is because, instead of expressing this
reality by those symbols which are words, I preferred
to express it through cinema: to express reality
through reality.
—Pier Paolo Pasolini (1969)

INFUSED WITH A SENSE of cultural and ideological crisis, Pasolini's theoretical discussions of cinema are—like his literary essays of the 1950s—
stamped by a very personal blend of linguistics, politics, and existential
concerns. Whereas, however, his reflections on literature were of particular interest to Italians, the scope and audience of Pasolini's film essays
were decidedly international. Pasolini was one of the many theorists—
from Great Britain and the United States as well as the Continent—who,
in the course of the late 1960s, sought to define the nature of film language. Whether or not Pasolini can be credited, as one critic suggests,
with having "inaugurated the use of semiological investigation" in Italy,[1]
he was certainly one of the most active, and probably the most controversial, participant in the theoretical debates of those years. His first major essay on film, "Il cinema di poesia," was, in fact, delivered at the 1965
Pesaro Film Festival during the round-table discussions that first sparked
international interest in film semiology. Significantly, other participants
at this important conference included some of the most influential theorists of the 1960s: Umberto Eco, Galvano Della Volpe, and Christian
Metz.

But if Pasolini had much in common with other theorists, in at least
two critical respects he also stood apart from them. As the only working
director in their ranks, his essays often had a special resonance, a particular relationship to praxis—not only to his own films but also to those of
others. Secondly, the impassioned, intensely personal cast of his essays—
where linguistic reflections slide into meditations on poetry and prose,
history and neurosis, or life and death—distinguished them sharply from

---

[1] Tommaso Anzoino, *Pasolini* (Florence: La Nuova Italia, 1974), p. 94.

the detachment, the rigorously maintained neutrality, of a Christian Metz or an Emilio Garroni. In the climate of the 1960s—which placed an almost religious (and, in retrospect, naive) faith in the "science of meaning"—the iconoclastic cast of Pasolini's essays exposed him to patronizing remarks, to charges of being "unscientific" or (worse still!) of approaching these issues as a "poet." Only as the years went by did it become clear that the continuing interest of these essays lay, precisely, in Pasolini's poetic intuitions, his adamant insistence on the subjective, his refusal to separate linguistics from the broader domain of human life and thought.

Since these various issues run throughout Pasolini's essays, it seems best to approach his theoretical writings from a thematic, rather than strictly chronological, viewpoint. For this reason, I shall examine them from a perspective that concentrates on three major areas of concern: (1) cultural and political analyses of film and filmmakers of the 1960s; (2) film semiology; (3) and—what I think is most important—Pasolini's concept of the "cinema of poetry" and its relation to his own films.

On the whole, Pasolini's reflections on film are less explicitly political than his literary meditations of the preceding decade. But one important essay, with the disarming title of "Confessioni tecniche" ("Technical Confessions"), does return to an ideological question that had preoccupied Pasolini throughout the 1950s: how, or in what way(s), can intellectuals and artists play a social role? But if, simply by asking this question, "Confessioni tecniche" forms a kind of bridge between Pasolini's writings of the 1950s and those of the 1960s, the pessimistic answer it offers reveals how deeply the political crisis he experienced in the mid-1960s—and expressed in *Uccellacci e Uccellini*—had affected him. For, like that watershed film, "Confessioni tecniche" leaves no doubt that Pasolini has, in truth, lost almost all faith in the concept of the intellectual's "mandate"—a concept fundamental to the political and cultural hopes of the preceding decade. As "Confessioni tecniche" progresses, it becomes clear that, far from changing society, writers and filmmakers can do little more—and even this is problematical—than offer passive resistance to the irresistible tide of technological neocapitalism.

Before he arrives at this somber conclusion, Pasolini confronts what has long been a vital issue in Marxist aesthetics from Engels down to Lukács and Brecht: that is, the relationship between capitalism and realism. Concerned, as always, with the links between culture and ideology, Pasolini's interest in this particular issue also reflected his long meditation on realism—or, more precisely, his aversion to it. Imbued with a "horror of naturalism," he had, after all, always insisted on the gulf between him and the neorealists. In "Confessioni tecniche," which was written in

1966, Pasolini's lifelong antipathy to realism takes on a political and even prophetic cast: two years later, after the tumultuous events of 1968, the political indictment of realism found in this essay would be echoed by a number of militant critics and directors. For example, Jean-Luc Godard, undoubtedly the best-known figure among the militants, would denounce realistic films (especially those of the American variety) as allies of capitalism insofar as they created an illusion of reality that served to mask the real facts of existence—ideological and social—from the viewer. (And, of course, the fact that cinematic realism was associated with Hollywood, and hence with the ugly face of American imperialism in Vietnam, only confirmed this theoretical opposition to it.)

Unlike Godard or a number of militant French critics, however, Pasolini went beyond the somewhat simplistic equation between capitalism and realism. In "Confessioni tecniche" his argument is at once less polemical and more complex than many of the discussions—or, more precisely, denunciations—of realism written after 1968. For one thing, Pasolini does not view capitalism as a monolithic, unchanging entity: rather, he draws an important distinction between nineteenth-century "paternalistic" capitalism and modern-day "neocapitalism." Basing his argument loosely on certain ideas associated with the French Marxist critic Lucien Goldmann—who maintained that artistic structures parallel mental structures in a given social group—Pasolini proceeds to observe that the traditional nineteenth-century novel reflects the bourgeois mentality of paternalistic capitalism. So far, of course, he is in agreement with most Marxist critics. But now he goes one step further and makes an observation—one that would be (deliberately?) ignored by post-'68 critics—with important ramifications for the avant-garde art of his own era. Arguing that modern capitalism has created new forms of expression, he draws a parallel between the "new novel"—such as that of Robbe-Grillet—and contemporary neocapitalism. For Pasolini, the absence of plot and characters in these novels, their seemingly objective descriptions that frequently have no discernible significance or function, reflect a world from which human elements, coherence, and meaning have been banished.

To a degree, of course, Pasolini's observations were in line with those of Lukács, who felt that modernism itself—a modernism embodied, for example, in Beckett's plotless, semi-characterless novels—reflects the alienation produced by modern capitalism. Needless to say, unlike Lukács, Pasolini did not judge Beckett or the "new" novelists, nor did he come to the same conclusions as the Hungarian philosopher, who seemingly advocated a return to the past, to the tradition of Mann rather than that of Kafka and Beckett. Eager, instead, to avoid both the traditional realism of paternalistic capitalism—and mimetic cinema would fall into this realm—as well as the alienated world of modern capitalism, in a much quoted passage Pasolini declared:

In the event that the author, insofar as he is a bourgeois, cannot represent, in a first phase, other than novelistic characters who imitate similar real men in the free-enterprise capitalistic society or, in a second phase, can only represent the disappearance of characters similar to the disappearance of individuals in monopolistic capitalistic societies, then, the sole liberating operation is not to imitate closely such situations . . . but to make such situations into the very object of the narrative. . . . I must say that ideological irony—which takes as its subject the very problem of the novel or film—seems extremely fertile to me.[2]

This passage was written in relation to *Uccellacci e Uccellini*. But the questions Pasolini raises here, of course, far transcend any single novel or film. He is virtually asserting that the only way an author can avoid being conditioned by capitalistic society—that is, can create "non-bourgeois" films or novels—is to take as the subject of a work the problem of its own creation. The following year, in one of his most famous essays, "Il cinema di poesia," he would valorize this self-reflexivity still further. That essay concludes, in fact, with the observation (which seems less a logical inference than an ardently held wish) that the meta-cinematic "cinema of poetry" may well be part of a "possible revolution" in bourgeois culture— an "internal" revolution effected by a "neocapitalism that questions and modifies its own structure and, in this case, restores to poets a late humanistic function: the myth and the technical awareness of form."[3] So, the argument goes, if poets cannot intervene directly in cultural and political life, let them make us aware of form since this awareness will allow us better to know (and perhaps change) the structure of capitalism itself.

Clearly, if Pasolini's defense of a meta-cinematic, essentially formalist, art reflected his belief that it was the only form of resistance still open to committed writers and directors, it was also deeply rooted in his lifelong attraction to a symbolist poetics, which is the very incarnation of literary hermeticism and self-reflexivity. Before his political crisis of the mid-1960s, however, Pasolini had fought against this tendency, had sought to balance it with ideology. Now, on the contrary, he not only embraced a difficult, self-reflective art but, as the above remarks reveal, found an ideological justification for it—a justification that clearly raised difficult questions. To begin with, how can a movement that is essentially bourgeois, irrational, and elitist (albeit self-reflexive) encourage us to modify the basic structures of capitalism? Further, do the self-reflexive novels of Proust, or the meta-cinema of Godard, escape historical determinants any more than Balzac or Griffith, whose mimetic works have not—at least not thus far—encouraged critics to place them in the modernist camp? Or,

[2] Pasolini, *Uccellacci e Uccellini* (Milan: Garzanti, 1966), p. 54.

[3] Pasolini, *Empirismo eretico* (Milan: Garzanti, 1972), p. 191. This important volume has recently been translated into English: *Heretical Empiricism*, trans. Ben Lawton and Louise K. Barnett (Bloomington: Indiana University Press, 1988).

for that matter, is the nonnaturalistic, symbolic *Uccellacci e Uccellini*—which appears to demonstrate the "disappearance of the individual in monopolistic capitalistic society"—less historically determined than *Accattone* or *Mamma Roma*? These questions concerning the social implications of modernist self-awareness seem to belie Pasolini's ideological justification of self-referential art even as they raise the specter of arguments that, in the past, Marxists often applied to Mallarmé and the French symbolists: that is, when writers feel totally alienated from a society that no longer responds to the values they represent or embody, all they find left to write about is the process of creation itself. And, as this argument suggests, an involuted, hermetic art that foregrounds the process of creation—an art, in Pasolini's words, that "takes as its subject the very problem of the novel or film"—is no less historically determined than any traditional, or realistic, work.

No one was more aware of these problems than Pasolini himself. Discussing the ideological implications of hermetic or symbolist poetry in his *Officina* essays, he had observed that an art turned inward upon itself, "filled only with its own aesthetic consciousness," is incapable of dealing with the outer world. And, in 1971, Pasolini returned to this earlier view even as he questioned the importance he had ascribed only a few years earlier to meta-cinema or meta-literature. In an interview entitled "Ancora il linguaggio della realtà" ("Once Again the Language of Reality"), he made it clear that he did not disagree with more traditional Marxist critics who viewed the late nineteenth-century preoccupation with poetic style and language as a bourgeois phenomenon.

> The meta-linguistic consciousness that somehow, for the first time, made language sacred was a classist phenomenon of entropy: it was a phenomenon lived completely within the bourgeoisie. . . . For the working class and for Marxist ideology, language remained a simple function . . . a means of communication.[4]

The *Officina* essays, as well as the change of heart Pasolini experienced in the 1970s, leave no doubt that he knew he was on very slippery ground in asserting that a meta-cinema, or one devoid of traditional characters, might have an ideological impact. His argument must have sprung less from ideological conviction than from deep personal tensions exacerbated, no doubt, by political disillusionment. Always torn between ideology and passion, between a (Gramscian) populism and a (symbolist) hermeticism, his embrace of "artistic experiments"—which were deemed "gratuitous" a decade earlier—represented one swing of an inner pendulum. It was, however, an important swing—from 1966, the year of *Uccellacci e Uccellini* and "Confessioni tecniche," to the beginning of the 1970s—which would lead him to an increasingly difficult and self-reflec-

---

[4] *Con Pier Paolo Pasolini*, ed. Enrico Magrelli (Rome: Bulzoni, 1977), p. 96.

tive cinema, and to theoretical essays (later collected in the 1972 volume *Empirismo eretico*) devoted, precisely, to the "myth and technical awareness of [cinematic] form."

> Les temps étaiant à la semiologie, à la marxologie,
> aux vilains mots plombés, langues de bois, lexiques
> de fer.
>   —Jean-André Fieschi (1985)
>
> (It was the time of semiology, of Marxology, of mean
> leaden words, wooden languages, iron lexicons.)

The "technical awareness of form" that runs throughout Pasolini's essays of the late 1960s bears not only upon cinematic style—in the way, for example, that his essays of the 1950s involved literary style—but also upon the very nature of film language. In this respect, his concerns dovetailed with those of other theorists like Christian Metz and Umberto Eco. But if Pasolini's essays reflected the general climate of that era, they also continued a personal meditation on the filmic sign that had, in fact, begun well before semiology came into vogue.

In earlier years, this meditation had often taken the form of a comparison between verbal and cinematic language. On more than one occasion, for example, he had expressed the conviction—at the heart, he said, of his attraction to film—that cinema is closer to reality than literature. As early as one of his *Officina* essays, he remarked that neorealism lends itself particularly well to cinematic expression since film "places the senses in front of the material object represented . . . [in an] unmediated way."[5] A few years later, in a 1961 essay published along with the script of *Accattone*, he alludes once again to the immediacy of cinema even as he notes its affinity to one particular mode of written expression: poetry. Discussing the presence of poetic devices such as anaphora and repetition in cinema, Pasolini differentiates film from literature, observing: "The fact that cinema can resemble a narrative, but a narrative which is above all musical, might demonstrate that cinema possesses a certain irrational quality—archaic and fantastic—when compared to literature."[6] After hinting at cinema's "musical" and "irrational" nature, as well as its "archaic" substratum—themes he would develop at length in "Il cinema di poesia"—he proceeds to examine the exact nature of film language. Deeming the choice of images a kind of lexicon, and the camera movements and framings a syntax, he compares verbal to filmic language: "The important thing is to see if the relationship between the word as a

[5] Pasolini, *Passione e ideologia* (Milan: Garzanti, 1977), p. 338.
[6] Pasolini, *Accattone* (Rome: FM, 1961), p. 18.

'sign' and the signified is similar to the relationship between the image as a 'sign' and the signified."[7]

These meditations on the "grammar" and nature of film language, as well as the "fantastic" or "poetic" quality of cinema, adumbrate what were to become major directions in his theoretical essays of the late 1960s. The nature of the filmic sign would, in fact, become the locus of his most heretical or scandalous pronouncements. As the 1960s progressed, he became increasingly convinced not only that such signs are inherently different from verbal ones—that is, from words—but that they do indeed coincide with reality itself. And the more this theme seemed to outrage other theorists, the more stridently he returned to it—in essays, as well as in interviews and even poetry. The Christ of *La ricotta*, he insisted in the poem "Bestemmia," is nothing other than "reality reproduced with reality."[8]

"Il cinema di poesia," written in 1965, hints at this issue, but in a tentative, embryonic way: Pasolini postulates infinite and noncodifiable "natural communicative archetypes" at the base of cinematic language. At this point, as Roberto Turigliatto points out in a fine essay,[9] Pasolini was not that far removed from the French semiotician Christian Metz, who deemed cinema a language system (or "langue") rather than a language ("langage") because it differs from verbal or written language in at least two crucial respects: (1) unlike written language, cinematic language cannot be codified in, say, a grammar or dictionary; (2) the link between the object and its filmic representation or sign is not an arbitrary one as in written language (where the word "house" and the object it designates bear no resemblance to each other). But from here on the paths taken by Metz and Pasolini diverged. The following year Pasolini noted a "profound disagreement" between himself and Metz: one should not, he argued, speak of film as an "impression of reality" as did Metz, but of "reality pure and simple." Instead of compelling cinema to fit the linguistic model of verbal/written language, we must, said Pasolini, enlarge our very definition of language.

> Cinema is a language . . . which obliges us to broaden our notion of language. It is not a symbolic, arbitrary, and conventional system. It does not possess an artifical keyboard upon which you can play signs like Pavlov's bells: signs that evoke reality, just as the bell evokes nothing other than cheese to the little mouse and makes his mouth water.
>
> Cinema does not evoke reality as literary language does; it does not copy reality like painting; it does not mimic reality like theater. Cinema *reproduces*

---

[7] Ibid., p. 19.

[8] Pasolini, "Bestemmia," *Cinema e film* Vol. I, No. 2 (Spring 1967), p. 224.

[9] See Roberto Turigliatto, "La tecnica e il mito," in *Lo scandalo Pasolini*, ed. Fernaldo di Giammatteo, special issue of *Bianco e Nero* No. 23 (1976).

reality: image and sound! In reproducing reality, what does it do? Cinema expresses reality with reality.[10]

To a Saussurian tradition—which understood language as a system of meaning separate from reality, and viewed object and sign (or signified and signifier) as separate entities—this was heresy. And Pasolini went even further, bringing into play phenomenological, hermeneutical, and even metaphysical considerations. Defining cinema as the most basic language—that is, the language of human action (composed, in turn, of the language of behavior, physical presence, and written-spoken language)—in "La lingua scritta della realtà" ("The Written Language of Reality") he argued that when we act, we ourselves make cinema.

> In reality we ourselves make cinema by living it: that is, by existing practically; that is, by acting. *All of life, in the whole of its actions, is a natural, living, cinema: in this, it is linguistically the equivalent of oral language in its natural and biological dimension.*
>
> By living, therefore, we represent ourselves, and are present at the representation of others. The reality of the human world is nothing other than this double representation in which we are both actors and spectators: a gigantic happening, if you like.[11]

As the space where "we represent ourselves and are present at the representation of others," reality becomes a kind of "cinema *in natura*" that needs only a camera to be reproduced. Conversely, by reproducing reality, cinema becomes the "written" moment of this natural language of action. From this belief stemmed Pasolini's conviction that cinematic "writing" has the same "revolutionary importance" as writing: just as writing "revealed" oral language to men by making them conscious of language as representation, so, too, does cinema—as a "writing" of reality—make us aware of the "language of action," that is, of a social praxis hitherto taken as natural.

> As long as it was natural, the language of reality was outside consciousness: now that we see it "written" through cinema, we cannot remain unaware of it.

---

[10] Pasolini, *Empirismo eretico,* p. 139. The smallest units of cinematographic language are, maintained Pasolini, the "various real objects of reality constituting a shot." Insisting that cinema possesses the double articulation of written or spoken language, he likened these objects or "cinemi" to phonemes, while calling the shot a "moneme." Pasolini's postulation of a double articulation in cinematic language was objected to by other semioticians for a variety of reasons. See, for example, Umberto Eco's *La struttura assente* (Milan: Bompiani, 1968), pp. 154–155; Emilio Garroni's "Popolarità e communicazione nel cinema," in *Teorie e prassi del cinema in Italia, 1950–1970* (Milan: Mazzotta, 1972); Christian Metz's "Some Points in the Semiotics of Cinema," in *Film Language: A Semiotics of the Cinema,* trans. Michael Taylor (New York: Oxford University Press, 1974).

[11] Pasolini, *Empirismo eretico,* p. 210.

The written language of reality will make us know first of all what the language of reality is; and it will wind up modifying our way of thinking about it—transforming at least our physical relations with reality into cultural ones.[12]

As our "physical" relations become cultural ones—that is, as we become conscious of them through [cinematic] "writing" or "representation"—we will be better able to recognize the ways in which our lives are immersed in pragma.

From the great action poem of Lenin to the brief page of action prose of an employee of Fiat or of a ministry, life is clearly moving away from classical humanistic ideals and is becoming lost in pragma. *Film* (along with other audiovisual techniques) *seems to be the written language of this pragma.* But it may also be its salvation, precisely because *it expresses it*—and it expresses it from within: producing itself from it and reproducing it.[13]

In a pattern that would hold true for his political writings of the 1970s, in some essays Pasolini grew more strident ("the only language that can be called LANGUAGE is the language of natural reality"), while in others he tempered and qualified his controversial positions. The most important of these qualifications turned on a distinction between Cinema—seen as a kind of metaphysical, abstract, and absolute totality, a "primordial and archetypal notion"—and individual films. Drawing a comparison with verbal language, he remarked that just as we know "words" rather than language—or as we know "men" but not "humanity," or "poems" but not "poetry"—so, too, do we know films but not Cinema. Whereas Cinema, a kind of "continuous and infinite long-take," resembles the flow and continuity of reality, individual films are "texts" or "fictions" where the natural, unbroken aspect of space and time is altered and fragmented by human will and desire in the form of camera angles, stylistic conventions, and, above all, montage or editing. The important role Pasolini conferred upon montage in individual films led him, in fact, to what may have been his most personal and striking analogy. Evoking Sartre's belief that only at the moment of death can we judge the significance of a life, as well as Cocteau's epithet that cinema captures "death at work," he drew a kind of metaphysical contrast between, on the one hand, the infinite long take (or plenitude of the real) inherent in Cinema and, on the other, the limitations (culminating in death) imposed by montage in individual films.

It is therefore absolutely essential to die because, *as long as we are alive, we lack meaning* and the language of our life . . . remains untranslatable—a chaos

[12] Ibid., p. 239.
[13] Ibid., p. 211.

of possibilities, a quest for relations and meanings. . . . *Death achieves a dazzling montage of our life.* That is, it chooses the truly significant moments of this life (which can no longer be modified by other possible contrary or incoherent moments) and puts them end to end, turning our infinite, unstable, and uncertain present—[a present] which therefore cannot be described linguistically—into a clear, stable and certain past, and hence [a past] which can be perfectly described linguistically (precisely in the framework of a General Semiology). *Thanks to death alone our life serves to express us.*[14]

This remark epitomizes the existential and metaphysical impulses at work in Pasolini's essays—impulses which led him to reject, often violently and polemically, the dry positivism of many of his theoretical colleagues. His comparison between cinema and plenitude (or life itself) sprang from a deep wish to embrace and encompass reality; he wanted not only to penetrate to the heart of the real but to decipher it, interpret it, wrest its secrets from it as from a text. Refusing to separate cinema and life, he desired, above all, to overcome the impossible gap between the real and the "represented"—the gap that had haunted him since the age of fourteen when he sat down to draw a meadow. "Perhaps the real tragedy of every poet," he confessed to Jean Duflot, "is that he only reaches the world metaphorically, in accord with the rules of a magic which, in the last analysis, can appropriate the world in only a limited way."[15] It was a desire to transcend these tragic limits that inspired his passionate opposition to those who analyzed film as a system of signs, removed from "reality," that obeys its own codes. In a very personal and even Freudian vein, in 1969 he told interviewers from the Italian film journal *Cinema e film* that his view of cinema as the written language of reality stemmed from his "hallucinatory, childlike, and pragmatic love of reality. A religious love in that it somehow merged, by analogy, with an immense sexual fetishism."[16] But, of course, the very violence of this "hallucinatory" love, this "fetishism," rendered its inevitable failure even more dramatic: the more Pasolini fixed people and places with his camera as if seeking to identify or to become one with them, the less his filmic world—where everything was, as he said, "stopped and isolated in the flux of time"[17]— resembled our own.

Pasolini's impossible desire—to seize the world directly without the mediating screen always implicit in artistic creation—is clearly part of a long poetic tradition that may have reached its apogee in the symbolist

[14] Ibid., p. 245.
[15] Cited by Jean Duflot in *Entretiens avec Pier Paolo Pasolini* (Paris: Belfond, 1970), p. 17.
[16] Pasolini, *Empirismo eretico*, p. 233.
[17] Ibid., p. 234.

poets he so loved. In one famous poem, Rimbaud speaks of "seizing" the dawn, while the extraordinarily hermetic Mallarmé, who dreamed of turning the world into a "book," wanted the very sounds of words to evoke, to correspond with, meaning. (The symbolist quest could almost be seen as a hermetic echo of primitive man's refusal to separate words and things, a refusal that evoked lyrical praise from Pasolini, who described it thus: "Magical formula, prayer, and miraculous identification with the thing pointed to."[18]) Transposing into semiological terms the symbolist insistence on the "real" itself, Roland Barthes could well be discussing one of Pasolini's most fundamental attitudes:

> For the symbolist mentality, the symbol is much less a (codified) form of communication than an (affective) instrument of participation. The word *symbol* is now a bit dated; it is eagerly replaced by *sign* or *signification*. [Although] this terminological slippage translates a certain wearing away of the symbolist mentality—notably as far as the analogical nature of signifier and signified are concerned—this mentality still remains typical of any analysis which is not interested in the formal relationships among signs. . . . For the symbolist mentality is essentially a refusal of form; in the sign, it is the signified which interests it: the signifier is never more than what has been predetermined. [19]

In retrospect, it is clear that Pasolini's evident disinterest purely in what Barthes calls the "formal relationships among signs" could hardly have been articulated at a worse time. In the mid-1960s, film critics and theorists—inspired first by structuralism and later by semiology—were intent on establishing rigorous codifying systems where, based on the model of linguistics, object and sign (or signified and signifier) would be seen as totally distinct entities. (Ironically, perhaps, Pasolini's position *was* echoed by one of the great linguists of this century; reiterating a remark first made in 1933, in a 1967 interview Roman Jakobson observed: "For me, St. Augustine was the first theoretician of cinema. In his classification of signs, he asserts that one can imagine a system of signs where the object becomes the sign of the object itself: that's cinema!"[20]) Looking back on

---

[18] Ibid., p. 268.

[19] Roland Barthes, "L'imagination du signe," in his *Essais critiques* (Paris: Seuil [Points], 1964), p. 208.

[20] Roman Jakobson, "Entretien sur le cinéma avec Adriano Aprà and Luigi Faccini, in *Cinéma: Théorie, Lectures*, ed. Dominique Noguez, special issue of *La revue d'Esthéthique* (Paris: Klincksieck, 1973), p. 66.

Pasolini's insistence that the world can be deciphered like a text finds an interesting echo in a passage where Roland Barthes compares the structuralist pursuit of meaning with the Greek sense that meanings were inherent in the natural world. For Barthes, as for Pasolini, structuralism does not seem to exclude a "semiology of reality." "According to Hegel," Barthes writes, "the ancient Greeks were astonished by what was *natural* in nature; they constantly listened to it, interrogated the meaning of streams, mountains, forests, storms.

those years, two Italian theorists, Gianfranco Bettettini and Francesco Casetti, later remarked: "Between 1964 and 1970, all seriously undertaken semiological investigations concerning filmic communication always tried ... to repel and exorcise the specter of analogy which, however, always reappeared in the form of inevitable methodological choices."[21] It was obviously this "specter of analogy" that, a generation earlier, had inspired the writings of the great French theoretician André Bazin and that, in the 1960s, lay at the heart of Pasolini's desire to equate reality and film. Observing that cinematic theories tend historically to fall into two opposing camps on precisely this issue, Bettettini places Pasolini in the line of Kracauer and Bazin as he notes:

> Theories of cinema reveal an eloquent bipolarity in the way they understand the relationship between reality and its representation: on the one hand, cinema [is] understood as the representation of the world ... that represents itself in the image; on the other, cinema [is understood] as a linguistically autonomous place, whose language is not a mediation-reflection of that of objects, but a semantic exercise. Along with Bazin and Kracauer, Pasolini is associated with the "realistic" perspective since he once again proposes the models suggested by his two predecessors but within the perspective of a linguistic formulation.[22]

It was, perhaps, as much Pasolini's "linguistic formulation" that outraged and scandalized critics as the issue of analogy itself. (After all, as Bettettini and Casetti suggest, all the attempts made to exorcise the "specter of analogy" implied a degree of failure; and, as Luigi Faccini observes, Pasolini was not alone in his preoccupation with the analogical nature of cinema, with the "reality pre-existing cinema, reality seen in its objects,

---

Without knowing what all these objects said to them nominally, they perceived in the vegetal or cosmic order an immense *frisson* of meaning to which they gave the name of a God: Pan. Since then, nature has changed, she has become social: all that is given to man is *already* human, including the forest and the river that we cross when we travel. But in front of this social nature, which is quite simply culture, structural man is not different from the ancient Greeks. He, too, listens to the natural in culture and constantly perceives in it not so much stable, finite, and 'true' meanings as the *frisson* of an immense machine which is nothing other than humanity in the process of indefatigably pursuing the creation of meaning." See Barthes, "L'activité structuraliste," in *Essais critiques*, p. 218.

[21] Gianfranco Bettettini and Francesco Casetti, "La sémiologie des moyens de communication audio-visuels et le problème de l'analogie," in *Cinéma: Théorie, Lectures*, ed. Noguez, p. 88. In 1972, Metz, too, noted: "At the beginning of visual semiology, we established a marked opposition ... between analogy and codes. Semiology came from linguistics, where arbitrariness and codes, both at their height, were temporarily confused. Early semiology could not imagine that analogy itself could result from certain codes." See Metz, *Essais sur la signification au cinéma, II* (Paris: Klinksieck, 1972), p. 12.

[22] Gianfranco Bettettini, *Produzione del senso e messa in scena* (Milan: Bompiani, 1975), p. 182.

acts, functions."[23]) And there is little doubt that, although Pasolini's remarks corresponded to deep existential impulses, he also enjoyed manipulating semiological and linguistic terms to bait critics whose use of those very terms implied the Saussurian view of language as an autonomous system of signs. Not many opponents were as harsh as Aldo Rossi, who noted contemptuously that Pasolini liked to think of himself as a "professor of semiology."[24] Still, theoreticians who agreed on little else were united in their opposition to Pasolini's "semiology of reality." Christian Metz distinguished film from reality, saying that "reality does not tell stories"; accusing Pasolini of a "singular semiological ingenuousness," Umberto Eco wrote that the director's views contrast "with the most basic aim of semiology which is eventually to transform natural data into cultural phenomena."[25] For Emilio Garroni, Pasolini's "semiology of reality" was nothing short of a contradiction in terms: "You can doubtlessly describe reality but it is really this description, and not reality, which can be studied from a semiotic viewpoint. . . . Reality, insofar as it is the condition or material presupposition of every possible code, is not a code."[26]

Nor did theorists object to Pasolini's views merely on philosophical and linguistic grounds; charges made by Italian critics, in particular, hint at a sub-text infused with the political and moralistic accusations that had always dogged Pasolini. Emilio Garroni, for one, felt that by postulating a universal, natural cinematic language anchored in reality, Pasolini ignored the way language is conditioned by culture and ideology. For Garroni, this was nothing less than a resurrection of the "old neorealism, with all its implications, including significant traces of the 'populism' which has already detracted from Pasolini's literary position."[27] The faint

[23] Luigi Faccini, "Lettura come spazio critico," *Cinema e film*, September 1967, p. 411. As Faccini also points out, Metz himself constantly wrestled with the issue of analogy and the codes of reality. In 1969, for example, Metz acknowledged that "the semiology of the image cannot take place outside of a general semiology." See Metz, "Au-delà de l'analogie, l'image," in his *Essais sur la signification au cinéma, II*, p. 154.

[24] Aldo Rossi,"Le nuove frontiere della semiologia: Cinema e narratività," *Paragone* No. 212 (October 1967), p. 108. In this same article Rossi also gleefully reports that when Pasolini presented his concept of the "semiology of reality" at Pesaro as if it were a new discovery, Greimas and Metz circulated a list detailing the many examinations of visual and gestural codes that had been undertaken in the past.

[25] Metz, *Film Language*, p. 23; Eco, *La struttura assente*, p. 152. Eco went on to say (p. 154) that film is not the "miraculous surrender of reality but a language which speaks another pre-existing language, both interacting with their systems of conventions."

[26] Garroni, "Popolarità e communicazione nel cinema," pp. 125–126.

[27] Ibid., p. 138. Moralism aside, Garroni's charges against Pasolini were also, I think, a bit unjust. While Pasolini's evocation of "reality" did privilege physical presence, certainly his postulation of a language of "human action"—which includes the language of *behavior and oral-written language*—was impregnated with social and cultural factors. He made this quite clear in an essay entitled "I segni viventi e i poeti morti." Equating physical presence

echoes of Asor Rosa and other "orthodox" Marxists—always quick to criticize Pasolini's "decadent" populism and his "distance" from reality, that is, from history and ideology—heard in Garroni's remarks become loud and clear in an article by Antonio Costa. Accusing Pasolini of "semiological heresy" and "irrationality," Costa declares that the director's "concept of the poetry of cinema appears to be the latest incarnation of his regressive series of subversions of the institution of language." Pasolini's theories, an indignant Costa concludes, are of no value "for the development of a scientific semiology of the cinema, nor for film theory and/ or film criticism."[28]

True, such harshness and stridency were probably more the exception than the rule.[29] Furthermore, a number of critics did admit that Pasolini raised important questions even if they disagreed with him on most points. (Garroni was not the only one who agreed with Pasolini's rejection of Metz's notion of cinematic codes based on narrative or syntagmatic models.[30]) Still, only well after Pasolini's death did it gradually become apparent that he had, in fact, raised crucial issues. As the years passed, his own provocative stance receded into the distance while—even more significantly—the cultural climate changed. The binary oppositions, linguistic models, and abstract self-regulating systems of structuralism and semiology gave way to a world view that analyzed texts in the light of "psychic and social determinants," that explored how the "conscious or unconscious subject" produced signs, and that was concerned less with narrative systems than with multiplicities or layers of meaning.[31] In this

with "pure" language, he asks: "While a poplar speaks a pure language, do I, Pier Paolo Pasolini . . . speak a pure language? Obviously not. This pure language is contaminated above all by the first social contract, that is, by language, first in its spoken and then in its written form; and then by all the infinite nonsign languages which I experience as a result of my birth, my economic station, my education—by society and the historical moment in which I live." *Empirismo eretico*, p. 255.

[28] Antonio Costa, "Pasolini's Semiological Heresy," in *Pier Paolo Pasolini*, ed. Paul Willemen (London: British Film Institute, 1977), pp. 38, 41.

[29] Costa's moralism did, however, make it across the Channel. It is felt, for example, in the following remark by Stephen Heath: "Against the false hypostatisation of 'reality' in Pasolini should be set Godard's insistence that 'we are condemned to an analysis of the real.' The *realism* of cinema, as that of the novel, is to be understood not in terms of some immediate mirroring of some Reality (though its definition in these terms may be a major ideological strategy), but in relation to the representation of 'reality' a particular society proposes and assumes." See Heath, "Film/Cinetext/Text," *Screen* Vol. 14, No. 1–2 (Spring–Summer 1973), p. 110.

[30] In Garroni's eyes, narrative codes don't "account for the legibility of the filmic message, but only for its banality or originality: horizontal semiology is no more than a poor tautology which says only that a given object can be seized in its internal articulation if, in fact, it is articulated." See Garroni, "Popolarità e comunicazione nel cinema," p. 126.

[31] The terms in quotes have been taken from those suggested by Marc Blanchard to describe the transition (proposed by Julia Kristeva) from "semiology" to "semiotics." See the

new climate—which admitted not only individual subjects but even the sub-conscious, which insisted on the play of ambiguities in meaning— Pasolini's theories no longer appeared marginal or eccentric but, rather, strangely prophetic.

Commenting, in fact, upon Costa's dismissal of Pasolini for being un-scientific, Teresa de Lauretis, one of the first to reexamine Pasolini's essays in light of subsequent theoretical developments, was moved to remark: "The development of a *scientific* semiology of the cinema, which never was Pasolini's concern, is no longer a concern at all: it is a moot case."[32] Calling for an "unconventional, less literal or narrow reading of Pasolini's pronouncements," de Lauretis argues that many of the director's concerns—which clearly did not fit the parameters governing the "theoretical discourse of semiology"—raised issues that took on a new importance in the 1970s. Pasolini's emphasis on physicality and dreams, for example, "recast in psychoanalytic terms, were to become central to film theory's concern with visual pleasure, spectatorship, and the complex nexus of imaging and meaning that Metz was to locate in the 'imaginary signifier.' "[33] Similarly, Pasolini's insistence on the existential and the subjective—condemned at the time for being ahistorical or asocial— pointed the way toward

> the current notion of spectatorship as a site of productive relations, of the engagement of subjectivity in meaning, values and imaging, and therefore suggest[ed] that the subjective processes which cinema instigates are "culturally conscious," that cinema's binding of fantasy to images institutes, *for* the spectator, forms of subjectivity which are themselves, unequivocally, social.[34]

De Lauretis's essay appeared in a 1980 volume commemorating the fifth anniversary of Pasolini's death. A similar volume, published that same year in France, contains an article by Alain Bergala which, although concerned principally with Pasolini's films, also sheds light on changing attitudes toward his theories. Bergala begins by noting that Pasolini's films seemed out of place initially because they appeared at a moment when European directors—epitomized by those of the French New Wave—saw and defined film in relationship to cinema itself, especially to

---

introduction to Blanchard's *Description: Sign, Self, Desire—Critical Theory in the Wake of Semiotics* (New York, Paris, The Hague: Mouton, 1980).

[32] Teresa de Lauretis, "Re-reading Pasolini's Essays on Cinema," *Italian Quarterly* No. 82–83 (Fall–Winter 1980), p. 159.

[33] Ibid., p. 163.

[34] Ibid., p. 164. Elsewhere, de Lauretis points out that Pasolini's idea that cinema is both representation and performance, that it emerges from human practice but that it also reveals it, similarly suggests way(s) in which cinema interacts with subjective processes. See her *Alice Doesn't: Feminism, Semiotics, Cinema* (Bloomington: Indiana University Press, 1984), p. 193.

classical American genres. But as a new generation of filmmakers (Syberberg, Schroeter) emerged, other concerns—bearing, for example, on the nature of silence in film or the relationship between film and spectacle/theater/epic—came to the fore. Turning their back on "films born of other films," a number of directors, says Bergala, went in search of a more "archaic" cinema. And this search led them to confront the "question of representation [with] a primitive frontal violence"—a confrontation that brought them close to the path taken by Pasolini years earlier:

> A path that Pasolini, through his fetishism for what he called Reality (at a time when the filmmakers of modernity fetishized cinema), through his quest for sacredness (at a time when these same filmmakers were seeking a truth which came from cinema and only from cinema) was virtually alone in exploring during his fifteen years of activity as a filmmaker.[35]

If Pasolini's films were out of step with dominant European currents of the 1960s, so, too, were his theories—and for much the same reason(s). Like his films, his theories were concerned less with (to use Bergala's term) the "inscription of things" than with things themselves, less with representations than with the mythic layers underpinning our inner selves and our most seemingly rational impulses and constructions. This temperament found the notion of autonomous signifying systems as alien as it did "films born of other films." Only when film theory itself evolved, and began to look outward from the text to issues of reception, perception, and subjectivity, did Pasolini's theories and films both take on a new cast, a new significance.

Still, to date, the only writer to have addressed the profound issues implicit in Pasolini's theories is the post-structuralist French philosopher Gilles Deleuze. His two-volume work devoted to cinema—*L'image-mouvement* (1983) and *L'image-temps* (1985)—offers not only the "less literal" interpretation of Pasolini's theories called for by de Lauretis but a masterful (re)reading of them. Another great iconoclast in revolt against the rationalist tradition of the Enlightenment, Deleuze rejects the Cartesian dualism underlying Saussurian linguistics even more markedly, perhaps more consciously, than does Pasolini. (Deleuze, after all, deliberately subverts the binary oppositions that still govern Pasolini's work. Of course, the French author may have derived a certain advantage from his nationality. As Pasolini once remarked, perhaps a bit enviously, the French spirit of classification, or what he called the "great catalogue of French rationalism," encompasses even irrationalism itself.[36]) It may well

[35] Alain Bergala, "Pasolini, pour un cinéma deux fois impur," in *Pasolini cinéaste*, special unnumbered issue of *Cahiers du cinéma* (Paris: Editions de l'étoile, 1981), p. 7.

[36] See "Le cinéma selon Pasolini: entretien avec Pier Paolo Pasolini par Bernardo Bertolucci et Jean-Louis Comolli," *Cahiers du cinéma* No. 169 (August 1965), p. 24.

be the conscious nature of this rejection that allows, indeed impels, Deleuze to assert that no single system—be it (Saussurian) linguistics or (Lacanian) psychology—can account for the phenomenon of cinema, which, as a "new praxis of images and signs," demands an equally new "conceptual praxis": "Cinema itself is a new praxis of images and signs [and] its theory must be created by philosophy as a conceptual praxis. Because no technical determination, either applied (psychoanalytic, linguistic), or reflexive, is sufficient to constitute the concepts of cinema itself."[37]

It is in the course of elaborating this new "conceptual praxis" that Deleuze rereads and, in fact, reshapes many of Pasolini's central intuitions. Thus absorbed into a broad philosophical context, transformed into moments or points of departure in Deleuze's own theoretical constructs, Pasolini's ideas often assume a more nuanced and profound coloration. For example, Pasolini's concept of an absolute and abstract cinema—a concept that seemed so eccentric in the 1960s—finds warm support from the French philosopher. Maintaining that Pasolini's deliberately naive slogans about cinema and reality were misread, or taken at face value, by (academic) semiologists who were truly naive, Deleuze asserts that Pasolini wished to establish the ontological ground for cinema (or for what Pasolini called Cinema as opposed to film):

> It is [his] study of the preliminary conditions that Pasolini's critics have not understood: these are the necessary conditions which constitute "cinema" although cinema does not, in fact, exist outside of a given film. In truth, therefore, the object can be only a referent in the image, while the image is analogical and refers back to codes. . . . The whole of Pasolini's thesis loses its meaning as soon as one neglects this study of necessary conditions. If a philosophical comparison were valid, one could say that Pasolini is post-Kantian (the necessary conditions are those of reality itself), while Metz and his disciples remain Kantian (the necessary [conditions] are collapsed into the fact itself).[38]

But Deleuze and Pasolini share more than an inclination toward metaphysics and ontology. According a primary role to the image rather than the narrative unit in film analysis, both emphasize the sensations, the conscious and unconscious processes evoked by the physical, sensorial qualities of such images. Echoing Pasolini's concept of a "semiology of reality," and his conviction that cinema "reveals" the world to us, Deleuze suggests that we "read" images as we "read" the world. Stressing the "voyeuristic" quality of modern cinema which privileges "seeing" in favor of "acting," Deleuze plays on the French word *voyant* (which means both "seeing" and "seer") as he writes: "For the eye of the *voyant* as for

---

[37] Gilles Deleuze, *Cinéma II: L'image-temps* (Paris: Minuit, 1985), p. 366.
[38] Ibid., p. 43.

that of the fortune-teller, it is the literalness of the perceptible world that constitutes it as a book."[39] And, for Deleuze, the world thus revealed is not, or not necessarily, or not at first, a conceptual one; rather, to use Pasolini's terms, it is a world of "physical presence," a pregrammatical and preverbal world where the "non-said" may be more important than the said, a world where bodies themselves "speak." Filmmakers such as Dreyer and Rossellini, observes Deleuze, are able to give back to us a "belief in the world. . . . [This means] returning discourse to the body and, to do so, reaching the body before discourse, before words, before things are named. . . . Returning words to the body, to flesh."[40]

Unwilling to sever cinema from this primal, nonconceptual world of matter and presence that constitutes its ontological base, Pasolini asked that we broaden our defintion of language. Less a prisoner of his Cartesian background than Pasolini, Deleuze takes this one step further. But the step he takes is a radical one, for it leads to a conclusion that is at once totally different, and yet implicit, in Pasolini. For Deleuze's belief in the material base of images, in the pregrammatical, premorphological nature of cinema, leads him to the conclusion that cinema is *not* a language. Cinematic shots, he says, constitute a kind of "plastic mass, a non-signifying and non-syntactic matter, a matter which is not linguistically formed."[41] Akin to thought, cinema *precedes* language:

> Cinema is not a universal or primitive language system ("langue") nor even a language ("langage"). It brings forth an intelligible matter, which is like a presupposition, a condition, a necessary correlation through which language constructs its own "objects" (unities and signifying operations). This correlation . . . consists of movements and processes of thought (prelinguistic images), and ways of seeing these movements and processes (presignifying signs). Language derives from it linguistic enunciations with unities and sense operations, but what is enunciated itself, its images and signs, are of another nature. It would be what Hjelmslev calls "matter" [which is] not linguistically formed, while language operates by form and substance. Or rather, it is the first signifiable, preceding every significance, which Gustave Guillaume saw as the condition of linguistics. Hence one understands the ambiguity running throughout semiotics and semiology: semiology, inspired by linguistics, tends to enclose the "signifier" and to cut language off from the images and signs which constitute its elementary matter.[42]

[39] Ibid., p. 34.
[40] Ibid., pp. 224–225.
[41] Ibid., p. 44.
[42] Ibid., p. 342. Félix Guattari, co-author, with Deleuze, of *L'Anti-Oedipe: Capitalisme et Schizophrénie* (Paris: Minuit, 1972), takes Deleuze's conclusion one step further; he pushes it onto a political terrain that was implicit in Pasolini's theoretical writings of the 1960s and that would become explicit in the 1970s. Linking dominant signifying systems to reigning political and social structures, Guattari writes: "If you want to make cinema

The kinship Deleuze postulates between "thought processes" and the "prelinguistic" images of cinema is at the very heart of Pasolini's most important essay, "Il cinema di poesia." Although this was also his first major foray into film theory, I have left it for last since it stands apart from subsequent essays for several reasons. Less deliberately polemical than later essays, "Il cinema di poesia" raises difficult questions—concerning the very nature of the "cinema of poetry," the relationship of film to the unconscious, and the problem of free indirect discourse—that fell by the wayside as Pasolini pursued the "semiology of reality." At the same time, this initial essay also contains what is certainly Pasolini's most elaborate and suggestive socio-linguistic analysis of modernist films and filmmakers—an analysis that, together with the theoretical concerns of this essay, says a great deal about his own cinema.

The issues raised in "Il cinema di poesia" may have been out of tune with the semiological climate of the 1960s, but they *were* part of a long tradition in film analysis, dating back to Soviet theorists of the 1920s. In all probability, Pasolini's essay was influenced by a number of Russian formalists who were being rediscovered and translated during the course of the 1960s. Pasolini himself was in charge of a book series that included an anthology of formalist writings on cinema (*I formalisti russi nel cinema* [Milan: Garzanti, 1971]). This anthology contained two essays of particular interest in light of the questions raised in "Il cinema di poesia." In "Problems of Film Stylistics," Boris Eikenbaum compares film language to a kind of inner monologue reminiscent of the primitive language Pasolini postulates in cinema; Viktor Shlovsky's "Poetry and Prose in Cinema" turns on the distinction—fundamental to Pasolini's essay—between cinematic prose and poetry. It is less certain whether Pasolini knew still another early Soviet thinker, Mikhail Bakhtin, who has come into prominence more recently for his theories concerning, to borrow a phrase from George Steiner, "pluralistic patterns of speech and points of view in literary constructs."[43] But the points of contact between Pasolini and Bakhtin—especially on the issue of free indirect discourse—are indeed striking: for Gilles Deleuze, in fact, Bakhtin is nothing less than "the best theoretician of 'free indirect discourse' before Pasolini."[44]

---

into a totalitarian machine, simply bring it under the rule of signifying semiologies, because cinema fulfills its function first of all in the order of images, movement, and sounds, that is, of pre-signifying or a-signifying semiotics. . . . The more cinema enriches itself in the domain of a-signifying semiotics and enlarges its range of esthetic possibilities, the more power tries to enslave it to signifying semiologies, that is, to dominant meanings." See Guattari, "Al di là del significante," in *Erotismo, eversione, merce*, ed. Vittorio Boarini (Bologna: Cappelli, 1974), p. 90.

[43] George Steiner, "The Good Books," *The New Yorker*, January 11, 1988, p. 94.

[44] Deleuze, *Cinéma II*, p. 244.

If "Il cinema di poesia" ends with suggestions of Bakhtin, it opens, essentially, with an issue addressed by Eikenbaum: the relationship between thought—or what the Soviet thinker calls "inner speech"—and cinema. Comparing the viewer to a person watching "someone's dream," Eikenbaum notes:

> For the study of the laws of film (especially of montage) it is most important to admit that perception and understanding of a motion-picture is inextricably bound up with the development of internal speech, which makes the connection between separate shots. . . . The film viewer must perform the complex mental labour of connecting the frames (construction of film-phrases and film-periods), a form of labour practically non-existent in everyday life where the word covers and eliminates all other means of expression. . . . though the audible word is eliminated from film, the thought, i.e., internal speech, is nevertheless present.[45]

In complete agreement with Eikenbaum's suggestion that film language resembles "internal speech" rather than "audible words," Pasolini begins "Il cinema di poesia" by showing why, or in what ways, the signs of cinematic language—which he calls *imsegni* (or "im-signs" from image-signs)—are different from those of verbal language, that is, from words. To begin with, says Pasolini, visual signs—that is, cinematic images—are unlimited: unlike words, they could never be codified in any possible dictionary. Moreover, cinematic signs are rooted not in logical, rational discourse but in memory and dream: whenever we try to remember something, a series of "significant images" (or "im-signs") passes through our mind. This series, clearly linked to our subconscious, is also akin to dreams, which are similarly composed of a free flow of images, often marked by abupt shifts, by condensation, displacement, and metaphor. And whether it occurs while we are awake or asleep, this image series shares many of the characteristics of film language since it lends itself to close-ups, long shots, details, and so forth. Together with images stemming from gestures and the physical world ("signs coming from the environment"), these images of memory and dream prefigure, and even constitute, the "foundation of cinematic communication."

Unlimited in number, derived from memory and dream, visual images

[45] This citation comes from an English translation of Eikenbaum's essay, "Problems of Film Stylistics," which appeared in *Screen* Vol. 15, No. 3 (Autumn 1974), p. 14. On the resemblance between cinematic language and thought (as opposed to spoken language), Emilio Garroni agrees with Eikenbaum—and, for once, with Pasolini. Garroni maintains that cinematic language often resembles thought in two important ways: it is both more abbreviated or condensed than verbal language and able to do without an explicit (or stated) frame of reference provided the filmic context is standard and recognizable. See Garroni's "Langage verbal et éléments non-verbaux dans le message filmico-télévisual," in *Cinéma: Théorie, Lectures*, pp. 111–128.

also differ from words since they are not part of an elaborate system of conventional signs. Just as no dictionary could contain them all, no grammar could encompass their infinite combinations. For this reason, Pasolini—foreshadowing Deleuze—calls them not only "premorphological" but also "pregrammatical." Visual images, he says, are "crude, almost animalistic . . . prehuman, or at the border of what is human."[46] And since Pasolini defines poetry in terms of its primitive or prerational nature, it is precisely the irrational and oneiric qualities of cinematic images that render the language of cinema essentially poetic. (Elsewhere he suggests that their visual, or concrete, nature may make cinematic images more "mysterious," "ambiguous," and full of "polyvalent meanings" than even poetry itself.[47]) The inchoate nature of images means that the task of filmmakers differs from that of poets or writers: before they can stamp images with their personal or "aesthetic" vision, filmmakers must undertake a "linguistic" quest for images, a quest that leads deep into the dark night of the unconscious, into a "chaos where there is only the possibility or the shadow of mechanical or dreamlike communication."[48]

But, Pasolini goes on in dismay, a central paradox has marked the history of film practice: after early, truncated leanings toward poetry—especially in evidence before the introduction of sound—the metaphorical, oneiric, and irrational qualities constituting the very core of film were pushed aside in favor of the realistic narrative conventions marking a cinema of prose.[49] Still, affirms Pasolini, just as primitive societies lie buried beneath technological civilizations, even the most rational and realistic film covers an irrational and mythical sub-stratum that hints at cinema's elemental nature.

> [Cinema] immediately underwent a rather foreseeable and inevitable desecration. In other words, all its irrational, oneiric, elemental, and barbarous elements were forced below the level of consciousness; that is, they were exploited as unconscious elements of shock and persuasion. A whole narrative conven-

[46] Pasolini, *Empirismo eretico*, p. 173.

[47] Cited by Oswald Stack in *Pasolini* (Bloomington: Indiana University Press, 1969), p. 153.

[48] Pasolini, *Empirismo eretico*, p. 174. Eco and Garroni, as well as Metz, disagreed with Pasolini's suggestion that images come from some shadowy zone, untainted by the cultural and grammatical history surrounding words.

[49] The systematization that cinema was prey to after the introduction of sound (a systemization that Pasolini lamented and linked to the advent of "prose") evokes a not dissimilar political interpretation from Guattari, who writes: "Silent cinema was able to express, generally in a more incisive and authentic manner than sound cinema, the intensity of desire in its relation to the social field. This was the case not because silent cinema was less rich at the level of expressive matter, but because it escaped from a signifying semiology that offers in "talkies" many more concrete possiblities for the transmission of the values of power." See Guattari, "Al di là del significante," p. 91.

tion—which fueled useless and pseudo-critical comparisons with the theater and the novel—was rapidly built upon this hypnotic *"monstrum"* which always constitutes a film. This narrative convention clearly belongs, by analogy, to the language of prose communication . . . [but] its foundation is the mythic and childlike film which, by the very nature of cinema, runs beneath every commercial film.[50]

But what shape has this "mythic" film, this "hypnotic *monstrum*," taken today? This is the real subject of Pasolini's essay and, to answer it, he raises the second important theoretical issue of "Il cinema di poesia": is there a cinematic equivalent of what is known in literature as "free indirect discourse"? Very simply put, literary free indirect discourse denotes the technique whereby an author conveys a character's thoughts or speech without either the quotation marks that accompany direct discourse or the "he/she said" of indirect discourse. For example, in the following passage taken from *Un coeur simple*, Flaubert, through the use of free indirect discourse, expresses the thoughts of Madame Aubain, whose daughter has just died: "First she rebelled against God, finding him unjust for having taken her daughter from her—she who never did anything bad, and whose conscience was so pure! But no! she should have taken her to the South of France. Other doctors would have saved her!"

Pasolini's discussion of free indirect discourse suggests that he was drawn to this issue—with its cluster of social and formal implications—for many of the same reasons as Bakhtin. The socio-linguistic approach characterizing Bakhtin and Pasolini—an approach, in both cases, that owed much to Leo Spitzer and other German philologists—meant that both accorded an important role to speech, whose changing patterns and different layers are emblematic (as Pasolini had always insisted in his remarks about dialects) of the way language itself is embedded in social and historical structures. Wary of any approach that failed to take full account of the changing, protean, essentially *social* nature of language, Bakhtin had, in fact, argued against Saussurian linguistics, which, in his view, defined language as an abstract, ideal identity.[51] Not surprisingly,

---

[50] Pasolini, *Empirismo eretico*, pp. 176–177.

[51] For Bakhtin, individual consciousness is shaped by language and, in particular, by speech, which, in turn, is part of a historical-social process. In his view: "The evolution of individual consciousness will depend upon the evolution of language, in its grammatical structures as well as its concretely ideological ones. Personality evolves along with language. . . . As for the evolution of language, it is an element in the evolution of social communication and cannot be separated from this communication and its material bases. The material base determines the stratification of society, its socio-political structure, and divides hierarchically individuals who are there into relations of interaction. These are the elements which engender the place, the moment, the conditions, the forms, and the means of verbal communication. In turn, the latter determines the destinies of individual enunciation at a given

one of the essential social aspects of speech for both Bakhtin and Pasolini involved free indirect discourse: for here, by definition, one discourse, or enunciation, is incorporated, layered, into another. By its very nature, as Deleuze remarks, free indirect discourse is not a simple combination, or admixture, of "two totally constituted subjects of enunciation" but, rather, the "differentiation of two correlative subjects in a system which is itself heterogeneous." For Deleuze, in fact, free indirect discourse is nothing less than *the* "fundamental act of language" insofar as it "bears witness to a system which is always heterogeneous, never in equilibrium."[52]

This "fundamental act of language" is—as Bakhtin's analyses make clear—both meta-literary and social. As the Soviet thinker observes, whenever and however a text conveys another's speech or discourse— whether in a direct or indirect manner—it always involves a "discourse about discourse, an enunciation about enunciation."[53] Of course, the distance between narrator and speaker may vary greatly. In modern writers, epitomized by Proust, the conveyed discourse often seems to merge with the narration. In such a case, where "hero and author express themselves together," the line of demarcation, or boundary, that separates the narration from the discourse it conveys becomes weak and indistinct: "Within the limits of one and the same linguistic construction, the accents of two different voices resonate."[54] And the distance, or lack of distance, between narrator and speaker (as well, one might add, as the tone characterizing the enunciation) has social—that is, class—implications. Once again, this is very clear in Flaubert's *Un coeur simple*, where the free indirect discourse applied to Madame Aubain's servant marks her as a peasant. An indication of class relations, the bond between hero and author, or between narrator and speaker, may well contribute to the heightened quality of imagination that, for Bakhtin, is an important characteristic of free indirect discourse.

> In truth, for the artist involved in the creative process, his phantasms constitute reality itself: he does not only see them, he also hears them. He does not give them words as in indirect discourse, he hears them speak. And this animated impression produced by voices heard as if in a dream can only be directly rendered in the form of free indirect discourse. It is the form of the imaginary par excellence. . . .
>
> In using [this] form, the writer also addresses himself especially to the read-

---

moment in the evolution of language." See Mikhail Bakhtin, *Le marxisme et la philosophie du language* (Paris: Minuit, 1977), pp. 211–212.

[52] Deleuze, *Cinéma I: L'image-mouvement* (Paris: Minuit, 1983), p. 106.

[53] Bakhtin, *Le marxisme et la philosophie du language*, p. 161.

[54] Ibid., p. 198.

1. Echoes of neorealism: Accattone and his family in the *borgata*.
2. *Accattone*: A "frontal, massive, romantic, chiaroscuro world."

3. Pasolini with Anna Magnani at his side on the set of *Mamma Roma*.

4. The two "directors" of *La ricotta*: Pasolini and Orson Welles.

5. Jacopo da Pontormo's *Deposition*.

6. Pasolini's re-creation of Pontormo's *Deposition* in *La ricotta*.

7. "Documentary movements" of *Il Vangelo*: (a) the Flight from Egypt;
(b) **opposite page:** Salome prepares for her dance.

8. Painterly influences upon *Il Vangelo*: (a) the Pharisees as seen by Piero della Francesca and (b) by Pasolini.

9. The Christ of *Il Vangelo*: distant, "hieratic," and violent.

10. Pasolini's mother, Susanna (center), as the aged Mary in *Il Vangelo*.

11. The three travelers of *Uccellacci e Uccellini*: Totò, Ninetto, and the Marxist crow.

12. Totò and Ninetto "talk" with the sparrows in the medieval episode of *Uccellacci e Uccellini*.

13. *Uccellacci e Uccellini*: the need for Marxism to embrace new realities such as the Third World.

14. Totò embraces a "life force" in the shape of a prostitute.

15. *La terra vista dalla luna*: "Lacking a language or style to express in writing, verbally, this type of comedy, I was forced to write the screenplay . . . by drawing Totò and Ninetto in various situations precisely as in *fumetti* [comic books]."

16. *Edipo Re*: a samurai-like Oedipus at the fatal crossroads.

17. The epilogue of *Edipo Re*: an aged Oedipus is led through modern-day Bologna.

18. *Teorema*: Terence Stamp as the "divine visitor."

19. *Teorema*: "scandalous loves" and a "fetishizing" camera.

20. Silvana Mangano as the love-starved mother of *Teorema*.
21. The "miracles" of *Teorema*: the servant (Laura Betti) levitates.

22. Pierre Clementi as the young cannibal in *Porcile*.
23. *Porcile*: the "disobedient" sons are punished by society.

24. *Porcile*: Herr Klotz plays the harp as he hears the gruesome details of Nazi atrocities.

25. A majestic Maria Callas plays the title role in *Medea*.

26. The "primitive barbarity" of Medea and her people.

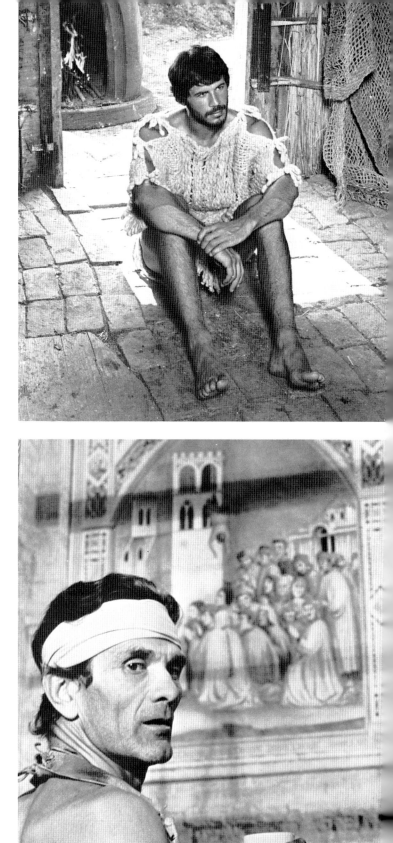

27. *Medea*: the "pragmatic" and "bourgeois" Jason.

28. Pasolini as a disciple of Giotto in *Il Decamerone*.

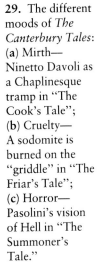

29. The different moods of *The Canterbury Tales*: (a) Mirth— Ninetto Davoli as a Chaplinesque tramp in "The Cook's Tale"; (b) Cruelty— A sodomite is burned on the "griddle" in "The Friar's Tale"; (c) Horror— Pasolini's vision of Hell in "The Summoner's Tale."

30(a) and **(b).** Scenes of Oriental splendor in *Il fiore delle mille e una notte.*

31. *Il fiore delle mille e una notte*: an underground chamber hosts a fatal encounter.

32. *Il fiore delle mille e una notte*: Zumurrud's complacent bride.

33. Modern art in the villa of *Salò*: a villa that might have been confiscated from some "rich deported Jew."

34. Victims and libertines await a performance in *Salò*: formal symmetry in a "perfectly calculated world."

35. The "performances" of *Salò*: (**a**) a mock marriage; (**b**) the libertines choose the most beautiful ass.

36. The end of *Salò*: (**a**) the guards dance; (**b**) the libertines celebrate the final sadistic orgy.

er's imagination. What he seeks is not to relate a fact or some product of thought but to communicate his impressions, to awaken in the soul of the reader images and living representations. He does not speak to reason but to imagination.[55]

In "Il cinema di poesia" Pasolini builds upon the web of formal and social implications that Bakhtin discerns in the use of free indirect discourse. Although he places a new emphasis upon psychology, he does not neglect the social, or class, relationship between the narrator and the character whose speech or thoughts are conveyed. Taking on a character's language—as he himself did in his early novels set in the *borgata*—means that the author immerses himself in his character's "soul" as well as his social milieu. But this also implies, he goes on, *that if the language of author and character(s) is the same,* or almost so, we lose all awareness of class differences even as we slip into what he calls "bourgeois" literature.

> In bourgeois literature, which lacks class consciousness (that is, in which there is identification with all of humanity), "free indirect discourse" is often a pretext. The author constructs a character, who may even speak an invented language, in order to express a particular interpretation of the world. It is in this "indirect" pretextual discourse . . . that you can find a narration written with many elements taken from the "language of poetry."[56]

In this passage, then, Pasolini adds new dimensions—which will be of particular importance later in his argument—to the notion of free indirect discourse: he postulates a "pretextual" discourse or character through whom the author speaks in his own voice as well as an intimate connnection between free indirect discourse and the "language of poetry."

Before he can continue this train of thought, however, Pasolini must confront a very difficult theoretical issue: how can the notion of free indirect discourse, so embedded in verbal language, be translated into cinematic terms? According to his own definition, unlike verbal language, that of film is a universal one (which, implicitly, does not betray social or class differences); moreoever, it is a universal language in which individuals, that is, directors, create their own grammar, their own lexicon and syntax, by the way they manipulate "im-signs." To overcome this philosophical hurdle, Pasolini takes us out of the domain of language into that of style: and not only does he manage to postulate a cinematic form of free indirect discourse—which he labels "free indirect subjectivity"—but he places it at the very heart of the "cinema of poetry."

Although this complex issue is central to the whole of "Il cinema di

[55] Ibid., p. 204.
[56] Pasolini, *Empirismo eretico*, p. 180.

poesia," it is presented rapidly—almost as if it were a digression. Pasolini begins by acknowledging that you cannot codify the difference between the way a peasant and an aristocrat look at something the way you can codify the language spoken by each. But, he continues, they do indeed see the world differently: "The 'gaze' of a peasant . . . embraces another kind of reality from the gaze which a cultivated bourgeois directs at this same reality: the two actually see a 'different series' of things; and even the same thing appears different to the two 'gazes.' "[57] And while film cannot convey this essential difference through language, it can and does, he argues, convey it through *style*. After this important declaration (which echoes Bakhtin's emphasis on the stylistic factors at work in free indirect discourse[58]), Pasolini makes a rather sudden and abrupt jump. Returning to the oneiric and barbaric nature of cinema, to the "*monstrum*" lying beneath every film, he asserts that free indirect subjectivity, which conveys a "gaze" or set of feelings not contained in the narrative, allows the "*monstrum*"—the "expressive possibilities stifled by the convention of traditional narrative"—to come to the fore. Free indirect subjectivity, then, fuels a style that restores to cinema its "original oneiric, barbaric, unconventional, aggressive, and visionary quality. In short, it is 'free indirect subjectivity' that establishes a possible tradition of a 'technical language of poetry' in cinema."[59]

Clearly, this definition raises at least two fundamental problems: how does free indirect subjectivity differ from what have traditionally been called "subjective" shots, that is, shots usually used to convey feelings and emotions, where, as a consequence, the world is seen through the character's eyes? And if, as Pasolini suggests, "free indirect subjectivity" is linked to a "technical language of poetry" which, presumably, infuses the *entire* film with a visionary and barbaric quality, what role is played by individual characters and/or the way they see the world?

Not surprisingly, these difficulties did not escape critics.[60] Once again

---

[57] Ibid., p. 182.

[58] For Deleuze even (written) free indirect discourse is essentially stylistic rather than linguistic. "Free indirect discourse does not fall within the jurisdiction of linguistic categories because these only concern homogeneous or homogenized systems. It's an affair of style, of stylistics, as Pasolini says." See Deleuze, *Cinéma I*, p. 107.

[59] Pasolini, *Empirismo eretico*, p. 183.

[60] For example, in an article devoted to the problem of free indirect subjectivity, Elena Dagrada raises both these points. Observing that Pasolini confuses "subjective" and "subjectivity," she notes that he uses free indirect subjectivity to denote both a stylistic register where the character's viewpoint coincides with the Weltanschauung or "subjectivity" of the author, as well as other shots ("technico-stylistic elements able to produce lyrical and poetic effects") where no subjectivity is involved. The latter shots, she contends, "have really nothing to do with what is subjective, and far from being limited to single [subjective] shots, they are at work directly throughout the filmic work and constitute its presupposition, its stylistic

though, perhaps only Deleuze tried to unravel them, to see what Pasolini really meant. Treating the two issues separately, Deleuze begins by addressing what is certainly the less fundamental and more technical issue: the difference between subjective shots and free indirect subjectivity. He first notes that many shots exist that are neither totally "objective" nor "subjective." We may, for example, see what someone is looking at even if we do not see the object of his gaze through his eyes. Such cases, observes Deleuze, prompted the film historian and theorist Jean Mitry to propose the category of "half-subjective image" which encompasses shots where the camera is not "fused with the character, nor inside him, but with him."[61] Since, continues Deleuze, natural perception lacks an equivalent for this, Pasolini had to invent a linguistic analogy that is, precisely, that of free indirect subjectivity.

But as Deleuze clearly senses, Pasolini did not elaborate this complex notion merely to define a certain category of shots. Coming closer to the heart of the issue, Deleuze now suggests that free indirect subjectivity refers to a kind of mimesis between a character's subjective vision and the camera, which sees both the character and his vision in a transformed manner.

> The camera does not simply give a vision of the character and his world; it imposes another vision in which the first vision is transformed and reflected. This doubling is what Pasolini calls 'free indirect subjectivity'. . . . it is a question of going beyond the subjective and the objective towards a pure Form which rises up as an autonomous vision of the content.[62]

There is no doubt that the presence of "transformed and reflected" visions—infused by what Pasolini called "contamination" and pastiche—is crucial to his notion of free indirect subjectivity. But I am not at all sure that a transcendence of the "subjective and the objective" is really what the concrete and earthy Pasolini has in mind. In fact, his analysis of this

---

given." See Dagrada, "Sulla soggettività libera indiretta," *Cinema e cinema* Vol. 12, No. 43 (May–August 1985), p. 54.

[61] Deleuze, *Cinéma I*, p. 106.

[62] Ibid., p. 108. Elsewhere, placing this concept of free indirect subjectivty at the heart of the deliberate "falsity" of contemporary cinema, Deleuze remarks that "Pasolini postulates a transcendence of the two viewpoints of traditional narrative—the objective indirect narrative from the camera's viewpoint and the direct subjective narrative from the character's viewpoint—to arrive at a very special form of 'free indirect discourse,' of 'free indirect subjectivity.' By establishing a contamination between these two sorts of images such that the unusual visions of the camera . . . express the character's singular visions, the latter are expressed in the former while giving the whole over to the power of what is false. The narrative no longer refers to an ideal of the truth which would constitute its veracity, but becomes a kind of 'pseudo-narrative,' a poem, a simulating narrative or rather a simulation of narrative." See Deleuze, *Cinéma II*, p. 194.

phenomenon in the work of other directors, which also reveals much about his own cinema, points at something quite different. Before returning to the theoretical difficulties, I would therefore like to take a closer look at Pasolini's examination of the way(s) three of his contemporaries—Antonioni, Bertolucci, and Godard—use free indirect subjectivity.

Pasolini begins his analysis of these modernist directors by observing that their films are peopled by neurotic, bourgeois characters. It is through such characters, he argues, that each director is able to express his own irrational world view—one marked by an obsessive relationship with reality. This hypothesis allows him, finally, to come to the important relationship he sees between free indirect subjectivity and the "technical means" characterizing the cinema of poetry: for he now declares that each director's own obsessive vision—expressed through the "pretext" of neurotic characters—is also one that endows reality with a poetic intensity not found in "prose" films. In the case, for example, of *Il deserto rosso (Red Desert)*, Antonioni immerses himself totally in the "look" of his neurotic heroine; her neuroses allow him to substitute his vision—a vision "delirious with aestheticism"—for hers: "a substitution justified wholly by the possible analogy of the two visions." In other words, with free indirect subjectivity comes the poetic liberty whereby Antonioni may indulge his obsessive view of reality—in which landscapes and objects assume an almost ontological density and vibrancy—and, ultimately, his aestheticism.

After establishing that free indirect subjectivity constitutes the grounds, the "pretext," for this poetic liberty, Pasolini then analyzes precisely *how* such liberty manifests itself. In passages where he might often be describing his own films—which are therefore quoted at some length—he explores the "technical means," the "stylistic operations," through which each director creates a poetic or obsessive intensity. In his view, Antonioni favors the following two-part operation:

1. The sequential juxtaposition of two viewpoints, scarcely different from each other, directed toward the same image: that is, the succession of two shots which frame the same portion of reality—first from up close, then from *a little* farther away; or else, first frontally and then *a bit obliquely*; or else, finally, actually on the same axis but with two different lenses. This gives rise to an insistence which becomes obsessive, like the myth of the real and anguishing autonomous beauty of things.

2. The technique of having characters enter and leave the frame, so that, in a sometimes obsessive way, the editing consists of a series of, let's say, informal "pictures" [*quadri*] into which the characters enter, say or do something, and then exit, leaving the picture once again to its own pure and absolute significance as a picture. This is followed by another similar picture where the char-

acters enter, say or do something, and so forth. In this way, the world appears to be ruled by the myth of pure pictorial beauty that—it is true—the characters invade but [only] by submitting to the rules of that beauty instead of profaning them by their presence.[63]

Whereas Antonioni substitutes his vision for that of his protagonists, in *Prima della rivoluzione (Before the Revolution)* Bertolucci's vision "shades" into that of the protagonist. "Inevitably anologous," these two visions, says Pasolini, "demand the same style."[64] Moreover, during intensely expressive moments of "naked and crude subjectivity," Bertolucci actually frees his own vision from that of his characters. Adding an important dimension to the concept of free indirect subjectivity, Pasolini now suggests that at these expressive moments—which are brought to our attention by the "insistences" of the framings and the montage rhythms—we begin to sense the presence of a "second" film. And this second film is *conveyed primarily by style*.

Such an insistence on details, particularly on certain details in the digressions [*excursus*], represents a deviation from the system of the film: *it is the temptation to make another film.* In short, it is the presence of the author who, through an abnormal freedom, transcends his film and continually threatens to abandon it, detoured by a sudden inspiration—an inspiration of latent love for the poetic world of his own vital experiences. . . . In short, beneath the technique produced by the protagonist's state of mind—which is disoriented, uncoordinated, beset by details, given to compelling anxieties—the world constantly surfaces as it is seen by the equally neurotic author: dominated by an elegant, elegiac, and never classicist, spirit.[65]

The specter of this "second" film—but this time far from "elegiac and elegant"—also haunts Godard. Unlike the two Italian directors, Godard is concerned with cinema itself rather than reality ("his poetics is ontological: its name is cinema"); still, to express his "technical liberty" he also needs neurotic protagonists. Hence his characters are almost pathological, ill but not in treatment. In their obsession with details and gestures they are specimens of a "new anthropological type"—the "exquisite flowers of the bourgeoisie." In Godard

there is neither the cult of the object as form (as in Antonioni) nor the cult of the object as symbol of a lost world (as in Bertolucci). Godard has no cult and puts everything on the same level, frontally: his pretextual "free indirect" [subjectivity] is the frontal and undifferentiated arrangement of a thousand details

[63] Pasolini, *Empirismo eretico*, 184.
[64] Ibid., p. 185.
[65] Ibid., pp. 185–186.

of the world . . . edited with the cold and almost smug obsession (typical of his amoral protagonist) of a disintegration which is reconstructed and unified through that unarticulated language. . . . Beneath the events of his films, beneath the long "free indirect subjectivity" that imitates his protagonists' state of mind, there always unwinds a film made for the pure pleasure of restoring a reality [which has been] fractured by technique and reconstructed by a brutal, mechanical, and discordant Braque.[66]

In each of the three directors, then, Pasolini postulates an intimate bond between free indirect subjectivity—which always implies a degree of mimesis between the author's vision and that of his neurotic protagonists—and an "abnormal" stylistic liberty; this liberty, in turn, betrays an obsessive relationship with reality even as it breaks with the conventions of film syntax. It is—finally—this stylistic liberty that lies at the very heart of the "cinema of poetry" for, through it, the director creates another film, an "authentic" and "irrational" film that springs from cinema's deepest, and most essential, poetic sub-stratum. This "other" film—one that the "author would have wanted to make even without the visual mimesis of his protagonist"—is "totally and freely of an expressive-expressionist sort."[67] *Since this "other" film is created totally through formal means, its true protagonist—and, by extension, the true protagonist of the cinema of poetry—is style itself understood, essentially, as a stylistic liberty that calls attention to itself by breaking the rules.* Discussing the stylistic transgressions that characterize the cinema of poetry—and that subsequently become the basis of a new canon, a new set of conventions—Pasolini could virtually be describing the films he would make in the late 1960s.

The camera is felt and for good reasons. The alternation of different lenses . . . on the same face, the abuse of the zoom with its long focuses which adhere to things and expand them like loaves with too much yeast, the continuous and deceptively casual shots against the light which blind the camera, the tremblings of the hand-held camera, the exasperated tracking-shots, the mistakes in editing done for expressive reasons, the irritating opening shots, the shots held interminably on the same image, etc., etc.—this whole technical code was born almost from an intolerance of the rules, from the need for an unusual and provocative liberty, from an otherwise authentic and delicious taste for anarchy. But it immediately became a canon, a prosodic and linguistic heritage, which now interests filmmakers all over the world.[68]

Although Pasolini implicitly distances himself from the three directors analyzed in "Il cinema di poesia," the fact is, as several critics were quick

[66] Ibid., p. 187.
[67] Ibid., p. 187.
[68] Ibid., pp. 189–190.

to observe, that he had a great deal in common with them. True, his style was far less consistent than theirs; his camera often—but not always— less intrusive. (He himself noted that, unlike his first two films, in *Il Vangelo secondo Matteo* "the camera makes itself greatly felt—there are many zooms and false continuity shots, if you like, somewhat close to the technique of certain films by Godard."[69]) As far as editing techniques are concerned, moreoover, there is no doubt that he was as unconventional as they: on his own admission, he discarded "normal narrative rhythms" in order to create a kind of rhythmic disequilibrium where "details are greatly dilated [while] moments classically considered important are touched upon very rapidly."[70] Further, and perhaps most significantly, this editing—as he himself repeatedly acknowledged—betrayed a relationship to reality that was not only obsessive but even, to use his own word, fetishistic. (One critic, in fact, analyzes two of Pasolini's later films, *Porcile* and *Teorema*, in terms of the double "stylistic operation" Pasolini discerns in Antonioni.[71]) The insistences of his lingering and fragmenting camera constantly endow objects and faces with a heightened reality, a symbolic cast. His repeated shots of rocky and volcanic deserts, for example, appear impelled by a desire to wrench secrets from nature's most inanimate and unyielding face. If the object is pure "form" for Antonioni, and symbol of a "lost world" for Bertolucci, for Pasolini it is the phenomenal carapace behind which lurk deep mystical currents, hidden myths, and forbidden sexual impulses.

But now an interesting question arises. In light of this obsessive relationship to reality—so fundamental to his own cinema as well as that of Antonioni, Bertolucci, and Godard—why did Pasolini seek to distance himself from the "cinema of poetry"? Much of the explanation lies in a number of revealing remarks—*which bear on the ideological nature of the "cinema of poetry"*—made toward the end of his essay. Only as he is about to conclude does Pasolini acknowledge that the "pretextual" use of neurotic bourgeois characters, through whom directors may express their "irrational" view of reality, is a sign of the bourgeoisie—of a bourgeoisie that "once again identifies itself with the whole of humanity, in an irrational interclassism." And the deliberate desire to ignore class distinctions is part of a larger, even more reactionary phenomenon: it indicates a general movement, on the part of bourgeois culture, "to recuperate territory . . . lost in the battle against Marxism." [72]

Even apart from his personal aversion to the bourgeoisie, it is clear that Pasolini would decidedly not want to align himself with a counterrevo-

[69] "Le cinéma selon Pasolini," p. 25.

[70] Ibid., p. 77.

[71] See Noel Purdon's "The Film of Alienation," in *Pier Paolo Pasolini*, ed. Paul Willemin (London: British Film Institute, 1977).

[72] Pasolini, *Empirismo eretico*, p. 191.

lutionary moment, a victory of bourgeois culture. It is now that we come
to the real reason for his insistence, despite all the theoretical problems it
raises, on the necessity of free indirect subjectivity in the cinema of poetry.
By defining this cinema as one where a mimesis of vision occurs between
the director and neurotic members of the bourgeoisie, Pasolini could
thereby distance his own films from a phenomenon he deemed reactionary, from a cinema whose involuted and narcissistic world view typified
the bourgeoisie he despised. After all, in terms of characters, his cinema
is markedly different from that of the three directors he analyzes. By depicting sub-proletarian characters in his early films or, in the case of films
made after 1966, bourgeois characters too grotesque and unreal to solicit
or allow audience identification, Pasolini does, indeed, avoid the impli-
cation that the "bourgeoisie constitutes all of mankind." Conversely, his
declaration that mimesis was at work in *Il Vangelo*, that all is seen
through the eyes of a believer, was an attempt to distance himself from
the religious aspect of the film. He even confessed at one point that it was
the problems posed by *Il Vangelo*—where he was telling a story in which
he did not believe—that gave rise to his theory of free indirect subjectivity.[73] If we accept the hypothesis that the critical role Pasolini attributed
to mimesis of vision—at the heart, after all, of free indirect subjectivity—
sprang from ideological and existential factors, then it becomes clear why
the usually lucid Pasolini was so slippery when discussing the nature and
function of free indirect subjectivity in relation to the cinema of poetry.
For in addition to the theoretical problems raised earlier—bearing on the
distinction between subjective and subjectivity—an even more basic question now comes to mind: is free indirect subjectivity, or mimesis of vision
between character and director, really necessary—as he repeatedly seems
to maintain—to the cinema of poetry? A number of remarks indicate that,
despite the whole tenor of his argument, even Pasolini wavered on this
essential point: for example, in his discussion of Antonioni and Godard,
at several points he hints that the director's vision does not merge with
that of his characters but actually "replaces" it.

   More than anything that is stated in the essay, however, it is Pasolini's

---

[73] "It was while thinking of *Il Vangelo* that this idea of free indirect discourse, which I
consider so important, came to me. The Gospel raised the following problem for me: I could
not film it as a classic narration, because I am an atheist, not a believer. . . . I had to narrate
a story in which I did not believe. I could not be the one to tell it. It's in this way, then,
without precisely wanting to, that I was led to reverse my whole cinematographic technique
and thus was born this *stylistic magma* which belongs to the 'cinema of poetry.' Because, in
order to narrate the Gospel, I had to plunge myself into the soul of someone who believed.
That is where you have free indirect discourse: on the one hand the narrative is seen through
my own eyes; on the other, through those of a believer. And it is the use of free indirect
discourse which is the cause of this stylistic contamination, of the magma in question." See
Pasolini, "Le cinéma selon Pasolini," p. 25.

own films that suggest that the expressive possibilities of the cinema of poetry may exist without the pretext—usually furnished by neurotic bourgeois characters—of free indirect subjectivity. This is not to deny the presence of mimesis in Pasolini's cinema. Quite the contrary. But, *contrary* to the theoretical model proposed in "Il cinema di poesia," it does not flow from a contamination of vision between director and characters, be they bourgeois or proletarian. The same year Pasolini published "Il cinema di poesia," in fact, a French critic, Jean-Louis Comolli, raised this very issue. Shifting the entire focus of Pasolini's essay, Comolli observes that, although a "second" film is clearly discernible in Pasolini's cinema, it does not involve free indirect subjectivity. "It seems to me," notes Comolli, "that it is precisely one of the traits of *Mamma Roma*, for example, to involve two films: the first, a kind of documentary about the life dramas of the humble people on the outskirts of Rome; the second, in filigree behind the first, a kind of Christian parable."[74] And the point Comolli raises here was echoed, years later, by Deleuze. Unlike Comolli, Deleuze does not drop the notion of free indirect subjectivity, but his description of it, the way he envisions the "two" films at work in Pasolini's cinema, implicitly denies the characters any vision of their own.

> What characterizes Pasolini's cinema is a poetic awareness which . . . is mystical or "sacred." This allows Pasolini to carry the . . . neurosis of his characters to a level of lowness and bestiality . . . while illuminating them in a pure poetic awareness impelled by something which is mythic or "sacred making." Here is the permutation of the trivial and the noble, the connection between the excremental and the beautiful, and the projection into myth that Pasolini diagnosed in free indirect discourse [seen] as the essential form of literature. And he succeeds in making it into a cinematographic form capable of grace as much as of horror.[75]

Deleuze's remark hints at the real nature of mimesis in Pasolini's films. I would argue that this mimesis, which takes place *without* the mediation of free indirect subjectivity, stems from a series of stylistic "permutations" or "connections" whereby, for example, the "excremental and the beautiful," or the "trivial and the noble," may clash, coexist, be superimposed upon each other, in such a way that each transforms the other. Concerned, like Bakhtin, with the interminglings of different languages or stylistic registers, Pasolini was always imbued with a heightened form of what the Soviet thinker called a plurilinguistic consciousness. Throughout his career, for example, he made great use of parody, pastiche, and dialect—all of which imply that one language is "enunciated in

---

[74] Ibid., p. 24.
[75] Deleuze, *Cinéma I*, p. 109.

light of another" or that two social languages are expressed "within one enunciation."[76] Indeed, long before he conceived of the notion of free indirect subjectivity, Pasolini's penchant for plurilinguistic effects was strongly in evidence: as early as 1959, Franco Fortini remarked that "linguistic plurality" and "stylistic contamination" constituted the poet's "expressive instruments." In a similar manner it was this "linguistic plurality"—*unmarked by a mimesis of vision between author and character*—that gave a special tone to Pasolini's early films. There, after all, it was essentially plurilinguism that governed the mixture of the sacred and the profane, as well as the "rereading" (or "reaccentuation," to use Bakhtin's term) of past language—that is, neorealism—in *Accattone* and *Mamma Roma*; that impelled the clash of stylistic registers and the use of parody (of mannerist painting as well as silent film comedy) in *La ricotta*; and that encouraged both the application of a documentary style to sacred events and the subversion of traditional iconography in *Il Vangelo secondo Matteo*. But if Pasolini's taste for "stylistic contamination" was clear from the beginning, it is also true that—showing the deep link between theory and praxis in his work—it was *after* writing "Il cinema di poesia" that this tendency became most extreme even as style itself became the undisputed protagonist of his films.

In several essays devoted to seemingly diverse subjects but all published in 1965, the year of "Il cinema di poesia," Pasolini makes it absolutely clear that his plurilinguistic concerns went way beyond the issue of free indirect subjectivity or mimesis of vision. One of these essays, "La sceneggiatura come 'struttura che vuol essere altra struttura' " (The Screenplay as a "Structure that Wants to Be Another Structure"), describes the film scenario itself in terms of multiple languages. As a literary text that demands a visual embodiment, the scenario, asserts Pasolini, is perched precariously between two "languages"; it is "a structure imbued with the will to become another structure." Thus set under the sign of movement or process, rather than stasis or structure, the scenario is fueled by a "dynamism" or "tension" that causes it to move "without departing and without arriving, from one stylistic structure (that of narrative) to another stylistic structure (that of cinema) and, at a deeper level, from one linguistic system to another."[77] The two "linguistic systems" that Pasolini perceives in the film scenario may also operate within a single literary text. This phenomenon is the subject of another essay, entitled "Intervento sul discorso libero indiretto" (Notes on Free Indirect Discourse). Here Pasolini describes the ways in which an author may absorb or ma-

---

[76] Bakhtin explores these plurilinguistic effects at length in his *Esthétique et théorie du roman* (Paris: Gallimard, 1975), especially in the chapter entitled "Du discours romanesque."

[77] Pasolini, *Empirismo eretico*, p. 199.

nipulate his characters in order to express his own vision through them. And, significantly, this takes place *without* any mimesis of vision. Thus acknowledging what he refused to admit in "Il cinema di poesia," Pasolini writes:

> Entire novels are really entire Free Indirect [Discourses] in that either the author identifies totally with a character, or the characters are a pseudo-objectification of the author, or the characters are mechanisms to express, in a substantially similar language, the author's thesis, or lastly—unconciously—the characters inhabit in exactly the same way the social and ideological world of the author.[78]

But the most illuminating essay written that year—one that might be seen as a very personal ars poetica—concerns neither contemporary novel nor film. Instead, it is devoted to Dante, that other great public poet whose presence haunted Pasolini's universe from the opening preface of *Accattone* to the last shots of *Salò*. I would not venture to say how much "La volontà di Dante a essere poeta" ("Dante's Will to Be a Poet") reveals about the towering figure of Dante; a number of critics certainly took issue with Pasolini's interpretation of his great predecessor.[79] But it does say a great deal about Pasolini. For the play of tensions—both formal and ideological—that he perceives in Dante is almost exactly the same as that characterizing both his literary and cinematic oeuvre.

At the core of this revealing essay lies Pasolini's conviction that *La divina commedia* has a "double nature"—one that stems from the presence of two opposing "registers." One register, turned to the "things of this world," is sociological; the other, allegorical and teleological. Pursuing the distinction between poetry and prose that informs "Il cinema di poesia," Pasolini proceeds to note that the teleological register, where a rapid, functional rhythm attempts to convince and convert, is—paradoxically— marked by the language of prose. Here the characters are presented as in a novel, and not with the "hallucinatory immediacy of poetry which transfixes figures in an absolute, inalienable moment which is also unanalyzable, stupendously arbitrary and impressionistic."[80] It is, rather, the sociological register—which records the political events and violent human dramas of Florence—that is marked by poetry: the "teeming details" of everyday life are presented through "slow rhythms" and "poetic fixations." Postulating—as he did for modernist cinema—an unconscious desire on Dante's part "to create poetry as poetry" ("dare poesia in quanto poesia"), Pasolini now asks where, precisely, this desire is located. Be-

[78] Ibid., p. 97.

[79] One of the harshest appraisals of Pasolini's essay on Dante came from Cesare Segre in his "La volontà di Pasolini 'a' essere Dantista," *Paragone* No. 190 (December 1965), pp. 80–84.

[80] Pasolini, *Empirismo eretico*, p. 112.

cause Dante separates the two registers, it is not found—and here *La divina commedia* is most unlike the "cinema of poetry"—in the lines of "suture" connecting the two registers, lines that might reveal "points of friction, of scandal, of expressive instability." Instead, this poetic irrationalism is embodied, in Pasolini's eyes, in the will to maintain an obsessive "unity"—a unity "inexplicable" and even "schizophrenic" in light of the double nature of the great poem.

Until his concluding remarks about Dante's "unity," Pasolini might well be describing himself. His work—like that of the great medieval poet—reveals a blend of the temporal and the teleological, of poetry and prose, of allegory and naturalism. Dante's "slow rhythms" find their cinematic counterpart in Pasolini's lingering camera, which fixes and isolates fragments of reality. But if Dante imposed an "obsessive unity" on his work, Pier Paolo Pasolini—who so desperately wanted to breach the distance between himself and the "things of this world"—did not. And it is precisely this lack of unity—that is, the "expressive clash" or unstable balance at the core of his work—that gave rise to so many different readings, so many scandals. From the very first, those who wanted to see only the social and temporal side of *Accattone* complained about the film's mythic overlay and charged Pasolini with a lack of historicity; when, after his death, *Salò* was finally released, critics objected to the highly charged presence of history at the heart of an allegory.

Even from film to film, this balance seemed to sway and change as it rendered Pasolini a more protean figure than anyone else in the world of film. Of all his films, *Uccellacci e Uccellini*—which he called a "poetic operetta in the language of prose"—is perhaps the most delicately balanced between the "real" world and that of myth, between poetry and prose, naturalism and fable. After this watershed film, Pasolini appeared to enter an allegorical universe marked by poetic leitmotifs, hieratic tableaux, and chiseled structural patterns. But even this mythic world was not devoid of naturalistic elements: his versions of the dramas of Oedipus and Medea carry a tremendous charge of physical presence, of corporeality. It is these films—so clearly marked by the "language of poetry"—that are the subject of the next chapter.

V

Myth: The Other Side of Realism

PUNCTUATED BY EXTREME stylistic ruptures and expressive clashes, Pasolini's films of the late 1960s bear witness to virtually all the artistic and existential concerns that animate his theories. Here the savagery and barbarism that he locates at the heart of cinema inform not only the hypothetical *"monstrum"* behind each film but the narrative itself—a narrative propelled by dark and savage impulses that well up from the unconscious of individuals and from mankind's archaic past. History gives way to myth as the linear time of Christianity is eclipsed by what Mircea Eliade—the famous ethnologist much admired by Pasolini—calls the "eternal return" of earlier religions.[1] In addition to Eliade, other ethnologists and anthropologists—Lucien Lévy-Bruhl and Sir James George Frazer—nourished Pasolini's fascination with prehistory, with what he called the "permanence of great myths in modern life." As if completing a circle, his depiction of archaic civilizations in the films of the mythic quartet would later move critics to praise the director's own ethnological bent.[2]

Inspiration for the cinematic re-creation of mankind's imaginary past came not only from works of anthropology and ethnology but also from journeys. Continuing the travels that had begun with trips to Palestine and India (the latter trip, undertaken with Moravia, resulted in his 1962 travel essay "L'odore dell'India" [Milan: Longanesi]), in the course of the 1960s Pasolini visited other countries of the Third World. Weaving his love of these places into his filmmaking activities, he used African and Middle Eastern locations for several of his films. He was particularly at-

[1] Pasolini discusses Eliade at some length in a review of the latter's *Myth and Reality*. See Pasolini, *Descrizioni di descrizioni* (Turin: Einaudi, 1979), pp. 367–371.

[2] Referring both to Pasolini's representation of the *borgata* in his early films as well as his re-creation of archaic civilizations in the mythic quartet, Alessandro Cappabianca calls him "the first and only great anthropologist of cinema." See Cappabianca, "Prodigi e incidenti sulle vie del cinema italiano," *Filmcritica* No. 244 (April 1974), p. 125. And, in a seminar devoted to "Visual Anthropology and Pasolini's Cinema," conducted at the University of Rome in 1984–1985, Massimo Canevacci suggested that *Medea* is a "masterpiece of visual anthropology." In his view, the opening sequence, which depicts an act of human sacrifice, captures basic human rituals: the "Dionysian sacrifice of death and resurrection (mystical and proto-eucharistic ecstasy), the great feast and the overturning of roles (flogging, laughter and revelry), the exchange of identities (masks and proto-theater), dances of mimicry (musical and bodily frenzy). A formal ritual that has been perpetuated by cinema."

tracted to Africa, which provided the inspiration for a series of poems; an unrealized screenplay, *Il padre selvaggio* (*The Savage Father*, [Milan: Einaudi, 1975]); and one of his most interesting and personal documentaries, *Appunti per una orestiade africana* (*Notes for an African Oresteia*, 1970).

Like his feature films of these years, both *Il padre selvaggio* and *Appunti per una orestiade africana* explore the ways in which age-old habits of thought and being persist in the modern world—physically, as in Third World countries; spiritually, as in poetry. Both works explore the clash, the mingling, of vastly different strands of civilization. *Il padre selvaggio* depicts a young African boy who is driven to the brink of madness when, spellbound by the teachings of a strangely attractive young European schoolmaster, he begins to feel alienated from his own culture. In *Appunti per una orestiade africana*, the clash of civilizations is seen in collective rather than individual terms. Within the film itself, Pasolini explores his desire to make a modern, African *Oresteia*—one informed by the parallels he perceives between the evolution of ancient Greek civilization and that of contemporary Black Africa. He is convinced, he tells us in the commentary, that just as the archaic moment of Greek civilization—a moment embodied in the Furies who hounded Orestes—gave way to the democratic state ruled by the Eumenides, so, too, in the last century has Africa gone from a tribal and "savage" state to one of "civil democracy." As the camera shows us the faces of contemporary Africans, Pasolini asks if this particular woman, this particular man, could be a modern Electra or an Orestes. Instead of having people embody the "irrational" and "animalistic" Furies, he muses, perhaps these archaic creatures might take the form of weirdly shaped African trees—"spectral" and "atrocious" trees that seem to come alive in the wind as they are captured by the camera. While discussing the evolution of the Furies in Aeschylus' *Oresteia*, Pasolini returns to the central idea of "Il cinema di poesia": it is works of art, he insists, that bear the traces of our savage past.

> The Furies who dominated the whole first part of the tragedy as Goddesses of a Tradition—a Tradition which was, precisely, full of blood and permeated by terror—are not destroyed at the end by the Goddesses of reason but transformed. Thus they remain irrational and archaic divinities; but instead of inspiring atrocious, obsessed, and degrading dreams, they reign over works of poetry, of affective imagination.[3]

Like his love for Friuli or his fascination with the Roman *borgate*, Pasolini's attraction to the Third World had deep existential roots. As the

---

[3] Pasolini, *Cinema in forma di poesia*, ed. de Guisti (Pordenone: Cinemazero, 1979), p. 80.

Italian film historian Guido Aristarco observes, Pasolini always sought companions and "brothers in the ruins, among primitives and 'savages.' "[4] Sexuality may have been the principal motive that drew him to these lands, but it was by no means the only factor. His longing for traditional civilizations seemed to grow as, increasingly, he felt repelled by the new Italy he saw emerging all about him. By the late 1960s he was convinced that the leveling forces of bourgeois consumerism had all but destroyed the regional differences—reflected in people, dialects, ways of life—that had formerly attached him to his native land. The imaginary barbaric, or archaic, civilizations envisioned in his films were essentially conceived, then, as polar opposites of a modern world he detested. Contrasting the contemporary world to what he called a "prehistoric" past, he remarked to one interviewer: "The barbarians that I depict are always outside history, they are never *historical*. The barbarians in *Medea* are invented: I reconstructed them by ethnological research and by my imagination. In my films, barbarism is always symbolic: it represents the ideal moment of mankind."[5]

The striking and idealized portrait of archaic civilizations found in Pasolini's mythic quartet foregrounds the contrast between past and present which, in various ways, had made itself felt throughout his films. After all, *Accattone* and *Mamma Roma* juxtapose a sacred past—evoked by the presence of Bach and Vivaldi as well as painterly allusions—with a degraded present; reversing the process, *Il Vangelo* depicts the life of Christ through analogies with the contemporary world. With *Uccellacci e Uccellini*, this essential contrast became explicit even as it determined the very structure of the film: the tale told by the crow is set in the past and framed by the modern episodes. With the exception of *Teorema*, Pasolini's films of the late 1960s resemble *Uccellacci e Uccellini* in that narrative divisions correspond to, and reinforce, this fundamental dichotomy between past and present—a dichotomy, as the 1960s drew to a close, that became ever more absolute, permeated and heightened by a series of elemental oppositions that saw nature and culture, taboo and transgression, at war with with one another.

Imbued with primordial oppositions, the world of the mythic quartet is one ruled by Furies who have not yet shed their "archaic and irrational" form. But if these bloodthirsty Goddesses pursue all of Pasolini's doomed protagonists, the guise they assume—that is, the stylistic register they impel—differs greatly from film to film. Violent and barbaric in the two films based on Greek myth—*Edipo Re* (*Oedipus Rex*, 1967) and *Me-*

---

[4] Guido Aristarco, "Jung et de Seta, Freud et Pasolini," *Cinema 69* (Paris) No. 135 (April 1969), p. 98.

[5] Pasolini, "Interview with Michel Maingois," *Zoom* (October 1974), p. 24.

dea (1969)—in *Teorema* (1968) and *Porcile* (*Pigpen,* 1969) the Furies are, instead, cold and precise in their unrelenting cruelty. And because the stylistic differences separating these two sets of films are so great, I shall break slightly with chronology and, leaving *Edipo Re* to be discussed later with *Medea,* begin with a look at Pasolini's two modern parables, *Teorema* and *Porcile.*

In retrospect, it is clear that (with the brief exception of *La ricotta*) these two films opened a new chapter in Pasolini's cinema—a chapter devoted to the "diseased flowers of the bourgeoisie," to the class whose "complacency and vulgarity" aroused in him a hatred he described as "visceral and profound."[6] If he had not depicted the bourgeoisie before *Teorema,* he told Oswald Stack, it was because he could not "bear to live with characters [he] could not stand for months on end."[7] The hatred he felt for the contemporary bourgeoisie was, in fact, one of the dominant themes, perhaps *the* dominant theme, of a weekly essay Pasolini wrote for the newspaper *Il caos* in the course of these years, that is, from 1968 to 1970. Both the polemical tone and the striking metaphors that would become a trademark of his journalistic writings were evident in the very first essay he published in *Il caos*: emphatically declaring that the bourgeoisie is not a "class," he deemed it instead a "contagious illness," a kind of "vampire" that would not be satisfied until it had rendered all its victims "as pale, sad, ugly, lifeless, twisted, corrupted, uneasy, full of guilt, calculating, aggressive and terroristic *as itself.*"[8]

Inevitably, Pasolini's critique of the bourgeoisie—which grew ever more intense not only in his journalistic writings but also in his films, as he went, first, from *Teorema* to *Porcile* and, finally, to *Salò*—was exacerbated by a deep sense of self-hatred. Tremendously lucid and self-aware, he could never forget that he himself came from the bourgeois world he so despised, that he carried its mark and depended upon it. Seeing his own worst tendencies mirrored in this world, he bitterly observed that he, too—like his friends Moravia and Bertolucci—was a "bourgeois, or even a petit-bourgeois, an asshole, convinced that his stink was not only a perfume, but the only perfume in the world. I, too, am marked by the . . . aestheticism and humor which characterize petit-bourgeois intellectuals."[9] Moreoever—and this made his drama particularly painful—he was not only a petit-bourgeois intellectual: he was *also* a Marxist. Condemned, thus, to struggle against the very class that gave him, as he said,

---

[6] Cited by Jean Duflot, *Entretiens* (Paris: Belfond, 1970), p. 14.

[7] Cited by Oswald Stack, *Pasolini* (Bloomington and London: Indiana University Press, 1969), p. 155.

[8] Pasolini, *Il caos* (Rome: Riuniti, 1979), p. 39.

[9] Pasolini, *Edipo Re* (Milan: Garzanti, 1967), p. 11.

"the modes and means of production," his dilemma could hardly have
been more acute:

> In my mortal body, I live the problems of history *ambiguously*. History is the
> history of the class struggle: but while I live the struggle against the bourgeoisie
> (against myself), at the same time I am consumed by the bourgeoisie, and it is
> the bourgeoisie that offers me the modes and means of production. This con-
> tradiction is not healthy and [yet] it cannot be lived in any other fashion.[10]

Tout puème est un blason: il faut le déchiffrer.
  —Jean Cocteau.

(Every poem is a blazon: it must be deciphered.)

Doubtlessly fueled by this existential tension, this unresolved inner con-
flict, Pasolini's depiction of the bourgeoisie—and this is especially true of
Porcile—was stamped by an unprecedented charge of cold and savage
irony. And this ferocious irony brought with it other important changes.
For the first time, his films were dominated by professional actors: stars
of "bourgeois" Italian cinema like Silvana Mangano and Ugo Tognazzi;
French performers associated with the New Wave such as Jean-Pierre
Léaud, Pierre Clementi, and Anne Wiazemsky; the English actor Terence
Stamp; and even the director Marco Ferreri. The polished acting of these
stars contributed to a highly stylized universe that banished any trace of
spontaneity, any hint of naturalism. Here formal constraints—built
around governing metaphors—reflected, and heightened, the sense of
spiritual emptiness and alienation exuded by the bourgeoisie.

The abstract, formal, and metaphorical nature of *Teorema* is implicit
in its very title, since a theorem denotes a kind of logical or mathematical
problem with premises, (possible) permutations, and conclusion. And,
like a theorem, Pasolini's highly elliptical film is rigorously divided into
precise parts or movements—movements structured around the visit of a
mysterious stranger. The film begins with a brief prologue (later revealed
as a flash forward) that recalls television documentaries or *cinéma vérité*:
eager journalists are interviewing Milanese workers who have just
learned that the factory where they work has been given to them by its
owner. Brusquely, silence replaces the journalists' frenzied questions as
the sepia tones of old newsreels fill the screen: four protagonists—lips
moving soundlessly and eerily—pass before us. Soon we learn that they
are all part of the same bourgeois household—father, and factory owner,
Paolo (Massimo Girotti); mother, Lucia (Silvana Mangano); daughter,

---

[10] *Con Pier Paolo Pasolini*, ed. Enrico Magrelli (Rome: Bulzoni, 1977), p. 91.

Odetta (Anne Wiazemsky); and son, Pietro (Andrès-José Cruz). (In the eyes of one critic, even the names of the characters are allegorical.[11]) This sequence closes with the first overt indication of the theorem's symbolic and religious core: in a kind of annunciation, an angelic postman (Ninetto Davoli) comes to the family's stately mansion to deliver a telegram that reads simply, "I'm coming tomorrow." Handing the telegram to the family's servant, Emilia (played by Pasolini's friend Laura Betti), the postman departs gaily, his arms moving like the wings of an angel.

Color suddenly replaces black and white as voices break the silence: the mysterious visitor (played by the handsome Terence Stamp) has arrived. Asked to discuss the "premises" of his frequently mysterious theorem, Pasolini described the allegorical meaning of the visitor thus: "A mysterious character who is divine love arrives in a bourgeois family. It's the intrusion of metaphysics and the authentic which come to destroy and overturn an existence which is entirely inauthentic."[12] Five parallel narrations now trace the disquieting effect this handsome stranger, the incarnation of "divine love," exerts upon each family member and upon Emilia. Without exception, each experiences inner turmoil, an overwhelming desire that impels him or her into a carnal encounter with the beautiful stranger—a "scandalous" encounter that, in Pasolini's view, strips away all the "deceptive security" each has created around himself or herself. (The sexual encounters are both abstract or "unrealistic," to use Pasolini's word, and yet insistent, even fetishistic: for example, the mother seems to worship Stamp's discarded garments; the camera lingers on parts of his body, especially his loins, although he is clothed.) The allegorical, religious nature of this "scandalous" love is, perhaps, clearest in the scenes between the father and the visitor—scenes where the overtones of homosexuality and incest bathing the film are also strongest. (The visitor, as Pasolini observed, acts as a kind of "son" in the family.[13]) Before the visitor and the father go off into the woods, where they will make love, we hear a quote from Jeremiah that insists on the "divinity" of the stranger and the allegorical message at the heart of the film: "You have seduced me, God, and I let myself be seduced; you have raped me and you have triumphed. I have become an object of mockery every day, all

[11] Noel Purdon observes that the men bear Pasolini's own name (Paolo, Pietro), while Lucia evokes "light" and Odetta suggests the theme of sexual love and perhaps inversion in Proust's *A la recherche du temps perdu*. Emilia is the region where Pasolini was born. See Purdon, "Pasolini: The Film of Alienation," in *Pier Paolo Pasolini*, ed. Paul Willemin (London: British Film Institute, 1977), p. 44.

[12] Pasolini, "*Teorema*," *Jeune cinéma* No. 33 (October 1968), p. 7.

[13] He went on to say that in *Teorema* "incest is multiplied at least by five and is mixed with the idea of God." "Interview with Jean-André Fieschi," *Cahiers du cinéma* No. 195 (November 1967), p. 13.

make fun of me." Both music (Mozart's *Requiem*) and lighting (Stamp is given a kind of halo) further underscore the religious nature of the quote and, of course, of the film itself.[14]

After all the sexual encounters have taken place, the angelic postman delivers a second telegram, which signals the beginning of a new narrative division. The guest, it seems, must leave as abruptly and mysteriously as he arrived. Everyone is anguished at this news. But while a reverent and silent Emilia merely kisses the stranger's hand, the family members hasten to confide their deepest problems—of alienation, identity, misplaced love—to the visitor before his departure. He finally leaves: the "mystical night," the night of transgression and ecstasy, has come to an end. Deprived of the visitor's divine love, each family member is now prey to self-disgust and self-destruction. The shy daughter becomes catatonic; the artist son urinates on his paintings; the elegant mother first picks up young men (who resemble Stamp) and then, in desperation, enters a church. All is in vain: nothing will fill the void within them since, in Pasolini's words, "the bourgeoisie has lost the sense of the sacred." Or, as Guy Scarpetta observes: "The neo-fascism of consumption . . . has definitively prohibited any transcendence: art degenerates into gesticulation, mysticism into psychosis, and eroticism into vague prostitution. . . . At the end of the theorem there is nothing else to do except flee, leave, leave everything, tear oneself from the world."[15] It is the father who does, literally, "tear himself from the world": like a Biblical character cast out by his tribe, he sheds his old life—factory, home, family, and even clothes—and, naked, begins a life of exile in a strange, volcanic desert. (Repeated shots of the desert—which Pasolini called the "visual form of the absolute, of time outside history"[16]—have been mysteriously intercut throughout the film; only at the end do we understand their significance.) In the book *Teorema*, written contemporaneously with the film, as the father wanders in the desert he utters a tormented question that raises the essential question posed by the film: "What shall prevail?" he asks. "The barrenness of the world of reason—or religion, [this] scorned fecundity that history has left behind?"[17] As the father's anguish erupts in an inhuman cry—a scream

[14] Concerning the "celestial" lighting, Elie Maakaroun notes that in the scene where the mother offers herself to the visitor, the (clothed) sex of the visitor is lighted obliquely, through a door, by the sun. In her view, this shot, reminiscent of Caravaggio, furthers the "religious sense of the film." See her "Pasolini face au sacré ou l'exorciste possédé," in *Pasolini: le mythe et le sacré*, special issue of *Etudes cinématographiques* No. 109–111 (Paris: Minard, 1976), p. 53.

[15] Guy Scarpetta, "Déracinements," *Tel Quel* No. 89 (Autumn 1981), p. 84.

[16] "Un cinéma de poésie: propos recueillis par Yvonne Baby," *Le monde*, October 12–13, 1969, p. 23.

[17] Pasolini, *Teorema* (Milan: Garzanti, 1968), p. 199.

Pasolini described as one of "vile hope" or "pure desperation"—the film draws to a close.

The father's question—where the "barrenness" of the modern, bourgeois world is opposed to the religious "fecundity" of earlier civilizations—touches on the fundamental contrast between the past and the present which so obsessed Pasolini in these years. Within the film itself, this contrast is embodied in the tremendous gap that separates the family members—symbols of the modern world—from their servant Emilia. Still tied to a peasant civilization, Emilia has not been contaminated by the bourgeois values that make "comfort and security" into a religion. Because she still possesses a sense of the divine, she reacts to the visitor's departure in a totally different way from the family members. Whereas they face only despair or madness after he leaves, she is touched by grace because she has understood, and accepted, the visitor's spiritual power. She becomes what Pasolini called a "crazy saint," or "a saint and a madwoman." (The "mad" or ironic cast that does, indeed, infuse Emilia's mystical gifts may be one more indication of Pasolini's deep religious ambivalence.) After returning to her rural birthplace, Emilia begins to work miracles: not only does she levitate herself but, in a scene that echoes one of Christ's miracles in *Il Vangelo*, she cures a little boy of terrible spots on his face. Finally, she requests that she be buried up to her eyes: before dying, she will shed tears that will become a source of life. In Pasolini's view, this fairly enigmatic scene was the most optimistic moment of the film. It reminds us, he said, that "preceding civilizations have not disappeared, but are only buried. Thus, peasant civilization remains buried under the world of workers, under industrial civilization."[18]

In light of the sexual and religious taboos broken by *Teorema*—where, after all, the divine takes the form of a beautiful young man and religious love is seen in (homo)sexual terms—it is hardly surprising that, with the exception of *Salò*, *Teorema* was probably Pasolini's most controversial film. Temporarily banned for obscenity, it was apparently deemed an "inadmissible" film by the pope himself. In retrospect, *Teorema* did, in fact, appear to inaugurate an era when Pasolini's bent for controversy took a deliberate, even calculated, turn. Its explicit portrayal of homosexuality, in particular, seemed designed to provoke violent reactions: critics called it an "autoconfession of the artist" and a "film on the difficulty of being a homosexual." One particularly harsh reviewer wrote: "The 'stranger' in *Teorema* resembles nothing so much as the symbolical figure at the center of the most homosexual fantasy, i.e., the 'emancipated' one moving among the uninitiated, covertly undoing their delusions of normal-

---

[18] Cited by Duflot, *Entretiens*, p. 109.

ity."[19] Compelled to defend his film, Pasolini moved from explanations and justifications—sexuality was used, he asserted, merely as a metaphor or "language" to depict an "authenticity" that could not be transmitted by words[20]—to counterattack. For example, as if to shock his critics further, he maintained that the divine visitor was no more "scandalous" than God himself.

If, as Pasolini's remarks suggest, the most controversial aspect of *Teorema* stemmed from its unorthodox blend of religion and sex, for many critics on the left it also had disturbing political implications. Unlike, say, *Il Vangelo*, which had focused on the *social* sins of those in power, here the bourgeoisie stood accused not of class exploitation but of spiritual emptiness. It was hardly surprising that one left-wing critic wanted the film to "auto-destruct" like the members of the bourgeois family; still another questioned the value of a "parable that is suspended in the air— like the servant—without contradictions, without proofs, without dialectical conflict?"[21] Even the father's renunciation of his factory was a source of ideological concern: in addition to showing the bourgeoisie in a good light, it suggested a decidedly non-Marxist path to social redemption.[22] Significantly, the film found more support among Catholics than among Marxists. For example, Marc Gervais, a Canadian priest who later wrote a book on Pasolini, observed that despite its "suspect" erotic sensibility, *Teorema*'s "mystical character cannot be questioned. It is an interrogation into the human condition. It is a work on the need to [reach] the

[20] The first remarks are cited by Luciano de Guisti in his *I film di Pasolini* (Rome: Gremese, 1983), p. 99. The last is found in *Films in Review*, June 6, 1969, p. 377.

[19] Alluding to the long stretches of silence in the film, Pasolini observed: "The relationship between authenticity and inauthenticity is impossible at the level of linguistic communication: in fact the young guest does not speak to the other characters nor seek to convince them with words but, rather, has a relationship of love with them. And it is here that the film is totally symbolic. When the guest leaves, the other characters are completely transformed . . . [but] they are not capable of understanding the authenticity that came to them. Thus the interruption of authenticity into an inauthentic world does nothing but put them into crisis, a crisis that is already a form of salvation." Cited by de Guisti in *I film di Pasolini*, p. 95. Originally in *Corriere della Sera*, November 10, 1968.

[21] Umberto Silva, "*Teorema*," *Filmcritica* No. 193 (December 1968), p. 549; Pascal Bonitzer, "Le carré," *Cahiers du cinéma* No. 211 (April 1969), p. 53.

[22] Asked specifically about the political meaning of the father's gesture in renouncing his factory, Pasolini observed that, like the reactions of all the family members, it was "suspended" and "open." Like the others, the father was going through a crisis he was powerless to resolve. Nonetheless, Pasolini continued, although the father's gesture was "absolutely negative" in a "strictly political and social context" (i.e., it was still the gesture of an owner), from a personal viewpoint it represented a certain liberation because "he is the only active character of the family although his secular, bourgeois education does not allow him, in spite of his mystical choice, a positive way out." See "*Théorème*: la démonstration de Pier Paolo Pasolini," *Cinéma 69* (Paris) No. 136 (May 1969), p. 112.

absolute and to reject the bourgeois condition that alienates man."[23] *Teorema* even won a prize from a Catholic group, the Office Catholique International du Cinéma. More conservative Catholics were enraged by this, and the ensuing polemics did nothing to lessen the aura of scandal surrounding the film.

Teorema's scandalous admixture of sex and religion was not repeated in Pasolini's next film about the bourgeoisie. Still, *Porcile was* extremist and desperate—a "poem," said Pasolini, "in the form of a cry of despair."[24] Its extremism clearly reflected a sense of political desperation which events of 1968 had brought to fever pitch: by the time he made *Porcile*, Pasolini (as I shall show in the next chapter) was estranged from the militant "new left" as well as the Communist party. And he was even losing his faith in the Third World: there, too, he sensed, the virus of consumerism was taking hold. At a time when other intellectuals still looked to China or Cuba as a revolutionary model, he pessimistically described the idea of a Third World revolution thus: "Ten years ago it was a myth, a poetic madness, a *raptus*. . . . Now it is clear that the force of this idea is purely psychological and mythical."[25]

The differences between *Teorema* and *Porcile* reveal how much the strife-torn year of 1968 had affected Pasolini. *Teorema*, after all, had shown a certain compassion toward the bourgeoisie; the torment experienced by the bourgeois family members is seen as a form of possible salvation. One year later, even this slight ray of hope had vanished. The bourgeois characters of *Porcile* are not pathetic but, instead, grotesque and despicable. And, while the humble servant of *Teorema* is moved by a religious, if "mad," impulse, the prehistoric protagonist of *Porcile* represents nothing more than pure, doomed defiance. Going from *Teorema* to *Porcile* clearly meant, as one critic phrased it, exchanging "a fragile hope for change [for] a declaration of impotence."[26]

Both figuratively and literally, *Porcile* begins where*Teorema* ends—in that same bleak, windswept volcanic desert (the desert sequences in both films were shot near Etna) where the father of *Teorema* uttered his last anguished cry. The implicit contrast between past and present in *Teorema* becomes explicit in *Porcile*, as Pasolini crosscuts between two narratives set in different eras. The so-called "prehistoric" narrative (which is absolutely silent until the very end) takes place in this lunar desert; the con-

---

[23] Cited by de Guisti in *I film di Pasolini*, p. 95. Originally in *Le nouvel observateur*, December 23, 1968.

[24] Cited by Duflot, *Entretiens*, p. 83.

[25] Cited by Ferdinando Camon, *Il mestiere di scrittore* (Milan: Garzanti, 1973), p. 115.

[26] Michel Estève, "Un cri de désespoir: *Porcherie*," in *Pasolini: Le mythe et le sacré*, p. 72.

temporary episode, which depicts another wealthy bourgeois household, unfolds in modern Germany. Although the two tales are linked only by the presence of Ninetto Davoli (who plays a witness or "spy" in both), the full meaning of each emerges only in relationship to the other. "Let's say that the 'ahistoricity' of the tale in the desert is reflected, explained," said Pasolini, "by the historicity of the German fable. And vice versa."[27]

As the "prehistoric" tale begins, a young man (with the singular features of Pierre Clementi) is hungrily foraging for food: eagerly, he devours grasses, butterflies, and snakes. In the course of his wanderings he comes upon a gun and, before long, uses it to kill a passing soldier. As he pulls the trigger, his face is lit by a strange and voluptuous expression. The soldier's body is quickly dismembered, the head tossed into the smoking volcano, the rest cooked and eaten. Before long, the young man is joined by a companion (Franco Citti) and a few women, and he becomes the leader of a little band of cannibals that preys on travelers. (Gruesome scenes depict another head thrown into the volcano, human limbs strewn around the fire, and so forth.) By chance, their terrible deeds are witnessed by a young peasant (Ninetto Davoli) who quickly carries news of the cannibals back to his town. The village elders stake a beautiful naked couple in the desert as a lure to trap the unsuspecting band members. The ruse is successful and the cannibals are captured and sentenced to death. Asked to repent, they cry and kiss a crucifix. All, that is, except their leader: refusing to yield to society, a proud Clementi thrice utters his first, terrible, words: "I have killed my father, eaten human flesh, and I am trembling with joy." Arms and legs outspread, he and the others are staked to the ground and left to be devoured by wild beasts.

In the modern episode (which has been intercut with the eerie "prehistoric" tale), bestiality replaces cannibalism as the governing metaphor. Julian (Jean-Pierre Léaud), the modern counterpart of the young cannibal, is the son of a German businessman. He is obsessed by a terrible secret and—indifferent to his girlfriend, Ida, as well as the family business—he falls into a catatonic state. Meanwhile, his wealthy father, Herr Klotz (Alberto Lionello), guided by his crafty business adviser (Marco Ferreri), plots to ruin his major business rival, Herr Herdhitze (Ugo Tognazzi) by revealing the latter's past as a Nazi criminal. The ex-Nazi parries this blackmail by threatening to expose Julian's terrible secret: the young man, it seems, loves pigs. Instead of destroying each other through mutual blackmail, the two practical businessmen decide to join forces. As they celebrate their merger, a group of terrified peasants (led by Ninetto Davoli) comes to report a hideous event: the pigs have killed and eaten

[27] Pasolini, "Un cinéma de poésie: Propos recuellis par Yvonne Baby," p. 23.

Julian. Ever pragmatic, ex-Nazi Herdhitze takes care to hush up the episode, making sure that literally no sign of Julian remains.

Even this brief summary suggests that the parable informing *Porcile* is
probably more closed and obscure than that of *Teorema*. In fact, when
the film was first shown at the Venice festival, Pasolini had *Porcile* accompanied by explanatory remarks clarifying the relationship between the
two tales. Declaring that *Porcile* was imbued with a "desperate defiance
toward all historical societies," he noted that the film shows that society
devours its sons, "both those that are disobedient, and those who neither
obey nor disobey. Sons must obey. That's all."[28] The "disobedient" son is
obviously the cannibal: while he may have eaten his first victim out of
hunger, it is clear, says Pasolini, that his cannibalism soon became a "kind
of madness, an ecstasy, a drug." A symbol of total revolt—like his confessed parricide—cannibalism, declared Pasolini, is a "semiological system," a form of "extremism pushed to the limit of scandal, of rebellion,
of horror. It is also a system of exchange or, if you prefer, one of total
refusal—therefore, [it is] a form of language, a monstrous refusal of normally accepted human communication."[29]

Unlike the young cannibal—whom Pasolini saw as a "saint of global
protest," a kind of Nietzschean intellectual who defies social norms—the
weaker Julian neither obeys nor disobeys. But his very passiveness, his
withdrawal, poses an implicit challenge to society: Julian, said Pasolini,
"makes poetry with his life and that is why society, totally dominated by
reason, devours him."[30] Drawn to both "sons"—who clearly represent
different aspects of himself—Pasolini remarked that he identified with the
"apocalyptic anarchy" of the young cannibal as well as with Julian's poetic, mysterious, and perhaps masochistic, nature. Noting that he felt
even closer to Julian than to the young cannibal, he explained his fundamental affinity for both of them, declaring simply: "As for me, I am on
the side of victims."[31]

While the alternation of the two tales suggests that every institutional-
ized society is repressive, the modern episode—explicitly set under the
sign of neocapitalism—has still further political ramifications. It hints at
the similarities—which would obsess Pasolini in the coming years—between what he called the "old" Fascism, that is, the Fascism of Hitler and
Mussolini, and the "new" fascism of contemporary neocapitalism. Go-

---

[28] "Note sur *Porcile*," *Jeune cinéma* No. 41 (October 1969), p. 16. Extracts from these
remarks are also included in de Guisti's *I film di Pier Paolo Pasolini* and in *Il cinema in
forma di poesia*.

[29] Cited by Duflot, *Entretiens*, p. 95.

[30] "Un cinéma de poésie: Propos recueillis par Yvonne Baby," p. 23.

[31] Cited by Piero Sanavìo in "*Porcile* o no tiriamo le somme su Pasolini," *Il Dramma* Vol.
45, No. 12 (September 1969), p. 85.

desberg itself, the West German town where Julian's family lives, provides a link between these two "fascisms": a resort town that now attracts wealthy West German businessmen, it was in Godesberg that Hitler delivered his ultimatum on Czechoslovakia. But the strongest link between Nazism and capitalism is embodied in the figure of Herr Herdhitze, a perfect Nazi turned successful businessman; the savagery that he formerly displayed toward Jews has now been channeled into making profits. The fact that Julian's father, a kind of latter-day Krupp, agrees to a merger with this brutal ex-Nazi—a merger that also incarnates, of course, the continuity between the two "fascisms"—demonstrates, said Pasolini, that the "alliance between the old and the new capitalism [is] cemented by the eternal hypocrisy of class."[32] As if to underline the ferocious nature of their "alliance," Pasolini implicitly compares the two businessmen to cannibals by the manner in which he crosscuts between the two episodes. Clearly, it is these wealthy "fathers," and not the innocent animals beloved by Julian, who are the real "pigs" of Porcile.

Not surprisingly, Porcile was Pasolini's least successful film. Neither its gruesome subject matter nor its abstract nature was designed to please audiences. Critics who had found Teorema too "cerebral" were undoubtedly only further dismayed by Pasolini's second parable about the bourgeoisie. To a large degree, this apparent disregard for audience sensibility was deliberate. As Pasolini repeatedly made clear in the course of these years—and I shall return to this issue later—he was possessed by a growing desire to make works that would not be easily "consumed" by the mass public. His very embrace of allegory seemed tinged with this defiance: long an unfashionable genre ("the critical suppression of allegory," observes the critic Craig Owens, "is one legacy of romantic art that was inherited uncritically by modernism"[33]), allegory is also one whose abstract nature seems particularly ill suited to the immediate and direct nature of cinema.

This is not to suggest, of course, that Pasolini was the first, or the only, filmmaker to venture onto the lonely terrain of allegory. Although this territory has appeared most beckoning during repressive eras when directors could not express themselves openly (in, say, occupied France or Franco's Spain), allegory has also attracted filmmakers as diverse as Cocteau, Buñuel, Fassbinder, and Wenders. Still, few have used allegory in as unequivocal and pronounced a fashion as Pasolini. Particularly in Teorema and Porcile, nothing—neither realistic characters nor believable

---

[32] Cited by Duflot, Entretiens, p. 84.

[33] Craig Owens, "The Allegorical Impulse: Toward a Theory of Post-modernism," October No. 12 (Spring 1980), p. 69.

events—is allowed to detract from the intellectual relationship between two texts which lies at the very heart of parable. As Pasolini himself noted, in these films there is never any doubt that "each thing represents another." The strange visitor of *Teorema* represents divine love just as surely as the cannibalism of *Porcile* is a symbol of disobedience. Other readings, particularly psychoanalytic ones, may build upon the intended parable, but none can afford to ignore it.

By making films that were clearly abstract and symbolic—that is, films demanding a process of interpretation—Pasolini was, of course, fore-grounding the hermeneutical impulse that marked his cinema from the very first. As a critic for *Cahiers du cinéma*, Serge Daney, remarked: "In-terpretation is a privileged theme in Pasolini, be it in *Il Vangelo*, the enigma of the Sphinx [in *Edipo Re*] or the language of the birds [in *Uccel-lacci e Uccellini*]."[34] A poet above all else, it is hardly surprising that Pa-solini was fascinated by the metaphors and symbols of allegory. Perhaps more noteworthy is the fact that he transferred this interest—which is usually seen as a literary one—to film. Soon after making *Accattone*, in fact, he observed: "The only serious difficulty that a writer must confront to express himself while 'shooting' is that metaphor doesn't exist."[35] But then, as if to test himself against this "serious difficulty," somehow to subvert filmic conventions, he proceeded to introduce metaphor into his films. At first, it took the shape of poetic leit-motifs, repeated images, and allegorical figures (such as the poor and hungry extra of *La ricotta*). By the time he made *Uccellacci e Uccellini*, however, metaphor had so thor-oughly infused the entire film that it became, to use Pasolini's word, a kind of fable. And it was a fable, as Daney suggests, that contained within itself still another fable—that is, the tale told by the crow—which con-cerned the very process of interpretation itself. Before the friars can teach the birds the nature of Christian love, they must decode the language of both hawks and sparrows. Noting that *Uccellacci e Uccellini* was, indeed, "permeated by metaphor," Pasolini proceeded to remark, "I wanted to make a film that would be metaphorical, that would continually allude to something, that would be both an apologue for something else and still have a value in itself."[36]

In respect to fable and allegory, as in so many other ways, *Uccellacci e Uccellini* was a watershed film. It was Pasolini's last film where allegory was muted by naturalism and humor, where the film was "both an apo-logue for something else and still [had] a value in itself." After that, as in the two surrealistic fables with Totò and Ninetto, Pasolini would turn away from the everyday world, from believable people and ordinary

[34] Serge Daney, "Le désert rouge," *Cahiers du cinéma* No. 212 (May 1968), p. 62.
[35] *Con Pier Paolo Pasolini*, p. 20.
[36] Ibid., p. 81.

events; instead, he would seek a "reality which [had] nothing to do with realism."[37] And it is this "reality"—stripped of any hint of realism or naturalism—that is evoked in *Teorema* and *Porcile*. Composed, in the words of one critic, of "metaphors and a multiplicity of signs,"[38] these films resemble hermetic, self-enclosed objects that have been sealed against the outer world. Significantly, the same year he made *Porcile*, that is, in 1969, Pasolini also returned to one of the parables he had depicted years earlier in *Il Vangelo*: in a ten-minute short, *La sequenze del fiore di carta*, he transposed into contemporary terms the Biblical tale of the innocent fig tree that is mysteriously struck down by God.[39]

An indication of his lifelong aversion to realism, the central role played by allegory in Pasolini's films of the late 1960s was also part of a complex system of formal and thematic changes—a system whereby style became, in Pasolini's words, "rigorous to the point of provocation."[40] In his view, this tremendous concern with form—which is also strongly marked in his theoretical essays of this period—was a reaction to the ideological and political crisis, the "collapse of a world," depicted in *Uccellacci e Uccellini*. In the course of a 1971 interview he remarked that after making that film he

> sought forms of stylistic crystallization that would confer guaranties of stability and "form" upon uncertainty and chaos. . . . [Faced] with a disintegrating world . . . I felt a more pressing need to create "objects": works which were like "slices of life" lived intellectually.[41]

The greater the threat of "chaos" and uncertainty, then, the more he felt that formal rigor and "stylistic crystallization" were absolutely essential. It seemed as if horror and chaos could be kept at bay, distanced, only through "great purity and formal clarity." Hence *Porcile*, where horror borders on the unthinkable, became a "rational mosaic of aberrant stories . . . an attempt to write a Petrarchian sonnet about a subject by Lautréamont."[42]

In these polished and self-contained artifacts, these intellectual "slices

---

[37] "Pasolini sur *Théorème*," *La Quinzaine littéraire*, March 1–15, 1969, p. 25.

[38] Pascal Bonitzer, "Le carré," p. 53.

[39] *La sequenza del fiore di carta* constitutes one of the episodes in *Amore e rabbia* (1969). As the film opens, Ninetto Davoli is gaily skipping down one of Rome's busiest shopping streets. As he does so, newsreel scenes of war and devastation—in Algeria, Cuba, Hungary—are superimposed on his smiling face. Ignoring the voice of God which urges him to pay attention to these events, he is struck down and killed because, like the fig tree, he "does not understand because he is immature and innocent and so at the end God condemns him and makes him die." Cited by Stack, *Pasolini*, p. 131. Pasolini went on to say that, in his view, this parable "expresses all that is inexplicable and contradictory" in the Gospel.

[40] Pasolini, "Io non cerco lo scandalo," *Cineforum* No. 85 (May 1969), p. 317.

[41] *Con Pier Paolo Pasolini*, p. 92.

[42] "Note sur *Porcile*," *Jeune cinéma*, p. 16.

of life," everything had to have a purpose, a place, a significance. This new rigor meant that incidental events and nonessential moments fell by the wayside even as everything came under the sway of a precise geometry. As suggested earlier, the very structure of *Teorema*—which is composed of two prefaces, three acts, and five parallel narrations—is rigorously mathematical. And if the structure of *Porcile* is less obviously geometrical, its bourgeois characters resemble mechanical or computerized puppets far more than the family members of *Teorema*: programmed to walk along straight lines, before speaking they carefully turn to face one another or align themselves along the points of a triangle. In turn, this stylized, implacable choreography is heightened by a camera that, as Noel Purdon observes,

> moves throughout the film with great clarity, like a compass describing a circle, or a ruler measuring the distance between two points, or a line meeting and bisecting. Typically, its frames are composed of straight lines receding into the distance, tramlines, roads, poplar avenues; and related to tangents by circles like those on the gate. . . . The effect is a sort of cubist still life. . . . This is passion . . . without blood.[43]

The formal patterns of these "cubist still lifes" demand, like everything else, that cultural allusions feed into, reflect, the ruling metaphor. Whereas earlier films had often evoked, say, paintings to alter the meaning of images—in the way that Mantegna's *Cristo morto* gives a sacred dimension to Ettore's death in *Mamma Roma*—now, instead, such references have a thematic, symbolic role. In this, they resemble *La ricotta*, where references to Pontormo suggest Pasolini's own mannerism as well as the unbridgeable gap between representation and reality. In a similar manner, a volume of Rimbaud's poems seen in *Teorema* hints at the divine stranger's Dionysian cast, at the scandalous love that he (like Rimbaud) calls forth; allusions to Bacon's paintings underline not only the son's thwarted artistic ambitions but also the torment and alienation of the family members. *Porcile*, too, uses cultural references to drive home a central message: for example, Grosz and Brecht become cultural icons even as Herr Klotz tells his wife:

> The era of Grosz and Brecht isn't over. And I could well have been drawn by Grosz as a great pig and you like a sad sow. We would be eating, of course, me with my secretary on my lap and you with your hand between the chauffeur's legs. And Brecht would have given us the parts of bad guys in a play in which the poor play the good guys.

Herr Klotz's sad admission is not only a reminder of the savage and grotesque portrait of the bourgeoisie found in Brecht and Grosz. It also epit-

[43] Noel Purdon, "Pasolini: The Film of Alienation," p. 47.

omizes, as Gian Piero Brunetta observes, the meaning of the *entire modern episode* of *Porcile*: that is, "the ability of the bourgeois world to absorb and digest any opposition."[44]

If these crystalline parables about the bourgeoisie reveal Pasolini at his most rigorously formal, they also carry what he saw as his mannerist "temptation" to its most extreme point. *La ricotta* may have mocked this temptation, but it did not exorcise it by any means: throughout Pasolini's cinema, it gave rise to startling formal and thematic contrasts, to ellipses and shifting tones, to static frontal shots and carefully composed images. Still, it was only in his films about the bourgeoisie—from *La ricotta* and *Teorema* to *Porcile* and *Salò*—that this temptation, *with its heavy dose of self-irony and implied distance from reality*, became most insistent. Only a mannerist simulacrum could, it seemed, capture the unreality and spiritual alienation of the bourgeois world. Here, what Deleuze calls the "demonic" character of the simulacrum—demonic because it replaces, *banishes* the real—both mirrors and creates a totally artificial world.[45]

Like Deleuze's discussion of the simulacrum, the notion of cinematic mannerism is relatively new. To my knowledge, the first extended discussion of it appeared in a 1985 issue of *Cahiers du cinéma*. And, not surprisingly, virtually all the *Cahiers* critics who have analyzed this phenomenon repeatedly refer to Pasolini's films. In fact, one critic, Pascal Bonitzer, places what is probably Pasolini's favorite shot—the "plan-tableau," or tableau shot (that is, a carefully composed, static shot that resembles a painting or tableau)—at the very heart of cinematic mannerism. Favored by filmmakers—like Pasolini—who prefer mise-en-scène and plastic values to narrative, the tableau shot, in Bonitzer's view, is emblematic of the unease and play of oppositions characterizing mannerism itself. Evoking Bakhtin's concept of "dialogism," the French critic argues that the tableau shot both plays upon, and subverts, the differences between painting and cinema.

> It is as if there were a quarrel, a struggle, in the film between cinema and painting. This inscribed difference, this marked disjunction between the movement of the shot and the immobility of the tableau, has a name: dialogism. The function of the plan-tableau is dialogic. Ambivalence, double discourse, unstable mixture of high (painting) and low (cinema), of movement (shot) and immobility (tableau).[46]

As an example of this "double discourse," Bonitzer turns to *La ricotta*, where the film-within-a-film not only plays on the difference(s) between

---

[44] Gian Piero Brunetta, *Forma e parola nel cinema* (Padua: Liviana, 1979), p. 105.

[45] Gilles Deleuze, *Logique du sens* (Paris: Minuit, 1969), p. 297.

[46] Pascal Bonitzer, "Le plan-tableau," *Cahiers du cinéma* No. 370 (April 1985), p. 18.

painting and cinema but is simultaneously an act of homage to Pontormo, albeit an ironic homage, and a grotesque parody of the "real" Passion.

> It must be emphasized that this homage is basically parodistic, and—in light of the theme of the film [which involves] hunger, cheese, and the poor extra who pulls the whole tableau toward the "low"—one that is, in fact, grotesque. Once again we have an unstable mix, a sort of static revolution in the hierarchy of low and high, epitomized in the *oxymoron* of the tableau vivant (which is an immobile movement).[47]

But, continues Bonitzer, the "oxymoron" of the immobile tableau shot does more than epitomize the "unstable mix" of painting and cinema. It also heightens the unease created by a cinema marked by inexplicable ellipses and startling shifts of tone and meaning. For the lack of action in such a shot means that the slightest movement is endowed with a mysterious significance, which is disturbing precisely because it is totally enigmatic: "The least batting of an eyelash, a facial tic . . . once again give rise to questions and interpretations. The whole representation becomes problematical. This living tableau ('tableau vivant'), this oxymoron incarnate, is a composite monster, a sphinx who poses riddles to Oedipus-the-spectator."[48]

There is little doubt that, like *La ricotta*, *Teorema* and *Porcile* embody the unease that Bonitzer discerns at the heart of cinematic mannerism— an unease that flows from the ambivalences of "double discourse," from mysterious and enigmatic shots, from a constant play of oppositions. Elliptical parables where parody and tragedy are in dangerous and disturbing proximity, these films demand a process of deciphering, of interpretation, even as they zealously work to guard their secrets from us. The uncertainties stemming from tableau shots—shots that constrain us, in the words of Guy Scarpetta, to seek meanings "beyond what is immediately visible"[49]—are heightened by many lacunae that punctuate the parable itself. Constant gaps of information make it impossible to reach a definitive, unequivocal, reading. As if *Porcile* were a Racinean tragedy rather than a "moving" picture, crucial scenes—like Julian's death among the pigs—are not witnessed but quickly recounted so that our desire to *see*, to *know*, is constantly thwarted. Forced, as Gian Piero Brunetta notes, somehow to complete the film ourselves, we can never emerge from the realm of the uncertain:

> The narrative elements in *Teorema* are reduced to the minimum . . . everything that happens in the course of the visitor's stay is never shown, but "suggested"

---

[47] Ibid., p. 18.
[48] Ibid., p. 18.
[49] Guy Scarpetta, "Pasolini sans légende," *Art Press* (September 1984), p. 37.

in such a way that each image involves the spectator—not emotionally, but in that he is forced to realize the work, to complete its meaning.[50]

The mannerist unease, the frustrating lacunae permeating these parables bring us back to an earlier suggestion that homosexual artists in particular often display a taste for mystery and ellipsis. Not surprisingly, the same might be said of cinematic mannerism: the names of Cocteau, Eisenstein, Murnau, and Carné immediately come to mind. Although he does not mention homosexuality in particular, another *Cahiers* critic, Patrick Mauriès, does hint at the current of hidden eroticism that drives the mannerist impulse. All too often, he remarks, discussions of mannerism slide over "its true erotic dimension which is that of ice(ing), [glaçage], of veiling, and consequently of deciphering."[51] Mauriès' observation is certainly borne out by Pasolini's cinema. Although an "erotic dimension" is felt throughout all of his films, it is strongest, certainly, in what might be called his mannerist trilogy—that is, *Teorema*, *Porcile*, and *Salò*. There a half-submerged yet powerful eroticism assumes a variety of (dis)guises. Evoking, moreover, the quintessential mannerist contrast between fire and ice, in these films burning and destructive passions are constantly repressed, checked, by the coldest of worlds imaginable. Calling *Teorema* a "constant paradox" for this very reason, Marc Gervais observes that the film "curbs its own passions, its own torment and anguish, behind an elegant and calm facade."[52] Feverish with passion and frustrated desire, the bourgeois victims of *Teorema* and *Porcile* are turned into laboratory specimens, into "pinned butterflies in a box,"[53] by a deliberately clinical style. Weightless puppets, constrained and imprisoned by precise narrative and temporal divisions, the characters move mechanically within a frozen world.[54] Hard and shiny surfaces (tiles, statues, countertops) dominate a mise-en-scène whose very colors—the yellows and mauves of Pontormo, the waxy white of dead flesh, dull grays and pinkish browns—speak of ice and death. For Julian, the pervasive yellow of *Porcile* is the color of "quinine," while to Noel Purdon it evokes a "beautifully repul-

[50] Brunetta, *Forma e parola nel cinema*, p. 113.

[51] Patrick Mauriès, "Le cinéma, l'art et la manière," *Cahiers du cinéma* No. 370 (April 1985), p. 23.

[52] Marc Gervais, "*Teorema* appare come un continuo paradosso," *Cineforum* No. 85 (May 1969), p. 324.

[53] "Un cinéma de poésie: propos recueillis par Yvonne Baby," p. 23.

[54] Father Fantuzzi, a French Catholic priest who was a friend of Pasolini's, notes that while editing *Teorema* the director deliberately sought to make his characters appear weightless or unreal: "Pasolini took [out] the scenes where Terence Stamp and Anne Wiamzemsky were together on screen, where they sat, where bodies appeared in their solidity: these scenes were suppressed and replaced by more stylized, more allusive details. [Pasolini] sought to erase everything which would recall in too heavy a way the density of the body." See Fantuzzi, "Pasolini, le scandale et le sacré," *Art Press* (September 1984), p. 38.

sive decadence."[55] In a more psychoanalytic vein, Marco Vallora writes that the "chromatic poverty and corpse-like pallor" of Pasolini's colors hint at a "world of doubt and at a secret fear of life which makes the shield preferable to the body, the mask to the face."[56]

In this world of doubt and fear, language, too, is subject to the same formal constraints, the same disturbing contrasts and tensions, as everything else. In earlier films, Pasolini's refusal to use language in a conventional, naturalist fashion had led him to experiment both with poetic texts (such as the commentary of *La rabbia*) and with long silent sequences, which evoked, for him, the "rhetorical idea of cinema as pure image."[57] For example, the dream sequence in *Accattone*, Totò's communication with the birds in *Uccellacci e Uccellini*, and his gestural wooing of Assurda in *La terra vista dalla luna* are all perfectly silent. Almost as if these experiments had convinced him that language, or the lack of language, alters the images themselves ("The word," he wrote in 1968, "does not only complete the image but renders it 'formally' different."[58]) in the films of the mythic quartet Pasolini's radical approach to both speech and silence becomes more dramatic, more central, than ever before. In *Teorema*, for example, silence gives the characters an unrealistic cast even as it permits eroticism to emerge as the only language: "For the whole length of the film, he [the visitor] limits himself to a few sentences, to reading some poems by Rimbaud—this silent relationship and this whole system of erotic signs establish the only means of communication among the protagonists of the film."[59] And silence seems an inherent component of the savage and primordial landscapes, the archaic and mythic civilizations, found not only in *Porcile* but also in *Edipo Re* and *Medea*. Here, suggests Deleuze, the absence of words (as in films by Antonioni, Resnais, or Straub) seems to reveal a kind of archaeological or geological zone marked by traces of earlier civilizations.

> It is as if, once the word withdraws itself from the image . . . the image, for its part, brings forth the foundations of space, the "undercrusts," these mute pow-

[55] Noel Purdon, "Pasolini: The Film of Alienation," p. 49. On the same page, Purdon attributes an important role to Pasolini's yellow as he observes: "As the characters in *Teorema* reached the critical points of their dilemma, their faces were composed against backgrounds in which yellow gradually came to the fore, or formed half of a bisected frame. In *Porcile*, since the protagonist is over the clinical edge from the beginning, the yellow appears immediately. More than any other single element of the composition, it both establishes Julian's sick state and allows the director himself to be honest under the guise of *un rire jaune*."

[56] Marco Vallora, "Alì dagli occhi impuri," in *Lo scandalo Pasolini*, ed. Fernaldo di Giammatteo, special issue of *Bianco e Nero* No. 23 (1976), p. 202.

[57] Pasolini, "La parola orale, meravigliosa possibilità del cinema," *Cinema nuovo* No. 201 (September–October 1969), p. 365.

[58] Pasolini, *Il caos*, p. 207.

[59] Cited by Duflot, *Entretiens*, p. 89.

ers which precede or follow words, which precede or follow men. The visual image becomes *archaeological, stratigraphic, tectonic.* We are returned not to prehistory (an archaeology of the present exists), but to the deserted layers of our time where our own phantoms lie buried. . . . Here you find Pasolini's deserts where prehistory becomes an abstract poetic element, an "essence" coexisting with our history, the Archean base which reveals an interminable history underneath our own.[60]

If the zone of prehistory is a silent one, that of the modern world is, instead, virtually defined by language. Nowhere is the fundamental contrast between these two zones, embodied in the absolute difference between language and silence, clearer than in *Porcile.* Acknowledging civilization and, at the same time, transgression, the cannibal's first, and terrible, words—"I have killed my father, I have eaten human flesh, and I'm trembling with joy"—announce a modern era marked by incessant chatter.[61] Whereas the young cannibal clings to a silence that, implicitly, refuses civilization, the bourgeois characters never cease to declaim in a highly theatrical, and totally artificial, manner. (Their dialogue reflects an interest in theater that arose in Pasolini toward the end of the 1960s.[62]) Displaying their alienation from themselves and one another, the characters recite in deliberately false tones, remain utterly detached from the meaning of their words, respond—or, more often, fail to respond—in

[60] Deleuze, *Cinéma II*, p. 317. Deleuze also argues (perhaps less convincingly) that the insistence on the physical presence of the earth, on the soil, also raises the question of history and the class struggle, since the earth is always linked to peasant civilizations. "Grasping an event," he writes, "means reconnecting it to the mute layers of earth which constitute its true continuity or which inscribe it in the class struggle. There is something peasant-like in history." See Deleuze, *Cinéma II*, p. 332.

[61] This sentence—because it breaks such a long silence, as well as for what it conveys—has given rise to many interpretations. For example, in de Guisti's eyes, "The 'bridge' between the two episodes is constituted precisely by the cannibal's sublimated words in correlation with the sublime, poetic words of the repressive and rational . . . contemporary universe." See de Guisti, *I film di Pasolini*, p. 105. Jean-Michel Gardair argues: "Virtually the film's only goal is to evoke and seize, at the moment of birth, the formulation of the 'word.' The latter is consciousness (of transgression—that absolute conquest of liberty in the solitude of evil) freeing itself of the repression that it must institutionally undergo in any society." "Il *Porcile* di Pasolini," in *Il dialogo, il potere, la morte*, ed. Luigi Martellini (Bologna: Capelli, 1979), pp. 247–248. Originally in *Paragone* No. 296 (October 1969).

[62] Forced to rest during a convalescence from ulcers at this time, Pasolini began to write nonnaturalistic plays as well as theoretical essays hinging on the question of dialogue. Criticizing both the bourgeois theater of "chatter" and the anti-bourgeois theater of Artaud's "gestures and cries," he declared that these two main theatrical currents were both inspired by a "hatred of the word." Calling for a "theater of words" reminiscent of Greek drama, he wanted the text, instead of the proscenium, to provide the "frontal theatrical space" for this new "cultural rite." See his "Manifesto per un nuovo teatro," *Nuovi Argomenti* No. 9 (January–March 1968). *Porcile* itself was written as a play and published by Garzanti in 1979 along with two other plays: *Orgia* and *Bestia da stile.*

grotesque ways. (This grotesque behavior reaches its height toward the end of *Porcile*: while listening to gruesome details of Nazi atrocities, an imperturbable Herr Klotz continues to play delicately upon his harp.) As in a play by Ionesco, language becomes an entity in itself, a vortex of sounds composed of nonsense phrases, bizarre names, puns, and word games.[63] In *Porcile*, as never before, Pasolini emptied language of all meaning even as silence became both eloquent and awesome.

> Everything concrete is mystical.
> —Pier Paolo Pasolini (1969)

The stark formal and thematic contrasts of *Porcile* (past/present, speech/ silence, fire/ice) are part of a system of stylistic clashes that operate not only within each film but also, as suggested earlier, from one film to another. Hence the crystalline simulacrum of *Teorema* and *Porcile* stands sharply opposed to the baroque and elemental violence of *Edipo Re* and *Medea*. Dominique Noguez surely has the latter films in mind when he deems Pasolini a "baroque Racine," the "first pagan filmmaker of modern cinema."[64] Drawn from the cauldron of Greek myth, *Edipo Re* and *Medea* replace ice and artifice with a world of blazing sun, haunting and eerie folk songs, and violent human cries. Calling *Edipo Re* a "series of events that explodes in sounds and violence," Marc Gervais writes:

> With a whirling, prowling camera that blinks at the sun and gasps and breathes almost in unison with Oedipus, Pasolini . . . invests his film with a wild, tormented, baroque quality. Opting for certain realistic elements . . . he situates the tragedy "openly" in Morocco: the rocks, the desert sand, the mountains, the sun, the primitive walled cities, and above all the Arab faces of the extras, are rich in that "réalité ontologique" that Bazin prized so highly in cinema.[65]

If the modern episode of *Porcile*, with its mannerist parody and grotesque bourgeois characters, can be set under the sign of Brecht, then the "wild" and "tormented" world of *Edipo Re* and *Medea* (like the cannibal's tale of *Porcile*[66]) evokes that other great theoretician of modern theater, An-

[63] Noel Purdon has analyzed at some length the linguistic puns and games that run throughout the film. See Purdon "The Film of Alienation," pp. 52–54.

[64] Dominique Noguez, "Pier Paolo Pasolini," in *Dossiers du cinéma: Cinéastes II* (Brussels: Casterman, 1971), p. 130.

[65] Marc Gervais, "Pier Paolo Pasolini: Contestatore," *Sight and Sound* Vol. 38, No. 1 (Winter 1968–1969), p. 4.

[66] Noting that *Porcile* reveals the "direct influence" of both Brecht and Artaud, Gian Piero Brunetta observes that in its prehistoric tale, that is, the tale evoking Artaud, "Pasolini reaches . . . the purest form of representation in which one can still feel the sacred force of that rite which reintegrates the original and authentic values of spectacle." See Brunetta, *Forma e parola in cinema*, p. 106.

tonin Artaud. Both films seem to embody Artaud's demand for a total theater—in which lights, sounds, and images would be as important as, or more important than, words—of cathartic and metaphysical violence. Here striking Third World landscapes suggest the physical presence of archaic and sacred civilizations, of mythic layers of time. Oedipus' legendary tale unfolds not in Greece, that legendary land of reason and harmony, but in the shimmering and savage desert of Morocco; Medea's people live among weird rock formations in the sun-drenched Anatolian region of Turkey. Likening these rocks to the "backbone of a desert," Pasolini exaggerated only slightly when he called this landscape the "protagonist" of the film. (Like the land of the Tarahumara Indians in Mexico which "spoke" to Artaud, so, too, do the very rocks of this desert appear imbued with "meaning.") Music and costumes rival the barbaric splendor of these desert sites. To invent what Pasolini called the "archaic-arbitrary" style of costumes in *Edipo Re*, motifs were drawn from widely diverse civilizations so that, for example, both Aztec and Sumerian symbols mark the royal robes.[67] Similarly, the film's music cannot be situated in any particular era: Pasolini deliberately chose folk songs from Rumania (where he had orignally thought to set the film) because of their strange "ahistorical," "atemporal" blend of Russian and Middle Eastern qualities.[68] In deliberate counterpoint to these folk songs, which seem to come from a great distance, delicate Japanese music signals "the theme of Oedipus' destiny." Asked about the suggestions of Japanese cinema in *Edipo Re*—Mizoguchi had always been one of his favorite directors— Pasolini suggested that its influence could best be felt in the "violence of certain struggles which were . . . based on a cruel ritualism."[69]

Instead of the icy cruelty of *Teorema* and *Porcile*, *Edipo Re* and *Medea* are, as Pasolini suggests, marked by a violence that is not only ritualistic but, on occasion, almost sensual. In perfect accord with Artaud's insistence that "all the great Myths are dark . . . [enveloped] in an atmosphere of carnage, torture and bloodshed,"[70] Pasolini re-creates the primordial

[67] Observing that even Sophocles viewed the story of Oedipus as a far-off myth, Pasolini remarked: "For Sophocles, too, the fact occurred centuries or millennia before his life, just as for us: therefore I sought simply to create an archaic era that was true, palpable, concrete, popular and—at the same time—without historical limitations, outside history. Thus, in making the costumes, for example, [the designer] Danilo Donato and I had written a kind of slogan in the lab: 'Barbaric and arbitrary.' " "Ora tutto è chiaro, voluto, non imposto dal destino," *Cineforum* No. 68 (October 1967), p. 608.

[68] In Pasolini's eyes, these strange folk songs—along with certain images of the city (the plague, the mass shrouds)—replace Sophocles' chorus, which he could not use as such in the film. For him, these were "real songs—popular, realistic—of a people bent under the yoke of a plague epidemic or a tyrannical regime." See "Entretien avec Jean-André Fieschi," *Cahiers du cinéma* No. 195 (November 1967), p. 14.

[69] "Pierpaolo Pasolini e l'autobiografia," *Sipario* Vol. 22, No. 258 (October 1967), p. 27.

[70] Antonin Artaud, *The Theater and Its Double* (New York: Grove, 1958), p. 31.

violence that inhabits these two expiatory rites of Western culture. The
most important scene of *Medea*—a scene that might stand as a symbol
for the entire film—depicts a ceremonial ritual of human sacrifice. As for
Edipo Re, Pasolini's Oedipus massacres both his father and the latter's
soldiers with the violent cries and movements of a samurai warrior. As
the camera follows Oedipus, it, too, becomes violent, aggressively pounc-
ing on people and objects. Suggesting that Pasolini's homosexuality may
have prompted some of the wild movements and shifting frenzy of *Edipo
Re*, Barthélemy Amengual writes:

> Whether or not one wants to see this as a result of the author's sexual ambiva-
> lence (the relationship is clear in the works of Murnau, Sternberg, Carné, Coc-
> teau, and often those of the American underground) Pasolini's films—or rather
> his écriture—constantly swing between possession and loss of the world, in a
> fringe of mists (memory, premonition, nostalgia, despair) or flashes (sunlight in
> eyes, in the camera, marked shots against the light, blurrings, flutterings of re-
> flections and bursts of light), between aggression (brutal traveling shots which
> jump . . . on a back, a face, an object) and flight (hand-held camera, rolling,
> staggering, anguished), seizure and release (long shots regularly come to snatch
> and tear the subject from shots closer up . . .). Varying lenses become the weap-
> ons of this conflict.[71]

In this atmosphere of baroque instability, narrative divisions take the
shape of striking ruptures and sudden metamorphoses. The abrupt cuts
Pasolini had always favored—as he went, without transition, from close-
ups to long shots, or from one close-up to another—fragment the narrative itself as it slashes across time and space, the known and the unknown,
legend and imagination. By virtue of a cut, a baby born in Fascist Italy
becomes the mythical Oedipus of Greek legend; still another cut transports us from Thebes to modern-day Bologna.[72] Dramatic visual transformations echo and reinforce the psychological metamorphosis underlying the myths: initially a sighted man who cannot see, Oedipus becomes
a blind man who sees all; one glimpse of Jason turns the savage princess,
Medea, into a love-struck woman swooning with passion. In part, it is
the unreal mythological context—peopled by centaurs, oracles, and
sphinxes—that permits ruptures and transformations more extreme and
striking than ever before. But our knowledge of the myths is also important: it allows us to follow these films despite dramatic cuts and enigmatic

---

[71] Barthélemy Amengual, "Le mythe et l'histoire," in *Pasolini: le mythe et le sacré*, p. 80.

[72] Describing these ruptures, Yann Lardeau writes: "Inscribing onto the body of the film
the discontinuity of cinematographic operations accentuates the metamorphoses created by
every change in framing acting upon the possible metamorphoses coming from the varia-
tions in camera angles." See Lardeau, "Le mur des métamorphoses," in *Pasolini cinéaste*,
special unnumbered issue of *Cahiers du cinéma* (1985), p. 85.

ellipses. Taking full advantage of our familiarity with the myths, Pasolini radically "rereads" the Greek texts: consistently telescoping the well-known parts in favor of long "invented" sequences, he transforms plays in which the word was all-important into almost silent films.

Thus, like ancient civilizations that lie buried beneath our own, the mythic text is turned into a kind of silent and invisible presence support-ing the film's imaginary world. Every so often, the text breaks through and we hear familiar lines: in this pulsating and intensely physical world, they resonate strangely, as if they constituted another "voice" within the film.[73] In a highly meta-cinematic sequence of *Edipo Re*, for example, a long speech from the beginning of Sophocles' play is spoken by Pasolini himself. Playing the High Priest and Spokesman of the people of Thebes, he becomes, as he observed, "the author who presents the other au-thor."[74] But if Pasolini "presents" Sophocles' text, merely by uttering it in this context he also transforms it. For here the Greek play, which belongs to an era already marked by words and reason, seems to stand midway between the modern world (evoked by Pasolini's presence) and the silent world of the savage landscapes. Superimposing the present on different strata of a buried past, Pasolini takes us into a zone that, as Yann Lardeau remarks, lies somewhere between the "abstractions of written culture and the traditions and architecture of oral societies."[75]

The multiple temporal layers that inhabit the mythic films are announced, strikingly, at the very beginning of *Edipo Re*. After a rapid opening glimpse of a desert road stone pointing to Thebes—that is, to Oedipus' destiny—the film quickly cuts to a town in Fascist Italy where, as we see through the window of a house, a woman is giving birth to a baby boy. As we later discover, this child is both the modern infant Oedipus and, given the autobiographical cast of the film, Pasolini himself. Not one but three texts infuse *Edipo Re*: the Oedipus tale of Greek myth and drama, Freud's reading of that tale and his elaboration of the Oedipus complex, and Pasolini's references to his own childhood. Simultaneously evoking child and adult, past and present, beginning and end (of the myth and the film), the opening sequence places the film under the sign of a Freudian

[73] Speaking of Bresson or Rohmer, Deleuze notes that their characters speak and listen to their own lines as if they came from someone else: "Each character," he writes, "speaks as if he were listening to his own words conveyed by another in order to reach the *literalness* of the voice, to cut it off from any direct resonance, and to produce a free indirect speech." See Deleuze, *Cinéma II,* p. 315. Much the same could be said of the textual fragments in Pasolini's films, which always seem to come from elsewhere—as if framed by quotation marks.

[74] "Pasolini e l'autobiografia," p. 27.

[75] Lardeau, "Le mur des métamorphoses," p. 86.

dream where, as Leo Bersani writes, there is "no contingency, no past, no present, only a miraculous synchronicity in which everything and anything is possible at once."[76]

In this tripartite film, prologue and epilogue, set in the modern era, frame the tale of the legendary Oedipus. Or, as Pasolini poetically describes the divisions: "The prologue is the childhood of a little boy who could be any one of us, and who dreams the whole myth of Oedipus as it was told by Sophocles but of course with Freudian elements. At the end, the little boy is blind and old."[77] Briefly, masterfully, the silent prologue, full of autobiographical allusions, suggests the intensity of love and rivalry at the heart of the Oedipus complex. One shot of the prologue, in particular, will resonate throughout the film, evoking, as it does, the primordial and fateful bond between mother and son. Seated in a verdant meadow with her suckling infant at her breast, the mother looks directly into the camera for an unbearably long time. (The shot lasts almost a minute.[78]) A circling pan tilts upward to encompass the trees enclosing the meadow before the camera returns to mother and child as if they, seated in the meadow, were at the center of the universe. And, of course, each *is* the center of the world for the other. This is followed by a quick montage sequence: to the tune of martial music associated with the father, we go from a shot of the Fascist flag to the mother wheeling a pram with a much older child, to the father in military uniform looking at the child with hatred as sub-titles convey the jealousy he feels for his son: "You are here to take my place in the world . . . you have already stolen *her* from me." The prologue closes with another astonishing montage sequence: as the child's parents begin to make love, Pasolini cuts to a very rapid nighttime shot of the lush primordial meadow associated with mother/child love, and to a similarly quick shot of the child, before returning to the parents who have finished lovemaking and lie apart, without speaking. His eyes filled with hatred, the father goes over to the child's bed and shakes his son by the feet. A strange tune begins: suddenly, a rapid cut transports us to the world of myth where the legendary infant Oedipus, hands and feet strung to a pole, is being carried into the desert to be left to die.

The Freudian cast of the prologue persists in the world of myth. "Instead of projecting the myth onto psychoanalysis," Pasolini observed, "I

[76] Leo Bersani, "Freud's Reflexive Realism," *October* No. 28 (Spring 1984), p. 49.

[77] Interview with Jean Narboni, *Cahiers du cinéma* No. 192 (July–August 1967), p. 31.

[78] Analyzing this shot, and the sequence of short shots surrounding it, Maurizio Ponzi and Claudio Rispogli suggest that this very long close-up exemplifies the way Pasolini "immobilizes objects or people." See their "Esterno giorno: P.P. madre," *Cinema e film* (September 1967), p. 455.

have reprojected psychoanalysis on the myth."[79] Whereas Sophocles recounts Oedipus' tale *after* his meeting with the Sphinx, the film contains a number of sequences in which Pasolini imagines how Oedipus (Franco Citti) might have behaved even before that fateful encounter. And his imagination shapes a tragic hero whose doom is decreed as much by his own psyche as by the gods. Oedipus' later blindness about himself and his unacknowledged love for his mother are foreshadowed in scenes where he cheats at games with his companions and turns away from a naked woman who offers herself to him. But "blind" destiny also plays its part. At each crossroads on his journey to Thebes, Oedipus spins around, hands over his eyes, asking fate to decide his route: each time he comes to a stop at the road marker that points him to Thebes.

Once Oedipus enters the plague-stricken city, the well-known outlines of Sophocles' tale begin, but they, too, bear the unmistakable stamp of Freud. The awesome Sphinx has become a grotesque puppet; "desacralized" (to use Pasolini's term) by the gaze of a witness-messenger (Ninetto Davoli), this weird creature is but the visual embodiment of Oedipus' unconscious. Significantly, the Sphinx does not ask Oedipus a riddle but demands, rather, that the young man shed light on the mystery that he carries within himself—that is, his unacknowledged love for his mother. But Oedipus refuses to heed the Sphinx's allusions about his forbidden desire and "represses" the monster (that is, his own unconscious) by pushing the Sphinx into a chasm even as the creature protests: "It's useless, it's useless, the abyss into which you're pushing me is in you." The Sphinx's warnings are ignored: a deliberately unseeing Oedipus makes love with Jocasta. But here, too, Pasolini makes an important change: his Oedipus—unlike Sophocles'—makes love with Jocasta even *after* he knows she is his mother. (In Pasolini's view, even Sophocles' tragedy was permeated by a conscious, if not explicit, awareness of incest.[80]) Lastly, after blinding himself, Oedipus is led away not by his daughter, Antigone, but instead by a young man: a messenger, played by Pasolini's friend Ninetto Davoli, hands Oedipus a flute—symbol of the poet-prophet—as they begin their wanderings.

As Oedipus and his companion leave Thebes for a life of exile, another narrative rupture and metamorphosis signal the beginning of the epilogue, which, like the prologue, is silent. Now a blind musician in modern-day Bologna, Oedipus is playing delicate tunes on his flute for tourists. "Once Oedipus has blinded himself," remarked Pasolini, "he reenters society by sublimating all his faults. One of the forms of sublimation is poetry. He plays the pipe, which means, metaphorically, he is a

[79] Cited by Stack, *Pasolini*, p. 120.
[80] "Pasolini e l'autobiografia," p. 27.

poet."[81] Once again, like the explicit autobiographical references of the prologue (Pasolini grew up in northern Italy in the 1930s; his father was a military man), Pasolini's own life is grafted onto his tragic hero: not only did he attend university in Bologna but his early hermetic poetry—like the "delicate, ancestral" Japanese flute music played by Oedipus—is involuted and private. And, no less than Pasolini himself, Oedipus undergoes a social awakening: he leaves Bologna for industrialized Milan, where he plays a revolutionary air for the benefit of factory workers. But the workers, like the tourists, ignore him. "Oedipus," noted Pasolini, "goes away to sing, no longer for the bourgeoisie, but for the exploited classes. Hence, this long road towards the factories. Where another disenchantment awaits him without a doubt."[82] (Elsewhere, in a more self-ironic mood, Pasolini described Oedipus as a "petit-bourgeois who is going through a Marxist type of sublimation."[83]) And soon, like everything else, political disenchantment, too, must give way before the absolute. As the film closes, Oedipus returns to the meadow of the prologue, where, as beginning and end meet, he will die. Chillingly self-prophetic, Pasolini remarked of his doomed hero: "First Oedipus is a decadent poet, then a Marxist poet, then nothing at all, someone who is going to die."[84]

Although definite autobiographical motifs run throughout Pasolini's cinema, never before, as in *Edipo Re*, had he so explicitly alluded to events, people, and places in his life. Even visual details were drawn from a reservoir of personal memories: the lush green meadow of the prologue and epilogue, he said, "corresponds exactly to the meadow where my mother took me to walk when I was a child. I had the clothes (the mother's dress and yellow hat) reproduced from old photographs."[85] And beneath these allusions lies a private, essentially homosexual, mythology. Evoking, for example, the many "angels" in Pasolini's films (marble in *Accattone*, carnivalesque in *Uccellacci e Uccellini*, androgynous in *Il Vangelo*, handsome and divine in *Teorema*), his beloved friend Ninetto Davoli appears as an "angel" in both parts of *Edipo Re*: a companion named Angelo in the epilogue, he is a messenger (or, in Greek, an *angelos*) in the mythic centerpiece.[86] Similarly, the flute played by the blind Oedipus—a motif that Dominique Noguez links to Virgilian homosexual pastorals—

---

[81] Cited by Stack, *Pasolini*, p. 129.

[82] Cited by Duflot, *Entretiens*, p. 108.

[83] "Pasolini e l'autobiografia," p. 27.

[84] "Entretien avec Fieschi," p. 13.

[85] Ibid., p. 16.

[86] The presence of angels is another motif that Pasolini shares with the French poet-filmmaker Jean Cocteau. In Cocteau's first film, *Le sang d'un poète*, a guardian angel "absorbs" the dead poet and carries him off. Still another angel plays a central role in both the filmed and staged versions that Cocteau did of the Orpheus legend.

has sensual antecedents in Pasolini's own work. One of his earliest poems—composed for a letter to a friend—describes a flute player whose enchanting tunes lure the young boys of a village into a cave; there, the poem concludes, the flute will sing to them "of covetous violence during nighttime nakedness" (Vi narrerò, col suono del mio flauto/delle trascorse nudità notturne la cupida violenza[87]). And flute and angel come together in *Teorema*: in the written version of the parable Pasolini remarks that the angelic postman (played by Ninetto Davoli in the film) seems to be "playing *The Magic Flute* upon an invisible and joyful flute."

At the center of all the personal allusions in *Edipo Re* lies, of course, the Oedipus complex itself. Pasolini believed, or at least wanted to believe, that this deeply autobiographical and introspective film even constituted a catharsis of sorts:

> The profound difference between *Edipo Re* and my other films is that it is autobiographical while the others were not, or were less so, or were so almost unconsciously and indirectly. In *Edipo Re* I recount the story of my own Oedipus complex. The little boy of the prologue is myself, his father is my father, a former army officer, and the mother, a teacher, is my own mother. I recount my life, mythified, rendered epic, by the legend of Oedipus. But while *Edipo Re* is the most autobiographical of my films, it is [also] the one that I regard with the most objectivity and detachment because, although it is true that I recount a personal experience, it is an experience which is over and which hardly interests me any longer. . . . Deep within me, it is no longer alive and violent.[88]

Profoundly attached to his mother, Pasolini had, of course, depicted maternal love long before *Edipo Re*: such love consumes Mamma Roma and impels, perhaps, even Stella in *Accattone*. In the eyes of one critic, Dominique Noguez, the need for maternal love is implicitly present even in the films with Totò and Ninetto. Suggesting that the two are somehow in search of a wife-mother in *Uccellacci e Uccellini*, Noguez feels that in the short film made the following year, *La terra vista dalla luna*, Totò and Ninetto clearly become "a single being, a sort of double Oedipus, who seeks maternal affection and sexual satisfaction in the same partner or, rather, sexual satisfaction in and through the mother."[89]

But mother/son love is only half of the Oedipus complex. The other half—father/son rivalry and hatred—was conspicuously absent from Pasolini's films before *Edipo Re*. It was only around the time he made this film that he began to talk about what his father, and "fathers," represented for him. "My dramatic relationships," he observed in 1966, "come

---

[87] Pasolini, *Lettere* (Turin: Einaudi, 1986), p. 31.

[88] Interview with Narboni, p. 31.

[89] Dominique Noguez, "L'*Oedipe* de Pasolini," *Ça cinéma* (October 1973), p. 104.

with everything that is paternal. . . . This is fruitful if this relationship is
with, say, the State (which represents the father). This forces the son to
be a kind of living protest—this is the source of poetry, of thought, of
ideology, in short, of life."[90] The student revolt of 1968, which saw one
generation so clearly pitted against another, may have brought his own
feelings of protest and rivalry into even sharper focus; in 1969 he remarked unequivocally that "what produces history is the relationship of
hatred between father and son."[91] And it is precisely this hatred that is at
the core of *Porcile*, where fathers—seen as the embodiment of order, authority, and institutions—are "defied" by sons who, like Oedipus, transgress society's most fundamental taboos.

Perched between earlier films, marked only by the presence of mothers,
and later films where sons (and daughters, in the case of *Medea*) would
revolt against paternal authority, *Edipo Re* is the only film to explore
both the love and rivalry at the heart of the Oedipus complex. It is these
primordial emotions that infuse and link the three parts, which, at the
same time, embody one of the most subtle stylistic clashes in all of Pasolini's cinema. Playing against expectations as always, Pasolini renders the
mythic, supposedly "unreal" centerpiece decidedly realistic. One virtually
feels physical presences: bodies, animal skins, flesh, harsh sunlight, earth
and rocks are all vibrantly alive. In contrast to this "ontological" reality,
the lyrical, silent prologue is wraithlike and hallucinatory: shadows and
delicate materials, wide-angle lenses and soft focus create the impression
of a primal moment, a remembered dream. (Even the intense lush green
of the meadow, said Pasolini, was present as "an aestheticizing and fantastic element.") Somewhat differently, canted shots and distorting lenses
turn the epilogue into a de Chirico painting, into a geometrical world that
has come free of its mooring. To a *Cahiers* critic who referred to the
Borghesian quality of the film, where each part could be the "dream" of
the other, Pasolini responded: "It was a question of linking the two parts
stylistically. If I had shot the modern part in a realistic way, I would have
had an easy and boring contrast. That's why I showed it as a dream with
distorting lenses."[92]

Unlike, say, *Porcile*, where the two parts remain distinct, echoes of the
prologue haunt the centerpiece, as history and meta-history, Sophocles
and Freud, slide into one another, become inseparable. The central close-
up of the mother in the prologue—a close-up embodying all the force of
forbidden and fatal desire—is matched by a similar close-up of Jocasta.
The resemblance between these two close-ups, a resemblance that points

[90] Cited by Fernaldo di Giammatteo in "Pasolini: La quotidiana eresia," in *Lo scandalo
Pasolini*, p. 13.

[91] Cited by Stack, *Pasolini*, p. 120.

[92] "Entretien avec Fieschi," p. 16.

to the fundamental identity of Jocasta and the mother, further compels our attention because both women are played by the same actress, Silvana Mangano. Her strange and unsettling beauty endows both women, moreover, with the air of an immutable phantom. "With Jocasta," said Pasolini, "I represented my own mother projected into myth; and a mother does not change."[93] A host of visual details reinforces the essential identity of the two women. The film's set designer, Dante Ferretti, recalls that Jocasta's room was designed to echo that of the mother down to the brick red color of the walls and a vase of red flowers.[94] Other recurring motifs hint at psychoanalytic domains, keeping us aware of both past and present, myth and autobiography. The swollen feet and blindness of the mythical Oedipus are presaged in the prologue when the father seizes his son's feet and the baby places his hands before his eyes; the adult Oedipus who sucks his hand recalls the prologue shot of the nursing infant at his mother's breast. For Dominique Noguez, these last shots in particular are

> an evocation and reminder of the buccal phase, a key moment in psycho-sexual evolution in that, as Freud tells us, it is from that moment on that the Oedipus complex develops (normally or abnormally) and that it is through regression to this stage—in the degree to which auto-eroticism is manifested—that homosexuality in particular is explained.[95]

This observation comes from a splendid essay on *Edipo Re* in which Noguez examines how the three texts informing the film—Pasolini's archive of memories, the myth and drama of Oedipus, and Freud's reading

[93] Ibid., p. 14.

[94] Cited in Antonio Bertini's *Teoria e tecnica del film in Pasolini* (Rome: Bulzoni, 1979), p. 169.

[95] Noguez, L'*Oedipe* de Pasolini," pp. 102–103. Cf. Freud: "One of the first of such pregenital sexual organizations is the *oral*, or, if one will, the cannibalistic. Here the sexual activity is not yet separated from the taking of nourishment and the contrasts within it are not yet differentiated. The object of the one activity is also that of the other; the sexual aim then consists in the *incorporation* of the object into one's own body, the prototype of *identification*, which later plays such an important psychic role. As a remnant of this fictitious phase of organization forced on us by pathology, we can consider thumbsucking. Here the sexual activity became separated from the nourishment activity and the strange object was given up in favor of one from his own body." See Freud, "Infantile Sexuality," in *Three Contributions to the Theory of Sex* (New York: Modern Library, 1938), p. 597.

Like this remark, a number of Freud's observations concerning the oral stage (which signals the beginning of libidinal or sexual development) are of interest not only for *Edipo Re* but for *Porcile*, where Pasolini's preoccupation with cannibalism, with eating and being eaten, reaches its apogee. One thinks particularly of the scene where the young cannibal looks amorously at his first victim before killing and eating him. In that film, notes Francesco Dorigo, the cannibal "falls victim to his own rebellion, to the first impulse of his own libido." See Dorigo, "Pasolini da Marx a Freud," *Revista del Cinematografo* (April 1970), p. 140.

of the Oedipus complex and myth—are woven together without privileging any single text. Noting that, like Gide or Sartre, Pasolini "*rewrites* his childhood in order to read it," Noguez remarks that the myth continues the "direct confession" of the prologue, pursuing the "same discourse . . . in a different language."[96] Here Pasolini's constant urge to interpret (be it the great texts of the past or reality itself) is applied to his life, a life viewed in relationship to Sophocles' drama and Freud's interpretation of that drama. Given the film's autobiographical nature, observes Noguez, the process of interpretation could be likened to that of analysis itself, an analysis where Oedipus-the-patient is enlightened by the blind analyst, Tiresias.

Although, remarks Noguez, the presence of Freud hovers over *Edipo Re*, psychoanalysis is never used to "explain" the other texts, that is, Pasolini's memories or Sophocles' drama. The young Italian child of the prologue "dreams" the myth of Oedipus as told by Sophocles but with a Freudian overlay. In this "dream" he is the Oedipus of both Sophocles and Freud, while, conversely, the mythical Oedipus is also the young child of the prologue and the blind man of the epilogue (that is, Pasolini). The links between the various parts of the film and the texts infusing them are such that, in Noguez's words, the "Sophoclean-Freudian discourse [becomes] a Pasolinian discourse. Everything occurs as if Pasolini were using Freud . . . to 'delocalize' the story of Oedipus, and Sophocles as a pretext to 'demetaphorize' the Freudian récit."[97] In *Edipo Re*, then, Pasolini draws on Freud/Sophocles—as he has recourse to other great texts elsewhere—to weave what Noguez calls the "material of his discourse: debris torn from great universal myths which, reassembled in an unusual fashion, serve for the most special autobiography."[98]

Whereas *Teorema* and *Porcile* were built around the signs and symbols of parable (signs that always "represent" something else), *Edipo Re* is marked only by juxtaposition from what Noguez describes as one "semic" space to the next. Like a dream, Pasolini's film goes from the abstract to the concrete, from the fantastic to the realistic, changing time, space, and mode "without breaking the narrative thread." Intensely real and yet totally invented, marked by a blend of African and Oriental motifs, its prehistoric landscape embodies nothing other than the "Absolute Elsewhere of dreams." The relatively conventional shots of *Edipo Re* may make it, as Pasolini once observed, the most "cinematographic" of his films, but, as Noguez argues, its complex interweavings also render it an "original form of filmic discourse." In Noguez's view, *Edipo Re* "can best

[96] Noguez, "L'*Oedipe* de Pasolini," p. 99.
[97] Ibid., p. 104.
[98] Ibid., p. 105.

be seen as the most persuasive realization of an original form of filmic discourse: collage, harlequinade of false fables, fables that are the most magical when they mock the magical and the fantastic, and come closest to metaphorical depths when they are literally explicit."[99]

If *Edipo Re* shows the birth of forbidden sexuality, *Medea* begins at the point where passion, full-blown, is about to explode. Although, writes René Prédal, "all of Pasolini's films share a certain number of themes, each crystallizes around one in particular: in *Medea* it is devouring passion."[100] As in all the films of these years, in *Medea* "devouring passion" is embedded in a web of oppositions structured around the central and absolute dichotomy between a sacred past (represented by Medea and her people) and a profane present (embodied in the pragmatic Jason). In Pasolini's reading of the myth, Medea is not only a symbol of archaic civilizations but also—and this was probably less clear to viewers—of the contemporary Third World whose ancient and sacred values crumble when exposed to the technocratic West. And his tragic heroine can be seen in still another, more personal light: a barbarian princess who abandons all to follow her faithless lover to a foreign land, she also appears to incarnate, as Jean Duflot observes, the "marginality" and "exclusion" that Pasolini himself felt so keenly at this time.[101]

At the heart of the film, and the point where all the dichotomies and various readings converge, is one of the strangest and most poetic creatures in all of Pasolini's films: the gentle and wise centaur, Chiron (played by the French stage actor Laurent Terzieff[102]), who, legend has it, raised the young Jason. No less than the talking centaur in Cocteau's autobiographical film *Le testament d'Orphée*, Pasolini's mythical beast is a highly symbolic and personal creature.[103] In fact, a few years after making *Medea*, Pasolini would explicitly identify himself with the centaur by en-

---

[99] Ibid., pp. 106–107.

[100] René Prédal, "Pier Paolo Pasolini," *Avant-scène du cinéma* No. 75 (November 1976), p. 18.

[101] Duflot, *Entretiens*, p. 113.

[102] Brunetta interprets Terzieff's presence as one more indication of Pasolini's link to Artaud, since Terzieff played the double role of a man and a horse in a production staged by Jean-Louis Barrault, a director associated with Artaud. In Brunetta's view, Pasolini attempts to revive the "primitive ritualism present in the theater and particularly in certain experiments of French theater of the 1930s (Jacques Copeau, Jean-Louis Barrault)." See Brunetta, *Forma e parola nel cinema*, p. 117.

[103] The centaur motif, with its erotic connotations (the resemblance between centaurs and satyrs is striking), constitutes one more link between Cocteau and Pasolini. Incidentally, Pasolini was well-acquainted with Cocteau's unsigned autobiography in which the French poet describes how he was first sexually aroused by the sight of a nude boy on a horse. See Pasolini, *Descrizioni di descrizioni*, p. 112.

titling a volume of personal and revealing interviews *Il sogno del centauro* (*The Centaur's Dream*).

The kinship Pasolini felt for the legendary centaur associated with Jason is not difficult to understand. In general, centaurs are not only a symbol of ancient civilizations but also erotic beings whose double nature rendered them fundamentally different from all others. In addition to this, Chiron in particular was both a teacher of young men and a sage endowed with prophetic gifts. In *Medea*, Pasolini's affinity with the centaur leads him to give the latter an authorial cast. In a work marked by temporal and spatial ruptures more extreme than ever before, it is the centaur who explains the motives of the characters, and even the sense of the film, to us. In so doing, he announces the explicit authorial figures—to be played by Pasolini himself—of subsequent films. "There is always a narrator," observes Yann Lardeau of Pasolini's later films,

> who coordinates image and dialogue. . . . as witness and speaker, he is the link between the spectator and the film—Pasolini himself in *The Canterbury Tales*, Ninetto Davoli in the two episodes of *Porcile*, the Centaur in *Medea*. This character appears furtively, on the periphery. . . . [But] his presence and the role he plays are nonetheless essential to the seduction exerted by the images: it is he who makes certain the images are linked to an invisible, but primary, text.[104]

But the centaur does more than act as a figure of continuity, a link between text and image. Soon after the film begins, he undergoes a metamorphosis—from mythical beast to "rational" man—which incarnates, in the most physical way imaginable, the tremendous gap separating Medea's archaic, "hieratic" civilization from the technological and pragmatic world of Jason. At the outset, the centaur appears in his mythical form. Half-man, half-beast, he is seen standing in a lush green and fertile landscape—in a marshy plain that suggests a primal era of beginnings. In this distant past, the centaur, who acts as both mother and father to the infant Jason, is explaining to his young charge that that "everything is sacred . . . there's nothing natural in nature." The centaur elaborates upon this theme—in a series of rapid cuts—as Jason goes from childhood to adolescence. But, like humanity itself, once Jason grows up, he loses his faith in fables and in fabulous creatures like the centaur. And so, when Jason becomes a man, the centaur, too, must undergo a transformation: in a rapid cut, he loses his mythic appearance and becomes wholly human. Now, like Jason, the centaur is part of a modern bourgeois era—an era whose faith in "success" and "progress" is matched only by its rejection of metaphysics and the sacred.

This fundamental metamorphosis is followed by still another dramatic

---

[104] Lardeau, "Le mur des métamorphoses," p. 85.

rupture as, suddenly, the scene shifts to an arid landscape. We are in Colchis, Medea's home, a land still ruled by archaic and sacred values. Cruel but exalted, the ancient pagan religion of Colchis is infused with a "primitive barbarity," which, in Pasolini's eyes, contained "something that is pure and good; ferociousness only appears in rare exceptional cases."[105] This barbarity sets its seal on the next sequence—one of the most striking, certainly, in all of Pasolini's cinema. To the accompaniment of eerie chants (not a word is spoken), a majestically robed Medea (Maria Callas), High Priestess of Colchis, presides over a fertility ritual of human sacrifice. A young man is tied to a cross and daubed with paint; then, in ceremonial fashion, his neck is broken, his body dismembered, and his blood spread on the fields to encourage the arid earth to yield food.[106]

After this chilling scene, Pasolini begins to trace the well-known outlines of Medea's tragedy. Far more than in *Edipo Re*, he quickly passes over the familiar and lingers on invented sequences. Jason is promised a kingdom if he can capture the fabled Golden Fleece, which is seen not merely as the symbol of the archaic religion of Medea's people but as its vital embodiment. He accomplishes this dreadful theft, which signals the end of the ancient civilization of Colchis, with the help of Medea—who swoons with love (and a foreboding of disaster?) when she first sees him—and her handsome younger brother. As they flee with the Golden Fleece, Medea's passion inspires another terrible deed. To ensure their escape, she stabs her brother; after first dismembering him, she throws his limbs and head from their racing chariot so that the pursuing soldiers of Colchis will be compelled to stop in order to recover the young man's remains.

But Jason's feat and Medea's betrayal are in vain: despite his success, Jason is denied the promised kingdom. Now the couple takes refuge in the walled city of Corinth, which is perched in striking splendor atop a reddish mountain. Laying aside her priestess robes, Medea begins her new life with Jason, a life that will be spent not in the sun-drenched expanses of her homeland but in dark and claustrophobic rooms. Elliptically, the film jumps ahead ten years. Jason is about to abandon Medea in order to make an advantageous marriage to the young princess of Corinth. At this crucial juncture in his life, once again the centaur appears to

---

[105] Cited by Duflot, *Entretiens*, p. 94.

[106] This ritual sequence—central to the film—virtually illustrates an observation made by Roland Barthes concerning the primal relationship between the theater and the cult of the dead: "The first actors set themselves apart from the community by interpreting the role of the Dead. Getting made up meant designating oneself as a living and dead body at the same time: the whitened torsos of totemic theater, the man with the painted face of Chinese theater, the rice paste make-up of the Indian Katha Kali, the Japanese Noh mask." See Barthes, *La chambre claire* (Paris: Gallimard-Le Seuil, 1980), p. 56.

him. And his former mentor analyzes Jason's predicament in terms of the two forms—that is, mythic and human—that he himself assumes. (At one point we see both the mythic centaur and the wholly human one in the same scene.) The presence of these two forms, the centaur tells Jason, shows that the sacred is "preserved beside its new, nonsacred form"; and, continues the centaur, even Jason himself has a sacred part buried within him, untouched by calculations and self-interest. It is that part of Jason, insists the centaur, that still loves Medea and understands her spiritual catastrophe: she is lost and disoriented, an "archaic woman in a world that doesn't believe in anything in which she always believed. . . . The poor soul has had a reverse conversion and has never recovered from it."[107]

But the centaur's words fall on deaf ears. Like Oedipus, who "represses" the Sphinx (i.e., his own unconscious), Jason ignores the centaur's message and persists in his plan to marry the young princess—a plan soon met by Medea's vengeance. Spurred on by a voice that comes from the blood-red sun, after donning her ancient priestess robes Medea has a gift of clothes sent to Jason's prospective bride. Soon the young princess (poisoned? guilt-ridden?) jumps to her death from the high walls of the red city. A rare lyrical moment precedes the final tragedy: a tender Medea bathes and caresses her two young sons. Then she stabs them, sets the house afire, and prevents Jason from seeing their bodies as she screams from amidst the flames: "Nothing is possible any more."

Medea's terrible fate is, clearly, sealed from the very first moment that she sees Jason and is seized by desire, by an almost hallucinatory passion, for him. In this, she incarnates the forbidden and fateful sexuality that drives all the characters—Oedipus, the family members of *Teorema*, the "sons" of *Porcile*—of the mythic quartet. But even more than in previous films, in *Medea* passion exists in its own right: freed of any symbolism, it is neither a sign of spiritual thirst (as in *Teorema*) or of revolt (as in *Porcile*). Rather than a metaphor or revelation of the divine, it is, in Pasolini's words, a "substitute for lost religion." When Medea meets Jason, he writes, she "once again finds a sacred relationship with reality. . . . And it is with the gratitude of those who feel life reborn in them that she lets Jason possess her."[108]

But if passion opens upon the sacred, it is also, as always, the principal catalyst in a primordial drama of taboo and transgression, of guilt and atonement. No less than the family members of *Teorema*, Medea—like all the other protagonists of the mythic quartet—is prey to a "scandalous love, a love that destroys." It is a love that impels her first to transgres-

---

[107] Pasolini, *Medea* (Milan: Garzanti, 1970), p. 62.
[108] Ibid., p. 55.

sion, to betrayal and murder, and, finally, to death. Moreoever, like a film beneath a film, beneath this fatal passion lurks still another "scandalous" love: for although *Medea*, unlike *Teorema*, contains no explicit homosexual encounters, it is clearly this forbidden passion that sets its seal on several scenes. For example, during the flight from Colchis, it is not Medea who exchanges highly charged glances with Jason but her brother. And while Medea herself is middle-aged and somewhat forbidding, her brother is young, handsome, and intensely sensual, with features Caravaggio might have admired. Lastly, and probably most significantly, the camera movements leave no doubt that it is Jason, and not Medea, who is the object of desire. In two crucial sequences, the camera makes us feel Medea's longing for him as it travels over his youthful, virile body and stops, teasingly and insistently, around his loins.[109] One might well argue that these scenes, in particular, bring us to the brink of an explicit avowal that it is really homosexual passion that ignites not only Medea's desire but all the "scandalous" loves—cannibalism, bestiality, incest—of the mythic quartet.

It is, in fact, precisely because homosexuality *is* so inextricably linked to the notion of "scandalous" loves that I cannot agree with those critics who tend to discount its importance. This is the case, for example, of Dominique Noguez, who, in other respects, is certainly one of Pasolini's most subtle and perceptive critics. In what is otherwise a very eloquent and convincing passage devoted to the role of passion in Pasolini's films, Noguez limits his discussion of homosexuality to the one film, *Teorema*, where its explicit presence makes it impossible to ignore. And even there, suggests Noguez, it is relatively unimportant. "It is not by chance," he writes,

> that the father strips naked in *Teorema* right after he has been aroused sexually. In Pasolini, sexuality is fatality (fatality is sexual). To talk about a homosexual vision of sexuality does not say much. Of course, in the presence of the Stranger and/or after his stay, almost all the characters of *Teorema* including the mother (who picks up and uses young men like a pederast) display a homosexual type behavior. But this homosexual way of being is not evoked for itself, but only insofar as it justifies better than any other a sacred and dramatic reading of sexuality. As has often been said . . . more than anyone else the homosexual is condemned to *desire*. In that, more than anyone else, he is destined to sacredness and unhappinesss. . . . That is why, in short, although Pasolini's work is

[109] Ester Carla de Miro might well be describing this scene when she observes that "in spite of the fundamental role that [Pasolini] assigns to sexuality, eroticism is almost always absent except for those rare moments when the masculine body itself is somehow 'feminized' by the camera's eye." See de Miro, "L'érotisme selon Pasolini: libération ou mystification?" in *Pasolini*, special issue of *La revue d'Esthéthique* No. 3 (1982), p. 78.

partially a reaction against this inclination (cf. the slapstick of *Uccellacci e Uccellini*, *La terra vista dalla luna*), the space where he moves most spontaneously is the tragic one (moreover the grotesque is the other side of tragedy). In other words, the unhappiness of being homosexual is slight compared to the unhappiness of simply being.[110]

I have quoted Noguez at such length because, in most respects, his observations are acute and persuasive. There is no doubt that, in Pasolini's films, passion is fateful and sacred, fueled by a desire destined to remain unsatisfied. But I cannot agree with his conclusion that homosexuality is merely a different, or more unhappy, way of being sexual. It seems to me, on the contrary, that homosexual passion is an archetypal moment in a worldview that conceives of Eros only in relationship to transgression and the law, to guilt and atonement. Pasolini's heroes *must transgress and must be punished for their transgression*: otherwise they will not go through the "purification," as Pasolini remarked of Oedipus, that permits them to reach the sacred, "the domain of heroism or poetry."[111] As in the case of Oedipus, too, this process of "purification" must etch itself, painfully and agonizingly, upon every fiber of their bodies. Only a punishment that is intensely physical can atone for a transgression stemming from the deepest recesses of their bodily selves. "Whoever transgresses a taboo," writes Yann Lardeau,

> sees himself condemned to pay for it cruelly with his body: eaten alive by dogs, strangled, dismembered, throat slit, or crucified. Torture—be it Oedipus' bloody eyes or Christ's Calvary—has one aim: to strip the victim of his human appearance, to set him totally apart from the profane world, to make his body bear the inscription of his guilt, his crime against humanity, and—in the process—his accession to the sacred.[112]

Seen from this perspective, if homosexuality justifies, to quote Noguez, a "sacred and dramatic reading of sexuality," it is not because it suggests perpetually frustrated desire (though, of course, desire is necessary to impel passion and transgression) but because—like all the "scandalous" loves of the mythic quartet—it *breaks the law*. In so doing, it sets in motion the parabola that takes Pasolini's unhappy protagonists not only to punishment and death but to martyrdom and consecration. "Disobedience," as Lardeau writes, "can only be absolute: punishment confirms the criminal's definitive rupture with the human species and, at the same time, consecrates him."[113]

[110] Noguez, "*L'Oedipe* de Pasolini," pp. 100–101.
[111] Cited by Duflot, *Entretiens*, pp. 107–108.
[112] Lardeau, "Le mur des métamorphoses," pp. 86–87.
[113] Ibid., p. 86.

To underestimate the importance of "disobedience" or transgression is, moreoever, to ignore the central role played by revolt—an essential component not only of Pasolini's persona but also of his films. Whether consciously or unconsciously, willingly or unwillingly, in breaking fundamental taboos, *Pasolini's tragic martyrs become rebels against the social order*. Their "scandalous" loves embody nothing other than the rebellion at the heart of all perversion. It is precisely this phenomenon that Herbert Marcuse underscores when, in *Eros and Civilization*, he writes that perversions

> express rebellion against the subjugation of sexuality under the order of procreation, and against the institutions which guarantee this order. Psychoanalytic theory sees in the practices that exclude or prevent procreation an opposition against continuing the chain of reproduction and thereby of paternal domination—an attempt to prevent the "reappearance of the father."[114]

Not surprisingly, the revolt against "paternal domination" is bolder in *Medea* and *Porcile*—both made after the student rebellion of 1968—than in the earlier films of the quartet. Unlike Oedipus, who unknowingly kills his father, the young cannibal and parricide of *Porcile* consciously, and defiantly, breaks the most implacable of taboos even as he refuses speech, that essential thread in the social fabric. And Medea's crime brings the social nature of revolt into even sharper focus: in stealing the Golden Fleece and the (patriarchal) power invested in it, she seals the doom of her people and her civilization.

The social nature of Medea's crime, as well as the ritual of human sacrifice over which she presides, means that here, far more than in previous films, individual transgression is seen against the larger canvas of human transgression and atonement. It is a canvas that, as in the case of *Edipo Re*, is unmistakably haunted by the memory of Freud. But whereas *Edipo Re* suggests Freud's study of infantile sexuality—in which he examines the development of the Oedipus complex in an individual—*Medea* evokes, instead, the author of *Totem and Taboo*. In that late work the father of psychoanalysis explores the primal collective consequences of the Oedipus complex. Reaching back into prehistory, in *Totem and Taboo* Freud puts forth the hypothesis that social rituals stem from a primordial, Oedipal murder—a murder in which the primal father was killed by his collective sons. Prey to an ambivalent mix of joy, fear, and guilt after this deed, the sons then (re)incarnated the dead father—whom death had rendered even more powerful—in a totem animal whom they sought to appease through sacrifice and ceremony. In these ritual ceremonies—which Freud sees as the beginning of all human ritual—the ta-

---

[114] Herbert Marcuse, *Eros and Civilization* (Boston: Beacon, 1971), p. 49.

boos surrounding the dead father (especially the primary taboos against patricide and incest, that is, the taboos broken by Oedipus) were transferred to a totem.

> If the totem animal is the father, then the two principal ordinances of totemism, the taboo prohibitions which constitute its core—not to kill the totem and not to have sexual relations with a woman of the same totem—coincide in their content with the two crimes of Oedipus, who killed his father and married his mother, as well as with the two primal wishes of children.[115]

Similarly, the ambivalence surrounding the killing of the dead father was also transferred to the death of the totem, which thus became a source of both exultation and grief.

> Psychoanalysis has revealed that the totem animal is in reality a substitute for the father; and this tallies with the contradictory fact that, though the killing of the animal is as a rule forbidden, yet its killing becomes a festive occasion—the fact that it is killed and yet mourned. The ambivalent emotional attitude, which to this day characterizes the father-complex in our children and which often persists into adult life, seems to extend to the totem animal in its capacity as substitute for the father.[116]

Without doubt, the totemic rite of *Medea*—with its blend of dread and exultation, of death and resurrection—might almost be taken as an illustration of Freud's imagined primal drama. At the same time, however, this scene also represents a primordial moment in Pasolini's film; in the words of Claude Beylie, it is both the introduction to the film and its "symbol pushed to the furthest degree."[117] For if this rite reenacts, or looks backward to a primal moment, it also announces Medea's own drama of guilt and atonement—a drama that thereby takes on the cast of ritual. Linked to her victim as to a pole of opposition, Medea presides at a ceremony that will resonate throughout the film. Her role as high priestess is but a prelude to her own tragedy; the young man's death foreshadows her own terrible end. These two sacrificial deaths, moreover, are part of a system of doublings and echoes suggesting, no less than the ritual it depicts, that the film itself takes the form of an inevitable and prescribed rite. For example, the knife Medea uses to kill her children—a knife emphasized by close-ups—inevitably recalls the one she thrusts into the sacrificial victim. Both executioner and victim, Medea herself swoons twice (when she first sees Jason and when he leaves her) and wreaks vengeance twice—once in a dream, once in reality. And even her dream takes us

---

[115] Sigmund Freud, *Totem and Taboo* (New York: Norton, 1950), p. 132.

[116] Ibid., p. 141.

[117] Claude Beylie, "Sur trois films de Pier Paolo Pasolini," *Cinéma* (Paris) No. 146 (1970), p. 71.

back to the totemic rite celebrated by her people, since she imagines herself "returning to the 'archetypes' of life. She sees the human sacrifices
which took place then and is stimulated by this vision."[118]

If the totemic rite of human sacrifice is the "symbol" (to use Beylie's
words) of *Medea*, in a more general way it is also emblematic of all the
films of the mythic quartet. Not only do the sufferings of Pasolini's
doomed protagonists resemble those of the sacrificial victim, but these
characters inhabit a cinema that, like ritual, is built around primordial
moments—moments imbued with the "scandalous" loves, the forbidden
desires that, Freud tells us, both provoke and come from taboo. Embedded in the farthest reaches of the unconscious, these moments transport
us into what Pasolini, inspired by Mircea Eliade, saw as the realm of the
mythic and the sacred. In a work that Pasolini considered one of the "theoretical" bases of *Medea*, *The Myth of the Eternal Return*, Eliade describes these archetypal moments in the following way: "Every sacrifice,"
he writes,

> repeats the initial sacrifice and coincides with it. . . . And the same holds true
> for all repetitions, i.e., all imitations of archetypes; through such imitations,
> man is projected into the mythical epoch in which the archetypes were first
> revealed. Thus we perceive a second aspect of primitive ontology: insofar as an
> act (or an object) acquires a certain reality through the repetition of certain
> paradigmatic gestures, and acquires it through that alone, there is an implicit
> abolition of profane time, of duration, of "history"; and he who reproduces the
> exemplary gesture thus finds himself transported into the mythical epoch in
> which its revelation took place.[119]

Pasolini's films of the late 1960s unfold, of course, in this "mythical
epoch" where history is abolished and archetypal moments endlessly repeated. Oedipus relives his earliest desire for his mother when—in another incarnation and another universe—he meets Jocasta; still later, yet
another Oedipus, now blind, relives this same moment, with all its charge
of forbidden desire, when he returns to the meadow of his childhood. The
fundamental "disobedience" of the young cannibal in *Porcile* is evoked—
in another civilization—by the "modern" son, Julian; Medea reenacts the
ceremonial rites of her civilization when she returns to her "collective
origins" and carries out her vengeance. And these primal transgressions
are constantly evoked, underscored, in a variety of ways: the camera
seizes and fetishizes the blue chair used by the "divine visitor" in *Teorema*, turning it into a symbol of the stranger's "scandalous" power; hu-

---

[118] Cited by Duflot, *Entretiens*, p. 112.
[119] *The Myth of the Eternal Return*, trans. Willard Trask. (London: Routledge & Kegan
Paul, 1955), p. 35.

man bones strewn around the fire in *Porcile* are a constant reminder of the first instance of cannibalism; the infant Oedipus places his hands before his eyes as if moved by premonition of the crimes he will commit and the terrible destiny that awaits him. Built around these primordial moments, which return obsessively as they are "reseen" and "relived," this is a cinema characterized by the repetition and closure of ritual. Here all is known in advance and, as Pasolini tells us at the end of *Edipo Re*, "Life finishes where it begins."

There is little doubt that the tragic and ritualistic cast of Pasolini's mythic films corresponded to some of the poet's deepest impulses. But—given the militant political climate of the late 1960s, which decreed that art and culture must serve ideological ends—these were not impulses designed to please Italian critics. Never, in fact, had Pasolini been so deliberately, so scandalously, out of step with the times. At a moment when other filmmakers (Godard, Costa-Gavras, Petri) were at their most "committed," his cinema seemed to renounce history and politics, to reject the modern world, in favor of an imaginary past. Thus, although the films of the quartet, especially *Edipo Re*, are now ranked among his best, their initial reception was harsh indeed. At one point Pasolini was even moved to declare that he was making his films with French audiences in mind: in France, neither viewers nor critics were disturbed by his psychoanalytic and formal concerns. In Italy, however, these tendencies only confirmed the worst fears that many critics, especially those on the left, had always harbored about Pasolini. Convinced that the director had "left Marx for Freud," they dubbed his quest for archaic and mythic civilizations "nostalgic" and "regressive." Ignoring ideology and dialectics, Pasolini had "escaped," they charged, into an ahistorical, aestheticized world of Absolutes—a world where Death, Sacredness, and Myth ruled supreme. One of his most articulate and unforgiving critics on the left, Goffredo Fofi, wrote that by "indulging in unbridled subjectivity" and "psychoanalytic confession," Pasolini had allowed his "poetics of death" to blossom into "aesthetic voluptuousness." Voicing sentiments shared by many, an unequivocal Fofi declared that Pasolini could no longer be considered an artist on the left: his cinema signaled nothing other than "a return to historical Italian decadentism."[120]

In the face of such charges, Pasolini countered with arguments that were, perhaps, even more scandalous than the films themselves—arguments that could only further inflame his implacable critics. Aggressively defending his apolitical stance, he denounced the very concept of "com-

---

[120] Goffredo Fofi, *Il cinema italino: servi e padroni* (Milan: Feltrinelli, 1971), pp. 110–112.

mitted" art. It was his conviction that such art was nothing more than a new form of "socialist realism" promulgated by "left-wing fascists." Insisting that a work of art had to be "mediated," he argued polemically against an overtly political cinema that "vulgarizes and simplifies problems"—a cinema whose only feat is "to quiet the bad conscience of the bourgeoisie."[121] Since, he reasoned, it is neocapitalism that exalts action and usefulness above all else, by destroying culture and demanding militant art one merely furthers neocapitalist or bourgeois values.

> Once the young militants abandon culture in favor of action and utiltarianism they resign themselves to being positioned where the system attempts to insert them. This is the crux of the problem: in their fight against neocapitalism they resort to arms which, in fact, carry its trademark and which are destined only to reinforce its tyranny. Although they think they are breaking the circle, they are only reinforcing it.[122]

In addition to "committed" art, he also opposed what was then called "materialist" criticism—associated with French reviews such as *Tel Quel* or *Cinéthique*—which chose to regard books and films as "products." In his view, this critical approach also furthered a neocapitalism that valued things, or products, more highly than people. Running counter to much left-wing theory and practice of those years, he repeatedly argued that "poetry"—symbolic of all true art—is not a "product."

> Since poetry, in fact, is not mass produced, it is therefore not a product. And a reader of poetry can read a poem a thousand times without ever consuming it. Rather, strange to think, the poem might well seem more strange, new, and scandalous the thousandth time than the first. Moreover, there is no refrigerator or shoe . . . which can also be consumed by posterity.[123]

Nor did his defense of poetry, of authentic culture, stop there. He also maintained that, unlike militant film and "materialist" criticism, true art—understood, characteristically, as an art of innovation and controversy, an art that subverts conventions and frustrates expectations—constitutes a genuine protest against the social order. Using one of his striking metaphors, he declared that the simple presence of a real intellectual was as revolutionary as the "face of a Negro at an all-white Anglo-Saxon cocktail party."[124]

Imbued with elitist overtones, Pasolini's defense of authentic art, of the inherent value of culture, was, clearly, meant to provoke. This stance has never been very popular on the left and, in the militant climate of the late

---

[121] Cited by Giammatteo in "Pasolini: la quotidiana eresia," p. 26.
[122] Cited by Duflot, *Entretiens*, pp. 68–69.
[123] Pasolini, *Il caos*, p. 100.
[124] Ibid., p. 99.

1960s, it bordered on heresy. Only when the passions of those years cooled did it become evident—as a number of critics have observed quite recently—that Pasolini's position had much in common with that taken years earlier by Theodor Adorno, one of the philosophers of the Frankfurt School. Comparing Pasolini to the German philosopher Lino Miccichè, for one, suggests that both men opposed not only the existing order of things but also the "existing modes of opposing such an order." Perhaps, says Miccichè,

> the role of Pasolini can be explained in an Adornian key, if Adorno is seen as the man who best described contemporary society as one in which the order of the Enlightenment turned into barbarianism, where thought ceased to think itself, where the destruction of Myth . . . created the new myth of Reason (and its order of the "rational"). For Adorno, in fact, and in general for all "negative thought," the mandate of intellectuals and artists . . . [to] merely oppose what exists . . . winds up by reflecting . . . the barbarity of what exists.[125]

In the case of both Pasolini and Adorno, the opposition to an art of pure protest went hand in hand with an aversion to mass culture, to what Pasolini called the degraded "circuits of mass consumption." It was hardly surprising, then, that as the 1960s drew to a close, Pasolini began to echo—with increasing stridency and despair—Adorno's polemical argument that the "social content" or worth of a work of art is virtually defined by the degree to which it contests "social reception" (that is, mass consumption).[126] For example, declaring that "only culture can purify," in 1969 Pasolini told one interviewer that the "aristocratic" language of his latest films—that is, *Medea* and *Porcile*—was a refusal to cater to popular taste, a kind of revolt against the vulgarization of culture: "If, at the moment, I appear to seek a precious and hermetic language . . . it is because I consider the tyranny of the mass media as a form of dictatorship to which I refuse to make the least concession."[127]

The same year that Pasolini made this inflammatory remark he also wrote an important article entitled "La parola orale: meravigliosa possibilità del cinema." Here he presented further arguments to justify not only the "precious and hermetic" language of *Porcile* and *Medea* but, in a sense, the tremendous preoccupation with form that is evident in all his work—theoretical essays as well as films—of this period. The essay be-

[125] Lino Miccichè, "Contestazione e controcontestazione," in *Per conoscere Pasolini* (Rome: Bulzoni e Teatro Tenda, 1978), p. 52.

[126] Theodor Adorno, "Sette tesi sulla sociologia dell'arte," *Cinema nuovo* No. 240 (March–April 1976), pp. 94–95. Walter Benjamin, too, urged the writer "to *think*, to reflect on his position in the process of production." See Benjamin, *Reflections* (New York: Harcourt, Brace, Jovanovich, 1978), p. 236.

[127] Cited by Duflot, *Entretiens*, p. 58.

gins as Pasolini implicitly attacks his critics on the left. Although, he tells them, intellectuals have long hoped that cinema would provide a means of realizing Gramsci's ideal of national-popular art, the time has come to admit that this hope is merely a "marvelous illusion." For, he continues, "mass culture has suddenly relegated Gramsci to the past, along with his 'people' and the 'people' of our youth—[that is, the people] seen as a revolutionary social class, distinct from the dominant class for political, historical, and, I'd say, racial reasons."[128] We are, he asserts, in a radically new era: one marked not only by the disappearance of the "people" but also—and now he touches on a theme that would dominate his writings of the 1970s—by the "false democracy" of television. Although he grants that militant cinema offers one way of resisting this "false democracy," he himself, he declares, has chosen instead to embrace a "nonconsumable" and "aristocratic" art. Using one of his favorite metaphors, he defiantly proclaims that his own films cannot be "digested"—consumers might swallow them but they would immediately "spit them out or spend the night with a stomach ache."[129] And, he goes on, if his films have become "indigestible," it is because he has followed the "ancient" path of formal invention—a path marked, in particular, by the radical experiments with silence and language that characterize the films of the mythic quartet:

> I do not place much faith in action, unless it is really and truly action—that is, physical blows and a real upheaval of institutions. I prefer to follow the classical paths of formal invention (not formalist—even if some mannerism may sometimes be a divine temptation). There are two of these paths and they are equally restrictive: either you do silent cinema or cinema that is completely and exclusively spoken.[130]

Pasolini's admission that he was deeply drawn to "formal invention," to stylistic experiments, did not, of course, come as a surprise. If, in earlier films, he had used various weapons (irony in La ricotta, humor in Uccellacci e Uccellini) to subdue this attraction, to make "ideology" as important as "passion," the mythic quartet left no doubt that after Uccellacci e Uccellini he had ceased to struggle against the "divine temptation" of mannerism. And even the political justifications he offered for his preoccupation with style were not totally new: after all, his 1965 essay, "Il cinema di poesia," hints at this when it concludes with the hope that the "myth and technical awareness of form" might enable artists to effect a "possible" revolution in bourgeois culture. Still, in looking back at "Il

---

[128] Pasolini, "La parola orale," p. 364.
[129] Ibid., p. 364.
[130] Ibid., p. 364.

cinema di poesia," one is, perhaps, struck less by lines of continuity than by the dramatic changes that had overtaken Pasolini in a few short years. Instead of the tentative tone and complex reasoning of that earlier essay, his writings and remarks of the late 1960s reveal a polemical intransigeance and singlemindedness, an almost ferocious subjectivity.

The aggressive stance that characterized Pasolini at this time—and would remain with him until his death—clearly stemmed from several factors. Not only was he prey to a growing sense of alienation and despair in these years but—and I shall return to this in the next chapter—his lifelong need to remain "different," to challenge all political and cultural orthodoxies, had become more pressing than ever before. As far as his defense of "nonconsumable" art was concerned, moreoever, inner conflicts may well have intensified his defiant tone: after all, the man who, in the late 1960s, proudly declared that his works could not be "digested" was also the man who—more than twenty years earlier—had criticized the symbolist tradition for its "involution" and self-conscious aestheticism. At some level, as I argued in the previous chapter, Pasolini never really renounced this earlier belief; he always knew that the formally perfect poem or film was nothing other than, in the words of Terry Eagleton, "the commodity as fetish resisting the commodity as exchange."[131] The tensions that must have been at work in the course of these difficult years would, in fact, soon be confirmed by still another dramatic turn in his filmmaking career. With his next, and immensely popular, film, *Il Decamerone* (1971), Pasolini would exchange the hermetic, mythic, and tragic space of *Medea* for the teeming and grotesque sub-proletarian world of medieval Naples.

[131] Terry Eagleton, *Against the Grain* (London: Verso, 1986), p. 140.

VI

The Many Faces of Eros

Hope is a horrendous thing invented by political
parties to keep their members in line.
—Pier Paolo Pasolini (April 1975)

THE PROHIBITIONS governing discourse, as Michel Foucault noted in his
inaugural address to the Collège de France, become most intense at the
"danger spots" of sexuality and politics. It was, of course, precisely Pasolini's embrace of these "danger spots" that had always rendered him a
figure of controversy. Still, from the late 1960s to his death, his lifelong
concern with both sexuality and politics took on a new intensity even
as—for the first time—it led him in two quite distinct directions. If he
broke sexual "taboos" with the popular and spectacularly erotic films of
the "trilogy of life," it was, instead, as a political commentator that he
created one ideological scandal after another. His journalistic denunciations of "mass culture" and the "new" fascism sparked heated debates
throughout Italy when they appeared in widely read and respected news-
papers such as *Il Corriere della sera*. Indeed, the inflammatory tone and
ferocious nature of his newspaper writings—later published in two volumes entitled *Scritti corsari* (Milan: Garzanti, 1975) and *Lettere luterane*
(Turin: Einaudi, 1976)—earned him, as these titles suggest, the sobriquets
of "Pasolini corsaro" (that is, an attacking "corsair") and "Pasolini lute-
rano" (a "Lutheran" moralist).

Pasolini first emerged clearly as a "corsair," a latter-day Rousseau at
odds with society, toward the end of the strife-torn 1960s. In the wake of
student demonstrations in Rome in 1968, he wrote a poem entitled "Il
PCI ai giovani," which epitomizes the infuriating yet vital public role he
would play until his death. In this piece of "civil poetry," Pasolini stood
opposed to virtually everyone on the left. Outraged by the students' attitude of moral superiority—an attitude that implied they knew more
about revolution than the generation of Communist organizers and intellectuals who had fought Fascism in the 1940s and worked in the harsh
social struggles of the 1950s—he defended the police against the students.
Although the police were on the "wrong" side, he argued, they *were sons
of poor peasants*. The students, instead, came from a middle-class background; devoid of real sympathy for the underprivileged, they were

caught up in an anarchic and exhibitionistic revolution that could lead only to the "restoration of the bourgeoisie." If the worldwide media favored the young radicals, he continued, it was simply because the media, too, was bourgeois. In verses calculated to provoke the students and their many sympathizers, he began the poem thus:

> It's sad. The polemic against
> the PCI [Italian Communist party] should have been made during the first half
> of the past decade. You're late, children.
> And it's not at all important that you weren't born then. . . .
> Now the journalists of the whole world (including those of television)
> kiss (as I think they still say in the language
> of the University) your ass. Not I, friends.
> You have the spoiled faces of your fathers.
> Blood doesn't lie.
> You have the same evil eye.
> You're fearful, uncertain, desperate
> (fine!) but you also know how to be
> arrogant, blackmailers, and smug:
> petit-bourgeois prerogatives, friends.
> Yesterday at the Valle Giulia when it came to blows
> with policemen,
> I sympathized with the policemen!
> Because policemen are sons of the poor.[1]

The poem left no doubt that while many intellectuals hailed 1968 as a prelude to revolution, for Pasolini it was a time of anguish. In his view, the many protests and demonstrations signaled not the birth of a new revolution but, instead, the death throes of the struggle for social justice which had appeared so compelling to him and others of his generation after the war. And whereas, he said, that earlier fight had involved social, or class, inequities, the students' revolt was simply the last internecine struggle of the bourgeoisie—a kind of "Civil War" in which the students placed their "bourgeois world into crisis in order to reify it."[2] While Pasolini subsequently tempered his harsh judgment of the students, he never changed his mind concerning the bourgeois nature of their "revolution." In 1974, for example, he described the students' revolt as a "scream of pain," a last desperate and impotent cry that came from the unacknowledged, and probably unconscious, realization that an era was over: "tech-

---

[1] Pasolini, *Empirismo eretico* (Milan: Garzanti, 1972), p. 155.
[2] Pasolini, "Anche Marcuse Adulatore," *Nuovi Argomenti* No. 10 (April–June 1968), p. 252.

nological capitalism" had triumphed and its victory precluded "any possible relation with Marxism."[3]

As the 1970s progressed, events appeared to justify the overwhelming sense of historical despair that had distanced Pasolini from so many in the heady days of 1968. In Italy, the worldwide recession of the early 1970s announced a difficult and divisive era in which the *dolce vita* and "economic boom" of the late 1950s and early 1960s gave way to worker demands, strikes, inflation (partly triggered by soaring oil prices), and aggravated political tensions. Social mores, too, were rapidly changing as mass communications and emigration—from South to North, from country to city—hastened the destruction of regional customs and dialects, of age-old patterns and beliefs. Within a few brief years, traditions that had underlain the fabric of Italian life for centuries were overturned as people voted for legislation permitting divorce (1974) and abortion (1975). The Communist party's seeming indifference to these social changes and others—concerns about the environment, the quality of life—dismayed young people in particular. As a result, splinter movements or "extra-parliamentary" groups formed on the left, ranging all the way from the established Manifesto to the progressively radical Lotta continua and then, alas, to groups advocating violence (Potere operaio) and, finally, to the out and out terrorists of Gruppi di Autonomia Operaia and Brigate Rosse. (From 1969 to 1982, in a kind of steady escalation, terrorist groups carried out 14,255 attacks, killing 415 persons. Not until 1982 did the tide turn: in the course of that year, Italian police executed a spectacular rescue of U.S. Army Brigadier General James Dozier, who was being held by members of the Red Brigade. Several of Dozier's kidnappers cooperated with the police, who, armed with this information, went on to make a number of decisive arrests.)

As one might have expected, Pasolini's reaction to the rise of splinter groups and the emergence of a young, militant left was complex and often ambivalent. On the one hand, many of the attitudes characterizing the young radicals deeply repelled him. As suggested earlier, their disdain for culture and their espousal of political art went counter to his deepest impulses. In his eyes, too, their "conformism" was but a new form of the "old provincialism" and "moralism" that he had always condemned. Further, he feared that this "moralism" fueled demands for immediate political action—demands that risked becoming a form of "left-wing fascism." Prophetically sensing the coming wave of left-wing terrorism, in 1974 he remarked:

> I know that pragmatism and empiricism are very dangerous: they burst out, they can burst out into the myth of irrational actions which then become the

[3] Pasolini, "Oltre le rabbie manichee," *Il Dramma* No. 3 (March 1974), p. 19.

basis of fascism. Pragmatism becomes a kind of myth of action . . . and fascism, in Italy, bases itself on this myth of action [which] is a form of irrationalism. . . .

The danger of thought prevailing over action has also occurred . . . in the extra-parliamentary movements of the left with their immediate interventions, their neoterrorism in literature, their advocacy of subjugating everything to action and immediate practical utility.[4]

Although, as this remark suggests, Pasolini was fundamentally opposed to the intransigeant "moralism" and "irrationalism" that characterized the young militants, on specific issues he sometimes found himself in agreement with them. On one such occasion, he actually collaborated with a left-wing group, Lotta continua, on a militant film designed to reveal governmental hypocrisy and corruption.

Entitled *Dodici dicembre*, the film concerns a sequence of events that began on December 12, 1969: announcing the terrorist attacks of the coming decade, bombs exploded at the Banca Nazionale dell'Agricultura in Milan and killed seven people. But the deaths did not stop there. In what many saw as an official coverup—whereby the government sought to place the blame for the terrorism on leftists—one anarchist, Pietro Valpreda, was accused of the attack while another, Pino Pinelli, "fell" from a window during a police interrogation. It was these last developments—part of what came to be known as the *strage di stato* (the state slaughter)—that prompted Pasolini to work with Lotta continua on *Dodici dicembre*.[5]

In light of his repeated opposition to political art, Pasolini's decision to collaborate on a militant film took many by surprise. He was careful to note that his support for the radicals did not mean that he had embraced miliant art. To do so, he declared, would mean that he, too, had turned into a "left-wing fascist." But, he continued, certain events were so critical they virtually compelled intellectuals to take action. In his view, the *strage di stato* was just such an event: not only did it signal a coldblooded inhumanity new to Italy but it constituted a threat to formal democracy itself. Affirming his solidarity with the radicals, he expressed his conviction that

a real revolutionary tension—the same as that in the distant years of '44 or '45 (although less pure and essential)—is being lived by minorities of the extreme

---

[4] *Con Pier Paolo Pasolini*, ed. Enrico Magrelli (Rome: Bulzoni, 1977), p. 102.

[5] The first part of *Dodici dicembre* contains interviews with an old Communist militant, various people involved in the Pinelli case (including his widow), and ex-partisans of World War II: the latter bitterly remark that they fought for a republic that now opens fire upon workers. In the second part, we see various workers: some are faced daily with a dangerous environment; others are out of work and live miserably. Still other sequences involve street fights in Reggio Calabria, the arrival of southern immigrants in Turin, and so forth.

left. I find myself in complete agreement concerning the substance (if not the form) of their global and almost intolerant critique of the Italian state and capitalist society. Therefore, as long as I am capable, and I have the strength, I will stand with them.[6]

If, as in the above remark, Pasolini experienced moments of political faith and conviction during these difficult years, his prevailing mood was still deeply pessimistic. As if making a disabused, and secular, Pascalian wager, he once noted that he stood ready to act even though he had lost all faith in the value of his actions. "I participate," he said, "and contribute as I have always done, in line with a certain ideology and a certain political position. I do this even if it is a sacrifice, and if, in truth, I no longer believe in the outcome."[7]

Skeptical and ambivalent not only toward the student radicals but toward all political activity, Pasolini maintained an uneasy, irresolute position that was exacerbated by the dramatic social changes taking place. On the one hand, he had good reason to feel successful: the repressive, clerical mentality and laws he had fought throughout his life were now, unquestionably, in retreat. But, on the other hand, as the climate grew increasingly liberal, his role of *provocateur*—a role forced upon him, perhaps, but also embraced—seemed less and less relevant. Even his homosexuality—the *diversità* that he had used polemically throughout the years—was rendered less controversial by what he saw as the "false" tolerance of the new power. For him, this tolerance was not only worse than repression but the most "intolerable" and "humiliating thing in the world."[8]

Looking back at these traumatic years, Pasolini would later observe bitterly that the events of 1968 marked his transition from being a "son"—a symbol of revolt and "disobedience"—to being a "father." Worse still, he did not belong with other "fathers" of his generation. For if he was at odds with the new left, with the militant "sons" of '68, he was also critical of their "fathers"—that is, of the old left or Communist party, which, by this time, was well on its way to becoming the new power. Although a variety of factors alienated him from the students, the truth is that he shared their disdain for the centrist, success-oriented course that the Communist party had come to embrace. The pragmatic "historical compromise" (*compromesso storico*) that the Communists were proposing in order to share power with the bourgeois Christian Democrats was, he declared unequivocally, an attempt to reconcile "two historically irreconcilable moments." Like the students, he, too, felt that

---

[6] Pasolini, *Cinema in forma di poesia* (Pordenone: Cinemazero, 1979), p. 97.
[7] *Con Pier Paolo Pasolini*, p. 101.
[8] "Le interviste: Pasolini," *Fiera Letteraria*, November 11, 1974, p. 8.

the party had become "bourgeois"—that it had accepted capitalistic models and goals in its singleminded pursuit of economic progress. This meant, he observed both sadly and prophetically, that even if the left assumed power in Italy, the "ideology of consumerism" would still emerge triumphant.

The disabused view of both radicals and Communists that characterized Pasolini at this time was, moreoever, merely one aspect of a still deeper historical pessimism. It was his conviction that the social dislocations brought about by rapid economic growth were creating nothing less than an "anthropological revolution" in Italy—a brutal revolution in which an age-old agricultural and paleocapitalist universe was being abruptly replaced by a totally new, and "other," civilization. Polemically comparing contemporary Italy to pre-Hitler Germany, he argued that Italy was experiencing a disastrous form of cultural and social leveling, or "homologization."

> There is, perhaps, only one precedent for the Italian trauma stemming from the contact between plurilingual "archaicness" and industrial leveling: pre-Hitler Germany. There, too, the values of diverse individual cultures were destroyed by the violent homologizing brought about by industrialization, an industrialization which was followed by the formation of those enormous masses— masses no longer archaic (i.e., peasants, craftsmen) and still not modern (i.e., bourgeois)—which constituted the savage, aberrant, and imponderable body of Nazi troops.[9]

Deliberately polemical, estranged from both the radical and the traditional left, Pasolini found himself, perhaps willed himself, more alone than ever before. The acute sense of persecution he experienced at this time was intensified by his inability to realize a cherished project for a film about St. Paul—a film that would transpose the saint's drama into the contemporary world. The published scenario leaves no doubt that Pasolini viewed the father of the Church in a deeply autobiographical light: a lonely prophet, St. Paul is struck down by a mysterious illness of the flesh after he witnesses a young man in the process of undressing. Like Pasolini, this unhappy saint is misunderstood and mocked by the progressive intellectuals who should best have understood him; at one point he is even booed by young radicals who arrogantly dismiss his "irrationalism."[10]

During these lonely years, Pasolini's deepest affinities seemed to lie with thinkers outside his native land. His concern with "false tolerance," and with the devastating effects of mass consumerism, echoed sentiments

---

[9] Pasolini, *Scritti corsari* (Milan: Garzanti, 1981), pp. 159–160.
[10] See Pasolini, *San Paolo* (Turin: Einaudi, 1977).

voiced by Herbert Marcuse and the American new left in general; his meditation on power was not unlike that of Michel Foucault. Above all, his semiological readings of cultural phenomena brought to mind the Roland Barthes of *Mythologies*. But while Barthes was frequently playful and detached, Pasolini was invariably intense and polemical. Under his scrutiny, everything—fashions, advertising slogans, gestures—became a sign of the "anthropological revolution" and the "new" fascism that were devastating Italy. For example, in an essay that became notorious, he used an irreverent advertising slogan for jeans (Christ's words "He who loves me follows me" were inscribed on the backside of an attractive woman in tight jeans) to demonstrate that the power of consumerism had triumphed over the Church. "Fascism," he said, did not even touch the Church, while, today, neocapitalism destroys it."[11] Even more polemically, he insisted that the "new" fascism was even worse than the old because, unlike Nazism-Fascism, neocapitalism distorted not only the behavior of Italians but the very way they thought: "The consciousness of the Italian people," he charged, "[has reached] the point of an irreversible degradation—something which didn't happen during Fascist Fascism, a period in which behavior was completely disassociated from consciousness. . . . When Fascist Fascism fell, everything was the same as before."[12]

To no one's surprise, these inflammatory comparisons met with severe charges: at best, Pasolini's glorification of a rural past was "nostalgic" and "romantic"; at worst, instead of being an organic intellectual, he was seen as a "reactionary" and "regressive" one. Critics did not hesitate to point out that, despite his condemnation of neocapitalism, he himself—as the costly and lavish films of the trilogy made amply clear—was exploiting one of its showiest markets: that of film.[13] (Still harsher critics pointed to his involvement in another "market"—that of masculine prostitution.) The more he saw himself attacked, the more his condemnation of contemporary life encompassed everyone and everything. For example, while virtually all of Italy interpreted the 1974 vote legalizing divorce as a victory of the left, Pasolini described the measure, rather, as a triumph of "the hedonistic ideology of consumerism and [the] ensuing modernistic tolerance of the American sort."[14] As for a similar measure legalizing

[11] Pasolini, *Scritti corsari*, p. 16.

[12] Ibid., pp. 160–161.

[13] Pasolini himself was unequivocal on the impossibility of reconciling art and the (cinematic) marketplace: their coexistence was, he said, "a monstrosity: a mermaid, half woman and half fish, or a hermaphrodite, half man and half woman—in short, a carnival attraction. You cannot oppose art and the marketplace because the two concepts belong to two incommensurable and different universes." Pasolini, "L'ambiguità," *Filmcritica* No. 247 (August–September 1974), p. 310.

[14] Pasolini, *Scritti corsari*, p. 48.

abortion, which was passed the following year, Pasolini, to the dismay of feminists in particular, maintained that abortion is useful only to "bourgeois" couples, who, unlike their proletarian counterparts, would rather consume than procreate. While others welcomed a sexual freedom new to Italy, he, instead, declared that it turned sex into "a convention, an obligation, a social duty, a social anxiety, and an inevitable part of the consumer's quality of life."[15] Moreover, beneath the smiling face of this "new" tolerance he discerned a repressive and conformist mentality that "ignored and rejected all that is sexually different with a violence found only in . . . the camps."[16] He feared, too, that this violence might well be directed against homosexuals in particular since their very nature made them a threat to the "repressive libidinal economy which supports the whole structure of industrial society."[17]

As this last remark suggests, the hatred Pasolini felt for the "anthropological revolution" taking place in Italy was intensified by the conviction that it had especially adverse consequences for homosexuals. He pointed out, for example, that the process of cultural leveling or "homologization" signaled the end of traditional societies (such as that characterizing Sicily)—societies where the sequestration of women had frequently encouraged homosexuality. Moreover, as regional differences weakened and the media grew more powerful and all-invasive, young men were increasingly pressured to reject the past, which had often included homosexuality, and to ape, instead, the "uniform" model of life seen on television—a model incarnated in the "bourgeois couple." In several instances, as Pasolini commented, this urge to repress and reject all that was "abnormal" in the past led bands of youths to turn on homosexuals and attack them. (Referring to one such incident that took place in Sicily, Pasolini remarked: "This little world of Sodom has been destroyed by a ferocious Gomorrah modeled after Milan."[18]) Whether or not part of this larger pattern, an atmosphere of physical and mental violence appeared, increasingly, to shroud Pasolini's own sexual adventures: it is said that young men, knowing who he was, used to blackmail him, or attempt to blackmail him, after an encounter. And these sexual difficulties were

---

[15] Ibid., p. 120.

[16] Ibid., p. 121.

[17] Pasolini, *Il sogno del centauro*, p. 159. Cf. Herbert Marcuse: "Against a society which employs sexuality as means for a useful end, the perversions uphold sexuality as an end in itself; they thus place themselves outside the dominion of the performance principle and challenge its very foundation. They establish libidinal relationships which society must ostracize because they threaten to reverse the process of civilization which turned the organism into an instrument of work. They are a symbol of what had to be suppressed so that suppression could prevail and organize the ever more efficient domination of man and nature." Marcuse, *Eros and Civilization* (Boston: Beacon, 1971), p. 50.

[18] Pasolini, "Le mie *Mille e une notte*," *Playboy* (Italy), July–September 1973, p. 124.

undoubtedly exacerbated by a growing concern with aging (he turned fifty in 1972) and by the deep distress he experienced at the marriage, in the early 1970s, of his beloved friend and frequent companion Ninetto Davoli.

Del resto l'amore per la verità finisce col distruggere tutto, perchè non c'è niente di vero.
—Pier Paolo Pasolini (1971)

(Besides, the love of truth winds up destroying everything—because nothing is true.)

The deep, and oft-expressed, despair that assailed Pasolini in these years was, certainly, one of the factors that made his decision to film Boccaccio's bawdy tales in *Il Decamerone* (*The Decameron*, 1971) one of the most unexpected of all the twists and turns that had punctuated his career. But there were other reasons for surprise. Not only did he turn his back on the tragic universe of the mythic quartet, and on the social and political concerns that preoccupied him as a journalist, but—and this was, of course, the most "scandalous" aspect of the film—he depicted sexuality with an explicitness and daring new to Italy. For the first time, Italian audiences saw scenes of unabashed nudity as well as frequent close-ups of genitals, erections, and lovemaking in all positions. Noting that he confronted the "theme of sex" in a way that touched upon pornography (the films of the trilogy were, in fact, soon followed by a flood of pornographic "sequels" on the order of *Decamerone II* and *A Thousand and One Nights in Italy*), Pasolini deemed this sexual explicitness "a traumatic thing which has the value of a rupture, a value of liberation both on the right and the left."[19]

If, as the above remark suggests, this "traumatic" rupture was impelled by Pasolini's desire for scandal (and, perhaps, by a wish to recover the audience lost during his "aristocratic" period), other factors were almost certainly at work. He himself spoke, for example, of his constant need for innovation: with *Medea*, he said, he had come to the end of the formal

[19] This remark was made at a 1974 conference that was reported on in *Il Messaggero* on November 1, 1976. Reproached with opening the door to pornography, Pasolini argued that his films helped create a liberalized climate allowing serious directors such as Bernardo Bertolucci and Marco Ferreri to make important works. He also argued polemically that even a pornographic film was better than television: "I prefer the vulgarity of pornography and the most traumatizing violence to the total absence of reality on TV. Violence and vulgarity are at least sometimes mitigated by the fact that they belong, sadly, to reality: the falseness of television is truly immoral." See "Le interviste: Pasolini," p. 8.

experiments that had begun with *Uccellacci e Uccellini*.[20] And, above all, he stressed his conviction that the films of the trilogy—*Il Decamerone* was quickly followed by *I racconti di Canterbury* (*The Canterbury Tales*, 1972) and *Il fiore delle mille e una notte* (*Tales of a Thousand and One Nights*, 1974)—were inspired by a changed perspective concerning life itself. It was a perspective, he said, that reflected both the depth of his political despair and the "onset" of old age: "After a series of disillusionments you wind up by seeing reality as a horrendous, intolerable thing—as a perfidious game played by some devilish god . . . or else as a game."[21] Disillusionment and age, together with the consequent sense of "life's brevity," had inspired in him, he insisted, a desire to laugh, to "reconcile" himself with life. And by "life" Pasolini meant, decidedly, not the historical and social changes that were the subject of his newspaper articles but, rather, physical or "ontological" realities embodied in the sexual act, the "corporeal moment by definition." It was, he insisted polemically, precisely their "rejection" of history that allowed the lusty Neapolitans of *Il Decamerone* to reach a "pure" state of reality.[22]

Not unexpectedly, while the overt sexuality of his films disturbed critics on the right, his defiant rejection of history and ideology drew the wrath, yet again, of left-wing critics. This time, they charged, Pasolini had taken refuge in erotic dreams, in an "idealized" version of the Middle Ages.[23] In the face of such accusations, Pasolini—also not unexpectedly—counterattacked as forcefully, as polemically, as ever. Still, as if moved by inner uncertainties, for the first time he appeared to embrace simultaneously several different, and not totally reconcilable, lines of defense. On the one hand, *implicitly separating sexuality and politics*, he maintained that it was "racist" and "conformist" to suggest that sexual themes were worse than, say, political or religious ones.[24] But, on the other hand, he

---

[20] Pasolini, "C'est le *Décameron* qui m'a choisi," *La Galerie* (Paris) No. 111 (December 1971), p. 88.

[21] "Intervista con Pier Paolo Pasolini," *Cinema sessanta* Vol. 12, No. 87–88 (January 1972), p. 99.

[22] *Con Pier Paolo Pasolini*, p. 100.

[23] For critical attacks against the trilogy, see *Da Accatone a Salò, Quaderni della Cineteca* (Bologna) No. 4 (May 1982), pp. 102, 107, 109.

[24] Pasolini's belief that one must not distinguish between "social" and "erotic" themes in cinema was shared by Félix Guattari, who wrote that "all themes are at once social and transsexual. There is not a political cinema and an erotic cinema. Cinema is political whatever its subject; every time that it shows a man, a woman, a child or an animal, it makes a political choice in the class micro-struggle for the reproduction of the models of desire. . . . You can make a film [that is] in favor of the revolution but [that is] fascist from the viewpoint of the economy of desire. Therefore, what is politically determining in cinema? Not words and ideas, but a whole series of asignifying messages that escape from dominant semiologies: images, noises, rhythms, the whole of movements that shape desire indepen-

contended that his portrayal of sexuality *was itself political*. And this was so, he seemed to suggest, for two major reasons. First, it was his conviction that the explicit sexuality of the trilogy was nothing less than a "political protest" against the reification and alienation imposed by modern capitalism. ("A body," he defiantly declared, "is always revolutionary because it represents what cannot be codified."[25]) Second—and here Pasolini's argument clearly touched on issues central to modern thought—he also maintained that the *very way we perceive, and represent, sexuality is itself political*. Thus when critics from the radical left complained about the lack of "ideology" in his films, he retorted by accusing them of ignoring the inseparable links between sexuality and ideology. In deliberately scandalous terms he told them that the "ideology" of his films was "really there, above their heads, in the enormous cock on the screen."[26] Clearly distressed by these youthful radicals who attacked him with the same narrow-mindedness that their Communist "fathers" had displayed in the 1950s and 1960s—and who, moreoover, saw *him* as a "father"—he went so far as to declare that the explicit sexuality of the trilogy was largely conceived as a protest against the rigid moralism of the extreme left. Indicting not only his intransigeant critics but also the puritanical cast of Marxism itself, he observed that the trilogy stemmed from the desire to

> oppose both this excess of politicalisation and utilitarianism on the part of leftists as well as the unreality of mass culture. To make films where you could find the existentialist sense of the body, of what is physical, the *élan vital* which is being lost. In my trilogy I tried—in a total and absolute way—to anchor myself in the existential. . . . Now, the extreme point of corporeality is sex. . . . Let me add something else. It is not true that sexual problems are external to politics— they are political. Why haven't Marxist texts talked about free love for forty years? Why? Marx spoke about free love. . . . It is that Marxism has re-absorbed the customs of the culture which gave birth to it.[27]

But if, as these remarks suggest, Pasolini was disturbed by left-wing attacks, in a curious way he obviously relished the opportunity they afforded for continuing polemics. Almost, in fact, as if he clung to the embattled and misunderstood position implicit in such polemics, he hardly appeared to acknowledge, much less enjoy, the general success enjoyed by the trilogy. ("Success," he remarked revealingly in the course of one

dently of the ordering values of power." Guattari, "Al di là del significante," in *Erotismo, eversione, merce*, ed. Vittorio Boarini (Bologna: Capelli, 1974), pp. 93–94.

[25] Cited by Tommaso Anzoino in his *Pasolini, Il Castoro* No. 51 (February 1974), pp. 7–8.

[26] Pasolini, "Tetis," in *Erotismo, eversione, merce*, pp. 100–101.

[27] "Pasolini ne triche pas avec le public," *Jeune cinema* No. 74 (November 1973), pp. 10–11.

television interview, "is but the other face of persecution."[28]) His own remarks contain little hint of the fact that the general public was clearly entranced by his films: for the first time in his life, Pasolini achieved a huge popular success. Even most reviewers (though ardent admirers of earlier films were probably not among them) welcomed the trilogy. Many of them saw these films not only as a happy departure from the elitism of the mythic quartet but even as a return to the populist world of *Accattone* and *Mamma Roma*—a world that, by now, they regarded with intense nostalgia.

This was a view that obviously pleased Pasolini. In fact, he was quick to underscore the resemblances between his early, sub-proletarian films and those of the trilogy. He pointed out, for example, that both sets of films used popular milieus, nonprofessional actors, and regional dialects.[29] Further—despite earlier, oft-repeated declarations that his Gramscian phase was over—he even suggested that the films of the trilogy had a national-popular cast. Almost as if to root these films in what Gramsci might have called the "humus" of popular culture, he observed that each of the three films was based on a book that had founded not only a literary tradition but an entire culture. "At the same time that [these books] establish a literature," he wrote,

> they offer, for the first time, a premature and prophetic image of what a society will be like. That is, Boccaccio's *Decamerone* already contains the Italian bourgeoisie and the world of Italy. . . . *The Canterbury Tales* already contains Shakespeare and the modern English world. And the tales of *Le mille e una notte*, although anonymous, nonetheless establish a world, a nation, a culture.[30]

And elsewhere—clearly in a more polemical vein—he went so far as to liken *Il Decamerone* to what was probably his most national-popular work, *Il Vangelo secondo Matteo*. "If you look at *Il Vangelo* and *Il Decamerone* with a critical eye," he said, "the style and the idea are the same: sex has taken the place of Christ, that's all, but it is not a big difference."[31]

Pasolini's desire to link the trilogy to the beloved figure of Gramsci and to his early films—icons of happier times—is not difficult to understand. And there is, as he noted, a distinctly populist cast to the trilogy. But, in

---

[28] Cited in *Pasolini: Una vie future*, ed. Laura Betti and Sergio Vecchio (Rome: River Press, 1987), p. 375.

[29] In *Il Decamerone*, Neapolitan dialect replaces Boccaccio's erudite language, while a mix of northern Italian accents and dialects is used to dub the English actors of *The Canterbury Tales*. Even the black Africans and Arabs of *Il fiore delle mille e una notte* are dubbed by speakers from the south of Italy.

[30] "Pier Paolo Pasolini," Interview with Michel Maingois, *Zoom* (October 1974), p. 24.

[31] "Entretien avec Pier Paolo Pasolini," *Image et son* No. 267 (January 1973), p. 84.

truth, just as the difference between Christ and sex is greater than he suggested, so, too, is the gap between the bawdy tales of the trilogy and the
tragic universe of his first films much wider than he cared to admit. Differences in tone and emphasis constantly overshadow more superficial
resemblances. In the trilogy, after all, Pasolini's earlier portrayal of proletarian life—a portrayal so accurate that many consider *Accattone* an
ethnological document—gives way to a mythical universe where little distinguishes medieval Englishmen from their Neapolitan counterparts. (As
if to justify this surprising indifference toward the specific nature of various cultures, Pasolini remarked of *Le mille e una notte* that "one popular
culture equals another popular culture; my polemic was against dominant eurocentric culture."[32]) In this mythical universe, the tension between "passion and ideology" at the heart of Pasolini's early films is
mowed down by an all-powerful Eros, while, on the formal level, the epic
style and "technical sacredness" of *Accattone* and *Mamma Roma* are replaced by an art that insistently declares that it wants only to play, to
please, to tell tales solely for the "pleasure of telling."

In the political climate of the early 1970s, Pasolini's repeated insistence
on the pleasure of art (a modern formulation, perhaps, of "art for art's
sake") was almost as scandalous—if less spectacular—as the sexual explicitness of his films. Deliberately polemical, he returned to this theme
again and again: a work of art, he declared, is nothing other than a
"dream," a "game," a "fantasy." Speaking of *Il Decamerone*, he told the
writer Dario Bellezza, "I do not claim to express reality with reality (or
men with men or things with things) in order to create a work of art, but
simply in order to 'play' with a reality that jokes with itself."[33] And even
within the films themselves, we are reminded of their unreal and imaginary nature: the preface to *Le mille e una notte* tells us that "a work of
art is made up not of one, but of many dreams"; *Il Decamerone* closes as
Pasolini, playing an artist, muses: "Why make a work when it is so much
nicer just to dream about it?"

The most "pleasurable" aspect of the trilogy stems, perhaps, from its
sheer visual beauty. Visibly modeled after schools of painting—Giotto
and Giotto's school (*Il Decamerone*), English and German miniatures
(*The Canterbury Tales*), and Arab miniatures (*Il fiore delle mille e una*

---

[32] Pasolini, *Il cinema in forma di poesia*, p. 162. Still—showing some of the tensions at
work in these years—Pasolini's professed indifference toward the specific nature of popular
cultures was far from consistent. Despite proclamations of this sort concerning his films, in
the collection of literary reviews entitled *Descrizioni di descrizioni* (Turin: Einaudi, 1979)
he continued to insist that authors must be scrupulous and precise when using dialect.

[33] Pasolini, "Io e Boccaccio," *L'Espresso* No. 47 (November 22, 1970), p. 18.

notte)[34]—the lavish costumes and elaborate sets constantly evoke analogies with the fine arts. Jean Sémoulé, for example, writes enthusiastically that the rich and warm "palette" of *The Canterbury Tales*—marked by sumptuous reds and strident yellows—pointed ahead to the "international gothic [style] and beyond that, to Cranach and especially Grünewald."[35] And, like paintings in whose depths lurks a small self-portrait of the artist, the first two films of the trilogy contain a performance by Pasolini himself: in *Il Decamerone* he appears as Giotto, or, more precisely, as a pupil of Giotto; in *The Canterbury Tales* as Chaucer. Pensive and solitary creatures given to bursts of creative frenzy, these authorial figures—portrayed with heavy self-irony by Pasolini—underscore, he noted, the artist's "detachment, the distance separating him from the world or from society."[36]

Playing a writer and a painter, Pasolini seems to locate film somewhere between these two forms of art. Ironically, perhaps, he is closer to Giotto than to Chaucer: the fresco painter's obvious pleasure in confronting the physical realities of his art—realities embodied in oozing paints and imposing stone walls—seems to echo his own lifelong desire to "seize" reality in a tangible way. The affinity he felt for Giotto is suggested by the deliberate analogies he created between himself and the medieval painter. In *Il Decamerone*, he observed,

> I created a perfect analogy: I played the role of a Northern Italian artist who therefore comes from historical Italy and goes down to Naples to paint frescoes (exactly according to this ontology of reality) on the walls of the Church of Santa Chiara. And, in fact, I am a Northern Italian from the historical part of Italy who goes to Naples to make a realistic film. Thus, there is an analogy between the character and the author . . . a work within the work.[37]

Still other affinities between Pasolini and Giotto have struck the imagination of critics. Millicent Marcus, for example, observes that both the fresco artist and the filmmaker "narrate through visual images, thus potentially reaching a much broader, more democratic audience than literature can, and both juxtapose a series of still frames to tell a story which unfolds in time and space."[38] Another American critic, Ben Lawton— who notes that Pasolini depicts Giotto surrounded by a team of helpers

[34] See the recollections of Dante Ferretti, set designer for the trilogy, in Antonio Bertini's *Teoria e tecnica del film in Pasolini* (Rome: Bulzoni, 1979), p. 191.

[35] Jean Sémoulé, "Réflexions sur le récit," in *Pasolini: Un "cinéma de poésie,"* special issue of *Etudes cinématographiques* No. 111–112 (1970), p. 160.

[36] "Entretien avec Pasolini," *Image et son*, p. 84.

[37] "Intervista con Pier Paolo Pasolini," *Cinema sessanta*, p. 96.

[38] Millicent Marcus, "*Il Decamerone*: Pasolini as a Reader of Boccaccio," *Italian Quarterly* No. 82–83 (Fall–Winter 1980–1981), p. 178.

and by extensive scaffolding—remarks that both mural painting and film-making require "collective effort" and "massive machinery." In Lawton's view, too, the analogies between Giotto and Pasolini are underscored by one sequence in particular, where the medieval painter behaves exactly like a filmmaker on location:

> We . . . see Pasolini/Giotto's pupil in the marketplace where he looks at differ-ent people and frames them with his fingers. The people he frames are individ-ually framed by the film itself as the director/painter turns to the camera, lowers his hands, and smiles directly at us (and the camera). As we move into the next episode . . . we discover that the people who were framed at the marketplace by the artist are now the protagonists.[39]

In the last scene of the film, as Lawton proceeds to observe, the two sep-arate visions—that of the filmmaker and the painter—actually merge as the Bosch-like tableau of the Last Judgment "dreamed" by Giotto's dis-ciple becomes the scene filmed by Pasolini.

Highly personal authorial figures, Giotto and Chaucer have still an-other important meta-cinematic function: appearing at intervals through-out the films, they serve to anchor or join a series of unconnected tales. In this way, they play a vital role in the so-called "frame narrative"—that is, a narrative where disparate tales are loosely grouped together in an open-ended fashion—which structures these films and aligns them formally. (One critic suggests that the Arabian *Tales of a Thousand and One Nights*—a collection of tales that Pasolini loved as a child and that he re-created in the last film of the trilogy—should be seen as the prototype of this frame narrative, a prototype that influenced both Boccaccio and Chaucer.[40]) If the arrangement of tales in the trilogy reflects Pasolini's longstanding love for sharp narrative divisions, for a narrative that calls attention to itself, it also serves to distinguish these films from earlier ones. Whereas the narrative divisions of previous films underscored the-matic and ideological contrasts—especially the fundamental contrast be-tween past and present—the separate tales of the trilogy have, instead, no connection to one another. Linked only by a frame, they belong to a world where, as Pasolini said, "form explodes for its own sake."[41] And

---

[39] Ben Lawton, "Theory and Practice in Pasolini's Trilogy of Life: *Decameron*," *Quar-terly Review of Film Studies* Vol. 2, No. 4 (November 1977), pp. 406–407.

[40] See Katherine Slater Gittes, "*The Canterbury Tales* and the Arabic Frame Tradition," *PMLA* xcviii, No. 2 (March 1983), p. 241.

[41] Interview with Michel Maingois, *Zoom*, p. 24. Pasolini's remarks notwithstanding, some critics did attempt to discern an order in the tales. For example, speaking of *The Canterbury Tales*, Jean Sémoulé proposed what he called certain "affinities." In his view, "in the first and last two tales supernatural forces intervene—either in a mysterious and discreet, or in a decorative and emphatic, way; the four tales in the middle . . . embody a

the more he delved into this world of narrative intricacies and gamelike patterns, the more he found himself entranced by what he called the "marvelous formal adventure of pure narration." Describing his fascination for the age-old genre of the tale, he remarked, "I wanted to pit myself against the (pure and simple) tale, to penetrate the great intricacies of the ontology of the tale, which are far more mysterious and universal than any other narrative form."[42]

"Pitting" himself against the tale meant, of course, deciding how to weave tales together, how to interlace frame and narrative. And for each film of the trilogy, Pasolini—who obviously loved playing with narrative permutations—chose a different solution. *Il Decamerone*, for example, is divided into two narrative blocks: the first of these is framed by the tale (split in two parts) of Ser Ciappelletto, the second by the adventures of Giotto's disciple. As if to insist on the affinities between these two framing or "meta-linguistic" characters, Pasolini has a close friend, Franco Citti, play Ser Ciappelletto, while he himself plays the medieval painter. (The fact that Boccaccio describes Ser Ciappelletto as a homosexual sinner suggests still another affinity between the two characters.)

The implied link between frame and narrator in *Il Decamerone*—provided by Pasolini's own presence—becomes explicit in *The Canterbury Tales*. There Pasolini abandons Chaucer's pilgrims—the presence of several narrators would, he said, have proven "mechanical and awkward" in the film[43]—in favor of a single character, the fictional Chaucer. Invented solely to narrate (unlike Giotto or Ser Ciappelletto, Chaucer is not embedded in a tale of his own), named after the author of the tales and played by the author of the film, it is this fictional Chaucer who clearly bears, as Pasolini said, the "meta-linguistic meaning of the film."

Both the narrative complexities of *Il Decamerone* and the textual layering of *The Canterbury Tales* become most extreme in the last film of the trilogy, *Il fiore delle mille e una notte*. Here there are no specific framing characters like Giotto and Chaucer. Instead, frame and tale constantly interact—like an infinite series of Chinese boxes—as tales encase other

---

much denser gaiety and remain more "earthy." See Sémoulé, "Réflexions sur le récit," p. 150.

[42] "Pasolini répond à huit questions," *Le Journal du Dimanche*, November 26, 1972. As this remark suggests, Pasolini's attraction to tales may have been heightened by their populist cast. Rooted in the "humus" of popular culture, tales always constitute, to use Walter Benjamin's term, an "artisanal form of communication." See Benjamin, "The Storyteller," in *Illuminations* (New York: Schocken, 1969), p. 91

[43] Pasolini, *Il cinema in forma di poesia*, p. 144. Elsewhere, he observed that Chaucer's narrators "chatter rather than narrate: the tales they recount are a pretext for marvelous comic-moralistic bravura pieces. . . . [This] gives rise to the distance from one's own tale, the irony toward one's own tale, that is typical of Anglo-Saxon literature." See "Libertà e sesso secondo Pasolini," *Corriere della sera*, February 4, 1973.

tales, breaking off abruptly only to resume at a later point. Discussing the attraction he felt for this kind of "limitless narration," Pasolini noted: "The proliferation of tales one within another, the possibility of telling infinite fables [*affabulazione*], of narrating for the sake of narrating (sometimes lingering over unexpected details) . . . —this, and the absence of an end, conquered me more than anything else."[44]

In the complex ways it interweaves frame and narrative, *Il fiore delle mille e una notte* announces the intricate structure of Pasolini's next and last film, *Salò*. Here, too, he based his film on a work that uses a variation of the frame narrative: *120 Journées de Sodome* (*120 Days in Sodom*), a novel by the Marquis de Sade. And it is noteworthy that, while still at work on the last film of the trilogy, Pasolini wrote a literary essay concerning the adroit integration of frame and narrative in *120 Journées de Sodome*. In a passage where he might almost be describing some of the narrative processes at work in both *Le mille e una notte* and *Salò*, Pasolini observes that Sade's narrators both act and relate tales—in a kind of *mise en abime*—that mirror their actions. "Sade's great discovery," he remarks,

> was not only to render the framework—a framework that, in Boccaccio, was pretextual and literary—alive and real but to do so in a way that creates a specular relationship between the framework and the narrative itself. The framework and the narrative "corpus" are linked by a series of situations which are subtly analogical rather than identical. This results in an infinite iterative accumulation (that of the central tale which acts as a framework) which, together with another iterative accumulation (of the 600 tales), carries a charge which expands to a point beyond the grandiose.[45]

The taste for narrative intricacies radiating from this passage, as well as the trilogy itself, reflects, certainly, Pasolini's lifelong passion for formal issues—the passion of an artist who wants to shape and mold a world of his own making. And perhaps the more the outside world made him feel vulnerable and powerless, the more he experienced the need to make the machinery of this fictional world as complex, as absorbing, even as autonomous, as possible. But if this was the case, then to some extent his labors were in vain. Despite himself, he could not prevent his true feelings from seeping into the trilogy, from contaminating this imaginary world which was to have been one of life and joy. Indeed, I would argue that, *like a film beneath a film, Pasolini's bleak and disabused view of human nature—and especially of sexuality—continually subverts the supposedly "joyful" Eros of the trilogy's many tales.*

[44] Pasolini, "L'idea delle *mille e una notte*," *Il Mondo*, May 31, 1973.
[45] Pasolini, *Descrizioni di descrizioni*, p. 275.

Although the dark underside of the trilogy would become increasingly apparent with each successive film, even when *Il Decamerone* was first released, a few reviewers did sense a somber note. One, for example, was struck by Pasolini's "furtive Eros" and his "dark" view of Boccaccio, while another went so far as to suggest that this supposedly lighthearted film echoed the "ferociousness" of *Porcile* and the "dark chasm" of *Medea*.[46] In all probability, the memory of the mythic quartet was evoked by one tale in particular of *Il Decamerone*—that of the "basil plant." For this haunting episode—which generally struck critics as the most beautiful moment of the film—does indeed reverberate with all the sensuous violence and death-haunted passion that mark, say, *Edipo Re* or *Medea*. In this tale, the brothers of a beautiful young woman discover her making love with a servant. Outraged, they kill the poor lad and hide his body. But their grief-stricken sister finds the corpse; she cuts off her lover's head, places it tenderly in a flowerpot, and plants a basil plant over it. In this way, she says, it will always remain close to her—a reminder, in the words of Edoardo Bruno, of the nights of "ecstasy" spent with her lover.[47]

This was, admittedly, the only tragic tale in the film. But, aside from one other episode that also features young lovers, the Eros of the other tales is less joyful than it is frenzied, grotesque, compelling. The contortions of the nude bodies in *Il Decamerone*, writes Lino Miccichè in an important article on the trilogy, communicate not physical or instinctive joy but, instead, a "dark and animalistic obsession mixed with blood and sperm, excrement and sweat."[48] For the most part, the lovers of *Il Decamerone* are fleshy, crude, and unattractive beings who are blindly driven by unbridled instincts. Stereotyped and "episodic" beings, to borrow a phrase from Jean Sémoulé,[49] these characters are jerked about like puppets activated not by strings but by a current of insistent sexuality. Lust makes them the perpetrators, and the butt, of cruel jokes: a priest sodomizes a woman by telling her husband that this will transform her into a useful donkey; a thieving woman has a youth robbed and dropped into a cesspool; a wife manages to hang up her husband in a basket so she can cuckold him with a student.

[46] Aggeo Savioli, Review of *Il Decamerone*, in de Guisti, *I film di Pier Paolo Pasolini*, p. 121 (originally in *L'Unità*, September 19, 1971); Giorgio de Vincenti, "Un nuovo corso," *Cinema sessanta* Vol. 12, No. 87/88 (January 1972), p. 101.

[47] Edoardo Bruno, "La sacralità erotica del *Decamerone* di Pasolini," *Filmcritica* No. 217 (August 1971), p. 344.

[48] Lino Miccichè, "Pasolini: la morte e la storia," *Cinema sessanta* No. 121 (May–June 1978), p. 10.

[49] "The men and women of the trilogy," writes Sémoulé, "remain episodic in the fullest sense . . . they emerge from the crowd only to be plunged back into it soon afterwards." See Jean Sémoulé, "Réflexions sur le récit," p. 153.

With the next film of the trilogy, *The Canterbury Tales*, the jokes and pranks took an even crueler and coarser turn. Only one truly lighthearted tale graces this film—a tale that, interestingly, features Pasolini's friend Ninetto Davoli. In a sequence that pays homage to Chaplin, Davoli plays a medieval tramp who creates havoc wherever he goes. But if, as always, Davoli radiates "joy" and "innocence," still another friend of Pasolini's, Franco Citti, becomes the very embodiment of evil in this film. In the most sinister and disquieting episode of *The Canterbury Tales*, Citti plays a devil who loves to spy upon homosexuals so that he can catch them in *flagrante delicto* and blackmail them. When one of his miserable victims is too poor to pay the sum demanded, Citti gleefully denounces the wretched sinner to the authorities. And, as the poor man is burned (or "fried") at the stake, this greedy devil hawks *fritelle* (fried things) to viewers who have come to see the spectacle. Nor is this the last we see of the devil. As if to set the entire film under the sign of evil, in the last scene of *The Canterbury Tales* he reappears in his true habitat—the inferno—as he farts demonic friars into the smoky air.

Epitomized by the scenes with the devil, the darkness and cruelty of *The Canterbury Tales* are so striking that even critics who had liked *Il Decamerone* cried out in dismay: epithets ranged from "bad taste" and "intellectual narcissism" to "acute pessimism," "desecrating cruelty," and "an increasingly ungovernable homosexual instinct." Forced to acknowledge the film's disturbing undertow, Pasolini remarked that this second film might be seen as a kind of "hiatus" in the trilogy, which, he confessed, reflected a moment of deep unhappiness on his part. (This was around the time of Davoli's marriage.) Still, as if to suggest that he himself was not totally responsible for the film's gloomy underside, he went on to observe that Chaucer himself was more somber than Boccaccio. In a remark laced with obvious personal overtones, he noted that whereas the Italian author lived at the beginning of an exciting "new era"—when the nascent middle class was still close to the people—Chaucer, instead, seemed to sense the eventual decay of the bourgeoisie. Imbued with a "metaphysics of death," Chaucer's work, noted Pasolini, was marked by an important dichotomy: "on the one hand, there is the epic aspect with the vulgar and vital heroes of the Middle Ages who were full of life; on the other, the essentially bourgeois phenomena of irony and self-irony which are the sign of a guilty conscience."[50]

Whether or not Chaucer did indeed suffer from "irony and self-irony"—and there is no doubt, of course, that the creator of *La ricotta* and *Salò* certainly did—the medieval author can hardly be made to shoul-

---

[50] "Un drôle d'uccello pour Pasolini: Interview with Gerard Langlois," *Les lettres françaises*, March 1, 1972, p. 16.

der all the blame for the film's dark and disquieting cast. As Lino Miccichè points out, it is, after all, Pasolini who manipulates Chaucer's tales.
And by choosing some tales and eliminating others, Pasolini creates what
Miccichè calls an "obsessive erotic ideology"—an ideology imbued with
the fatal and sin-ridden view of sexuality that had always characterized
his work. With this film, asserts Miccichè, Pasolini transforms a literary
document informed by nascent Protestantism into a film marked by the
dark and unsettling Catholicism of the Counter-Reformation. In his view,
Pasolini's vision of sexuality

> appears more fecal than fatal, more linked to a conception of matter as con-
> demnation and of sex as a mournful instinct placed "*intra foeces et urinam*"
> . . . than to even a rough and confused search for a lost "principle of pleasure."
> Here teratology becomes scatology, sex is only an interpersonal variation on
> collective violence; human relationships are supervised by the devil in person,
> nature appears estranged and hostile, and the images of sinners sodomized by
> winged monsters or of women raped with hot irons seem to prefigure the infa-
> mies of *Salò*.[51]

Nor, finally, does Miccichè view *The Canterbury Tales* as a "hiatus" in
the trilogy. Quite the contrary: he goes so far as to argue that all three
films constitute less a "trilogy of life" than, together with *Salò*, a quartet
or "tetralogy of death."

If, as Miccichè suggests, all the films of the trilogy can be said to prefigure *Salò*, it must also be noted—and this qualification is an important one
that has been missed by many critics—that the last film, *Il fiore delle mille
e una notte*, does so in very different ways from the first two. In many
respects, *Il fiore delle mille e una notte* (*The Tales of a Thousand and One
Nights*)—usually seen as the high point of the trilogy and, sometimes, as
one of Pasolini's best films in general—is most unlike *Il Decamerone* and
The Canterbury Tales. Again, one can speculate on the reasons for this
change. It may be that, despite protestations to the contrary, Pasolini took
to heart the criticisms of *The Canterbury Tales*; or perhaps even he felt
that the grotesque carnival had gone far enough. Or, impelled by one of
the inner swings that punctuate his career, he may have wanted to exorcise what he called the "irony and self-irony"—those quintessential
"bourgeois phenomena"—that had given *The Canterbury Tales* its special tone. Whatever the reason, or reasons, in *Il fiore delle mille e una
notte* he abandons the very physical world of medieval Europe for a totally imaginary and stylized universe. No longer dense, weighty, and "ontological," reality now springs from, and merges into, pure appearance:
narratives woven into tapestries start to unfold in "real" life, which be-

---

[51] Miccichè, "Pasolini: la morte e la storia," p. 8.

comes, as a consequence, one more fiction. "A series of realistic figures," said Pasolini, "that you gradually see embedded in other realistic figures becomes a series of fictional figures."[52] In this weightless and elegant universe, where life is no more than a "dream within a dream," flying carpets and magic spells replace coarse jokes and earthy humor. The flesh of middle age gives way to the grace of adolescence in willowy youths who, unmarked by a physical or psychological presence, resemble, in Pasolini's words, "gazelles" and "palm trees."[53]

At this time in his life, perhaps the only beautiful universe Pasolini could imagine had to be totally imaginary and unreal. Still, the stylized elegance of *Il fiore delle mille e una notte* also reflects his love for the exotic people and places of the Third World—Eritrea, Yemen, Iran, and Nepal—where the film was shot. His intense feelings about this remote world inspired a beautiful documentary which, although shot a few years earlier, was released the same year as *Le mille e una notte*. Entitled *Le mura di Sana'A* (*The Walls of San'A*, 1974), this short film depicts San'A, the capital of Yemen, an ancient and exquisite city that Pasolini described as "a small, savage Venice perched not at the sea, but on the dirty dust of the desert between gardens of palm and grain."[54] Within the film itself, Pasolini appeals to UNESCO to rescue San'A from the building speculation and greed that have ruined European cities. (The medieval panorama of the Italian town of Orte is shown ringed by ugly modern high-rises.) The film concludes with a poetically insistent, repeated panorama from right to left of San'A's ancient walls, as Pasolini reiterates his plea that the town be saved in the name of the "revolutionary force of the past, before it is too late."

No less than *Le mura di Sana'A*, *Il fiore delle mille e una notte* vibrates with Pasolini's love for this ancient and remote world—a world characterized, in his eyes, by "peasant superstition, homosexual love, and feudal civilization."[55] It is these essential traits that infuse his film, propelling the inexplicable events and moments of erotic intensity that punctuate the seamless surface of the interlaced tales. Freed of grotesque frenzy, of sin, the sexuality of this world is "mysterious and hidden," tragic, perhaps,

---

[52] *Con Pier Paolo Pasolini*, p. 110.

[53] Suggesting that the stereotyped characters were, like sets and costumes, merely one element in the tale, Pasolini remarked: "In *Le mille e una notte* psychology does not have as much importance as in Boccaccio: it is very stereotyped. Now a stereotyped psychology also demands a more stereotyped language. In Boccaccio, for example, when a character talks, he expresses linguistically his social condition. When an Arab character [of *Le mille e una notte*] talks, he does not express that. In *Le mille e una notte*, the real function is *the story*, while in Boccaccio, and especially in Chaucer, the real function is the *character*. "Interview with Michel Maingois," *Zoom*, p. 24.

[54] Pasolini, "Le mie *Mille e una notte*," p. 126.

[55] Ibid., p. 124.

but "exalted."[56] Describing his deliberate efforts to create a "purified" and stylized Eros in the last film of the trilogy, Pasolini remarked:

> May I say, a bit tautologically, that for me eroticism is the beauty of the boys of the Third World. It is this type of sexual relation—violent, exalting and happy—that still survives in the Third World and that I have depicted almost completely in *Il fiore delle mille e une notte* although I have purified it, that is, stripped it of mechanics and movement [by] arranging it frontally, almost arresting it.[57]

As this remark suggests, the "violent and exalting" Eros of these tales concerns love between men as often, and perhaps more often, as love between men and women. In striking contrast to *Il Decamerone* and *The Canterbury Tales*, in *Le mille e una notte* homosexuality is free not only of irony and sin but even of "otherness." (Precisely for this reason, at least one critic considers it an important moment in film history.[58]) In several tales, morever, homosexuality is imbued with what Pasolini called a particular "exquisiteness" or "ambiguity." In one of these tales, a middle-aged black poet-king—perhaps the most delicate autobiographical figure in Pasolini's cinema—invites three lads into his tent so that "they can give pleasure to each other and to him." The camera implies that the boys are already giving visual pleasure to the film's director for, as the sequence draws to a close, it focuses on their nude loins seen, and framed, through the opening of the tent. And an even more "ambiguous" scene closes the film. In this tale, a young man, Nur-ed-Din, finally finds the beautiful slave girl, Zumurrud, who was abducted from him as the film began. (Their tale frames all the others.) But he fails to recognize his beloved because, by a strange set of circumstances, she has become a king and is dressed as a man. In her manly disguise (which one critic sees as an "amused denial of the patriarchal, virile investiture of power"[59]), Zumur-

---

[56] For Barthélemy Amengual, the Eros of this film, which he locates between Arab courtly love and Hindu tantric love, represents nothing less than the "path to the absolute." See Amengual, "*Les Mille et une nuits* ou les nourritures terrestres," in *Pier Paolo Pasolini: Un "cinéma de poésie*," p. 178.

[57] Pasolini, "Eros e cultura: Interview with Massimo Fino," *Europeo*, October 19, 1974.

[58] Noting that Pasolini's films go beyond the "tentative representation of homosexual desire" (found, say, in a Visconti), G. Nowell-Smith writes: "With Pasolini something far more radical is happening—the beginnings of an effective undifferentiated treatment, in which there is no privileged role attributed to the male heterosexual vision, but all are, so to speak, within the reach of all. This is most clearly exemplified . . . in the scene in *Arabian Nights* where the older man and woman are watching the sleeping bodies of the adolescent boy and girl and speculate over which one is (to them) the more beautiful, and which will fall in love with the other first and most passionately." See Nowell-Smith, "Pasolini's Originality," in *Pier Paolo Pasolini*, ed. Paul Willemin (London: British Film Institute, 1977), p. 18.

[59] See Adelio Ferrero, *Il cinema di Pasolini*, (Venice: Marsilio, 1977), p. 132.

rud orders the terrified slave, Nur-ed-Din, to pull down his pants, turn on his stomach, and prepare to be mounted. Fearing the worst, he obeys . . . as he does so, his hands discover her real identity and they embrace in ecstasy.

This teasing ambiguity is, however, merely one guise that a protean Eros likes to assume. In other tales, a dark and violent sensuality impels the characters to the violent doom suffered by Oedipus and Medea. And, as two very similar tales reveal, here, too, homosexuality and heterosexuality are treated identically. Both these tales of fatal passion take place, suggestively, in a dark and forbidden underground chamber. In the homosexual tale, where passion is implicit, a shipwrecked prince comes upon a young lad who has been hidden in such a chamber in order to forestall a prophecy announcing his imminent murder. The prince laughs at the boy's fears; they bathe, caress each other, and fall asleep in the same bed. But destiny is not to be thwarted: the prince awakens in a trance, slips off the sleeping lad's clothes, and stabs him to death before climbing back into bed. In the heterosexual tale, the inhabitant of the underground chamber is a young girl who has been imprisoned by a jealous demon (Franco Citti). She, too, is discovered by a handsome youth and, defying the terrible demon, they make love. But once again passion calls forth violent death: when he learns of their love, the vengeful demon dismembers and decapitates the girl and then turns her lover into a monkey. His human form is restored to him only by the sacrificial death of another young girl, who, as if consumed by love of him, vanishes in a burst of flames.

As these tales reveal, in this legendary universe, Eros is the lure, the tool, used by an all-powerful destiny seen here at its most naked— stripped of psychology, history, and ideology. Observing that destiny is usually hidden, Pasolini remarked that every so often it "wakes up, makes a sign to us, 'appears' and there is an anomaly." Every tale in the film, he continued,

> begins with an "appearance" of destiny which manifests itself through an anomaly. Well, there is no anomaly that does not generate another. So a chain of anomalies is established. And the more this chain is logical, tightly knit, and essential, the more beautiful (that is, vital and exalting) the tale. The chain of anomalies always tends to return to normalcy. The end of each tale in *Le mille e una notte* consists of a "disappearance" of destiny which sinks back into the happy drowsiness of everyday life.[60]

Since the "sign" made by destiny involves the birth of desire, the film itself becomes a chain of desires, an erotic current that seizes its mesmerized

[60] Cited by G. L. Rondi in his *Sette domande a 45 registri* (Torino, s.e.i., 1975), p. 213.

victims and carries them along, sometimes to happiness but more often
to death. These passive beings may suffer from what Pasolini called "epis-
temological anxiety" concerning their fate, but they know that all resistance is vain: "What God wants will happen," murmurs one, "what God
does not want will not happen." The camera itself shares, and heightens,
their passivity. "Aside from two or three panning shots," said Pasolini,
"[the camera] is never present. I let the profilmic world flow by, just as
dreams and reality flow by. . . . Moreoever, in arranging its heroic game
of events, Destiny certainly does not need the camera's help. The latter
can only be contemplative."[61]

Marked by an inexorable destiny, a chain of "anomalies," *Le mille e
una notte* underscores the fatalism implicit in Pasolini's films from the
beginning. Here, destiny itself—embodied in the onward flow of a limitless narrative—has become a protagonist governing characters more sub-
missive and passive than ever before. Pawns of desire, the stereotyped
beings of *Il fiore delle mille e una notte* announce the faceless victims of
Pasolini's last film, *Salò*. There, destiny will take the form of four diabolical puppeteers, while Eros, impelled by a grotesque and precise nihilism,
will cast off all disguise, all other forms, as it becomes one with Thanatos
itself.

Toute lune est atroce, tout soleil amer.
  —Arthur Rimbaud, "Le bateau ivre" (1871)

(All moons are atrocious; all suns bitter.)

Completed weeks before his death, *Salò* is not only Pasolini's most scandalous and chilling film but one of the most disturbing and radical films
in the history of cinema. It represents the last, and most violent, swing of
Pasolini's inner pendulum—a swing that also led him to write a renunciation, or, in his words, an "abjuration," of the "trilogy of life" soon after
completing *Il fiore delle mille e una notte*. And, even as this highly theatrical document reiterates the polemical ideas voiced throughout Pasolini's
journalistic writings of this period, it also announces the dominant motifs
of *Salò*.

In the abjuration, Pasolini declares that it has become impossible to
make films, like those of the trilogy, about a beloved past. For even the
past, he charges, has been contaminated and destroyed by an abhorrent
present. The "unreality" of neocapitalism, he insists, has rendered the
impulses behind the trilogy "archaic" for three major reasons: 1) the old
struggle for free expression and sexual liberation—a struggle fundamen-

[61] Ibid., pp. 215–216.

tal to the "progressive tension" of the 1950s and 1960s and embodied in the trilogy—has been made irrelevant by the "false tolerance" of the new power; 2) the "innocent" bodies of the trilogy, bodies whose sexuality was marked by an "archaic" and "vital" violence, have been manipulated and destroyed by the "new human era"; 3) on a personal level, the fascination and pleasure that he took in sexuality have, like the "innocent" bodies of the trilogy, been swept away: "Private sexual lives (like mine) have been subjected to the trauma of false tolerance and/or corporeal degradation: what constituted joy and sorrow in sexual fantasies has turned into suicidal disillusionment and amorphous ennui."[62]

Infused with this "suicidal disillusionment," *Salò* carries us to the depths of the modern inferno announced at the beginning of *Accattone*. A "re-reading" of the Marquis de Sade's *Les 120 journées de Sodome* (*120 Days of Sodom*), *Salò* places people and actions imagined by Sade against a background informed by Dante and by modern history. Set in the last days of the Republic of Salò—the northern Italian town where Mussolini set up a short-lived "republic" after his flight from Rome in 1943—*Salò* echoes the "theological verticalism" of *The Inferno* as, like a descending spiral, it takes us from one circle of horrors to the next.

The film begins with a prologue, or "anti-inferno": in its only lyrical moment, quasi-neorealist shots depict a lush and peaceful rural landscape.[63] But the beauty of nature is soon shattered by human violence: bombardments are heard in the distance as, acting on the orders of four powerful libertines (a duke, a bishop, a magistrate, and a banker), armed soldiers are seen rounding up young male and female peasants. (As they do so, we see an ominous road sign pointing to Marzabotto, a town where acts of the Resistance triggered a terrible Fascist massacre.) Once the victims are assembled in the villa, they are read the precise rules of conduct, the formal code of sexual practices and perversions, that will henceforth govern their lives.

Inside the villa, we follow the victims' inexorable parabola as they descend from one circle to the next. Beginning with the circle of perversions (or "mania"), they proceed to that of "shit" (dominated by coprophagy) and, finally, to that of "blood" (torture and death). Each circle is introduced by a different middle-aged female narrator: dressed like the madam

---

[62] Pasolini, *Trilogia della vita* (Bologna: Capellelli, 1975), p. 11.

[63] Ugo Finetti views these opening scenes, with their long shots and panoramas of the outdoors, as an obvious reminder of neorealist films like *Paisà*: "We have the external world," he writes, "historical givens and the concrete reality of peasant life. The victims are torn away from all this and taken toward a Calvary with a growing loss of the sense of reality, toward an oneiric dimension which is the negation of history." See Finetti, "Nella struttura di *Salò*: la dialettica erotismo-potere," *Cinema nuovo* No. 244 (November 1976), p. 431.

of an elegant brothel, each relates scabrous anecdotes designed to excite the libertines, to stimulate them to perform acts similar to those described. For most of the film, a fourth middle-aged woman accompanies these anecdotes on the piano until—propelled by horror? by despair?— she jumps to her death from a window. In the film's final orgy, victims die in agony as skulls are cut open, eyes slashed, and dead bodies sodomized. As the film reaches its dreadful climax, we hear, as if broadcast by Fascist radio, Canto 99 by Ezra Pound: "The whole tribe is from man's body/ The father's word is compassion/ The son's filiality."[64]

Whereas the violence of earlier films was often left to our imagination—for example, the bestiality of *Porcile* is never seen—here every horrible detail is cherished and prolonged: the camera lingers on the blood oozing from the victims' mouths when they swallow food spiked with nails, and on the excrement smearing their lips during a coprophagic banquet. What Pasolini saw as Sade's "arid rationalism"[65]—a rationalism built upon a "series of cold and inexpressive pieces of information"—is conveyed not only by the precision and literalness of the bureaucratic libertines but by the film itself. Like Pasolini's other modern parables—*Teorema* and *Porcile*—the world of *Salò* is one where everything is mathematically composed, geometrically balanced, endowed with a precise function and meaning. Using metaphors drawn, significantly, from the inorganic world, Pasolini noted that he wanted *Salò* to be as exact and perfect as a "crystal," to have the "precision" of unreality. To achieve this end, as he told Gideon Bachman, he had to change his usual methods.

This time I want even the nonprofessional actors to act like professionals. Instead of choosing, in the cutting room, the most successful of the improvised

[64] Norman Mac Afee comments on this reference to Pound in "I am a Free Man: Pasolini's Poetry in America," *Italian Quarterly* No. 82–83 (Fall–Winter 1980–81). A great admirer of the American poet, Pasolini did a moving interview with Pound for Italian television and commented upon him in a number of his literary essays. In light of of *Salò*'s theatricality, one of his comments about Pound is of particular interest. Noting that Pound's choice of Fascism was a "totally theatrical gesture," Pasolini went on to say that Pound's politics "is gestural. Once a 'gesture' is made, every justification of it is superfluous, if not impossible. A gesture explains itself." See Pasolini, *Descrizioni di descrizioni* (Turin: Einaudi, 1979), p. 76.

[65] Describing Sade's "arid rationalism," Pasolini observed: "As in works of pornography, [Sade's writing] consists of a series of cold and inexpressive bits of information (whose linguistic characteristics of arid rationalism and feeble irony never create a stylistic tension). Nonetheless, the linguistic nature of these bits is transmuted by their virtually infinite accumulation. It is this infinite accumulation that replaces "expressiveness": for, if the first piece of information (a monk who has a child urinate in his mouth) is cold and inexpressive, the second is less so, and the thousandth not at all. And because accumulation is also repetition, the effect achieved, mechanically but very expressively, is that of litanies." See Pasolini, *Descrizioni di descrizioni*, p. 274.

lines that I have collected in the camera, and then reiterating them by synchro-
nisation or post-dubbbing and thus ending up with having to use cut-aways to
bridge the obvious gaps in continuity, this time I refuse to use cut-aways and I
now insist on exact delivery of lines so as to create a streamlined, dramatic
structure. Formally I want this film to be like a crystal, and not magmatic, cha-
otic, inventive and out-of-proportion like my previous ones. It is all perfectly
calculated.[66]

Jewel-like and polished, Salò is Pasolini's ultimate mannerist parable,
a simulacrum where nothing disturbs the seamless surface of the unnatural and the unreal. Deemed "the ultimate post-hermetic poem" by one
critic, still another wrote that Salò was as "glacial and opaque as marble,
as pure and cutting as diamond."[67] In Pasolini's elegant lager, everything
speaks of formal precision and abstract lifelessness: dark and somber colors (grays, blacks, browns); icy tile floors with geometrical patterns; and
mathematical combinations—sixteen victims (eight female, eight male),
four libertines, four middle-aged women. More strongly than any words,
the precise geometry and formal rituals of the film make it clear that no
spontaneity or life, no jouissance, is possible; nothing can break the
downward spiral of horrors, just as no one can escape the enclosed, win-
dowless rooms of the infernal villa. The one brief moment of revolt is
quickly extinguished: a young man caught in the "forbidden" act of making love naturally and spontaneously just has time to make the Communist sign of upraised arm and clenched fist before he is shot by the libertines.[68] Contrasting the relatively open nature of Teorema—where the
visitor comes from the outside world to create a "problem" within the
theorem—with the enclosed universe of Salò, Gilles Deleuze observes that
in Salò "there is no problem because there is no outside: Pasolini does not
even present Fascism in vivo, but rather Fascism at bay—shut up in the
little community, reduced to a pure innerness which coincides with the
conditions of closure where Sade's experiments unfold. As Pasolini desired, Salò is a pure dead theorem, a theorem of death."[69]

[66] "Pasolini on de Sade," Interview with Gideon Bachman, Film Quarterly Vol. 29, No. 2
(Winter 1975–1976), p. 43.
[67] Mac Afee, "I am a Free Man," p. 100; Marcel Martin, "Salò ou Les 120 Journées de
Sodome," Ecran (July 1976), p. 49.
[68] While some critics felt that this scene suggests that even the lager cannot wipe out all
hope and rebellion, the unrelenting blackness of the film leads me to agree with Ugo Finetti's
more pessimistic interpretation. For him, the gesture of the upraised fist is nothing more
than a "symbol," an icon of a past when revolutionary hope was still conceivable. Deeming
this moment the only ray of normalcy or reality in the film, he notes that even this "reality"
is reduced to a "dream," a "legend," since Pasolini depicts it with "an aureola, having recourse to the by-now mythical image of 'socialist realism.' " See Finetti, "Nella struttura di
Salò," p. 432.
[69] Gilles Deleuze, Cinema II: Image-temps (Paris: Minuit, 1985), p. 228.

A "theorem of death," the world of *Salò*—as historical allusions and visual echoes make clear—is set in the deadliest of eras. References to the Fascist epoch are both explicit (like the film's very title) and implicit. The villa itself—with its severe Bauhaus décor and paintings by modern artists like Léger, Severini, and Duchamp—was meant, noted Pasolini, to suggest a home that might have been confiscated from some "rich deported Jew." And the frontal, symmetrical arrangement of people on the set was to evoke what he called the solemn efficacy of Nazi "choreography." In their combination of "decadence and military simplicity," the libertines of *Salò* were, he felt, "cultured in the same pseudo-way as the German and Italian party hierarchy were, with pseudo-scientific ideas and pseudo-racist rationalizations. It was what Hitler and Mussolini called a 'decadent' world, it was to be destroyed but exerted its fascination upon these louts."[70]

Intermingled with historical references are literary ones. Dante and Sade are only slightly more important than a number of modern French commentators on Sade who are cited, often in the original, by Pasolini's cultured libertines. As if to make it absolutely clear that his film constitutes one more stitch in an intertextual web that is at once very cerebral, and very French, Pasolini prefaces *Salò* with a list of works by these authors: Pierre Klossowski's *Sade mon prochain?* (1947); Simone de Beauvoir's *Faut-il brûler Sade?* (1951–1952); Maurice Blanchot's *Lautréamont et Sade* (1963); Roland Barthes's *Sade, Fourier, Loyola* (1971); Philippe Sollers's *L'écriture et l'expérience des limites* (1968).[71] (One of Pasolini's friends recounts that the director, who had always felt better understood in France than in his native land, wanted *Salò* to be the most "French" of his films.[72]) But if references to Sade's erudite modern interpreters emphasize the serious nature of the film, they also, as Pasolini observed, create a "link with our time; Sade is read in a more modern and rational way. If I limited the characters' consciousness to that of Sade, I would have to leave out psychoanalysis, i.e., the modern world."[73]

[70] Cited by Gideon Bachman in his "Pasolini and the Marquis de Sade," *Sight and Sound* Vol. 45, No. 1 (Winter 1975–1976), p. 52.

[71] Toward the end of *Intersections* (University of Nebraska Press, 1981), a book devoted to Sade and his French commentators, Jane Gallop notes that what she calls the "net Bataille-Blanchot-Klossowski" has recently been reread by the "net Derrida-Lacan-Barthes." One might add that both these nets have now been reread by *Salò*.

[72] Jean-Claude Biette observes that Pasolini, who wanted a dubbed French version of *Salò* shown in France, considered *Salò* "like a French film, a little the way he must have considered *The Canterbury Tales* an English film. Ideally, to dub his characters, he would have wanted Klossowski, Rivette, and Simsolo." See Biette, "Dix ans, près et loin de Pasolini," in *Pasolini cinéaste*, special unnumbered issue of *Cahiers du cinéma* (Paris: Editions de l'étoile, 1981), p. 62.

[73] Pasolini, *Il cinema in forma di poesia* (Pordenone: Cinemazero, 1979), p. 164.

No less than *Edipo Re*, Pasolini's first explicitly "psychoanalytic" film, *Salò* is a dense cultural and historical web where—collapsing past and present, the real and the imaginary—he weaves in and out of personal memory. Asked, in fact, how he brought Sade up-to-date, Pasolini responded that he did so "in an autobiographical way, as it were. Recalling the days I lived in the Republic of Salò in Friuli. This had become a German region. . . . It was an epoch of sheer cruelty, searches, executions, deserted villages, all totally useless, and I suffered a great deal."[74] A savage rereading of his youth, and of the petit-bourgeois world evoked so nostalgically and lyrically in *Edipo Re*, *Salò* even contains a scene where Pasolini mocks, explicitly and ferociously, his former, idealistic self. As the victims of *Salò* observe one of their number being brutally sodomized, they woefully sing an old Alpine song that contains a line—"La meglio gioventu va soto tera" (The best youths go underground)—that Pasolini had chosen as the title of a collection of his Friulian verse, *La meglio gioventù*. A mournful reminder of a happier era, sung in this context, the song suggests that just as that earlier epoch has been annihilated by a dreadful present, so, too, has the young poet of Friuli become the desperate and cynical creator of *Salò*.

Not surprisingly, when the initial series of bans on *Salò* were lifted and the film finally released, these complex interweavings were eclipsed by its graphic sadism and polemical analogies—analogies between, on the one hand, the "old" and the "new" fascism and, on the other, between sadism and Fascism. By that time, too, Pasolini's violent murder had cast its long shadow over the filmed atrocities. Behind *Salò* lay grisly and unforgettable newspaper photographs of Pasolini's bloody and disfigured corpse. Cries of outrage were shrill, verging on hysteria. Ugo Finetti recounts that, upon leaving the projection room, one critic—referring to Pasolini's recent death—cried out: "Luckily, they killed him." Still another wrote: "Rest assured that whoever is courageous enough not to see *Salò-Sade* will not miss anything."[75] A number of critics, disturbed by films like Liliana Cavani's *Portiere di notte* (*Night Porter*, 1974) and Lina Wertmuller's *Seven Beauties* (1976), saw *Salò* as one more film where Fascism had become a pretext for titillating sadomasochism. Even as late as 1982, this was a view espoused by Nancy Huston, a feminist critic: "Like Cavani's *Night Porter*," she wrote, "Pasolini's film is an unfortunate attempt to reinject eroticism into genocide."[76]

Huston is usually a very perceptive critic, but here she is deeply in error. Admittedly—and I'd like to return to this shortly—the implied analogy

[74] "Pasolini on de Sade," *Film Quarterly*, p. 41.
[75] Cited by Finetti in "Nella struttura di *Salò*," p. 431.
[76] Nancy Huston, *Mosaique de la pornographie* (Paris: Denoel/Gonthier, 1982), p. 165.

between Fascism and sadism in *Salò is* disturbing. Still, in essential ways, Pasolini's film differs markedly from virtually all the other films, set in the Fascist era, of the so-called "retro" phenomenon. Such films include not only *Night Porter* and *Seven Beauties* but also Visconti's *La caduta degli dei* (*The Damned*, 1969), Louis Malle's *Lacombe Lucien* (1974), Bernardo Bertolucci's *Novecento* (*1900*, 1976), and Diane Koury's *Coup de Foudre* (*Entre nous*, 1983). These films are, of course, different from one another in important ways: some (like *Entre nous*) use Fascism as a kind of stylized backdrop; others (*Lacombe Lucien* and *Novecento*) are obviously infused with a deep historical awareness and a sense of moral dilemmas; still others (*Night Porter* and *Seven Beauties*), as I've suggested, polemically reduce Fascism to sadomasochistic theatrics.[77] But however serious or exploitive, these films resemble one another in that all are realistic melodramas—that is, all rely heavily on characters and psychology in an attempt to provoke audience sympathies and identification. *Salò, instead, is an icy parable that resolutely turns its back on realism, on psychology, and on conventional characters.* Instead of engaging the sympathies and emotions of viewers, it does all that it can to distance, even repel, its audience.

Nor is *Salò*'s cerebral approach, its deliberate rejection of audience complicity, the only factor that distinguishes this film from others of the "retro" phenomenon. Its portrayal of sexuality is also unique. Whereas the others—although, admittedly, to vastly different degrees and ends—cast Fascism, or Fascists, in an erotic light, Pasolini seemed impelled, rather, by a desire to strip his Fascist libertines of any hint of sexual energy or fascination. *Instead of rendering sadomasochism erotic—and, here, of course, he was fundamentally different from Wertmuller and Cavani in particular—he tried to remove every cloak, every veil, conferred upon it by a tradition of romance and or pornography.* Several critics did, in fact, perceive that Pasolini's film is not about sex but, rather, "the death of sex"—less a hymn to eroticism than its "funeral dirge."[78] Perhaps the mass public understood this best of all: while it flocked to *Night Porter* and *Seven Beauties*, once its initial curiosity was sated, it shunned *Salò*.

Even when, as in the trilogy, Pasolini had tried to portray Eros in a joyous light, his dark view of sexuality made itself felt. And, after all, *Salò* was conceived as the mirror image, the infernal opposite of the trilogy; it

[77] This aspect of both films enraged a number of critics. For example, Bruno Bettelheim argues against *Seven Beauties* in "Surviving," *The New Yorker*, August 2, 1976, pp. 31–52; Pascal Bonitzer attacks *Night Porter* (and the "retro" phenomenon) in "Le bourreau derrière la porte," in his *Le regard et la voix* (Paris: U.G.E. [10/18], 1976), pp. 98–117.

[78] Cesare Musatti, "Il *Salò* di Pasolini: regno della perversione," in *Da Accattone a Salò*, p. 131; Henry Chapier, "L'érotisme selon Pasolini," in *Cinéma d'aujourd-hui* Vol. 4 (Winter 1975–1976), p. 116.

was designed to show not the "joy" of sex but, rather, the commodification, the reification, of the human body. While this in itself could not guarantee that no one would find *Salò* arousing, the film does—consistently and deliberately—work against eroticism. To begin with, Pasolini's cold and clinical portrayal of sexual combinations and perversions—a portrayal that the viewer of a film, unlike the reader of a book, cannot soften by his own desires and imaginings—lacks the cinematic foreplay, the elements of "strip-tease," that Roland Barthes, for one, considers fundamental to an "erotic" work. (For this reason, Barthes believes that Sade himself is not "erotic."[79]) In *Salò*, sexual acts are brutal, without preamble; its victims do not undress but appear nude, lined up as if awaiting the gas chamber.

Moreoover, this film gives little hint of the sexual pleasure that an erotic work seems to require. Its tortured victims bear no resemblance to the heroines of a certain pornographic tradition who, as Nancy Huston observes, achieve pleasure through pain.[80] And even their executioners, that is, the libertines, do not attain the pleasure they so endlessly seek. These monsters are, in fact, driven not by energy or the pulsing of desire but by impotence and frustration. Pasolini's libertines are neither Sade's aristocrats nor Byron's satanic heroes but, instead, meticulous bureaucrats who try to codify, quantify, pleasure. In their erotic excesses, their refusal to obey the dictates of convention and morality, they are not—and, significantly, this dismayed some scholars of Sade[81]—romantic or revolutionary figures but, rather, banal and grotesque ones. *Salò*, as Adelio Ferrero remarks so eloquently, is "a macabre fable and a chilling metaphor about impotence in power: masturbation, make-up, voyeurism, and coproph-

---

[79] "We are constantly told," observes Barthes, "that Sade is an 'erotic' author. But what is eroticism? It is never more than a word since (erotic) practices can only be codified if they are known, that is, spoken. Now, our society never enunciates any erotic practice but only desires, preambles, contexts, suggestions and ambiguous sublimations so that for us eroticism can only be defined by a word that is perpetually allusive. In this perspective, Sade is never erotic: as has been noted, with him there is never any sort of 'strip-tease,' this essential apologue of modern eroticism." Barthes, *Sade, Fourier, Loyola* (Paris: Seuil, 1971), pp. 31–32.

[80] In pornographic novels, says Huston, the heroines' pleasure "comes from their pain and is inextricably linked to it; punishment is a necessary step on the road to *jouissance* (that of their partner and also their own)." Huston, *Mosaique de la pornographie*, p. 137.

[81] Admirers of Sade—who often saw the "divine marquis" as a revolutionary, anti-establishment figure—were disturbed by Pasolini's unflattering portrait of the libertines. Fulvio Accialini protested that it was unfair to take Sade out of his own historical context, while Jean Chérasse, author of a book on Sade, criticized Pasolini for refusing to see that *Les 120 Journées de Sodome* was really a "libertine utopia" that stood opposed to "scholastic ideology, religion, and hypocrisy." Chérasse's remarks are cited by Marcel Martin in his *Salò ou Les 120 Journées de Sodome*, p. 49. For those of Accialini, see *Da Accattone a Salò*, p. 138. Originally in *Cinema e cinema* No. 7–8 (April–September 1976).

agy take up the time and the thoughts of the verminous quartet. A darkly monotone and repetitive ritual of substitutions."[82]

If *Salò* avoids the romantic fascination with evil as well as its latter-day counterpart—that is, the temptation to view Fascism, and Fascists, as sexy—its obsessive literalness also sets it apart from the metaphorical readings proposed by Sade's most important modern commentators. Klossowski and Blanchot, for example, consider Sade's universe as one of metaphysical revolt; Barthes and Sollers view it as one of discourse. But the irony here is that the contemporary fascination with Sade—clearly perceptible in all these commentators—reflects modern horrors that were only too real. It was, after all, largely the experience of the Holocaust that made Sade's imaginary world—a world not thought possible, imaginable, before then—a compelling one for the modern imagination. As a number of commentators have observed, Sade even envisaged methods of humiliation and degradation that were, in fact, used by the Nazis in the camps.

Still, to point to resemblances between the Sadean universe and that of the camps is not, by any means, to draw an analogy between the two or to equate them in any way. It is not merely that no analogy is possible between, on the one hand, the horrors of fiction and, on the other, those of the gas chamber. It is also because any such analogy—whereby the complex social, historical, and economic phenomenon of Fascism is reduced to sexual pathology—would be simplistic and dangerous. But having said this, we are left with a basic question: if this analogy is so dangerous, why did Pasolini come so perilously close to it by deciding to set Sade's novel at the time of Nazism-Fascism—a decision, to some degree, that certainly suggestes a correlation between (imaginary) sadism and the very real phenomenon of Italian Fascism. It was, after all, a deliberate decision—one that he considered crucial to the film and repeatedly tried to explain, to justify, even before *Salò* was completed. But, significantly, his very explanations—where contradictory impulses were clearly at work—raised, perhaps, more questions than they answered.

In justifying this decision, Pasolini seemed, in fact, to embrace two different, if not irreconcilable, lines of defense. On the one hand, he kept suggesting that the fascism of *Salò* was merely "symbolic"—that is, it referred to fascism in general rather than to the particular historical phenomenon of Nazism-Fascism. The obsession with precise formulas and bureaucratic regulations that characterizes his libertines represented, he declared, the strategies embraced by *all* power in its drive to codify and ritualize its own "pure arbitrariness, that is, its own anarchy." He chose to set his film at the Fascist moment, he said, simply because it was an "archetypal" instance of power, the "last time that the human power

---

[82] Ferrero, *Il cinema di Pasolini*, p. 148.

drive expressed itself in such direct, linear, and almost symbolic terms."[83] But even as he argued that the fascism of Salò was emblematic of "all" power, he also maintained that it represented a precise historical phenomenon. Moreoever—and here he added a new twist to his argument—he insisted that, *despite the setting of the film,* this precise phenomenon was not to be equated with Nazism-Fascism but, rather, with the "new" fascism of neocapitalism. Returning to the controversial comparison between the "old" Fascism and the "new," which dominates his journalistic writings of this period, he defiantly called Salò his "first film about the modern world." This work, he insisted, was the oneiric "representation of what Marx called the commodification of man, the reduction of the body (through exploitation) to a thing. Therefore sex is still called upon in my film to play a horrible metaphorical role. Precisely the contrary of the 'trilogy.' "[84]

Pasolini's insistence that Salò be seen as a kind of double parable—concerning both power in general and a specific instance of power—clearly evokes the memory of *Porcile.* But the very memory of that earlier film serves, in a sense, to underscore the ambiguities of Salò. In *Porcile,* the juxtaposition of two highly imaginary episodes points to the film's allegorical core even as it suggests that contemporary power is but one instance of universal social repression. Instead of a similar juxtaposition of imaginary eras, Salò deliberately, and elliptically, collapses two historical eras—that of Sade and the postwar era of Sade's modern commentators—into yet a third, that of Nazism-Fascism, with the result that temporal/historical relationships, as well as the nature of power, are rendered far more obscure. And the one historical era (Nazism-Fascism) that is presented in an unequivocal way is doubly problematical: not only are we asked to see it as a symbol of the modern world but it is an era—unlike the imaginary epochs of *Porcile*—that is far too emotionally charged to function purely as a metaphor. And this last objection might also be directed toward the film's use of sexuality. Once again, whereas the distanced, unreal sexuality of *Porcile* (cannibalism, bestiality) is obviously allegorical, the graphic sadism of Salò constantly threatens to exceed the bounds of the symbolic.

These considerations make it difficult to dismiss the profound difficulties at the heart of Salò. And indeed the most serious and thoughtful adverse criticism of the film concerned, precisely, Pasolini's problematical

---

[83] Cited by Bachman in "Pasolini and the Marquis de Sade," *Sight and Sound,* p. 52.

[84] Pasolini, "Il sesso come metafora del potere," *Corriere della sera,* March 25, 1975.

For Adelio Ferrero, Salò is, in fact, the "absolute" and "tragic" embodiment of Pasolini's conviction, expressed throughout his polemical writings, that "Buchenwald exists within the heart of progress." See Ferrero, "*Salò*: metafore della morte borghese," in *Da Accattone a Salò,* p. 139. Originally in *Cinema e cinema* No. 7–8 (April–September 1976).

mixture of the real and the imaginary, of history and allegory. The respected novelist Italo Calvino spoke for many when he declared that the
horrors of Nazi-Fascism could not be presented in an "imaginary" way.

> The idea of situating Sade's novel in the times and places of the Nazi-fascistic
> republic seems the worst possible one from all points of view. The horror of
> that past which is in the memory of so many who lived it cannot serve as back-
> ground to a symbolic and imaginary horror constantly outside the probable
> such as is present in Sade's work (and justly represented in a fantastic vein by
> Pasolini). . . . The evocation of the Nazi occupation can only reawaken a depth
> of emotions that is the complete opposite of the paradoxical ruthlessness that
> Sade poses as the first rule of the game not only to his characters but to his
> readers as well.[85]

Calvino's contention that Sade's novel should not be situated in the Fascist era was shared by the French critic Roland Barthes. But Barthes approached the issue in a somewhat more theoretical fashion: he began by
drawing an important distinction between what he called "fascism-system" (a historical phenomenon like that of Nazism-Fascism) and "fascism-substance" (which can circulate anytime). By confusing these two
phenomena, Pasolini had managed, suggested Barthes, to distort them
both. Observing that the danger and complexity of "fascism-system"
(Nazism-Fascism) demanded more than the simple analogy offered by
Salò, Barthes declared: "Fascism *forces* us to think about it accurately,
analytically, politically. The only thing that art can do . . . is *demonstrate*
how it comes about, not *show* what it resembles; in short, I do not see
any other way of treating it than '*à la Brecht*.' " As for the protean, and
imaginary, phenomenon of "fascism-substance," there, too, Barthes
found *Salò* wanting. One cannot, argued the French critic, anchor "fascism-substance" in any particular historical event such as Nazism-Fascism since it "is only one of the modes with which political 'reason' hap-
pens to color the death drive which, in Freud's words, can only be seen if
treated with some kind of fantasmagoria."[86]

Barthes's distinction between "fascism-substance" and "fascism-system" goes unerringly to the fundamental ambiguity at the core of *Salò*.
Still, like everyone else, even Barthes—this most subtle of modern critics—allowed the distaste he felt for the film to color his perceptions. (Admittedly, Barthes had better reasons than most to dislike *Salò*: not only
did the film contradict his own reading of Sade but its savage portrayal of

---

[85] Italo Calvino, "Sade is within us," in *The Poetics of Heresy*, ed. Beverly Allen (Saratoga, Calif.: Anma Libri, 1982), p. 109. Originally in *Corriere della sera*, November 30,
1975.

[86] Roland Barthes, "Sade-Pasolini," in *Pasolini cinéaste*, p. 89. Originally in *Le monde*,
June 16, 1976. Translated into English in *The Poetics of Heresy*.

both culture and homosexuality—a portrayal I shall discuss shortly—must have offended him deeply.[87]) Simplifying issues that Pasolini had deliberately rendered complex, Barthes deemed Pasolini "naive" even as he himself missed the film's *deliberate and fundamental embrace of ambiguity*. For if *Salò*'s graphic sadism, in particular, makes the film seem all too "real," it is also true—as suggested earlier and *contrary to what Barthes contends*—that the film as a whole does indeed treat Fascism in a Brechtian manner. Marked by all the distancing devices of *Porcile*—which is explicitly set under the sign of Brecht—*Salò* forces us to reflect about the nature of power, of sadism, of—and I'll return to this later—spectatorship. And if Pasolini did set his film in the Fascist era, he also used strategies—for example, he had his libertines quote from contemporary critics—to make it clear that *Salò* is a *comment* about a past era, not a faithful reconstruction of it.

These deliberate ambiguities and displacements point to a "message" that Barthes ignored and that even Pasolini did not acknowledge. I would argue that Pasolini, *impelled by a desire to be scandalous*, deliberately placed *Salò* in that dangerous and controversial no-man's-land between metaphor and reality, a zone of shifting contours where, as Barthes indicates, "fascism-system" flowed insidiously, scandalously, into "fascism-substance." No one knew better than Pasolini that, like the film's explicit sadism, this choice would anger and disturb: according to his cousin Nico Naldini, before Pasolini's death he was looking forward with "excitement" to the release of *Salò*, as if to a coming "battle."[88] And in April 1975, he himself remarked to his friend Gideon Bachman that *Salò* "goes so far beyond the limits that those who habitually speak badly of me will have to find new terms."[89]

Such a remark leaves little doubt that Pasolini's decision to set Sade's novel in Fascist Italy—like the very choice of *Les 120 Journées de Sodome*—reflected nothing less than a desire to fashion one of the most extremist, perhaps *the* most extremist, films ever made. Often drawn to scandalous texts—one must remember that the Gospel was profoundly revolutionary, that *Il Decamerone* was expurgated during the Counter-Reformation—for *Salò*, Pasolini took *the* most notorious work by a man

[87] Maintaining that Sade's universe is one of discourse and hence cannot be represented, Barthes writes: "Remaining faithful to the letter of Sadean scenes, Pasolini winds up distorting the object-Sade and the object-fascism: therefore it is with good reason that Sadeans and men of politics are indignant and disapproving. Sadeans (readers enchanted with Sade's text) will never recognize Sade in Pasolini's film. The reason for this is a general one: Sade can in no way be represented." Barthes, "Sade-Pasolini," in *Pasolini cinéaste*, p. 89.

[88] These remarks by Nico Naldini, Pasolini's cousin, are cited in *Pier Paolo Pasolini: Une vie future*, p. 306.

[89] Ibid., p. 309.

who might well be history's most infamous author. A great *diverso*, Sade was judged intolerable, and imprisoned, by three totally different political regimes: the monarchy, the republic, the empire. (Even today, Sade's novel does not circulate freely in my university library.) Pasolini was doubtlessly attracted, as he claimed, by Sade's critique of Enlightenment "reason" and "progress." Above all, though, it was the marquis's extremism that enchanted him. "The pages of de Sade," he wrote, "are extremely revolutionary. I have created this lucid, extraordinary scandal of reason, a limitless and boundless scandal that I admire. That I admire along with Klossowski, along with Blanchot, along with the best of contemporary critics, in short."[90] Using this revolutionary text as a point of departure, Pasolini turned *Salò* into a last, deliberate act of transgression: its scandalous political analogies outraged intellectuals, while its horrific depiction of sex repelled the mass audience. No political party—neither the "old" left nor the "new"—could accept a film that denied all hope in the future, that showed the disappearance of the individual and, in Pasolini's words, the "inexistence" of history.

Still, in some ways, the "scandal" of *Salò* goes beyond politics, beyond ideology, beyond even sexual horror. The sense of numb and leaden helplessness that attacks the viewer of this film comes less, perhaps, from intellectual or moral outrage than from the way he (and, to a lesser extent, she) is positioned by *Salò*. Like the "pinned butterflies" of *Porcile*, spectators of *Salò* are inexorably drawn into a web of complicity with the monstrous libertines—a terrible web where they are compelled to see both Pasolini, and themselves, as one of their number.

   If the viewer's complicity with the libertines becomes clear only toward the end of the film, the similarities between Pasolini and the "verminous quartet" are, instead, unmistakable almost from the outset. Never in fact had Pasolini's lifelong bent for self-irony assumed such a savage and ferocious cast. Indeed, the film's autobiographical resonances are so striking that, if they delighted the director's critics (who naively considered them unintentional), they saddened and dismayed his friends (who knew better). Alberto Moravia, one of Pasolini's oldest and closest friends, even expressed the wish that the director's career had ended not with *Salò* but, instead, with *Il fiore delle mille e una notte*. Unlike *Salò*, Moravia remarked, in *Il fiore delle mille e una notte*

> homosexuality is viewed . . . with happiness, sympathy, with ingenuity and serenity. . . . In *Il fiore*, for the last time, Pasolini liked himself, that is, his own life, his own destiny, his own way of being in the world. In *Salò*, on the other

---

[90] Pasolini, *Il cinema in forma di poesia*, p. 175.

hand, he hated himself in the most radical way, to the point of self-calumny. I don't know why he did it. Probably from a sense of guilt.[91]

Gideon Bachman, too, who interviewed Pasolini while he was making *Salò*, was distressed by the fact that Pasolini seemed to echo the libertines whenever he spoke of sexuality: "Hearing him [Pasolini] discuss Klossowski's ideas of the eternal repetitiousness of the act of love, I realise the man is talking about himself, about his eternal reaching out, and his eternal disappointment. . . . Disappointment in man and in God."[92]

But it is not only his insatiable drive—a drive doomed to endless repetition and frustration—that Pasolini attacks so savagely in the libertines. Like their creator, the libertines are the spiritual heirs of late nineteenth-century decadent writers who, like Pasolini himself, were deeply influenced by the great tradition of symbolism. Whereas Sade's libertines push Enlightenment reason and method into the realm of obsession and hallucination, Pasolini's bureaucrats carry late nineteenth-century culture to *its* culminating point—a point, as *Salò* makes abundantly clear, deeply imbued with fascism, with sadism, and with death. Moreoever, *Salò* implies that the culminating point of the literature and culture that Pasolini had always loved—a culture whose worst crime he had formerly seen as that of "involution," of "elitism," of refusing to deal with the outside world—had been present from the beginning. Or, to phrase this in the words of Roberto Escobar, Pasolini roots Nazism-Fascism in the "bourgeois economy and culture that found its explict and clear expression in the great culture of the decadence, from Schopenhauer and Nietzsche."[93]

The clearest discussion of the implicit links between fin-de-siècle European culture and Nazism which underlie *Salò* are not found in the film itself but in one of Pasolini's literary essays—a 1974 essay devoted to *A rebours*, a minor symbolist novel by the late nineteenth-century French author J. K. Huysmans. In this essay, Pasolini analyzes Huysmans's aristocratic protagonist, Des Esseintes, in such a way that the character emerges as a forerunner of the libertines of *Salò*. Like Wilde's Dorian Gray, or Proust's Swann, or Villiers de L'Isle-Adam's Axel, Des Esseintes is a perfect fin-de-siècle aesthete and dandy. Prey to an exacerbated sensibility, Des Esseintes becomes obsessed with taste and culture, with rare and rarified objects. His repugnance for the crass outside world leads him to take refuge within his house, where he seeks to (re)create an artificial, cloistered world of refined and bizarre sensations. But all of Des Es-

---

[91] Alberto Moravia, "Dall'Oriente a *Salò*," *Nuovi Argomenti* N.S. 49–52 (1976), pp. 93–94.

[92] Bachman, "Pasolini and de Sade," *Sight and Sound*, p. 52.

[93] Roberto Escobar, "*Salò* o le *120 giornate di Sodoma*," in *Da Accattone a Salò*, p. 135. Originally in *Cineforum* No. 153 (April 1976).

seintes's strategies, observes Pasolini, are undermined by a fundamental paradox. For although this dandy cannot bear the philistine world of the bourgeoisie, his life—devoted not to work but, rather, to consumption and "possession"—means that he, too, is as bourgeois as those he despises.[94] Calling Des Esseintes a "mediocre superman" (*A rebours*, in fact, did appear in 1894, a year after *Thus Spake Zarathustra*), Pasolini argues that the dandy's impossible desire to reject both his inner (bourgeois) core and the outer world has led to nothing less than the "diabolical" and "suicidal" impulses of our own century:

> The mechanism of Des Esseintes is the mechanism of an anti-bourgeois bourgeois who commits suicide by destroying himself through an excess of his own culture. He finds himself in a moment of history in which the genealogical tree of bourgeois typology separates into two great trunks: at the base of one of these trunks you find the signpost bearing Hitler's name, at the base of the other you find the sign pointing to "hippies." The kinship between these two phenomena (i.e., Nazism and formal democracy)—phenomena that we erroneously consider opposite and irreconcilable—consists in the fact that in both cases a diabolical and self-punishing force destroys bourgeois Reason. . . . Although the coexistence of the S.S. and of hippies is . . . unexpressed and inarticulate in Des Esseintes, it is nonetheless perfect.[95]

The dilemma of bourgeois intellectuals or aesthetes who despise themselves and their heritage, who take refuge in a world of culture, was, of course, a dilemma that Pasolini had always experienced in a particularly acute manner. And if he analyzed this "mechanism" in Des Esseintes, he re-created it—endowing it with a savage self-irony—in the libertines of *Salò*. Through these erudite dandies he parodies both his own "excess" of culture and the terrible void that lies beneath it. In the mouths of these

[94] In an essay on Proust, Benjamin makes explicit Pasolini's implied connection between dandyism, (bourgeois) consumerism, and homosexuality. "For the attitude of the snob," he writes, "is nothing but the consistent, organized, steely view of life from the chemically pure standpoint of the consumer. And because even the remotest as well as the most primitive memory of nature's productive forces was to be banished from this satanic magic world, Proust found a perverted relationship more serviceable than a normal one even in love. But the pure consumer is the pure exploiter—logically and theoretically—and in Proust he is that in the full concreteness of his actual historical existence. He is concrete because he is impenetrable and elusive. Proust describes a class which is everywhere pledged to camouflage its material basis." See Benjamin, "The Image of Proust," in his *Illuminations* (New York: Schocken: 1969), p. 210.

[95] Pasolini, *Descrizioni di descrizioni*, pp. 52–53. Once again, Walter Benjamin makes much the same point. Discussing the right-wing aesthete Maurice Barrès in "Zum gegenwärtigen gesellschaftlichen Standort des französischen Schriftstellers" (The Present Social Position of the Writer in France"), he remarks: "These cultivated sensations never deny that they derive from an estheticism which is only the other side of nihilism." See Benjamin, *Angelus Novus* (Frankfurt: Suhrkamp: 1966), p. 266.

learned monsters, his own love of words and poetry disintegrates into artificial and absurd rhetoric marked by long, pompous speeches full of
meaningless exclamations. Similarly, his bent for parody and pastiche dis-
solves into disjointed quotes that are, significantly, frequently drawn
from the symbolist or post-symbolist authors he loved—that is, from
Baudelaire, Lautréamont, Proust, and Pound.[96] One of the libertines begins a sentence by citing, in French, the Proustian title, "A l'ombre des
jeunes filles en fleur," and ends with a phrase, "La bourgeoisie tue ses
propres fils" (The bourgeoisie kills its own sons), that refers at once to
Porcile, to Proust, and, above all, to *Salò*, where sadistic "fathers" might
be murdering their "children."

"Mediocre supermen" who have chosen the "signpost pointing to Hitler," the cultivated libertines of *Salò* share Des Esseintes's hatred of ordinary men, his separation from life itself. Libidos jaded, these connoisseurs
of torture and death must turn to artifice and fiction to become aroused;
in their search for a pleasure forever deferred, they demand ever more
perverse and "unnatural" practices. Instead of Des Esseintes's rare and
precious objects, these satanic dandies collect beautiful bodies, no less
than culture itself, that are fragmented, fetishized, and, ultimately, destroyed. This process is made strikingly clear in one scene where the libertines hold a contest to see which of their victims has the most beautiful
ass (that is, the one that most invites sodomization): with lights extinguished to hide faces and identities, the victims are forced to bend over
and present their backsides to the libertines who inspect them by flash-
light. The winner—a young boy—is rewarded with a "false death": a gun
is placed at his head, the trigger is pulled . . . but the bullet proves a blank.
The "moral" of this scene is then sententiously announced by one libertine who draws a parallel between death and sodomy: "The sodomitic
gesture has the great advantage that it can be repeated hundreds of times.
As you know, Monsignore, reiteration is indispensable because death is
reborn at the level of monstrosity."

Grotesquely pompous, the libertine's words nevertheless hint at the
links between sodomy and death that lie at the core of this apocalyptic
film. Occupying the role played by bestiality and cannibalism in *Porcile*,
sodomy, too, is a symbol of revolt and transgression—a dandy's protest
against a capitalist world where all is based on use and exchange, a lib-

[96] Interpreting Pasolini's extensive use of quotations in a somewhat different way, Giovanni Buttafava writes: "The principal figure of expression in *Salò* is, in short, the quotation, whose repressive and authoritarian nature is unmasked. The superabundant, and even
pedantically ostentatious use of quotations corresponds to the ruthless assembling of political, ethical, and religious relics conducted by Pasolini in the body of the work." See Buttafava, "*Salò* o il cinema in forma di rosa," in *Lo scandalo Pasolini*, special issue of *Biano e
Nero* Vol. 1, No. 4 (1976), p. 47.

ertine's revolt against the biological imperative to reproduce. But, like those other perversions, it is an act of protest that speaks of death. Sodomy, suggests Lino Miccichè in a discussion of *Salò*,

> corresponds—precisely because it cannot be *codified* in any norm of life—to a sort of progressive expropriation of vital functions. . . . *To exist totally and to be totally free*, and therefore not subject to codification, means reaching, from one transgression after another, the greatest of transgressions: that is, the annulling of oneself and of existence, the identification of the gratuitousness of pleasure (the non-procreative orgasm) with the gratuitousness of pain (death as a game), and the transformation of the organic into the inorganic.[97]

Set under the sign of death and transgression, infused with a ferocious self-irony, sodomy, remarked an obviously embittered Pasolini, is also the most "typical" of erotic acts because it is the most "useless, the one which best sums up the repetitiveness of the act precisely because it is the most mechanical."[98] Or, to quote his bombastic libertine once again: "The sodomitic act is the most absolute for its mortal thrust concerning the human species; the most ambiguous in that it accepts social norms in the aim of transgressing them; and finally the most scandalous because at the same time that it is the simulacrum of the act of generation, it derides it totally."

A derisory "simulacrum of the act of generation," the most "typical" of all erotic acts in its endless repetition, sodomy assumes its rightful place as the reigning metaphor of *Salò*—the perfect emblem of a world of dandies where artifice holds sway. The mock death accorded the boy with the most beautiful ass is but one of the endless rites or performances—complete with props and costumes—designed by the libertines in their frenzied efforts to re-create life, to turn everything into theater. Like the limitless tales of *Il fiore delle mille e una notte*—"dreams within a dream"— the endless performances of *Salò* imply that here, too, all is fiction. As in a play by Genet, where opposites melt into each other, showing that nothing is what it appears, the performances of *Salò* suggest that everything is equally unreal, equally illusory. In a mock marriage scene, for example, two of the victims are dressed as if for a "real" wedding; but when they begin to make love in earnest after the "ceremony," each is seized by an aroused libertine as a new performance, a new ritual, begins.

As in Genet, too, the performances staged by the libertines are characterized by exaggerated theatrics that grossly parody traditions drawn from stage, vaudeville, and cinema. The libertines declaim with the pomposity of has-beens in a mediocre melodrama, while the female narra-

---

[97] Lino Miccichè, "Pasolini: la morte e la storia," *Cinema sessanta* Vol. 19, No. 121 (May–June 1978), pp. 13–14.
[98] *Con Pier Paolo Pasolini*, p. 120.

tors—two of whom are played by famous actresses of Italian Fascist cinema—might be aging night-club *chanteuses*. Intensifying the parodistic and theatrical cast of Sade's novel, which echoes, plays off, the rhetoric of both religious and pornographic texts, Pasolini creates still more layers of satire and pastiche.[99] Observing that Sade turned what was "marble" in Dante into "papier-mâché," Pasolini might have been describing his own film, where horror may don a new mask or take a carnivalesque turn at any moment: here bloody executions turn into Grand Guignol as executioners perform a grotesque minuet amidst their victims' corpses. Steering a course between "seriousness" and the "impossibility of seriousness," *Salò* wavers between what Pasolini described as a "massacring and bloody Thanatos" and a "cheap Baubo." (Baubo, he added, was a Greek goddess known for her obscene and liberating laugh.)[100]

The theatrical numbers staged by the libertines are, of course, moments in the larger drama embodied in the film itself—a film that thus becomes a kind of diabolical meta-theater. Its three "circles," for example, clearly correspond to the acts of a play. As if to emphasize the division into acts, each "circle" is preceded by shots that depict one of the female narrators applying makeup before a mirror as if in a dressing room. The act itself begins with a theatrical "entrance" as she descends the stairway which takes her from the second floor of the villa to "center stage"—that is, to the front of the room where she will perform for the libertines and their victims. (One critic suggests that her descent evokes "Italian vaudeville theater of the 1940s or the Folies Bergères."[101]) Meanwhile, the camera, seemingly part of an unseen audience watching from the back, repeatedly pans along both sides of the room, where, as if at the edges of the proscenium, the inhabitants of the villa have lined up to await her performance.

A world of deadly theater, *Salò* becomes a ferocious re-reading of *La ricotta* as Pasolini savagely parodies his own tendency to turn everything

[99] The theatrical and parodistic nature of the Sadean orgy has long been the subject of commentary. On the subject, for example, of Sadean parody, Simone de Beauvoir notes: "It is both natural and striking that Sade's favorite form was parody. He did not try to set up a new universe. He contented himself with ridiculing, by the manner in which he imitated it, the one imposed on him." See de Beauvoir, *The Marquis de Sade* (New York: Grove, 1953), p. 49.

And a more recent critic, Marcel Hénaff, writes that in Sade "places and landscapes only appear as *décors*. . . . the narration (as in theater) *is not important* for its 'reality'; it is only a simulating machine, an experimental artifact, where something of historical and social reality is tested, exhibited, and proposed to the understanding of the reader/spectator in such a way that he must avoid the hypnotic trap of an imaginary identification." See Hénaff, *Sade: L'invention du corps libertin* (Paris: PUF, 1978), pp. 136–137.

[100] Pasolini, "*Salò* ou 'l'intolérance' du spectateur à saisir l'anarchie du fascisme et du pouvoir," *Nouvelle critique* (May 1976), p. 25. Originally in *Roma Giovanni*, No. 8 (October–November 1975).

[101] Buttafava, "*Salò* o il cinema in forma di rosa," p. 50.

into art, his immeasurable distance from reality. The isolation of *La ricotta*'s film director has become impotent and frenzied sexuality; his indifferent abuse of the poor extra, Stracci, has blossomed into sadism and torture; and his mannerist vision, now a demonic (rather than "divine") temptation, has engulfed, replaced, all of reality with a simulacrum, a facade stretched over a vertiginous void. In a world where only the villa and its theater exist, its rooms and stages have become the space of representation itself. "*Salò-Sade*," observes Franco Cordelli,

> is above all the description of its own language . . . and therefore a critique of language, an auto-critique, a masterly metafilm: Isn't the recruitment of the sixteen youths Pasolini's delirious desire for power—and isn't this what Pasolini is denouncing? Isn't the claustrophobic, sumptuous, funereal interior of the villa the aseptic and Lacanian white space of representation, where everything is reduced to a sign, where everyone is equal in the ass, in a "hole," in a "lack"? Aren't the violence and sex above all indifference, distance, a pure spectacle, that is, the epiphany of capitalism?[102]

In this ferocious meta-cinema, Pasolini indicts himself on several counts: a user of adolescent bodies in both life and film, he—like the libertines—manipulates bodies, tells stories, arranges "numbers." He, too, is a master of spectacle, an organizer of rites, an expert at turning violence into theater. But no one is innocent in the ninth circle and, to varying degrees, we are made to share his guilt. By the very way he depicts the victims, Pasolini ensures that we—like the libertines—will regard these adolescents as little more than beautiful bodies or interchangeable objects. To begin with, he keeps them naked and mute so that they are prevented from emerging as individuals, from entering the world that we, and the libertines, inhabit. ("The master," observes Barthes, "is the one who speaks, who disposes of the whole of language; the object is the one who keeps silent, kept away—by a mutilation more absolute than all the erotic tortures—from any access to language."[103]) Even more important, with the exception of the single moment of revolt, the victims are never seen in an admirable light. On the contrary, not only do these passive beings lack any sense of solidarity but they are easily induced to denounce and betray one another. This is made absolutely clear in the last scene of the film. Here two victims, who have apparently become soldiers, are seen dancing together as their companions are slaughtered. Totally indifferent to the massacre, one murmurs to the other: "What's the name of your girlfriend?" And the other answers: "Margherita." While some critics have perceived a ray of hope in this enigmatic sequence, the unrelenting

---

[102] Franco Cordelli, "Per *Salò-Sade*," *Nuovi Argomenti* N.S. Nos. 49–52 (1976), p. 91.
[103] Barthes, *Sade, Fourier, Loyola*, p. 36.

blackness of the film leads me to share Ugo Finetti's somber reading of it. In his view, the scene epitomizes the "process of corruption" at the heart of the film—that is, the libertines' success at transforming innocent victims into "perfect executioners."[104]

Defending his unattractive portrayal of the victims, Pasolini argued that Salò would have been unbearable had they begun to touch us as individuals. "If," he told Gideon Bachman, "I had nice victims that wept and tore at your heart, after five minutes you would leave the movie house."[105] Perhaps. Still, unable to feel for the victims as fellow beings, we become uneasy, unsure about the extent of our own humaneness. And this unease fuels, and is fueled by, a still greater malaise: as the machinery of torture takes its couse, we slowly become aware, consciously or subconsciously, that the very act of watching Salò turns us, like the libertines, into spectators of sadistic rites—rites that have been distanced by theater, by style, by the formal perfection of this crystalline film. As Leo Bersani and Ulysse Dutoit remark in a very interesting article on Salò: "Pasolini makes us into more willing, less purposeful spectators than his sado-fascistic protagonists. In a sense, this means that we never tire of being spectators; but it is the very limitlessness of our aestheticism which constitutes the moral perspective on sadism in Salò."[106] If the victims become "perfect executioners," then we are turned into "perfect spectators"—viewers repelled yet fascinated by the spectacle of aestheticized violence. And, as one libertine reminds us, our role is a vital one: in this satanic theater, the act of watching—or, in his words, "the intellectual joy of contemplation"—is as important as "the sublime joy of action and the abject joy of complicity." Mesmerized by the beautiful and polished images of Salò, we cannot deny the visual pleasure offered by a theater, a cinema, of violence.[107] Here the persistent hints of voyeurism in earlier films (Ninetto Davoli is a hidden witness to two acts of transgression in Porcile; lovers

[104] Finetti, "Nella struttura di Salò," p. 430.

[105] Pasolini, Il cinema di poesia, p. 164.

[106] Leo Bersani and Ulysse Dutoit, "Merde Alors," October No. 13 (Summer 1980), p. 31. Reprinted in The Poetics of Heresy, ed. Beverly Allen.

[107] To quote Bersani and Dutoit once again: "In short, we tend to sequester violence; we immobilize and centralize both historical acts of violence and their aesthetic representations. A major trouble with this is that the immobilization of a violent event invites a pleasurable identification with its enactment. A coherent narrative depends on stablized images; stabilized images stimulate the mimetic impulse. Centrality, the privileged foreground, and the suspenseful expectation of climaxes all contribute to a fascination with violent events on the part of readers and spectators. As Sade spectacularly illustrates, the privileging of the subject of violence encourages a mimetic excitement focused on the very scene of violence. All critiques of violence, to the extent that they conceive of it in terms of scenes which can be privileged, may therefore promote the very explosions which they are designed to forestall." Ibid., pp. 28–29.

are spied on throughout the trilogy) become explicit and central as *Salò*, turning on the viewer, denounces his or her voyeurism, that is, the visual pleasure he or she derives from beautiful images of sadism.

Like the sufferings of the victims, the viewer's unease is brought to its peak in the frenzied, totally meta-cinematic, climax of *Salò*—a climax that explicitly likens the spectator's voyeurism to that of the sadistic libertines. One after another, each libertine stands by a window and uses binoculars to watch the scenes of carnage taking place below in an inner courtyard. Pasolini then depicts the massacre as seen through the binoculars, which thus become a stand-in for the camera lens, so that we are forced not only to merge our gaze with that of the libertines but also compelled to acknowledge the voyeuristic lure that sadism and cinema, and, above all, a cinema of sadism, hold for us. As if to emphasize the analogy between the libertine's binoculars and the camera lens, the binoculars are held in reverse so that each scene witnessed is, quite literally, distanced, but also framed and miniaturized like the iris shots of early cinema.[108] Reinforcing this visual echo of old films, the sequence is silent except for light piano music in the room: the sight—but not the sound— of the victims' cries and screams heightens both the vividness and the unreality of the slaughter, a vividness and unreality that characterize not only *Salò* but also the very institution of cinema.

This scene makes it absolutely clear that *Salò* is not only a denunciation of Fascism or Fascim/sadism, or even an apocalyptic view of Western civilization and bourgeois "reason." It is also a ferocious attack upon director, film, and viewer. In this sense, even as *Salò* coerces us into sharing the libertines' sadism, it also places us in a masochistic position.[109] And I would argue that—more than its political analogies or graphic horrors— it is the web of sadomasochism that *Salò* compels us to enter which makes the film so disturbing, perhaps unbearable. For this reason, I believe that the few critics who have argued that *Salò*'s "real" message lies, precisely,

[108] For one critic, this most Brechtian of scenes evokes the end of Brecht's play *The Days of the Commune* where the bourgeoisie watches the destruction of the Commune from the ramparts of Versailles. See Edoardo Bruno, "La 'rappresentazione,' " in "*Salò*: due ipotesi," *Filmcritica* No. 257 (September 1975), p. 268.

Emphasizing the unreal cast of this scene, still another critic, Guy Braucourt, speaks of a "carnal abstraction where the sign replaces acts and images." Cited by Florence Mèredieu in "Théâtre de parole, oralité et cannibalisme," in *Pasolini*, special issue of *Revue d'Esthéthique* N.S. No. 3 (1982), p. 82.

[109] Interestingly, Pasolini himself felt that voyeurism—with its implied distance from reality—has a masochistic stamp. In an interview concerning *Il fiore delle mille e una notte* (where the camera insistently peeps through keyholes and door frames), he observed: "The pleasure of someone who watches a sexual act—an act that he has experienced—also consists in the pain of observing that he is fatally excluded from it." See Pasolini, "Le mie *mille e una notte*," *Playboy*, p. 123.

in its desire to be unbearable, that is, its refusal to be consumed, have been very close to the truth. Discussing *Salò*'s scenes of coprophagy—perhaps the most unbearable moments of the film—Pasolini deemed them a metaphor for the fact that "the producers, the manufacturers force the consumer to eat excrement. All these industrial foods are worthless refuse."[110] Denouncing a bourgeois public that consumes every piece of "worthless refuse," *Salò* deliberately makes itself "indigestible." As Renato Tomasino—playing, almost inevitably, on the theme of excrement—observes:

> *Salò* is not a value, neither of use nor exchange . . . it never sought a public—it enclosed and exhibited within a livid crystal the work of production, of fiction. . . . Hence *Salò* is not a product: it is the ultimate and definitive defeat of capitalism. . . . Of course, capitalism will swallow up even *Salò*—it will distribute it and give it a public; it will consume it and will make it into a social, political and human message; it may even transmute censorship and horror into a mass success of Art (with a capital A). . . . But it will be defeated just the same, because here the "Message" is one of shit.[111]

Even Tomasino underestimates *Salò*'s power to resist consumption. Pasolini's last film may be greatly admired by a fervent minority, but it has not entered the normal channels of distribution; as of this writing, *Salò* is not even available for rental in the United States. It remains, in fact, the perfect example of the totally "extremist" art espoused by Pasolini toward the end of his life. It was his contention that such art—by unmasking both the false nature of contemporary "tolerance" (true tolerance, he argued, has no limits) and the "purely economic reasons governing the liberalization of sex"—would reveal the repressive and dehumanizing nature of modern hedonism and consumerism. Now as never before, he declared in the course of a 1974 debate, "artists must create, critics defend, and democratic people support . . . works so extreme that they become unacceptable even to the broadest minds of the new State."[112] No one could deny, certainly, that with *Salò* he created precisely such a work.

[110] "Pasolini on de Sade," *Film Quarterly*, p. 45.
[111] Renato Tomasino, "Il vuoto della traccia," in "*Salò*: due ipotesi," *Filmcritica* No. 257 (September 1975), p. 269.
[112] Pasolini, "Contro la permissività di Stato," *Cinema Sessanta* (January 1976), p. 19.

VII

Epilogue

I poeti appartengono sempre ad un'altra civiltà.
—Pier Paolo Pasolini, *Bestia da stile* (1967)

(Poets always belong to another civilization.)

THE FUROR PROVOKED by *Salò* was not the last scandal surrounding Pasolini. That, alas, was reserved for his death: on November 3, 1975, he was found brutally murdered on the squalid outskirts of Rome. Although a young male prostitute he had met the previous night confessed to the bloody crime, many felt that this youth may not have been the assassin and, in any case, could not have acted alone. Thus shrouded in an atmosphere of homesexual violence and mystery, Pasolini's death evoked the greatest scandal of all.

After Pasolini's murder, it became virtually impossible to disassociate the sadomasochistic universe of *Salò* from the manner in which he lived his life and, above all, met his death. The many comparisons between art and life were sadly, perhaps inevitably, infused with the moralism that he had fought from the beginning. For example, calling the violence of *Salò* "existential" rather than "theoretical," the Brazilian film director Glauber Rocha remarked that it was his favorite film by Pasolini because there

> he tells the truth; he says: "There you are, I am perverted, perversion is fascism, I love fascist rituals, I am making *Salò* because it is the theater of this perversion and my character, my hero, loves torturers as I love my assassin." And after the film he died in an incident involving the exploitation of proletarian sex. Pasolini, a communist intellectual, a revolutionary, a moralist, abetted prostitution, that is, he paid poor boys, the "ragazzi di vita," for sex. He sought the poor, the ignorant, the illiterate and he tried to seduce them as if perversion were a virtue. . . . In *Salò*, Pasolini accepts his true personality.[1]

Obviously fascinated by the notion of sadomasochistic rites, Rocha—like so many others—tends to simplify, to mislead. The victims of *Salò* do *not* love their torturers; perversion is *not* seen as a virtue; Pasolini (who

[1] Glauber Rocha, "Le Christ-Oedipe," in *Pasolini cinéaste*, special unnumbered issue of *Cahiers du cinéma* (Paris: Editions de l'étoile, 1981), pp. 81–82.

always avoided the obvious) did *not* paint himself among the victims. Nor does Pasolini "accept his own personality": on the contrary, *Salò* is infused with savage self-irony, not to say self-hatred. But more importantly, above and beyond *Salò*, to say of Pasolini that he "loved fascist rituals" is, in some sense, to say that he demanded—or, worse still, deserved—the atrocious death he met; such a remark exculpates his assassin(s) even as it makes Pasolini responsible for his own murder. Violent homophobes took this reasoning one step further: in their eyes, Pasolini's alleged assailant—who maintained that he murdered rather than commit repellent homosexual acts—became a kind of hero. The homophobia evoked by the murder reached such a point that Jean-Paul Sartre was moved to write an article pleading that the court "not put Pasolini on trial."[2]

Still, if Rocha's remarks reveal a homophobic edge, the Brazilian director was by no means alone in his desire to "interpret" Pasolini's death, to draw lessons from it. Pasolini's admirers, too, were prey to this temptation. Their perspective was, of course, radically different from Rocha's: Pasolini's predilection for certain themes, his insistence on transgression, and his constant persecution prompted many of them to see his death as a kind of ultimate martyrdom. (Gay groups were, perhaps, the only ones who resisted the temptation to "explain" Pasolini's death, to distance its terrible existential immediacy. Pointing out that similar banal and dreadful deaths took place nightly in every major Italian city, they suggested that if Pasolini were a "martyr" to a conformist and repressive society, so, too, were hundreds of nameless and faceless others.) As the years passed, the note of martyrdom, even hagiography, became more and more insistent: in the course of one retrospective of his cinema, an early film was shown superimposed on photographs of his corpse; at an exhibit in Rome, the blood-stained jacket he was wearing the night of his death was displayed like a saint's relic; a Dutch documentary devoted to him (*He who tells the truth shall die*) ends with shots from *Il Vangelo* that depict Christ's—and, implicitly, Pasolini's—crucifixion.

In the end, though, I do not think the notion of sainthood would have displeased Pasolini. Obsessed with the idea of martyrdom, in a revealing passage of his youthful diary he described a fantasy where he identifies with Christ on the Cross. As he does so, he experiences a kind of voluptuous suffering. "This nude body," he confesses,

> scarcely covered with a strange band at the loins . . . evoked in me thoughts which were not openly illicit and yet whenever I looked at this swathe of silk (as if at a veil spread over a disquieting abyss) . . . I would suddenly direct my feelings to piety and prayer. Then there would clearly appear in my fantasies the desire to imitate the sacrifice Jesus made for others, to be condemned and

[2] Jean-Paul Sartre, "Non fate il processo a Pasolini," *Corriere della sera*, March 14, 1976.

killed despite my total innocence. I saw myself hung, nailed, on the cross. My loins were scantily wrapped by this thin strip and an immense crowd watched me. My public martyrdom wound up by becoming a voluptuous image and, bit by bit, I was nailed up with an entirely nude body. . . . With arms outstretched, with hands and feet nailed, I was totally vulnerable, lost.[3]

In various guises, this passage—with its blend of masochism and exaltation, of mysticism and sensuality—haunts all of Pasolini's cinema. Martyrs all, some of his protagonists even die in the position of the cross (Ettore, the victim of *Medea*, the homosexual burned at the stake in *The Canterbury Tales*). Others—taut and frozen like *Medea*, or limbs outstretched like the young cannibal of *Porcile*—await their death with a kind of voluptuous suffering and pride.[4] But it is not only Pasolini's overt images that betray a deep masochism. Whether censored, banned, or merely denounced, virtually every film of his was part of a pattern of transgression and persecution. It was a pattern that began when the first showings of *Accattone* provoked right-wing disturbances in Rome and that ended only with the banning of *Salò*. Judges, censors, and journalists alike were only too ready to fuel this pattern, to justify the sense of persecution that, toward the end of Pasolini's life, seemed to border on paranoia. The year of his death he lamented to Jean Duflot that public opinion, urged on by the Italian press, saw his homosexuality as "the very sign of an abominable human type."[5]

But if persecution was unbearable, it was also somehow desired. It was almost as if, seeing himself, knowing himself different, Pasolini had to transgress, to break the rules, to expose himself, so that others would perceive his *diversità* and punish him for it. He saw the world, as he told Jean Duflot in 1969, as an "ensemble of fathers and mothers toward whom I feel a total attraction, an attraction made of respect and veneration, and, at the same time, I feel the need to violate this veneration through a certain number of violent and scandalous desecrations."[6] The

---

[3] Pasolini, *Lettere* (Turin: Einaudi, 1986), pp. xx–xxi.

[4] Pasolini's films seem to buttress Gilles Deleuze's argument that certain formal proclivities (a taste for immobility, iciness, plans-tableaux) reveal a masochist sensibility. Discussing the novels of Sacher-Masoch, Deleuze could well be describing Pasolini's films. "Masoch," he writes, "has every reason to believe in art, in the immobilities and reflections of culture. Plastic arts, as he sees them, stretch out their subject, suspend a gesture or an attitude. . . . The taste for scenes which are frozen—as if photographed, stereotyped, or painted—manifests itself most intensely in Masoch's novels. . . . An experience of waiting and suspense belongs essentially to masochism. Masochist scenes involve veritable rites of physical suspension: tying up, hanging, crucifixion." Gilles Deleuze, *Présentation de Sacher-Masoch* (Paris: Minuit, 1967), p. 62.

[5] Cited by Jean Duflot, *Entretiens* (Paris: Belfond, 1970), p. 154.

[6] Ibid., p. 129. In a burst of characteristic self-irony, Pasolini followed this remark with

"need to violate" began early: not only did he write his earliest poems in a language that was officially frowned upon and that few could understand, he also became a Communist in a region so conservative and Catholic that, it was said, "only the radishes there were red." After he went to Rome and embraced the world of film, his transgression grew more scandalous, its masochistic cast more obvious, his martyrdom (to use his word) more public. He made autobiographical—some would say exhibitionistic—films even as he acknowledged that "confession and scatology are clearly forms of self-punishment: almost clinical sado-masochism."[7] Speaking of the student protests of the late 1960s, Pasolini might almost have been describing the masochism implicit in his own thirst for rebellion. In his view, their revolt was imbued with a "presentiment of death, a mythical masochism. Killing the father, even in this way, represents an absolute masochism, a constant sense of guilt."[8]

Even his theoretical writings are imbued with the terminology of masochism and martyrdom. Writing to the young director Marco Bellocchio in 1967, he questions the value of avant-garde films that—like his own or those of Bellocchio—break the "rules." What purpose, he asks, do such films serve since the vast public either rejects or ignores them, while the cultural elite—inured to scandal ever since the time of Rimbaud—can no longer be shocked. Perhaps, he suggests to Bellocchio, such extremist art does nothing more than bring its creator into a direct, and masochistic, relationship with the public. "Is it possible," he writes,

> that the act of scandalizing is an act that the author accomplishes so that it rebounds upon himself? An act of sadomasochism, let's say, or of self-punishment? An expressive act in that it's a public punishment of oneself? Therefore the value of scandal would not reside in the form or content of a work but [in the way] that it rebounds upon the author himself? Thus, by once again becoming action, pragma? Therefore the work would be merely an episode—with other intrinsic values but with the declared instrumentality of being the vehicle of a scandal—that puts the author directly in touch with his audience?[9]

Returning to this theme a few years later in 1970—in an article entitled, significantly, "Il cinema impopolare" (Unpopular cinema)—he remarks that avant-garde or transgressive cinema "wounds" the spectator, who, in turn, retaliates by rejecting or attacking such films, thereby enabling

---

the following aside to Duflot: "Oh! Come on. These are things that one says in an interview—this extraordinary literary genre."

[7] Pasolini, *Descrizioni di descrizioni* (Turin: Einaudi, 1979), p. 311.

[8] Pasolini, "A quattr' occhi con Pasolini," *Lui* No. 1 (June 1970), p. 8.

[9] Marco Bellocchio, *I pugni in tasca* (Milan: Garzanti, 1967), pp. 18–19.

the director to "enjoy equally the pleasure and pain of martyrdom."[10] (He himself, he confesses, often feels the "almost sensual effect of breaking the code" when shooting or editing a film.) But now he attributes a positive social value to innovative or extremist art: by challenging the code, he argues, such art questions and subverts the culture and society embedded in it. Assuming a martial tone, he urges artists to embrace "permanent invention" and "continuous struggle":

> Every volunteer who seeks a meaningful death "as exhibition" must deliberately present himself on the firing line: there is nowhere else where he can so rigorously carry out his course of action.
> Only the hero's death is a spectacle; and it alone is useful.
> Therefore martyr-directors, by their own decision, always find themselves, stylistically, on the firing line, and thus at the front line of linguistic transgressions. By dint of provoking the code (and therefore the world which uses it), by dint of *exposing themselves*, they wind up by obtaining what they desire so aggressively: to be wounded and killed with the weapons they themselves offer to the enemy.[11]

The very embodiment of the "martyr-director" envisioned here, Pasolini was continually, defiantly, on the "front lines" of linguistic and of social/political transgression. His cinema was but the most public and spectacular manifestation of a perpetual struggle for "permanent invention," a struggle constantly renewed as each new film opposed still another constellation of formal and social conventions. By a transgression that inevitably, and demonstrably, revealed the "infinite possibilities of modifying and enlarging the code," Pasolini challenged the cultural limits, the social vision, reflected and perpetuated in the code. His insistence on the moral implications of culture was, perhaps, frequently disturbing and often unfashionable, but it was largely this very insistence that made him one of the central figures of our time. Resolute and lonely, he stood, as Maria-Antonietta Macciocchi so rightly observes, at the intersection of "three great protests against the power of the state: political, sexual, and mystic."[12] Set under the sign of scandal, Pasolini's oeuvre incarnates nothing less than the extremism that Roland Barthes places at the very heart of literary creation:

> The social intervention of a text is not measured by its popularity . . . or by its faithfulness to the economic-social [order] it reflects . . . but rather by the vio-

---

[10] Pasolini, *Empirismo eretico* (Milan: Garzanti, 1972), p. 278. Originally in *Nuovi Argomenti* No. 20 (October–December 1970).

[11] Pasolini, *Empirismo eretico*, p. 279.

[12] Maria-Antonietta Macciocchi, "Pasolini: assassinat d'un dissident," *Tel Quel* No. 76 (Summer 1978), p. 38.

lence which permits it to *exceed* the laws that a society, an ideology, a philosophy, give themselves in order to appropriate . . . historical intelligibility. This excess has a name: writing.[13]

Undoubtedly, Pasolini's will to "excess" *was* impelled by existential factors. Moravia is not wrong when he compares Pasolini to Genet, saying: "For each of them, revolt is not really political, but comes from a homosexual or ideological malaise"; nor is Glauber Rocha wrong when he observes: "Pasolini sought an alibi for his perversion in the Third World."[14] But if Moravia and Rocha are not wrong, neither are they totally right. Fueled by his neuroses, Pasolini's scandalous art also transcends them. If his sexuality drew him to underdeveloped countries, his love for the Third World led to striking films dealing with the clash of civilizations, the very nature of the West. If an exacerbated sensibility, a sense of otherness, led him to denounce modern society as the "new" fascism, his fear of the media and cultural leveling has not, alas, been proven wrong. Pasolini was by no means the first prophet or moralist whose vision sprang from an inner malaise. As André Gide wrote in a book on Dostoievsky: "If we really look, at the origin of every great ethical reform we find a little physiological mystery, a dissatisfaction of the flesh, an unease, an anomaly."[15] It was, perhaps, this "dissatisfaction of the flesh," this "inner disequilibrium," that made of Pasolini not only a poet—a being that Walter Benjamin calls the "most different of living creatures"—but one of the most radical and prophetic voices of our century.

[13] Roland Barthes, *Sade, Fourier, Loyala* (Paris: Seuil/Points, 1971), p. 16.

[14] Marc Gervais cites Moravia's remarks in his *Pier Paolo Pasolini* (Paris: Seghers, 1973), pp. 177–178; for those of Glauber Rocha, see his "Le Christ-Oedipe," in *Pasolini cinéaste*, p. 81.

[15] André Gide, *Dostoievsky* (Paris: Plon, 1923), p. 265.

Filmography

Commentaries

1956   *Manon Finestra 2* (Short, dir. Ermanno Olmi)
1957   *Il Grigio* (Short, dir. Ermanno Olmi)
1958   *Ignoti alla Città* (Short, dir. Cecilia Mangini)
1960   *Stendali'* (Short, dir. Cecilia Mangini)
       La canta delle marane (Short, dir. Cecilia Mangini), based on a chapter of Pasolini's novel *Ragazzi di vita*

Subjects and Screenplays

1954   *La donna del fiume* (Dir. Mario Soldati) Co-scriptwriter
1955   *Il prigioniero della montagna* (Dir. Luis Trenker) Co-scriptwriter
1956   *Le notti di Cabiria* (Dir. Federico Fellini) Consultation on Romanesque dialogue
1957   *Marisa la civetta* (Dir. Mauro Bolognini) Co-scriptwriter
1958   *Giovani mariti* (Dir. Mauro Bolognini) Co-scriptwriter
1959   *La notte brava* (Dir. Mauro Bolognini) Subject and scriptwriter
       Morte di un amico (Dir. Franco Rossi) Collaboration on subject
1960   *Il bell'Antonio* (Dir. Mauro Bolognini) Co-scriptwriter
       La giornata balorda (Dir. Mauro Bolognini) Co-scriptwriter
       La lunga notte del '43 (Dir. Florestano Vancini) Co-scriptwriter
       Il carro armato dell'8 settembre (Dir. Gianni Puccini) Co-scriptwriter
       La dolce vita (Dir. Federico Fellini) Co-scriptwriter
1961   *La ragazza in ventrina* (Dir. Luciano Emmer) Co-scriptwriter
1962   *La commare secca* (Dir. Bernardo Bertolucci) Subject and co-scriptwriter
       Una vita violenta (Dirs. Paolo Heusch, Brunello Rondi), based on Pasolini's novel *Una vita violenta*
1966   *Il cinema di Pasolini/Appunti per un critofilm* (Short, dir. Maurizio Ponzi), includes clips from *Comizi d'amore*
1970   *Ostia* (Dir. Sergio Citti) Collaboration on subject and script; supervision of mise-en-scène
1973   *Storie scellerate* (Dir. Sergio Citti) Collaboration on subject and script

Directed

1961   *Accattone*
       Screenplay: P. P. Pasolini, with dialogue collaboration by Sergio Citti
       Assistant director: Bernardo Bertolucci
       Photography: Tonino Delli Colli

Art Direction: Flavio Mogherini
Music: J. S. Bach (coordinated by Carlo Rustichelli)
Editing: Nino Baragli
Cast: Franco Citti (Accattone), Franca Pasut (Stella), Silvana Corsini (Maddalena), Adriana Asti (Amore), Mario Cipriani (Balilla), Roberto Scaringella (Cartagine), Adele Cambria (Nannina), Stefano D'Arrigo (Judge), Elsa Morante (Prison inmate), Paola Guidi (Ascenza), Piero Morgia (Pio)
Producer: Alfredo Bini for Cino Del Duca and Arco Film
Running time: 116 minutes

1962   *Mamma Roma*
Screenplay: P. P. Pasolini, with dialogue collaboration by Sergio Citti
Assistant Directors: Carlo di Carlo, Gian Francesco Salina
Photography: Tonino Delli Colli
Art Direction: Flavio Mogherini
Music: Antonio Vivaldi (coordinated by Carlo Rustichelli)
Editing: Nino Baragli
Cast: Anna Magnani (Mamma Roma), Ettore Garofolo (Ettore), Franco Citti (Carmine), Silvana Corsini (Bruna), Paolo Volponi (Priest), Luisa Orioli (Giancofiore), Luciano Gonini (Zaccaria), Piero Morgia (Piero)
Producer: Alfredo Bini for Arco Film
Running time: 105 minutes

1963   *La ricotta* (Third episode of *Rogopag* or *Laviamoci il cervello*; other episodes by Roberto Rossellini, Jean-Luc Godard, Ugo Gregoretti)
Screenplay: P. P. Pasolini
Assistant Directors: Sergio Citti, Carlo Di Carlo
Photography: Tonino Delli Colli
Art Direction: Flavio Mogherini
Costumes: Danilo Donati
Music: Carlo Rustichelli
Editing: Nino Baragli
Cast: Orson Welles (the Director), Mario Cipriani (Stracci), Laura Betti (the Star), Edmonda Aldini (Another Star), Vittorio La Paglia (the Journalist), Ettore Garofolo (Extra), Maria Bernardini (Extra who does strip-tease), Elsa De Giorgi and Enzo Siciliano (two guests)
Producer: Alfredo Bini for Arco Film-Cineriz (Rome)/Lyre Film (Paris)
Running time: 35 minutes

La rabbia (First part; second part by Giovanni Guareschi)
Subject and Verse Commentary: P. P. Pasolini
Assistant Director: Carlo Di Carlo
Editing: P. P. Pasolini and Nino Baragli
Commentary spoken by Giorgio Bassani and Renato Guttuso
Producer: Gastone Ferrante for Opus Film
Running time: 50 minutes

1964   *Comizi d'amore*

Commentary written by P. P. Pasolini
Assistant Director: Vincenzo Cerami
Photography: Mario Bernardo, Tonino Delli Colli
Editing: Nino Baragli
Commentary spoken by Lello Bersani and P. P. Pasolini
Participants: P. P. Pasolini, Alberto Moravia, Cesare Musatti, Giuseppe Ungaretti, Camilla Cederna, Adele Cambria, Oriana Fallaci, Antonella Lualdi, Graziella Chiarcossi (in the role of the bride)
Producer: Alfredo Bini for Arco Film
Running time: 90 minutes

Sopraluoghi in Palestina

Subject: P. P. Pasolini
Photography: Aldo Pennelli, Otello Martelli
Participants: Don Andrea Carraro and P. P. Pasolini
Commentary and editing: P. P. Pasolini
Producer: Alfredo Bini for Arco Film
Running time: 55 minutes

Il Vangelo secondo Matteo

Screenplay: P. P. Pasolini (from The Gospel of St. Matthew)
Assistant Directors: Maurizio Lucidi, Paul Schneider
Photography: Tonino Delli Colli, assisted by Dante Ferretti
Art Direction: Luigi Scaccianoce
Costumes: Danilo Donati
Music: J. S. Bach, W. A. Mozart, A. Webern, S. Prokofiev, Negro spirituals, Russian revolutionary songs (Coordinated by Carlo Rustichelli and Luis Bacalov)
Editing: Nino Baragli
Cast: Enrique Irazoqui (Christ, dubbed by Enrico Maria Salerno), Margherita Caruso (the young Mary), Susanna Pasolini (the old Mary), Marcello Morante (Joseph), Mario Socrate (John the Baptist), Ferruccio Nuzzo (Matthew), Alfonso Gatto (Andrew), Enzo Siciliano (Simon), Rodolfo Wilcock (Caiphas), Francesco Leonetti (Herod II), Natalia Ginzburg (Mary of Bethany), Settimio Di Porto (Peter), Rossana di Rocco (Angel), Otello Sestili (Judas), Giacomo Morante (John the Apostle), Amerigo Bevilacqua (Herod I), Ninetto Davoli (young shepherd)
Producer: Alfredo Bini for Arco Film (Rome)/Lux Cie Cinématographie (Paris)
Running time: 137 minutes

1966   *Uccellacci e Uccellini*

Screenplay: P. P. Pasolini
Assistant Directors: Carlo Morandi, Vincenzo Cerami, Sergio Citti
Photography: Tonino Delli Colli, Mario Bernardo
Art Direction: Luigi Scaccianoce, assisted by Dante Ferretti
Costumes: Danilo Donati, assisted by Piero Cicoletti

Music: Ennio Morricone, title song by Domenico Modugno

Editing: Nino Baragli

Ornithological expert: Pino Serpe

Cast: Totò (the Father, Friar Cicillo), Ninetto Davoli (the Son, Friar Ninetto), Femi Benussi (Luna, the Prostitute), Rossana di Rocco (Friend of Ninetto), Lena Lin Solaro, Gabriele Baldini (the Dantesque Dentist), Francesco Leonetti (Voice of the Crow);

Producer: Alfredo Bini for Arco Film

Running time: 88 minutes

1967   *La terra vista dalla luna* (Third episode of *Le streghe*; other episodes by Luchino Visconti, Mauro Bolognini, Franco Rossi, Vittorio De Sica)

Screenplay: P. P. Pasolini

Assistant Directors: Sergio Citti, Vincenzo Cerami

Photography: Giuseppe Rotunno

Art Direction: Mario Garbuglia and Piero Poletto

Costumes: Piero Tosi

Sculptures: Pino Zac

Music: Piero Piccioni

Editing: Nino Baragli

Cast: Silvana Mangano (Assurdina Caì), Totò (Ciancicato Miao), Ninetto Davoli (Basciù Miao), Laura Betti (Tourist), Luigi Leoni (Tourist's Wife), Mario Cipriani (Priest)

Producer: Dino De Laurentiis Cinematografica (Rome)/Les Productions Artistes Associés (Paris)

Running time: 30 minutes

Edipo Re

Screenplay: P. P. Pasolini, inspired by Sophocles' *Oedipus Rex* and *Oedipus at Colonus*

Assistant Director: Jean-Claude Biette

Photography: Giuseppe Ruzzolini

Art Direction: Luigi Scaccianoce

Architectural Assistant: Dante Ferretti

Costumes: Danilo Donati

Music: Rumanian and Japanese folk songs plus original music coordinated by Pier Paolo Pasolini

Editing: Nino Baragli

Cast: Franco Citti (Edipo), Silvana Mangano (Jocasta), Alida Valli (Mereope), Carmelo Bene (Creon), Julian Beck (Tiresias), Francesco Leonetti (Servant), Ninetto Davoli (Anghelos/Angelo), P. P. Pasolini (High Priest), Luciano Bartoli (Laius), Jean-Claude Biette (Priest)

Producer: Alfredo Bini for Arco Film

Running time: 110 minutes

1968   *Che cosa sono le nuvole* (Third episode of *Capriccio all'italiana*; other episodes by Steno, Mauro Bolognini, Pino Zac, and Mario Monicelli.)

Screenplay: P. P. Pasolini

Assistant Director: Sergio Citti
Photography: Tonino Delli Colli
Sets and Costumes: Jürgen Henze
Music: Domenico Mondugno, P. P. Pasolini
Editing: Nino Baragli
Cast: Totò (Iago), Ninetto Davoli (Othello), Laura Betti (Desdemona), Adriana Asti (Bianca), Franco Franchi (Cassio), Ciccio Ingrassia (Roderigo), Francesco Leonetti (Puppetmaster), Domenico Modugno (Garbageman), Carlo Pisacane
Producer: Dino De Laurentiis Cinematografica (Rome)
Running time: 22 minutes

Teorema
Screenplay: P. P. Pasolini
Assistant Director: Sergio Citti
Photography: Giuseppe Ruzzolini
Art Direction: Luciano Puccini
Costumes: Marcella De Marchis
Music: W. A. Mozart, Ennio Morricone
Editing: Nino Baragli
Cast: Terence Stamp (the Visitor), Silvana Mangano (Lucia, the Mother), Massimo Girotti (Paolo, the Father), Anne Wiazemsky (Odetta, the Daughter), Andrès José Cruz (Pietro, the Son), Laura Betti (Emilia, the Servant), Ninetto Davoli (Angelino/the Postman), Susanna Pasolini (Old Countrywoman), Alfonso Gatto, Carlo De Mejo
Producers: Manolo Bolognini and Franco Rossellini for Aetos Film
Running time: 98 minutes

Appunti per un film sull'India
(Short film, made for Italian television, concerning a proposed film on hunger in India)
Subject and direction: P. P. Pasolini
Collaboration: Gianni Barcelloni
Editing: Jenner Menghi
Producer: Gianni Barcelloni for Italian television (RAI)
Running time: 32 minutes

1969   *La sequenza del fiore di carta* (Third episode of *Amore e rabbia*; other episodes by Carlo Lizzani, Bernardo Bertolucci, Jean-Luc Godard, Marco Bellocchio)
Screenplay: P. P. Pasolini (from an idea by Puccio Pucci and Piero Badalessi)
Assistant Directors: Franco Brocani, Maurizio Ponzi
Photography: Giuseppe Ruzzolini
Editing: Nino Baragli
Music: J. S. Bach, Giovanni Fusco
Cast: Ninetto Davoli (Youth), Voices of God: Graziella Chiarcossi, Aldo Puglisi, Bernardo Bertolucci, P. P. Pasolini

Producer: Carlo Lizzani for Castoro Film (Rome)/ Anouchka Film (Paris)
Running time: 12 minutes
Porcile
  Screenplay: P. P. Pasolini
  Assistant Directors: Sergio Citti, Fabio Garriba
  Photography: Tonino Delli Colli, Armando Nannuzzi, Giuseppe Ruzzolini
  Art Direction and Costumes: Danilo Donati
  Music: Benedetto Ghiglia
  Editing: Nino Baragli
  Cast: Pierre Clementi (Cannibal), Franco Citti (Second Cannibal), Jean-Pierre Léaud (Julian), Alberto Lionello (Klotz, the Father), Ugo Tognazzi (Herdhitze), Anne Wiazemsky (Ida), Marco Ferreri (Hans Gunther), Ninetto Davoli (Young Man/Marracchione), Margherita Lozano (Mrs. Klotz, dubbed by Laura Betti)
  Producer: Gian Vittorio Baldi for IDI Cinematografica, Orso Films, INDIEF (Rome)/CAPAC (Paris)
  Running time: 98 minutes
Medea
  Screenplay: P. P. Pasolini, inspired by Euripides
  Assistant Director: Carlo Carunchio
  Photography: Ennio Guarnieri
  Art Direction: Dante Ferretti
  Costumes: Piero Tosi, assisted by Piero Cicoletti and Gabriella Pesucci
  Music: Coordinated by Pasolini with the help of Elsa Morante
  Editing: Nino Baragli
  Cast: Maria Callas (Medea), Giuseppe Gentile (Jason), Laurent Terzieff (the Centaur); Massimo Girotti (Creon), Margaret Clementi (Glauce), Paul Jabara, Gerard Weiss
  Producer: Franco Rossellini and Marina Cicogna for San Marco Film (Rome)/ Les Film Number One (Paris)/ Janus Film and Fernsehen (Frankfurt)
  Running time: 110 minutes
1970 *Appunti per una Orestiade africana*
  Script: P. P. Pasolini
  Photography: Giorgio Pelloni, Mario Bagnato, Emore Galeassi
  Editing: Cleofe Conversi
  Music: Gato Barbieri
  Producer: Gian Vittorio Baldi for IDI Cinematografica
  Running time: 55 minutes
1971 *Il Decamerone*
  Screenplay: P. P. Pasolini, based on Boccaccio's tales
  Assistant Directors: Sergio Citti and Umberto Angelucci
  Photography: Tonino Delli Colli
  Art Direction: Dante Ferretti

Costumes: Danilo Donati

Music: Coordinated by Pasolini with the help of Ennio Morricone

Editing: Nino Baragli, Tatiana Casini Morigi

Cast: Franco Citti (Ser Ciappelletto), Ninetto Davoli (Andreuccio), Angela Luce (Peronella), Jovan Jovanovic (Rustico), Giuseppe Zigaina (Monk), P. P. Pasolini (Giotto), Silvana Mangano (the Madonna)

Producer: Franco Rossellini for PEA (Rome)/ Les Productions Artistes Associés (Paris)/ Artemis Film (Berlin)

Running time: 111 minutes

1972   *12 dicembre*

Concept: P. P. Pasolini

Subject and Script: Giovanni Bonfanti, Goffredo Fofi

Editing: Lamberto Mancini

Music: Pino Masi

Photography: Giuseppe Pinori, Sebastiano Celeste, Enzo Tosi, Roberto Lombardi

Producer: Giovanni Bonfanti for Lotta continua

Running time: 104 minutes

N.B. Although Pasolini's name is not on the credits, he directed about half of the film

I Racconti di Canterbury

Screenplay: P. P. Pasolini, based on the stories by Geoffrey Chaucer

Assistant Directors: Sergio Citti, Umberto Angelucci

Photography: Tonino Delli Colli

Art Direction: Dante Ferretti

Costumes: Danilo Donati

Music: Coordinated by Pasolini in collaboration with Ennio Morricone

Editing: Nino Baragli

Cast: Hugh Griffith (Sir January), Laura Betti (the Wife of Bath), Ninetto Davoli (Peterkin), Josephine Chaplin (May), P. P. Pasolini (Chaucer), Franco Citti (Devil), Alan Webb (the Old Man), John Francis Lane (Monk)

Producer: Alberto Grimaldi for PEA (Rome)/Les Productions Artistes Associés (Paris)

Running time: 111 minutes

1974   *Il fiore delle mille e una notte*

Screenplay: P. P. Pasolini, based on the *Arabian Nights*

Collaboration on the Screenplay: Dacia Maraini

Assistant Directors: Umberto Angelucci, Peter Shepherd

Photography: Giuseppe Ruzzolini

Art Direction: Dante Ferretti

Costumes: Danilo Donati

Music: Ennio Morricone

Editing: Nino Baragli, Tatiana Casini Morigi

Cast: Franco Merli (Nur-ed-Din), Ninetto Davoli (Aziz), Franco Citti
(the Demon), Ines Pellegrini (Zumurrud), Teresa Bouché (Aziza),
Margaret Clementi
Producer: Alberto Grimaldi for PEA (Rome)/Les Productions Artistes
Associés (Paris)
Running time: 148 minutes

Le mura di San'A
Script: P. P. Pasolini
Photography: Tonino Delli Colli
Editing: Tatiana Casini Morigi
Commentary: P. P. Pasolini
Producer: Franco Rossellini for Rosina Anstalt
Running time: 16 minutes

1975   *Salò o Le 120 giornate di Sodoma*
Screenplay: P. P. Pasolini and Sergio Citti, based on the Marquis de
Sade's novel *Les 120 Journées de Sodome*
Assistant Director: Umberto Angelucci
Photography: Tonino Delli Colli
Sets: Dante Ferretti
Costumes: Danilo Donati
Music: Coordinated by Ennio Morricone
Editing: Nino Baragli, Tatiana Casini Morigi
Cast: Paolo Bonacelli (the Duke), Giorgio Cataldi (the Bishop), Um-
berto Paolo Quintavalle (the Magistrate, Curval), Aldo Valletti
(Durcet), Caterina Boratto (Signora Castelli), Elsa De Giorgi (Si-
gnora Maggi), Hélène Surgère (Signora Vaccari), Sonia Saviange (Pi-
anist), Ines Pellegrini, Franco Merli
Producer: Alberto Grimaldi for PEA (Rome)/ Les Productions Artistes
Associés (Paris)
Running time: 114 minutes

Published Screenplays by Pasolini

La notte brava. Filmcritica Vol. 10, No. 91–92 (November–December
1959).
Accatone (Preface by Carlo Levi). Rome: F.M., 1961.
Mamma Roma. Milano: Rizzoli, 1962.
Il Vangelo secondo Matteo. Milano: Garzanti, 1964.
La ricotta. In *Alì dagli occhi azzurri.* Milan: Garzanti, 1965. This volume
also contains *La notte brava, Accattone,* and *Mamma Roma.*
La comare secca. Filmcritica Vol. 16, No. 161 (October 1965). Subject
and treatment of the film directed by Bernardo Bertolucci.
Uccellacci e Uccellini. Milan: Garzanti, 1966.
Edipo Re. Milan: Garzanti, 1967. French translation: *Oedipe Roi* in *L'a-
vant-scène du cinéma* No. 97 (November 1969). English translation:
Oedipus Rex. London: Lorrimer, 1971.

Che cosa sono le nuvole? *Cinema e Film* Vol. 3, No. 7–8 (Winter–Spring 1969).

Media. Milan: Garzanti, 1970.

Ostia (written with Sergio Citti). Milano: Garzanti, 1970.

Il padre selvaggio. Turin: Einaudi, 1975. Originally published in two parts in *Cinema e Film* Vol. 2, No. 3 and Vol. 2, No. 4 (1967).

Trilogia della Vita (*Il Decamerone, I racconti di Canterbury, Il fiore delle mille e una notte*). Bologna: Cappelli, 1975.

San Paolo. Turin: Einaudi, 1977.

Coccodrillo ————————————————————————

He broke bread—which was not very bitter but rather sweet—
with himself. He was born in the city of Koinè-Keltike,[1]
still emerging from the baked medieval earth, not yet
   swallowed up by cement.
But his grandmother came from Cascinale, the capital of a district
which later turned out to be the Land of self-mutilators and fags.
For centuries his father's family, on the other hand, had inhabited
Byzantain, that world of sentimental fuckers
(slightly more than a hand's breadth higher than the top of the
   Afflicted Sea.)
His conformity was, of course, ambiguous; but not as ambiguous
as his masochism (which was, moreoever, merely *verbal* and
   social).
While the latter (his masochism) came from parental
quarrels—that cast the son into such a state
that only the desire to be killed could rescue him—
the origin of the former (his conformity) was exclusively maternal.
It is very doubtful that his Teacher Mother, the Solitary Blackbird,
had read Hegel or Nietzsche: nonetheless she was a beautiful soul.
Thus in this mother—born in a village of Things (goats),
on the denuded plains of the Romance Forest,
with, however, its few etymons of woods and many proto-Europeans—
there was bourgeois snobbery, but in a form so
embryonic that little distinguished it from peasant
nature. Still, it was through this channel that erupted in him
—Teacher of Primroses[2]—bourgeois conformity.
In the PC[3] (to which he remained faithful despite idealistic
criticisms launched like strictly personal heroics—
and that he found odious as soon as they became public)
he sought the Authority *feared* by his mother
not the Authority *exerted* by his father—a Fascist,

This poem, where Pasolini "objectifies" himself by speaking of himself in the third person, was written in 1968 for the American review *Avant Garde*, but never published. In journalistic slang a "coccodrillo" is an obituary prepared for someone in the event of his death.

[1] Pasolini appears to be using two Greek words here: "Koinè" refers to commonly spoken Greek; "Keltike" is Greek for "Celt."

[2] The Italian word for "primroses," that is, *primule*, also refers to elementary schoolchildren.

[3] PC, that is, Partito Communista.

a poor creatue who came from Byzantain (mentioned above),
only to give pain and inspire still more pain,
and then to croak, as if it were a natural death, of disappointment.
In short, something called destiny—which includes him, mother
and son in a Thing polished off like a stone.
Now that this stone has rolled into the ravine,
it needs only a funeral elegy, briefly put,
therefore edited from *another* point of view—the Roman one.
(In fact, the Thing is over with, in today's light.)
This point of view is simply marvelous because it
lets one—without breaking the rules (of the oral
agreement)—objectify narcissism and dust it off
one last time. Ah! Not an observation
concerning this dammed life—whose stirrings
render doubtful all the most extravagant perceptions,
[and] groundless all the deepest insights *about oneself*—
but a narcissistic observation performed after death, when
montage, at any rate, is complete—and the story is ONE.
No object of narcissism was ever more fecund than a cadaver.
Therefore: his conformism—once again, of *maternal and not*
paternal origin—prevented him, for longer than is normal,
from understanding what liberty and rebellion were.
Because liberty and rebellion were his bread (which was, let's say,
not bitter but rather sweet—inexpressive routine daily food).
Accustomed to this taste, at the age of twenty (when a man decides
to be a warrior) he had already decided, already become a
warrior. Without knowing it he had already broken
what the youth of twenty deliberately breaks:
at eleven, and maybe earlier, he had already suppressed
his father! But what about Authority, disguised as idealism,
that came to him
from the adored world, from his gentle bourgeois mother?
Well, that Authority long remained deep within him; in fact,
it was never again erased. It was only erased (it's true)
when its resemblance to paternal [Authority] was obvious!
Thus he could never do without this oppression, remote
and rendered unrecognizable by rural gentleness.
He was one of those professors, or writers, described
by Chekhov in his stories, that Lenin must have known.
Strange, for an extremist, but that's how it is. Humanism
does not make psychological distinctions: it is sold in bulk.
Thus, although living as an outlaw, he was a humanist.
He abandoned his studies to wander around the city's edge
and to shoot films; but studies were within him;

idle hours filled by work that was in fact a drug.
Thus he reached his forty-sixth year, the age of this supposed death
and thus this display of narcissistic insight—in a series
of dispassionate and ironic obits: the death of a humanist!
It was precisely in 1968, a year in which without much regret
he experimentally expired,
that he had the first real crisis of his life. Why?
Because for the first time he realized he was a father.
Thanks, Avant Garde, for having given me the chance
to subject "him," once again . . . to
analyses that much crueler when more forgiving
(attempts at a secure loyalty and basic heroism).
Your million readers have, I suppose, the correct
and suitable number of children: and therefore well know
what a child is like, a child in the United States.
Lacking an analogous blessing, they cannot know
what a child is like in Italy, a child at the University
(we're talking in fact among respectable and well thought-of people):
This vigorous twenty year old is liquidating his fathers:
but, here, unlike in Dallas, he has two of them:
he must, therefore, liquidate two.
but if he liquidates the bourgeois father, which is simply logical,
the struggle is only internal.
If, instead, he liquidates the Marxist father
he, himself, objectively becomes bourgeois.
Poor youth!
But for a bachelor like me, what does all this mean
if not that my sons were like my fathers?

— — — — —

But no! Let's go back to the beginning. His life was
not affected: first,
by the place where he and his kin were born;
second, by his two desires—to obey and to die,
(they had become mere habit);
third, by that Student revolt which occurred in '68.
But no! Let's go back to the beginning;
exhuming everything that I have gone through.

— — — — —

The "persistent" Gramscian substratum ceased
suddenly.

Some intermittent substrati replaced it:
Don Milani, Malcolm X (while convalescing
from an ulcer, in 1965) and other *little read* authors.
Let's start it all again from the beginning and first of all
let's forget his name and what he knows about him.
Facts! Facts! Some Jews hated him
because they had not asked themselves about the problem of his
     diversità
They stupidly considered him normal by right.
Many Arabs loved him, because they saw in him chosen flesh.
He loved Jews, believing them (correctly) brothers.
Communists understood nothing and deemed him
(through intermediaries, those miserable people) a pitiful individual.
The bourgeois were drunk. They sang from morning to night
in *their* rooms, *their* stations, *their* squares.
Yes, Elsa,[4] I hated them because I loved them, you're right.
But I loved the man in them. When I was small
how could I make certain distinctions?
For me, there was only *man*, living in the *world*;
And he had chased me from there. How handsome and happy he seemed
     to me!
How I loved him! I did not even know, naturally,
that I was a victim who loved his persecutor.
The man and the bourgeois then became distinct
(or, to put it better, I was able to make such distinctions):
and in an annoying way I have continued to love the man,
and, in an equally annoying way, to hate the bourgeois.
Deprived of my place in the bourgeoisie, I was deprived
of my place in the world. Where does someone go, I wonder,
who lacks a place in the world?
When he dies, how will he be changed?
There is no doubt: I lived a life hardly worthy of being lived.
The strange thing is that almost without distinction all could
have been my Himmlers. Himmler (I repeat) among the Jews,
(Many) Himmlers among the Communists; many, many (almost all)
Himmlers in *the* world par excellence
the bourgeois world that claims to be all of history, asshole!
But, to tell the truth, only among the bourgeoisie as such
were there people who, I think, best showed
a certain charity toward my being.
Still very few of them were laymen (and, in that case, what

---

[4] The novelist Elsa Morante, a friend of Pasolini's.

kind of bourgeois were they?) Like a beggar I walked through ghettos
(leaving behind the convenient ghetto where poets are put).
And there I found a lot of understanding: the fields
for lovemaking were hundredfold and all stinking.
From there too came messages of hate: but it was . . .
a just hatred. A poor man's hatred, a worker's hatred.
A hatred full of gentleness. But didn't I say that
the Gramscian tune had ceased?
Perhaps I lied? Oh, well, you know, nothing ever ceases.
Thus, because of continuity in a lifestyle,
because of the immutability of a condition,
because of cultural determination,
he had an incredible experience: that
of being a father. Naturally, he behaved like one (he,
who had so filially killed his own).
But the image of his sons in their class arrogance
was a truly unbearable image; even more so
because they were sons he had been constrained to adopt.
My God, those thousands of faces like his father's!
Or if not like that of his father, like those of his professors,
his political enemies, his bad poet friends,
his weak and arrogant arriviste colleagues;
or simply like those of any citizens
belonging to the middle class who populate the world
as if they were innocent—assholes! undertakers!
Thanks, Avant Garde, for having let me shed—
in the face of cops and judges—
emotional tears about my dead self. It is well known
that this is one of the pleasantest things in the world.
Let's begin again.
The Arabs were more generous than Friulian peasants
whose mothers and fathers teach them to
place their seed in only one place—if not, look out!
All the Arabs, except for those of Tripoli,
trained, in fact, by Italian boors.
The inhabitants of Tangiers were very generous,
so beautiful they seemed as tranparent as ghosts
of the dead from other centuries; so too were the inhabitants
of Casablanca, and Marrakesh. There should be
peasants of the sea! How many seeds in the ports
of Aden, of Mombasa, of Bari, Barletta, Molfetta,
Reggio Calabria, Villa San Giovanni, Messina, Catania,
Syracuse, Beirut, Istanbul, Antioch! You cannot

make love in living rooms, nor even in beds.
You need a meadow outside the city, a stretch of desert,
a steppe, a heath—in short, any place
where grass is scarce, burned and hot; the Mediterranean
hillsides, where weeds grow that
mothers do not gather, mothers who remain
with their youngest in the little streets.
There are nights when it is absurd to do anything except make love.
He died after experiencing these nights of other centuries.
He belonged to one of the last generations so fortunate.
He was really an idiot to have sacrificed so many of these
nights to work, not to have spent his whole life
in Morocco, in Sicily, or even only in the Maremma.
Those nights were summer nights, and his love for summer
was perhaps the strongest feeling in his life . . .
Really? but how can you be sincere, if you are too exact
or too fatuous?
Let's begin everything again.
From the depths of the—Catholic and reactionary—world
emerged . . . sons of Catholic and reactionary bourgeois
(from the bourgeoisie whose origins the eternal Gramsci described so
    well)
although used to the idea
of Faith and Hope they could also
go over to the opposition—to the communism and socialism
of the left and beyond; therefore
finding themelves on the *just* side
they felt *justified*
in singing victory as if liberation had come:
in fact they sang shit with Faith and Hope.
Yes, because the great leap could have taken place
through (neurotics') BOURGEOIS Reason:
this is why they rediscovered
FAITH and HOPE but never CHARITY.
A fascism of the left took shape (I'm writing in 1968).
He died when he was fighting against
this: and died, perhaps, out of sorrow over this.
(A flight into death—better than a flight into Vietnam.)
(And thanks, Avant Garde, for having let me pronounce
this stoic conclusion, too, over the beloved cadaver.)
Let's begin again: it's true, power uses even death
"to accustom us to repression": still, still . . .
isn't resignation a sublime sentiment? Whereas

the consciousness of one's rights (a stupendous thing)
mayn't it be a disagreeable sentiment?
The class consciousness of workers is always gentle,
even when, with red banners held high,
they might have to fight.
The—bourgeois—consciousness of one's rights taught
to good bourgeois sons by good bourgeois fathers
at a time when realizing one's rights
seemed a dream—and thus, those fathers
became used to *mere dreaming*—
is not (in itself) redeeming.
Dying, he therefore left the sons
to fight for their rights without the gentleness of workers.
Moreoever, things known through learning never seem like dreams:
and thus generate scorn for dreams in the precocious learner.
Let's start everything again from the beginning: he spent his existence
divided exactly in half (he was, that is, ambiguous):
he believed in everything when he no longer believed in anything.
Like all people who are *not* normal and therefore *not* holy,
he left *no* regrets behind him; nor received any tears.
Only his mother, Graziella, and Ninetto[5] cried desperately for him.
Let's begin again, *chè il naufragar m'è dolce in questo mare.*[6]

[5] His cousin Graziella and his long-term friend Ninetto (Davoli).
[6] Citation from Leopardi's poem "L'infinito": "how sweet it is to drown in this sea."

Translated by NAOMI GREENE *and*
CESARE VESCO

Index

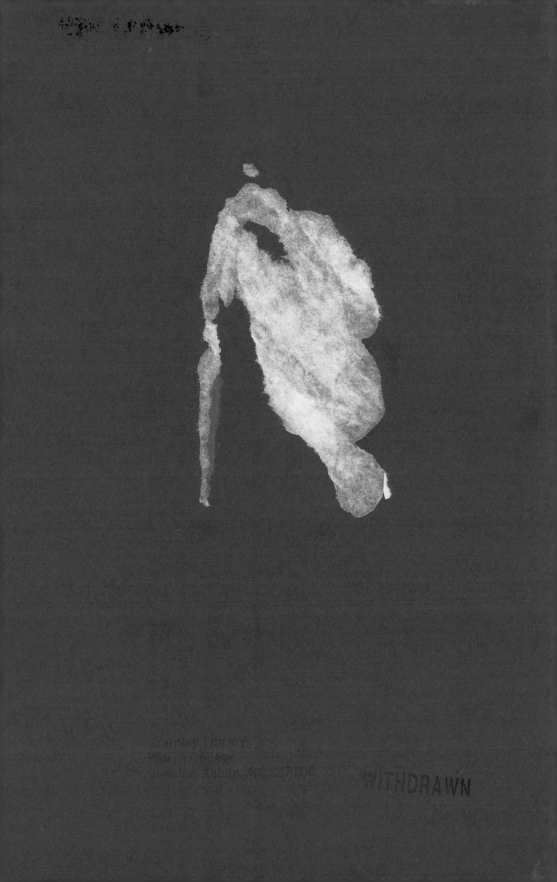